D0754661

Beijing

World Cities Series

Edited by
Professor R. J. Johnston and Professor P. Knox

Published titles in the series:

Mexico City *Peter Ward*
Lagos *Margaret Peil*
Tokyo *Roman Cybriwsky*
Budapest *György Enyedi and Viktória Szirmai*
Hong Kong *C. P. Lo*
Dublin *Andrew MacLaran*
Vienna *Elisabeth Lichtenberger*
Birmingham *Gordon E. Cherry*
Taipei *Roger M. Selya*
Rome *John Agnew*
Beijing *Victor F. S. Sit*

Forthcoming titles in the series:

Brussels *Alexander B. Murphy*
Buenos Aires *David J. Keeling*
Glasgow *Michael Pacione*
Harare *Carole Rakodi*
Havana *Joseph Scarpaci, Roberto Segre and Mario Coyula*
Johannesburg *Keith Beavon*
Lisbon *Jorge Gaspar and Allan Williams*
London *Michael Hebbert*
Melbourne *Kevin O'Connor*
Montreal *Annick Germain and Damaris Rose*
New York City *David A. Johnson*
Paris *Daniel Noin and Paul White*
Randstad *Frans M. Dieleman, Rein B. Jobse and Jan van Weesep*
Seoul *Joochul Kim and Sang Chuel Choe*

Other titles are in preparation

Beijing

The Nature and Planning of a Chinese Capital City

Victor F. S. Sit
University of Hong Kong, Hong Kong

JOHN WILEY & SONS
Chichester • New York • Brisbane • Toronto • Singapore

Copyright © 1995 Victor F. S. Sit

Published 1995 by John Wiley & Sons Ltd,
              Baffins Lane, Chichester,
              West Sussex PO19 1UD, England

              National   01243 779777
              International (+44) 1243 779777

Other Wiley Editorial Offices

John Wiley & Sons, Inc., 605 Third Avenue,
New York, NY 10158-0012, USA

Jacaranda Wiley Ltd, 33 Park Road, Milton,
Queensland 4064, Australia

John Wiley & Sons (Canada) Ltd, 22 Worcester Road,
Rexdale, Ontario M9W 1L1, Canada

John Wiley & Sons (SEA) Pte Ltd, 37 Jalan Pemimpin #05-04,
Block B, Union Industrial Building, Singapore 2057

Library of Congress Cataloging-in-Publication Data
Hsüeh, Feng-hsüan.
    Beijing : the nature and planning of a Chinese capital city /
Victor F.S. Sit.
        p.   cm. — (Belhaven world cities series)
    Includes bibliographical references and index.
    ISBN 0-471-94983-3
        1. City planning — China — Peking. 2. Urbanization — China —
    Peking   3. Peking (China) — Social conditions   4. Peking (China) —
    Economic conditions. I. Title. II. Series.
    HT169.C62P454   1995
    307.76'0951'156—dc20   94-46816
                                                                   CIP
British Library Cataloguing in Publication Data

A catalogue record for this book is available from the British Library

ISBN 0-471-94983-3

Typeset in 10/12pt Palatino from author's disks by
Mayhew Typesetting, Rhayader, Powys
Printed and bound in Great Britain by
Biddles Ltd, Guildford and King's Lynn

*This book is printed on acid-free paper responsibly manufactured from
sustainable forestation, for which at least two trees are planted for each one used
for paper production.*

Contents

List of figures

List of tables

Preface

I grew up in Hong Kong. Although a place largely of Chinese (95% of the population), Hong Kong has been planned and built under the sway of British ways modified by an obvious tint of colonialism. My exposure in Hong Kong and training in the University of London as an urban and economic geographer have brought me in contact with concepts and theories of the city of the Western industrialized countries. I only started to 'discover' the Chinese city at the beginning of 1970 when I for the first time walked the streets of Guangzhou, which gave me a strong feeling that it is a very different city under a unique system, yet a city to which I have been culturally and emotionally tied ever since.

My undergraduate training and long-held patriotic interest in Chinese history, Chinese philosophy and Chinese literature have nurtured in me a continual habit to read about China and the latest development in the PRC. Yet it was the 'mental shock', and/or 'love at first sight' of being physically present in a Chinese city that has hence started my frequent visits to the PRC and a devotion to uncover the real essence of the Chinese city.

Until the 1980s, the self-imposed isolation of the PRC due to ideology and politics, besides the separation of language and culture, had created a vacuum in contemporary urban geography so that the nature and state of affair of the Chinese city have largely been left unexplored. Since then the opening up of the PRC has paved the way for some research and publication on Chinese urbanisation and the Chinese city. My work: *Chinese Cities* (OUP, 1985) is the first comprehensive work (unfortunately) on these topics published in English in the West. Yet most such recent works focus on issues created by changed government policy as well as new market forces on the heightened pace of urbanization and urban development under the ruling philosophy of Deng Xao-ping i.e., economics first, politics second. How sustainable is Deng's sway and what is its impact on the Chinese city? Though these are interesting and important questions for research and have attracted most academic attention on the subject, two more fundamental questions have not been addressed, i.e., what is the nature of the Chinese city? Is there a Chinese city model that stands the test of time and change in governments and their ruling philosophies? Works by people such as Soothill (1951), Mote (1977), Chang (1977), Wright (1977) and Skinner (1977) that focus on the traditional Chinese city tell us that there is a unique Chinese urban model and a unique Chinese city model. Unfortunately no such work has been extended to the contemporary period and tested by post-1949 developments under the communist government of the PRC.

Post-1949 research by PRC scholars on the traditional Chinese city and its contemporary variates were prevalent in the 1950s. Unfortunately they are mainly descriptive and are unrelated to, even often unaware of, parallel developments in theory and methodology of urban geography in the rest of the world. Political movements of the late 1950s, early 1960s and the Cultural Revolution (1966–1976) dampened the research zest in all social sciences disciplines in the PRC and research on the Chinese city came to a standstill. Revival of interests and efforts after 1980 are nevertheless disappointing. Recent surge of activities and publication in this respect seems to reflect what exists outside of China, i.e. they are either descriptive studies on the traditional Chinese city or reviews, documentation and applied research on changes of the Chinese urban scene since the adoption of new market forces and relaxed official control over urbanization and urban development in 1978. The link between the traditional Chinese city as well as what the Chinese city had become under Maoist socialism in 1949–78 have not been explored.

The above situation is detrimental to a better and fuller understanding of the present day Chinese city and for projecting the likely path for its future development. The intention of the present volume is to fill such a vacuum, using Beijing as a detailed case study. As the capital of imperial China for 800 years during the Jin, Yuan, Ming and Qing dynasties, Beijing has preserved major elements of traditional Chinese city planning in the Forbidden City, the numerous ceremonial buildings in its inner city, the layout of the old city and its predominant courtyard houses. It has been a long Chinese tradition that all lesser cities are to be modelled after the capital in principle in its nature and layout. This principle has been followed in the PRC since 1949 under the dictate of central planning and Maoist ideology. Thus the exposition on what the national capital is in urban function, urban form, planning standards and urban life would shed light on general understanding of Chinese cities at lower levels of the PRC urban hierarchy.

A significant finding in this volume, however, is that the Chinese city arose in history not because of the economic needs for trade and concentrated development for handicrafts, but as an auspicious site for man's communication with the universe and the centre for dissemination of such information, and it drew on itself forces of growth because of such a specialization. For dispensing such a role, it took its early form from the institution called Ming T'ang. Then it was elaborated and codified in the *Kao Kung Ji* of *Zhou Li* about 2000–3000 years ago.

Post-1949 Beijing has grown rapidly as a consequence of a new dynamic, a vigorous programme of socialist industrialization. Yet the capital still retains the feudal role of being the national centre of 'communication and control', and serves the long tradition as the model for the rest of the country. In the latter, it has inherited the spirit of the Ming T'ang, the forerunner of the Chinese national capital, that the national capital should be the nation's centre of information, communication and control. Although in the post-1949 period the critical information is no longer 'blessing' from Heaven, they are the important factors and decisions regarding the political, social and economic developments of the country. Such a 'communication and control' role of the old and new Beijing could be linked to the recent concept of the global city by scholars like Friedmann (1986), who believe that the most important urban centres of the world are no longer production or trade centres. They are primarily centres of finance and corporation decisions. Their *raison d'etre* for national and international eminence lie not in productive activities of manufacturing and trade, but in the cities' information, communication and financial controls over material production and consumption of the country and all over the world. Post-1949 devotion to 'productive' activities and self-sufficiency in Beijing had not only constrained its primary role as the national centre of 'communication and control', it also brought to the city serious 'big city problems' such as inadequate urban infrastructure, congestion, excessive population and pollution. At present, the consensus of PRC planners and academics is clearly that there is an urgent need to suppress the 'productive role' of the city and to encourage high level tertiary activities that befit it as a national capital.

In this volume, I have explored the nature of Beijing through its long historical past as well as its post-1949 developments. Against such a background, I have examined urban planning, development of the urban economy, spatial distribution and fluctuation of the population, urban transport and housing, the urban environment, social areas and the city's spatial integration with its surrounding areas.

The findings revealed in this volume are minuscule compared to the vast treasure of the field of Chinese cities. I dedicate this volume to all those who would come after me and would be more successful in enriching our understanding of the field, and those who have assisted, encouraged and loved me in my search for the nature and identity of the Chinese city.

Victor Fung Shuen Sit
University of Hong Kong, January 1995

1

Nature of the Chinese city

Western definition of the city

It seems natural and obvious that cities arose in history owing to advancement in the technologies of production, transport and storage as well as humanity's increased capability in organization and management (Hauser, 1965; Johnson, 1967; Meadows, 1957). It is equally well known that the early cities emerged in different parts of the world in response to these innovations and their successful exploitation of the nearby environment, such as the emergence of Erech and Ur on the Euphrates around 3000 BC, the appearance of Memphis in the Nile Valley and Mohenjo Daro in the Indus Valley at about 2500 BC, as well as the early cities in the Shang Dynasty in China in the middle of the Huanghe Valley around 2300 BC (Meadows, 1957).

'Urban communities can be supported only when the foundation of life is such as to yield a surplus of food over and above the consuming needs of the food producers, and also when the means are available to concentrate this surplus at particular spots' (Turner, 1949). Such a material basis for city growth, resting on technological and social progress, has become the mainstay of the Western conceptualization of the origin and nature of the city. To many Western scholars, the stages in the development of technology and society have also been used to demarcate stages within the historical continuum of human society. For example, Sjoberg (1960) distinguishes three types (or stages) of societies: the folk or preliterate; the 'feudal' society (also termed pre-industrial civilized society or literate pre-industrial society); and the industrial-urban society. The last two contain urban agglomerations with diverse forms, character and layout, reflecting varying levels of technology and social structure. Sjoberg believes that the pre-industrial cities, whether they are in Medieval Europe, traditional China, India or elsewhere, closely resemble one another and in turn differ markedly from modern industrial-urban centres. Even today, one can still find pre-industrial cities, e.g. Kathmandu in Nepal, where the inhabitants continue their pre-industrial forms. In more or less the same vein, Reissman (1964) hypothesizes that the urbanization process, in general, works through four stages, i.e. primordial, definitive, classical and industrial, and that it shapes distinguishable urban (or non-urban) settlement communities and forms at each stage.

These concepts of the city acknowledge the intimate link between city and civilization, as Sjoberg does in the first sentence of his book, *The Pre-industrial City*:

> The city and civilization are inseparable: with the city's rise and spread, man at last emerged from the primitive state. In turn, the city enabled him to construct an ever more complex and, we would like to believe, more satisfying way of life. (Sjoberg, 1960)

However, they have hidden one main assumption, that of the *universalism* of the city. This may be further supported by another quote from Sjoberg regarding the modern industrial city:

> Vast and complex multi-function cities mirroring the vastness and complexities of an evolving industrial technology, sometimes typifying in their uniformity and standardization of machine technology, sometimes in their novel and individuality and specialization and creativity of the machine, such is one perspective at least of contemporary urbanism which is identified with a technology called industrialism . . . Industrial cities over the world are becoming alike in many aspects of their social structure . . . Modern technology . . . encompasses scientific knowhow . . . In turn, the scientific method seems to support and is itself sustained by an ideology that gives rise to and promotes the democratic process, and such forms of universalism and emphasis on achievement in modern bureaucracies. (Sjoberg, 1965).

Sjoberg has not only assumed a uniform technology, but a uniform value system and similar urbanization consequences of a democratic, modern and bureaucratic society. The notion of cultural differences therefore may be said to be non-existent or assumed absent in such a perspective. To this type of scholar the city form, the nature of urbanization, its extent and intensity, as well as the nature of the city, its number and size, are all just reflections of the qualitative and quantitative change process in a single dynamic, succinctly put in a simple formula by Smailes (1967), viz:

Industrialization → modernization → urbanization

While this conceptualization and the accompanying descriptions may be generally true of Western European cities that have evolved from Greek and Roman cities, there is serious doubt about their application to cities of other major cultures, particularly the Chinese cities. As Ginsburg (1972) has put it: 'There is reason to ask whether the urbanization process is unidimensional or multi-dimensional and whether it is culturally and areally, as well as temporally, differentiated.'

Agnew et al. (1984) referred to such economism as an 'enduring Western conceit' that comes out of a 'rational' economic calculus of profit and loss for the individual or group in the contemporary Western cultural context. This, when applied to other places and times, improperly projects recent Western experience onto other contexts, accounting in an invalid, *a priori* fashion for urbanization and urban life.

Berry (1973) has discerned a spectrum of urbanization experiences, from those obtaining under conditions of *laissez-faire* privatism to the highly centralized circumstances of socialist states, that argues strongly for a contrary view. He has observed that the diverse forms of public intervention adopted by different national governments on urbanization, city growth and urban planning, as well as the variety of goals sought by these governments, and the manipulation and manipulability of the population and economic activities and their whereabouts, have combined to produce an increasingly divergent path of 'deliberate urbanization'. On that basis, he has identified five different types of urbanization modes for the post-World War II period, each with varying characteristics of urbanization and city form and function. The US and Canada are given as examples of the 'free enterprise dynamics' model, whereby government intervention or guidance regarding urbanization and city development is limited, and the dominant factor in such matters is market forces. In countries such as Australia, Japan and France another model is said to be in practice, one of 'organizational market negotiation' where predominant interest groups such as unions and trade associations bargain for policy influence in a situation whereby the free market is also generally obtained. In countries in Western Europe, such as UK, the 'redistributive welfare state' model prevails in which strong government intervention is aimed at obtaining regional economic and population balances. In the former communist bloc of countries in Eastern Europe and in other countries subscribing to such ideology and way of governance, such as China and North Korea, another model, 'socialist directions', has been used to describe their urbanization and city development processes. These follow the common goals of a 'classless society', emphasizing the industrial role of cities (while downplaying the role of consumption), and the strong hand of the government through a rigid system of central planning, rather than the play of market forces, has been key in implementing related policies. Lastly, in many Third World countries yet another model is said to be in general application and is described as 'new radical policies of modernization combined with tribute to tradition'. This last model embodies a strong sense of nationalism and strives for political and economic independence, while the countries concerned are usually confronted with lack of economic development, large population growth, intense rural–urban influx, huge urban unemployment and underprovision of basic urban infrastructure and services, in addition to an unstable and bureaucratic, sometimes even dictatorial, government.

Berry's view has effectively cast doubt on the assumption that industrialization, modernization and urbanism necessarily lead from one to another and in consequence produce universal characteristics of the city and of urbanization. Clearly the application of modern technology and the prevalence of modern industries in the former Soviet Union and the US have not yielded cities in these two countries that function, look and feel the same (French and Hamilton, 1979; Bater, 1980). Of course, underlining the Soviet city is a different culture, or rather a subset of contemporary culture or ideology. To link culture and city closely together is true and relevant in a macro sense; if one acknowledges the fact that cultures do vary, so do the cities which develop within them.

Yet the economics and modernism so embedded in the Western conceptualization of the city, though reasonably apt and useful for understanding the evolution of Western European cities since the Renaissance and the development and nature of American cities in the past two centuries, may not be useful tools for comprehending cities in other cultures, particularly Chinese cities. A typical example of such a Western concept of what the city is may be gleaned from a quote from Mumford's famous book *The City in History* (1961):

> the city is a new settlement unit which is a leap from the old village culture. On this new plane, the old components of the village were carried along and incorporated in the new urban unit; but through the action of new factors, they were recomposed in a more complex and amicable pattern in a fashion that promoted further transformation and developments. This new urban mixture resulted in an enormous expansion of human capacities in every direction. It affected a mobilization of manpower, a command over long distances in space and time, an outburst of invention along with a large scale development of civil engineering and, not least, it promoted a tremendous further rise of agricultural productivity.

Mumford's 'city' is obviously the creature that emerged in Western Europe in the era of the 'First Industrial Revolution' and is both time and culture bound. However, in a different part of the same book when discussing the origin of cities, he has this to offer:

> What I would suggest is that the most important agent in effecting the change from a decentralised village economy to a highly organised urban economy, was the king, or rather, the institution of kingship. The industrialization and modernization we now associate with urban growth was for centuries a subordinate phenomenon, probably even emerging later in time . . . In the urban implosion, the king stands at the centre: he is the polar magnet that draws to the heart of the city and brings under the control of the palace and temple all the new forces of civilization. (47)

Although this quote from Mumford shows the germ of a very different interpretation of the origin of the city, it has not drawn attention among Western scholars. The economic origin of the city is still emphasized. To complete our Western definition of the city, we may refer to Mayer's short article (1971) in which he extracted from Western literature 18 definitions of the city, most of which are less time and culture bound than Mumford's version. In these definitions the city is regarded as a carrier of civilization. It is a collection of memories, customs and values, a concentration of the highest human achievements in art, literature and science, a source of freedom and democracy, a concentration of wealth, power, comfort and leisure. It is a type of community with distinct social correlates such as division of labour, of non-agricultural activities and of creativity. It is a protected place, a 'fortress' both physically (in history) and literally, a place of refuge of people and ideas; a place of 'crowds' and dense clusters of people, being protected by a world of people. It is a service centre with groupings of centralized and higher-grade services that distinguish it from the surrounding countryside. It is a market, the economic centre of its hinterland in which there is the seat of production of non-agricultural goods, and where both the urban and non-urban populations satisfy their needs for articles of trade and commerce. It is a meeting place and a transport centre, able to attract non-residents to it for communication and spiritual stimulus no less than for trade, and is a melting pot as well. Lastly it is an area of poor environment.

The images of the city presented in Mayer's summary of the 18 definitions certainly look all embracing. Some of them do apply to cultural settings other than those in Western Europe. The economics that underlie the 18 definitions are quite obvious too. To many people, the origin of cities may be ascribed to one factor, i.e. the economic factor based on the emergence of a sufficient surplus. Others regard alternative spheres of activities as basic, i.e. cities arise when political means are employed to convey food surpluses into authoritarian hands; or the important role played by religion which explained more of the origin of early cities. They point to the lack of clear evidence that a generalized desire for exchange is capable of concentrating political and social power to the extent attested by archaeological record, and that it can bring about the institutionalization of such power (Agnew et al., 1984, 10–11). Wheatley even went as far as saying that religion has at least an equal role to that of economic forces in the emergence of the city:

> It is doubtful if a single autonomous, causative factor will ever be identified in the nexus of social, economic, and political transformation which resulted in the emergence of urban forms, but one activity does seem in a sense to command a sort of priority . . . This does not mean that religion . . . was a primary causative factor, but rather that it permeated all activities, all institutional change; and afforded a consensual focus for social life. (Wheatley, 1971, 318–19)

The lack of congruence between Mayer's images and the traditional Chinese city is particularly notable. In traditional China, there was not such a rigid difference between the city and the countryside economically or culturally. The idea that the city represents either a distinct style or, more importantly, a higher level of civilization than the countryside is a cliché of Western cultural traditions (Mote, 1977). To Mote, China's cities were just knots of the same material, of one piece with the net, denser in quality but not foreign bodies resting in it. In his study on the subject, Trewartha (1952) concluded, 'Probably in no other country has the political influence on city development operated in such a pure fashion and, at the same time, so strongly and continuously through the centuries as in China' (pp. 82–83).

With the political factor prevailing, the form of the traditional Chinese city has also been distinctly regulated by the administrative philosophy behind it, so much so that Chinese cities are very uniform in plan and outlook. In each, the walls were oriented to the cardinal points of the compass; the major streets formed a similarly oriented grid; gates were surmounted by a gate tower; the seat of government occupied the most central or auspicious location of the city, either at the centre or the northerly central location, facing the major street and the main gate of the city in its southern wall. Not only are these the characteristics of the traditional Chinese city in its feudal history, to some extent they are still observable and some have been subconsciously retained as important principles behind the city planning of the People's Republic of China in the post-1949 years. During the Cultural Revolution (1966–1976) lowering the standard of urban housing and urban infrastructure provision was exalted as a means to minimize the difference between town and country. Indeed, Chinese socialist idealism calls for the eradication of the three contradictions: those between mental and manual labour, between higher-level coastal development and lower-level development of the interior provinces, and between town and country. The significance attached to cities as agents of industrialization and modernization in China has certainly never been as great as that given to cities in Western culture. We shall now turn to examine the 'Chineseness' of the traditional Chinese city, which obviously is the underlying dimension for understanding its contemporary capital city – Beijing.

The Chinese world view and the traditional Chinese concept of the city

Agnew et al. (1984) stated that culture refers to the ways of life and the system of meaning established by groups of people who form communicating networks, or did so at one time. The city in its cultural context therefore implies two things: (1) that networks of practices and ideas are drawn from the shared experience and histories of social groups; (2) that these practices and ideas can be invoked to account for specific patterns of urban growth and urban form. Studying the city in its cultural context does not imply the acceptance of the concept of urban culture, nor the idea of a universal rural–urban continuum, as has been discussed in previous paragraphs. Instead it emphasizes the practices and ideas that arise from collective and individual experiences in the varying circumstances of social, economic and political situations that have shaped group and individual existence.

In this section we shall examine the Chinese world view and how it is related to the Chinese concept of the city and its form.

All civilizations have traditions for choosing a fortunate site for a city and symbol systems for relating the city and its various parts to the gods and to the forces of nature. In ancient times, when old religions are strong, a people's beliefs and value system are reflected in where they locate a city and how they design it. Generally, as a civilization develops the authority of the ancient beliefs wanes and secular concerns – economic, strategic and political – come to dominate the location and design of cities. In most societies, then, the influence of early religious concerns is only accidentally reflected in their later cities. But the history of Chinese civilization offers an exception to this general pattern. Throughout the long period of Chinese city building we find an ancient and elaborate symbolism for the location and design of cities persisting in the midst of secular changes. (Wright, 1977, 33).

The symbolism that Wright refers to in this extract is the traditional Chinese world view developed from the core ideology of the Chinese culture, i.e. Confucianism. Although it is beyond our focus here to dwell on details of the Chinese culture, its main elements need to be mentioned in order to comprehend the cultural root of the Chinese city. The universe, according to this view, is a harmoniously functioning organism consisting of multitudinous objects, qualities and forces which, despite their seeming heterogeneity, are integrated into coherent patterns as they all have one source and are subsumed under one or other of the many numerical categories generated by the unity source. The unity source is the universe or *dao*, the Great Unity, from which two opposing and mutually interacting 'vital forces' or 'ethers' emerge. They are the *yin* (negative, passive) and *yang* (positive, aggressive) principles. The *yin* and *yang* ceaselessly interact to generate the eternal round of cosmic phenomena, which within the year follows the cycle of the four seasons. With the passing of the seasons so come the growth and decline respectively of *yin* and *yang*, creating a pattern of rain and dryness, or high and low temperatures. As the Chinese were and are still basically agricultural people, the significance of the seasons, of rain and sunshine and of natural hazards is well understood.

On such a basis, it is logical that the natural dynamic does not only cut across time and space but also bridges the human and natural worlds. To be able to understand and follow the sequence of natural changes such as the seasons and rain and sunshine through the creation of the calendar, for example, reflects the paramount significance of the response of humanity to nature. The two worlds are in fact seen by the Chinese to merge to form a single continuum (universe–man unity), the two halves of which are so closely interwoven that the slightest pull or strain on one spontaneously induces a corresponding pull or strain on the other. The Chinese then see the primary function of the ruler or sovereign as understanding and apprehending the law of nature and preventing or relieving pulls and strains caused by the imbalance of forces in the two halves. In the prehistoric or legendary period of China, this had given rise to the emergence of virtuous men, sages or *sheng ren* through whom Heaven would bestow on land or earth and its people the regularity of the elements of the four seasons and the potency of the soil, while withholding any natural mishaps. These sages were able to perform that role because they had obtained the mandate of Heaven, and because they paid due respect to Heaven through attending correctly to the rituals of sacrifices.

From old records, we can learn of Rao and Shun, the early sage kings. They governed by their personal virtue. Their rule is likened to the Pole Star, which remains in its place while all other stars bow towards or circle round it (Soothill, 1951, 1). The Confucian interpretation of the ancient sage kings is that they were so virtuous that Heaven's will and blessing or, in Confucian terminology, the *dao* (nature of things, law of nature) and *de* (the expression of *dao* or its application) shine through them without any activity on their part. What they did is merely order themselves in the right position, i.e. seated on the throne and facing the south, or the bright regions as in China the dark regions lie in the north owing to its location in the northern hemisphere. Their virtue was so admirable that without effort their moral example spread through the realm. The period of sage kings ended in the Xia Dynasty (2205–1765 BC) with the establishment of hereditary succession. As the divine and potent influence or *de* associated with the sage kings was essential for good government, so Confucian thought believes it should be characteristic of any truly royal throne, since unworthy occupants of that throne could prevent the virtue of Heaven from reaching the people. It therefore demanded of sovereigns virtue in their moral character in resemblance to the Pole Star and observance of rituals to sustain and reinforce the link between the sovereign and God on High. This is symbolic of the normal affinities of the two halves of the Chinese universe, the human and the natural worlds, as an essential part of these ethics. If true sincerity could be restored to the state rituals, then the *de* would shine forth as it did in the days of the sage kings. This view that the sovereign was the mainspring of government and acted as an agent on earth for Heaven (i.e. he was regarded as the Son of Heaven), and that he should position himself like the Pole Star, with other heavenly bodies around him, has espoused a host of ideas which affected both the Chinese world view and the perception and design of Chinese cities.

Most of these ideas had been quite well developed by the Zhou Dynasty (1027–476 BC). Wright (1977) labelled them the three main Zhou cults: worship of the God of Soils; ancestral worship; and worship of Heaven. For men of Zhou the universe was peopled with divinities, spirits and forces that worship, sacrifices and propitiatory rites could control. One of the most ubiquitous cults was that of worship of the God of Soils, a personification of the forces of fertility and self-renewal that reside in the earth. For the sovereign, the altar to this god was symbolic of the power of the state. Named also the 'Altar of Grains and Soils', it was located at the right side of the sovereign's palace. The god was worshipped at all levels, including small altars at the doorways of individual households. Similarly ancestral worship ranged from the sovereign's ancestral temple (*zhu-miao*) to the ancestral halls of a village clan and ancestral tablets within a commoner's house. The sovereign's ancestors, like his God of Soils, were believed to have the power to help assure good crops, victory in war, timely appearance of rain and sunshine, and were equally symbolic of state power as the Altar of Grains and Soils. As chief of all gods and spirits, the master of men, Heaven, or God on High, gave the 'mandate to rule' to those who deserve it. When their line showed signs of vice or incompetence he sent natural calamities to warn them and, if these went unheeded, awarded the mandate to a more virtuous prince. Only sovereigns should worship Heaven. Such Zhou cults linked humanity to the natural forces as well as the ancestors whose influences interact with nature in a seamless web. As Son of Heaven, the sovereign saw his main responsibility to lie in these important acts of worship and was himself the focus of the state religion that had evolved around them, for it was the prerogative of the sovereign and the source of his power and potency.

The essence and rationale of the Zhou cults of worship were formalized and made clear by Confucius and his disciples in *Li Ji*, a Chinese classic believed to be formally published in the Han Dynasty but taking its main ideas from the Zhou Dynasty. Indeed, the acts of worship are the basis on which Confucius developed the rites. They were taken as the basis for the rule of the country which Confucius urged that the sovereign must understand and his officials must organize and help to perform. The five main types of rites are: royal audiences; tours of the lords; sacrifices and burials; feasting; and marriage. *Li Ji* lays down very clearly the offer of sacrifices by the sovereign to the Altar of Grains and Soils for war and for a tour of the country, and to the Ancestral Temple four times a year corresponding to the four seasons. The acts of worship and sacrifices by the sovereign, his lords, officials, scholars and commoners were rigidly ranked. Collectively, the rites form the realization and expression of the *de*, the major means to rule the country, in the same way as a scale is for weighing and a rope and ink for making a straight line or a curve (Wang, 1986, 795).

The rites also express the world view that man and nature are closely interrelated. For that matter, secular behaviour and events of nature are mutually dependent. *Li Ji* spells this out fairly clearly: 'The rites are based on the Great Unity which was separated to form Heaven and Earth and thence transformed into *yin* and *yang*. The latter then changed into the Four Seasons.' *Li Ji* further elaborated the relationship between this basis of the rites, the two fundamental ethers of *yin* and *yang* and the numeric symbolism which form the key elements of the Chinese world view and affect very much the concept and design of Chinese cities. Because of this basic world view, Confucius said that sage kings all followed the natural laws when creating rules and regulations for their subjects, i.e. they used Heaven and Earth as the basis, *yin* and *yang* as the principles, the four seasons as the main key, the positions of the sun and the stars as the guides, the moon (month) as the time divisions, the gods and spirits as the companions, the five elements as the substance, the rites as the tools and humanity as the target, and the four talented beings as the domestic animals.

Thus by the end of Western Zhou (770 BC) there existed a clearly established Chinese world view. The Confucians, which some called ritualists (Wright, 1977, 44), had successfully preserved and codified this into a body of lore, practice and ideas, linked with the behaviour of the sovereign, his manner of rule, and the way that cities were to be planned. At the time of the founding of a unified and huge empire in the Han Dynasty (206 BC), the Confucians were successful in persuading the sovereign to adopt this body of ideas more or less as the state culture and state religion. Of course, the Han Confucians followed basically what had previously been presented. However, there were a few characteristic themes to the Han synthesis which made it more appealing, not only to the Han sovereign but to those other sovereigns in the dynasties to come, and which made 'ritualists' an occupational group and further promoted their ideological influence on statecraft and the Chinese city form. Wright (1977, 46) summarized these characteristics as: (1) archaism; (2) organicism; (3) centralism; and (4) moralism. The effect of archaism is to take Confucius' idealization of the Zhou period as historically true and integral. Organicism explains all the elements in the human and natural worlds in terms of their interactions. Centralism stresses the centrality of the sovereign in the world of men and the centrality of China, the Central Kingdom, in the universe. Finally, moralism involves belief in the moral right of the sovereign to rule, in the moral rightness of the social hierarchy and in classics (particularly the *Li Ji*) as containing the basis of morality and norms for proper social behaviour.

The Chinese traditional world view of mutual interaction of the human and natural worlds focused on the behaviour of one person, the sovereign, or Son of Heaven. Key elements of such Confucian ideology were behind everything and were symbolically expressed through the sacrifices of the sovereign and the design of his capital. The latter was obviously related to his periodic sacrifices to the natural world, as well as his day-to-day behaviour which was of immense symbolic significance in justifying and maintaining a peaceful and long-lasting rule. The Ming T'ang, or Hall of Light, embodies these demands and objectives of kingship in traditional China and is the forerunner of the principles for later designs of the Chinese city. What Mumford (1961) has claimed to be a bold suggestion that 'in the urban implosion, the king stands at the centre' can indeed be substantiated by detailed records of Chinese history, and has hence become part of its characteristic civilization based in Confucianism as well as of the design of the traditional Chinese national capital, which we are going to explore in the next section.

The Ming T'ang: early idea of the Chinese capital

A study of early Chinese kingship by Soothill indicates that it is intimately related to the astronomy which formed the foundation of the Chinese world view. It too is associated with an institution known as the Ming T'ang, Hall of Light, literally the bright hall where things were made clear (Soothill, 1951, 8). In fact the Ming T'ang was the place where the sovereign communicated with the God on High, observed the movements of the stars, and performed sacrifice to Heaven, the various gods, spirits and the ancestors. The sovereign too formed major policies, decided on major measures and gave instructions for their implementation from these. It is believed to be the physical site of the earliest form of state government:

> It appears that this royal and astronomical institution, originating in a stargazer's primitive thatched hut amidst the rudest conditions, became the means which drew into clear alliance untutored contiguous tribes and welded them into nationhood. The disclosures concerning the heavens, the sun, the moon and stars, which emanated from that hut, invested it with power, and made it the focus of the religious and governmental life of the growing nation. (Soothill, 1951, 8–9)

The Ming T'ang was where the sage king sprang up and proved himself to be the true leader of his people. It was a symbol of the conviction that law dominates the universe, that man's prime duty was to accord with that law and that for its harmonious working man's part was essential. The duty of the sage king was to act as guide and ruler, to be his people's link with celestial and terrestrial powers by embodying in himself the principles of this law.

Old Chinese records indicate that the Ming T'ang was first built by Sheng Nong, the Divine Farmer and the second legendary sage king (2736–2705 BC) according to the Yi (Book of Changes) of Fu Xi, the first legendary ruler (who died in 2852 BC), in the shape of an octagon symbolising the ba-gua or Eight Diagrams of Yi. Huang Di, the emperors of Rao and Shun, the Xia, Shang and Zhou dynasties were all in accord with Ming T'ang and maintained it:

> Maintaining it [Ming T'ang] in world-wide exactitude, they link up the ways of the three powers of Heaven, Earth and Man, and extended it throughout the seasons of spring, autumn, winter and summer. These Three

Powers and Four Seasons form the Seven Essentials, from which spring the
fulfillment of the nature of things in general and which, by aiding their
development and nurture, complete that which has already been ordained.
(Soothill, 1951, 70)

During earlier times, i.e. before Huang Di, the Ming T'ang was
situated in open secluded country, but very close to the residence of the
sage king. Its location in the countryside may be related to the
possibility of clear observation of the sky. There it was also surrounded
by still water, which added to the seclusion and acted as a mirror for the
reflected stars. In the Zhou dynasty the Ming T'ang was considered to
be three to seven *li* south of the palace, which is about the present
situation of its later offspring, the altars of Heaven and Agriculture, in
the palace city of Beijing.

The early Ming T'ang with nothing more than the thatched hut,
consisted of one structure, a single room. The central part was for
observatory purposes while the rest of it was divided into eights for
correct positioning of sacrifices according to the different parts of the
year. Under Huang Di, the Ming T'ang changed in its outlook. It was
divided into Five Houses or Five Rooms, growing into a more
complicated building with a central hall and four buildings attached.
Huang Ti also appointed officials for astronomical and weather observation, with a view to regulating the calendar. In the Zhou Dynasty, the
institution attained its fullest development. The Five Houses were
further developed into the Nine Rooms, representing the coordinate
scheme of the eight directions of the compass plus the centre, providing
the clockwise progression of the monthly sacrifices from the beginning
to the end of the year, as it was important that these sacrifices and the
ceremonies associated with them should be offered and performed in
the right and proper directions.

The most detailed and earliest plan of the Ming T'ang came from the
Han Shu (the *History of the Han Dynasty*, published officially during the
Han Dynasty), which described how Wu Di's minister Feng Kao
obtained an allegedly true plan of the Ming T'ang at Huang Di's time.
Based on it Wu Di built his Ming T'ang:

In the middle was a hall which had no four walls, and was covered with
thatch; it was connected with water, which surrounded the boundary walls
of the edifice; and over the water was a double approach. It had an upper
storey with an entrance from the south-west; the upper storey was called
kun-lun; and the Son of Heaven entered by it to worship and sacrifice to
Shang Di (God on High) . . . The surrounding water was outside the four
gates, which were in the boundary walls. It was circular, like the large jade
ring called the *pi*; hence this moat, or *Yong*, was called *Pi Yong*, or Jade-Ring
Moat. The upper storey was called by *Kong Yu-tai* or *k'un-lun* in which to

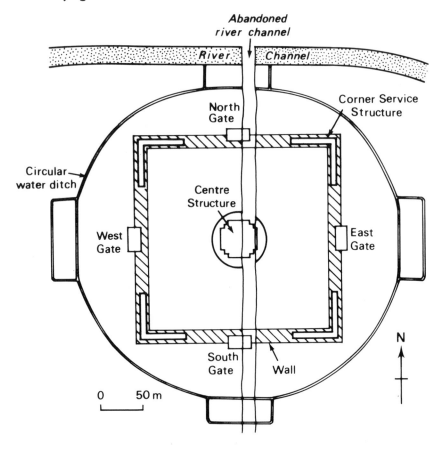

Figure 1.1   Plan of Ming T'ang of Han Dynasty uncovered in Xian. Source: Liu, 1980

sacrifice to *Shang Di*. (Soothill, 1951, 85; See Figures 1.1 and 1.2, the plan and reconstructed view)

That description is more likely to be a reflection of the Ming T'ang during its peak in the Zhou Dynasty. It was then also accorded various names underlining its diverse functions:

The *Da Miao* [Ming T'ang] had eight names, but was one entity. Because of its seclusion and quietness, it was called the *Qing Miao*, 'Pure or Quiet Fane'; because of the quinquennial and triennial sacrifices, and the arranging of the two ranks of ancestors, it was called the 'Great Fane'; because of the announcement of the new moon and the promulgation of the orders of government, it was called the *Ming T'ang*; because of the archery

A. Whole structure

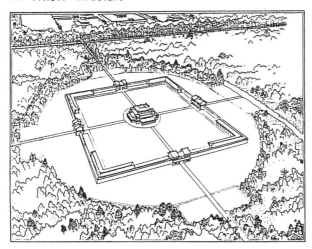

B. Centre structure

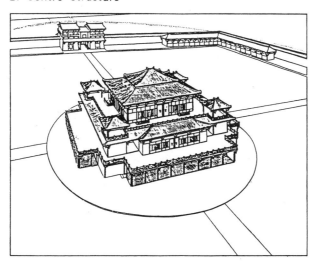

Figure 1.2 Reconstructed view of Ming T'ang. Source: Liu, 1980

tournament and the alimony given to the royal elders, it was called the *Pi Yong* or 'Jade-Ring Moat'; because of its meteorological inquiry for auspices, it was called the *Ling Tai*, or 'Observatory'; because of the four schools at the four gates, it was called the *Tai Xue* or 'Great College'. Its central building was called the *Da Shi*, or 'Great House'. And altogether, it was called *Gong* or a Palace'. (Quoted in Soothill, 1951, 82).

Two observations may be made about this quotation. First, the Ming T'ang was the seat of government, state religion, education and science. Similar functional roles of the Ming T'ang in the Zhou Dynasty were echoed in the Chinese classic *Da Dao Lu*:

> The *Ming T'ang* was the Son of Heaven's Great Temple, or *Da Miao*, for the *ti ji* or sacrifice to the founders of the imperial house. There were oblations to certain ancestors, the *zhong shi*; the spring and autumn audiences, or *Chao jin*; the ploughing of the sacred plot; the bestowing of food on the old relatives and officers; the distinguishing of worth; the archery tournament; the offering of captives of war; the regulation of the calendar; the observation of the clouds and weather; the announcement of the new moon; and the giving of orders of government. All these affairs were transacted within it; and therefore it was the hall, or palace, of Great Instruction. (Quoted in Soothill, 1951, 69–70)

Secondly, both passages summed up the varying roles of the Ming T'ang by the label of 'palace' or '*gong*' (Chinese character meaning palace). It provides us with the basis to infer that the sovereign's palace, the physical setting for him to perform his various duties, originates from the institution we describe as Ming T'ang. Ku's work (1984) has quoted quite widely from old classics which hinted at this:

> The *Ming T'ang* was a structure with thatched roof. The water outside it was called *Pi Yong*. Its doors were coloured red and windows white. The hall was 3 feet high and 9 *yin* wide in the east–west direction and 7 *yin* deep in the north–south direction. It had 9 rooms and 12 halls. Each room had four doors and each door two panels. It was also taken to be *Wei Huang's Da Miao*. (*Da Dai Li*)

> *Pi* is in a circle to symbolise Heaven, *Yong* means to flow water in a channel to symbolise the spread of education or rites . . . . The *Ming T'ang* was round on top and square at the base. It had eight windows and four sectors . . . It is the palace of administration and located at the southern side of the capital. The rounded upper part takes its form after Heaven and the square foundation symbolises Earth. The eight windows symbolise the eight types of winds and the four sectors, the four seasons. The nine rooms represented the nine provinces of China. The twelve halls represented the months. The 36 doors represented the 36 sectors of the lunar months while the 72 openings in the walls, the 72 breezes. (*Bai Hu Tang*)

> Offered sacrifices to *Wei Huang* in the *Ming T'ang* to pair with sacrifices to God on High. (*Xiao Jin*)

> *Ming T'ang*, the palace wherein the Son of Heaven announces his policies. (*Xiao Jin Zhu*)

The multi-functional characteristics as well as the symbolism in shapes and numbers were very much followed by designs of the palace city of sovereigns of various dynasties. Figure 1.2 shows the Ming T'ang built by Han Wu Di, based on successful digs in the 1950s. They have confirmed many of the points on its design and related symbolism contained in the early Chinese classics. As a physical group of buildings, the Ming T'ang declined from the later parts of the Zhou Dynasty. The seat of government moved to the Throne Room of the palace some distance away. The observation of the stars and the calculation of the calendar had been taken away from it too, to be housed in the Observatory and performed by specialist officials. Nor was it an ancestral temple in the usual sense of a temple to all the family ancestors. With the expansion of the sovereign's realm, his increasing desire for pleasure, comfort, his journeys from the capital and finally his laziness brought about the centralization of government in the palace. The Ming T'ang lost its former role as the real headquarters of imperial power. Some of its other functions were secularized and housed separately in institutions that through later dynasties still bore alternative names of the Ming T'ang, i.e. Ling Tai (Observatory), or Tai Xue (Great College).

Even as the centre of the state religion, the Ming T'ang was in many instances in history replaced by other arrangements such as the Altar of Soils, Altar of Agriculture and the Da Miao (Ancestral Hall). It was noted that in the later Zhou, though the building might have been maintained, the rites were no longer carefully observed within the Ming T'ang. By the time of Confucius, it was further noted, both in the imperial capital and in the capital of the state of Lu, that it had decayed even physically. Several times during the ensuing centuries, notably by Han Wu Di and Empress Wu of the Tang Dynasty, a new Ming T'ang was erected. These later structures had only very limited symbolic and little real function either in the administrative or religious sense. They too soon invariably fell into neglect. Soothill saw the Ming T'ang's final demise in the Ming Dynasty as Beijing was constructed as the new national capital:

> The Ming dynasty saw its final demise. Its primary astronomical and meteorological functions in aid of the calendar had long been undertaken by a separate office; the monthly sacrifice by the sovereign at the new moon had long ceased; the colleges had separate buildings; the scope of religion had widened and included other cults, such as Buddhism; the emperor had no longer claimed descent from one of the Five *Ti*, as was the case until the end of the Zhou dynasty; and the sacrifices to heaven, to earth, to the sun, the moon, and the other gods or natural phenomena, having now their distinctive and separate altars, and no longer attached to one place.
>
> Politically, the break-up of the feudal system was a main factor in the decline of the *Ming T'ang* with its state rites and in the wider dispersal of functions. Without the presence of the barons, by whom the Son of Heaven ought to 'stand surrounded', the glory had gone. Without the barons,

indeed, to whom could be delivered the calendar, or how could be carried out the ancient duties, save with shorn rites and meaning? (1951, 76–77)

The physical demise of the Ming T'ang may be interpreted quite differently to the perspective of Soothill. Indeed we see a gradual evolution of the Ming T'ang into the 'Palace City' of the Emperor, with his extending realm and increasing concentration of power. The basic roles of the Ming T'ang can easily be traced in the various buildings of the later Palace City. They were there to congregate and perform the same role as the single-room structure of Sheng Nong, or the thatched hut without walls in earlier times than that. The same principles that there was a need for the nation to be linked in harmony with the realm of nature; that the ruler was still for this purpose the one essential nexus; that the material, or rather the animated world, in all its operations, still depended on his cooperation in the trifold union of Heaven, Earth and Man, still remained the guardians in the planning and lay-out of the Palace City of the national capital until the Qing Dynasty. There is more sense in the view that the Ming T'ang had not fallen. Instead it evolved to become the basic concept of the Chinese national capital or, for that matter, the concept of the Chinese city in general.

A Japanese scholar compared the ancient records of the Shang Dynasty and those of comparable civilizations of other parts of the world and concluded that the early capitals of these different cultures share one common feature: the key element in their formation was the chieftain, or the sovereign. The central area of the capital was the palace. Its residents were either his officials or slaves. These ancient capitals were therefore all populated with the extended family of the sovereign. On top of that there may be some additional people for supplying food and for the upkeep of the city. Exchanges at that time might not be viewed as commerce (Ho, 1937). Referring specifically to China, Lao (1942) believes that the early capital was founded on the palace. There was little concern about municipal plans. Excavation of capitals of the Shang Dynasty brought out this point very well. Another hint he observed from these historical digs is that the palace was invariably in front of a stream, which he related to the *pi yong* of the Ming T'ang. Excavations in the 1970s threw further light on this. For example, the Long Pan City was surrounded on three sides by water and its palace had a thatched roof (Ye, 1986, Vol. 1, 81–83). In a Shang Dynasty palace site at Fu Feng County, found in 1976, the main building structure was reconstructed by archaeologists as having no walls on four sides. The first storey was almost square in shape with a central round upper storey crowned by a thatched roof (Ye, 1986, 98).

From a thatched hut to a one-room structure, then five-room

structure, then nine-room structure, and then more elaborate, the Ming T'ang moved forward to become the spiritual and physical model of the Chinese city. It is the physical expression of the Chinese world view which governed the relationship between man and nature and the role of the sovereign in mediating between these two different worlds. Thus the Chinese city does not have the same foundation as the 'natural' city developed out of economics or trade. It is the seat of governance and for maintaining orderliness and productivity, based on a set of cults embodying the sacrifices and symbolism and evolved out of a unique Chinese world view.

The Chinese city concept

There is no lack of Western literature that says Chinese cities have been for many centuries dominated by the administrative function. For example, Trewartha (1952) concluded that to a much greater extent than in those two other great population centres, one on either side of the Atlantic Ocean, cities in China originated and developed as a result of the stimuli associated with administration, and that these administrative functions are still more prominent in Chinese cities than they are in those of the Occident. He observed that since ancient times there appear to have been two primary forces in China stimulating the development and growth of cities: (1) the dynastic or administrative factor, and (2) the economic factor. This conforms with Mote's two categories of Chinese cities, i.e. the administrative city and the economic or natural city. The dynastic factor includes two elements: administration and defence. This factor has been so pure and pervasive that Trewartha thinks it is only within the last half century or so that the Chinese concept of a city as the seat of a public official, the visible evidence of which was the city wall, has been significantly modified. Indeed, for centuries in China the importance of a city was measured not so much in terms of its area or the number of its inhabitants, as by the rank of the government official who resided there. This dynastic influence increased in strength as the administrative factor operated to bring prosperity to a city in trade and industry, since the officials were a luxury-loving group and their presence in large numbers required many people for service and maintenance. The officials often acted as patrons of science, art and literature, so that they supported the related population and attracted many 'lookers on'. Moreover, there was also a tradition of the State absorbing profitable enterprises and making them government monopolies (Trewartha, 1952, 84). Thus, although the rank of a particular city originally had little relationship to its size and commercial importance, there was a natural tendency for cities of higher administrative rank gradually to develop important commercial and industrial functions.

The administrative ranking in terms of the political organization of the country is directly linked to the size of the city's wall, and hence the rank of its officials and the possible size of its economy, as reflected by the rule set up in the *Book of Yin*:

> Any metropolitan city whose wall is more than 3,000 cubits around is dangerous to the state. According to the regulations of the former kings, such a city of the 1st order can have its walls only a third as long as that of the capital; one of the 2nd order only a fifth as long and one of the least order only a ninth. (Legge, quoted by Trewartha, 1952, 73)

Though acknowledging a second factor as well as a second type of Chinese city, i.e. the economic, Trewartha categorically stated that most cities in ancient China possessed political or military functions and it was probably rare, if not unknown, for a sizeable urban community to develop solely with non-administrative functions. The term 'Chinese city' usually means the roughly 1500 to 2000 urban concentrations that were designated the seats of the administrative arms of the central government, that is, imperial and provincial capitals plus prefectural and county-level capitals (the *fu*, *zhou* and *xian* cities). In Chinese they are *zhen*, because their administrative significance gave them the right or the need to be walled. The administrative function, as noted by Mote, also contributed much to form: the walls, square or rectangular in shape, were oriented to the cardinal grid whose intersections were right angles; gates were surmounted by gate towers; and a moat surrounded the walls. Even though he recognizes the fact that all administrative cities of pre-modern China had a wall, he believes that the wall is only psychological rather than to offer a real physical defence:

> Perhaps in a large sense the walls of Nanking and of other cities rebuilt in Ming times served the primarily psychological function of reaffirming the presence of the Chinese state rather than the purely physical function of making cities and their inhabitants secure against possible sources of danger . . . The high walls and broad moats of Nanking did not protect the shrines of Heaven and of Earth, the tombs of the imperial ancestors, or even the major government entrepot and factories, and most officials who resided in government-built housing outside them. (Mote, 1977, 137)

Thus the walls around administrative cities did not divide off a zone of guaranteed safety from the rest of the population. More importantly, Mote believes that they did not divide an urban subculture from a rural one. The Ming founder certainly had some purely military functions in mind when he decided to include readily fortifiable points within the enlarged walls of Nanking, but:

> he ruled primarily by civil means, and these means included above all the ritual ordering of society and government and the reliance on a mystique of legitimacy expressed in the Mandate of Heaven. The city walls of Nanking were, like other acts of government, designed to reinforce that mystique and maintain the awesome sense of the government's presence. That, I would hypothesize, is their primary significance in Chinese cultural history and in the study of the city in traditional China. (Mote, 1977, 138)

Mote has surely identified the essential nature of the Chinese city. The traditional Chinese city, its role and its form, had been derived from the traditional Chinese world view described earlier which had shaped the philosophy of government and the way that rulers and their officials should govern and administer. This will be covered in more detail in a later discussion on the 'ideal' Chinese city plan. Here we shall dwell on the city–country convergence of traditional China which makes the city an integral part of the vast agricultural community rather than a distinctive, separable part of the body of China.

The Chinese civilization had not granted the same degree of importance to typical urban activities as has been accorded by other urban civilizations. Its values did not sustain a self-identifying and self-perpetuating urban elite as a component of the population. The idea that the city represented either a distinct style, or more importantly a higher level of civilization than the countryside, is a cliché of Western cultural traditions, and had never been the case in traditional China. Since the Zhou dynasty China, in theory and in practice, was an open society. The Chinese attained the rights to own land freely and to change their place of residence and way of life. There was frequent, and in many cases daily, movement of large numbers of people in and out of cities. They were not aware of crossing any definite boundary. The city wall was not in fact a boundary between an urban within and a rural without (Mote, 1977). The imperial magistrate in the city (county seat) was officially responsible for everyone and everything in the county (*xian*). He was closely assisted by unofficial, but often powerful, local gentry and peasant village elders or clans in the management of the bulk of the rural and hence *xian* affairs. The practical administration of the magistrate and his deputies, combined with the family, clan, gentry and the nearly universally accepted Confucian ethics, kept not just order remarkably well, but also effectively integrated the city and its surrounding countryside into one administrative, social and cultural unity.

This perceived unitary relationship between town and country was true of economic affairs as well. Traditional China was overwhelmingly agrarian. Cities were designed not only to control and tax the country-side, but most importantly to serve it. Trade and merchants flourished in these cities, but most commodities were of agricultural or rural origin. The primary responsibility of the city-based imperial officials was to ensure the productivity as well as the orderliness of the agricultural countryside. This was true most immediately for the *xian* magistrate, the official closest to the rural areas, but also for the emperor himself, at the head of the pyramid. His and the city magistrate's first concern was the well-being of the agricultural sector and the serving of it which was met most significantly by order, then productivity and protection. The city not only provided the 'place' where such needs were to be met, but also strengthened them through the symbolism embedded in its physical form (Murphy, 1984).

Thus Trewartha observed a cellular structure of economy and society built on the administrative walled 'city in the country' and its tributary agricultural area (1952, 70–71). This cellular structure was repeated indefinitely all over China and many of the features and functions remained the same under both Zhou feudalism and later imperial orders. In the fundamentally agricultural economy of traditional China, the walled city became essential as well as an integral feature of the landscape. In the more fertile parts of the country, one city could be reached by another in less than a day's walk and the cell was smaller. The expansion of the empire was said to proceed with the implant of the walled city and its cellular structure to the newly conquered or opened areas. Giovanni Botero wrote as early as the sixteenth century that China should rather be considered as 'but one body and but one city' (Mote, 1977, 105). Though a high degree of centralization and despotism was realized in China as early as the Qin Dynasty, partly because of the vastness of the country but more importantly owing to the concept of the city derived from the traditional world view, there was no corre-sponding urban development nor the rise of a single prime city as occurred in Europe after the Medieval period. Botero explained that China was not an agglomeration of semi-autonomous city-states, and that it was not a country in which island-states were surrounded by seas of rude peasants. All China, as it were, constituted one organizational entity as though it were one city. Mote further explains:

> Despite the political centralization that was so fully realized in the later centuries for the imperial era, there was no primate city that claimed for itself exclusively such characteristic metropolitan activities as (1) setting fashion, (2) providing the locus of intellectual, artistic, and creative developments, and (3) concentrating the cultural achievements of civilization in the form of libraries and art collections. The dispersion of

these activities throughout many urban and rural settings, and the consequent lack of any single great urban centre that was both the acme and the microcosm of Chinese civilization strengthens our awareness of rural China. The rural component of Chinese civilization was more or less uniform, and it extended everywhere that Chinese civilization penetrated. It is not the cities that defined the Chinese way of life. It was the net in which the cities and towns of China were suspended . . . To extend this metaphor, China's cities were but knots of the same material, or one piece with the net, denser in quality but not foreign bodies resting on it. (Mote, 1977, 105)

The cultural continuum from city to country was also maintained by the two-way flow of human resources, officials in the course of their duties or on furlough or retirement, and rural recruits moving into the commercial or bureaucratic world of the city. There was no denigration of rural circumstances and values, but rather, on the part of many of the urban elite, a longing for the countryside, to which they would retreat whenever they could and to which they almost invariably retired. Building structures, e.g. houses, business buildings, temples and government buildings, were essentially the same in principle in design, orientation, style and material, in cities as well as in the countryside. The parts of a single unit, be it a small house or large official building, are arranged to enclose and to include the use of open ground. The rural ideals of the upper class, which are part of Confucianism, the permeation of those ideals throughout the whole society and the tendency of the upper classes to alternate between living in town and living in the country helped to diminish the cultural and architectural differences between them. Equally, styles of dress, patterns of eating and drinking, means of transportation, and other obvious aspects of daily life did not display any characteristic dichotomies between rural and urban.

This deliberation on the nature of the city and its relationship to the countryside has provided useful background to the 'ideal' as well as the 'typical' pattern of the Chinese city form, as the latter is to a great extent affected by what the city is within the broad frame of the minds of the Chinese.

Layout of the ideal Chinese capital city

The earliest Zhou city building was recorded in the *Book of Songs*: the grandfather of King Wen, T'an-fu, founded a city at the foot of Mt. Chi (about 1352 BC) (Wright, 1977, 35). This was done with great ceremony. The founding noble was in full official dress. First he inspected the countryside to select a proper site. Shadows were studied to determine the cardinal points of the compass. He examined the declivities in sun and shade. Account was taken of the direction of the running water. Finally the tortoise shell was consulted to determine whether the chosen site met with the will of Heaven. If it did, the decision was confirmed and sacrifices were made to Heaven and the god of soils of the new city. Other records in the *Book of History* also confirmed this sequence of events in the founding of cities in the early Zhou period; similar procedures and rituals were followed in later dynasties. From these early descriptions, Wright has drawn four elements in city building in early Zhou, i.e.:

1. The city was pre-planned and the plan was reduced to written form.
2. The proposed city was staked out on its site according to the plan.
3. When this had been completed, there were two sets of animal sacrifices. One set – probably to Heaven and the Zhou primordial ancestors – took place at the altar outside the limit of the planned city, whereas the other set – fertility sacrifices – took place at the earth-mound that had been raised within.
4. The labour force was charged in advance with specific parts of the work.

With the exception of the last element, the observations are significant in our understanding of the plan of the ideal city in traditional China. There can also be observed from these records further key physical features of the plan and construction of the Zhou cities:

1. The city was placed in precise alignment with the four directions.
2. The city walls were built in the form of a square or rectangle. South is the favoured orientation of important temples, halls and all other important buildings, the main gate and even of the entire city. There is also an emphasis on the north–south axis.
3. Cities are located on level land near water.
4. Pounded earth platforms are used as foundations of politically or religiously important buildings.
5. The city plan is articulated into functional zones: a central area, usually walled, that contained the palaces and important buildings used by the aristocracy; surrounding the central area is a second walled area that included industrial and artisanal quarters, residences of the people, some farmland, commercial streets and markets; outside there is often a moat.

Points (1), (2), (4) and (5) are of ritual and symbolic significance. They have evolved from the early Chinese world view embedded in the Ming T'ang which later had been theorized by Confucianism. Cheng Zhou, built by King Wen, is a good representation of this city plan (see Figure 1.3).

Yet the ideal city form of traditional China has been further elaborated by passages that appeared in one of the Confucian classics, *Zhou Li*, in which three passages are particularly relevant:

> It is the sovereign alone who establishes the capital, gives the palace a central position and proper orientation to the four directions. He gives the capital its form and the countryside proper divisions. He creates the offices and apportions their functions in order to form a centre and a moral yardstick to which his people may look. (*Zhou Li, Tian Gong,* Lin (ed.), 1972, 1)[1]

> Here, where Heaven and Earth are in perfect accord, where the four seasons come together, where the winds and rains gather, where the forces of *yin* and *yang* are harmonized, one builds a royal capital. (ibid., *Kao Gong Ji*)

> The capital city shall be a walled square. Each wall measures nine-*li* and has three gates. There are nine north–south and nine east–west arterial roads, each of which shall have a width for accommodating nine chariot-ways. On the left-hand outside of the palace shall be the Ancestral Hall, while on the right-hand side shall be the Altar of Soils. In front of the palace shall be the Audience Halls. The market is to be located at the back side of the city, and measured one hundred paces on each side. The corner towers of the palace shall be five-*zhang* high, that of the imperial city seven and the outer wall nine. The major roads are to be nine chariot-ways wide, minor roads seven and those outside the capital only five. The capitals of the princes shall have city wall towers up to the height of the imperial city of the sovereign, whereas those of the lords may not be five-*zhang* high. Similarly, the main roads of the prince's capital shall be the same width as the minor roads of the emperor's capital and those of the lords of a width equal to roads outside the emperor's capital. (ibid., *Kao Gong Ji*)

This ideal city plan is graphically presented in Figures 3.5 and 3.6 in Chapter 3. Although *Zhou Li* expressly refers to the sovereign's capital, there is also clearly, as shown in the third passage, extension of the same principles and rules to capitals of the princes and lords, with a gradual reduction of the scale of the walls, gates and the width of the roads. We can further extend these principles and rules similarly to lesser-grade cities in the administrative hierarchy. Thus the ideal city plan governs, in principle, the layout of all cities in traditional China.

---

1. Wright translates *Guo* as 'state' whereas Huang took it as the capital city. The sentence on central position and the four directions was taken by Wright as referring to the city, whereas Huang believes that it refers to the royal palace. The Chinese character *ji* in the last sentence may be translated as 'a point' or 'an extreme'. Here it is more appropriate to take it to mean principle or moral yardstick, as has been so interpreted by Tang.

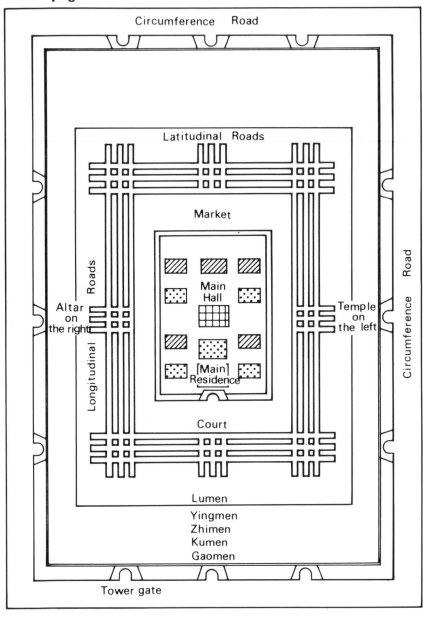

Minor Hall

Minor Residence

Figure 1.3   Plan of Cheng Zhou of Zhou Dynasty. Source: Yung Lo Da Din, 1425

In the first passage, we may infer that the sole purpose for constructing the capital is to provide the sovereign with a place in which he
could organize his administration and implement his rule according to
the basic Chinese world view which incorporates the concepts of
centrality, orderliness and paternity relationship between the ruler and
his subjects. The second passage elaborates on the centrality and
paternity element of the capital by referring to the requirement that it
should be where, symbolically, Heaven and Earth are in perfect accord.
In practice, this means a central location *vis-à-vis* an agrarian economy as
well as in the detailed layout of the capital, i.e. the location of the palace,
gates and various important ceremonial buildings in proper symbolic
positions. This reminds us of the changing shape and evolution of the
structure of the Ming T'ang. There is also the requirement of the exact
orientation for sacrifices in various months and the centrality of the
locale where the sovereign watched the sky to read messages from
Heaven. In large measure, the detailed layout represents the codified
version of a widely expanded departmentalization of the Ming T'ang as
the empire had grown in size. Though the symbolic as well as real
values of these various functions of the Ming T'ang remained, they now
took the forms of definitive buildings and important structures of an
entire city. We do not yet have sufficient evidence, but it is nevertheless
worthwhile to record the following speculation: that the square wall of
the ideal city takes its form from the wall of the Ming T'ang, as in the
traditional Chinese view the earth was square and it was the earth
where the sovereign ruled. The moat surrounding the wall may be the
circular channel of water that skirted the Ming T'ang, reminiscent of
heaven above, or the four seas that encircle the earth.

These ideas contained in *Zhou Li* have been critical in our hypothesis
that the nature of the city in traditional China and its form originated
from the traditional Chinese world view and that the city's physical
structure is related to the early institution of Chinese kingship, the Ming
T'ang. Obviously, ideas of later periods, such as the more elaborated
concepts of *yin–yang* and the Five Elements as developed in the Han
Dynasty, as well as concepts of the quasi-science called *feng shui*, also
contributed in some measure to the layout of the traditional Chinese
city. We will only elaborate on these when examining Beijing as the
example of the traditional Chinese city.

Conclusion

Before we end this chapter let us summarize the key elements of the ideal
Chinese city as reflecting the traditional world view of Confucianism:

1. Siting – central position relative to its subjects and natural environs.
2. Orientation – faces south (particularly the main gate) as the south represents the direction of potency as well as being the choice of the early sage kings, and purports a smooth and benevolent blessing from Heaven.
3. General layout – square and orderly, representing the need to conform with the orderliness of nature to avoid haphazard mishaps.
4. The palace or administrative quarter (in case of a lesser city than the capital) is located at the centre where the administrative head resides to symbolize centralization of power as well as the mandate from Heaven to rule.
5. The ceremonial building of the Ancestral Hall and the Altar of Grains and Soils reflect the lineage of the sovereign to the sage kings and his close relation to the potency of the earth. Regular rituals in these places substantiate his claim to legitimacy as well as continued blessing from both gods and spirits.
6. The wall – symbolizes the sovereign's reign on earth.
7. Location of the market in the most inauspicious location to the north of the city represents the lesser significance of trade and merchant classes and of non-productive pursuits in an agrarian economy.
8. The size and scale gradation of the hierarchy of cities reflects the rank ordering of society emanating from Confucian rituals as well as the practical delegation of power from the national capital to regions in the country.

Murphy (1984), in a paper on the relationship between city and culture, wrote that each culture has built cities which reflect, symbolize and affirm its character, its values and its distinctive set of solutions or non-solutions to common human problems. In reverse, the city is both a convenient and revealing key to culture, and is the clearest, most concentrated and most significant imprint which a culture produces on the landscape. The Chinese case is a special one only in that it has a long and largely continuous history of cities produced by a culture which remains 'at least in consciousness, essentially the same for well over two millennia, largely free of significant cultural admixtures of foreign origin and within a context of political–administrative continuity as well.' We feel that Murphy is generally correct, though we would add that the divergence between the Chinese case and those of other cultures, particularly the Western European ones, lies also in the basic fact that the Chinese cities are different in nature as well as in concept.

2

The emergence of Beijing

Location of the national capital

A national capital is usually a nation's political, economic and cultural centre. It concentrates not only the typical achievements of the people, but also reflects the cultural traits and the nation's strategic position at the time. There are numerous studies on China's changing capital locations which mostly take the view that it would bring better understanding on the economic, military, political and cultural aspects of Chinese history. Shi, a famous Chinese contemporary historical geographer, thus has proposed the founding of a new sub-branch of science – ancient capital study (Shi, 1987, 1).

Cornish (1922) proposes three factors that govern the location of ancient national capitals, i.e. crossway, granary and fortress. Crossway clearly emphasized waterways in the context of ancient times. Granary refers to the centrality of the national capital in respect of a region of high agricultural productivity. Lastly, the military or strategic consideration for the defence of the national capital and its convenient control over the rest of the country has also been an obvious factor. The actual location of a national capital, however, may be the result of one or a combination of the three factors. In approaching the subject, we have to give due consideration to the geographical diversity of different countries, the time period involved, as well as the predominant national problems and the related national strategies to meet such challenges at the time. Xia (1952, 422–3), based on his examination of national capitals of the world at different times, produced a useful typology of national capitals, taking into consideration the geography, time and strategy factors, viz:

Type A   *Coastal capitals*
Subtype: A1 For commanding a sea frontier – found in a maritime country whose economic base lies partly on land and partly in the sea, e.g. Rome, Athens and Copenhagen.

A2 For commanding a land frontier – beachhead port cities of colonies, e.g. Jakarta, Rangoon and Singapore.

A3 Power base – found in island states or coastal states whose largest concentration of land, productivity and population is found in a coastal plain, e.g. Colombo, Seoul, Helsinki.

A4 A4i Forward coastal capital of an inland state – for cultural and defence purposes, an inland state places its capital strategically on the coast for defence or for absorption of an alien culture; e.g. St. Petersburg in Russia and Constantinople of the Ottoman Empire.

A4ii Retreating coastal capital – mainly for easy defence of an ailing empire in face of threat from a powerful enemy, e.g. Hangzhou in the Southern Song Dynasty of China.

Type B   *Inland Capitals*
Subtype: B1 For counterbalancing neighbouring powers – found in inland states of square or round-shaped territory surrounded by powerful neighbours. The capital is located at the centre of the country for national security and defence purposes, e.g. Warsaw and Moscow (in the Middle Ages).

B2 Power base – found in the most densely populated and economically concentrated region of the country with little regard to its powerful neighbours or defence considerations, e.g. Ottawa, Bogota, Mexico City.

B3 Transport node – in control of the major transport routes of the country, e.g. Paris, Cairo, and Pataniputra in Indian history.

B4 B4i Forward inland capital – Inland empire with a forward defence national strategy, e.g. Xian in China in the Han to Tang Dynasties, and Delhi in India.

B4ii Retreating inland capital – capital founded by a retreating or ailing empire in times of crisis, e.g. Russia after World War I moved its capital from Petrograd to Moscow, and the Eastern Jin Dynasty of China moved its capital from Luoyang to Nanjing; both were pursuing a retreating national defence strategy.

In the five millennia of Chinese history, the location of the national capital changed many times. It is obvious that not a single subtype of Xia's typology is adequate to define the Chinese national capitals. The pattern and character of the varying Chinese national capitals have been discussed by Li and Liu (1986). They have drawn three main observations. First, the character of shifting locations is rarely found in most other countries. For example, the choice of capital in ancient and contemporary Egypt is much constrained within the delta of the Nile. Rome has been the consistent capital of Italy and so has Paris from the fifth century onwards of France. London has been the capital of England from the Middle Ages onwards. In China, excepting minor shifts, the location of the national capital changed six times in major eastward, westward, northward and southward shifts over long distances of more than 1000 km. Secondly, there had been many times a dual capitals system. In world history the only comparable examples are Rome and Constantinople of the Roman Empire. Within the huge Chinese empire, its significant north–south geographical and economic differences, as well as the need for defence, had made it necessary and strategically desirable at times to have more than one concurrent national capital. Finally, in the contemporary period, the influx of Western culture and capitalism have induced a new change regarding the role of the national capital. Since the mid nineteenth century in the Yangtze Delta, these newly imported elements have developed a new modern culture in an already prosperous economic and cultural region. It has since evolved into the cultural hub of the country, while Beijing can only retain the role of a political centre. For the first time since the Qin Dynasty, the political and cultural centre roles of the Chinese national capital have been split up and a new national cultural centre has been established outside the national capital.

Chinese literature on the choice of the location of the national capital can be traced back to the very early days of the Zhou Dynasty. Within the literature we may summarize that the foremost principle behind the choice of a capital is the maintenance of harmonies between men, as well as between man and the natural realm. This principle is closely related to the traditional world view that lies behind the concept and the design of the ideal Chinese city, as has been discussed in Chapter 1. In practice, the idea has evolved into the principle of centrality, the principle of military strategy and the principle of harmonious human relationship.

The principle of centrality has been clearly expressed in the old classic *Zuo Zhuan*:

> The sovereign is mandated to found his state. His capital should be at the centre of his territory to enable him to be at harmony with his realm and to obtain the positive interaction of *yin* and *yang*, to have a fair control of the four directions and a grip on the thousand vassal states. (Quoted in Ye, 1988, 20)

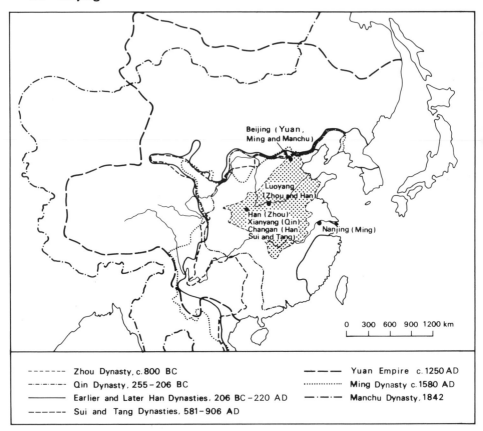

Figure 2.1 The territorial boundaries of the Chinese Empire from Zhou to Qing Dynasty and the locations of the national capital

When Zhou Gong chose Luo (Luoyang) as the new capital of the Zhou Dynasty he actually said it was 'at the centre of the world wherefrom the length of the tribute routes from all vassal states are similar'. City Luo was more or less the geographic centre of Zhou's realm (see Figure 2.1). The notion of centrality had also been developed into a concept similar to Christaller's (1933) central place theory and the concept of nodal region. *Shang Shu* elaborated a territorial administrative system whereby the emperor's realm was divided into five *fu*, i.e. the capital was treated as the centre and from it radiating in all directions the land is marked out into five *fu*, each of 500 *li* in depth. Thus the capital is to be 2500 *li* from the four edges of the empire, being at its centre. In *Zhou Li*, a similar system was mentioned, the nine *fu*, in which the capital was at the centre of a nodal region, about 5000 *li* from its rim. Such ideas of centrality and of nodal region had transcended lesser capitals of the princes and lords. 'In ancient times, the sovereign chose the centre of his 1000 *li* wide realm as capital; the lord chose the centre of his 100 *li* wide realm.' Such a notion has categorically expressed a hierarchy of centres, each at the midpoints of their respective nodal regions (Hou, 1989, 39).

The principle of centrality conforms with the traditional Chinese world view that the ruler was the Son of Heaven, and he acted as the mediator between man and Heaven. So he must be centrally located between Heaven and Earth. This positioning of the capital at balance with the four directions and harmony between man and Heaven played its part in cultivating a centripetal and loyal psychology in the traditional Chinese mind. The emphasis on geographic centre obviously facilitated the efficient dispatch of administrative orders, material flows for sustaining the army and the central bureaucracy, as well as the recruiting of peasants as soldiers. The centralizing force of the centre in a nodal region also produces other positive impacts on economic and cultural developments of the entire region. It too serves as an efficient model in the opening up of frontier regions. Thus it is well said by Zhou Gong that the benefit of City Luo lies in its ability 'to harmonize *yin* and *yang*, to balance north and south and to concentrate hundreds of material flows' (Hou, 1989, 38).

Military strategy or defence has been regarded by many Chinese scholars (Hou, 1989; Shi, 1986a, etc.) as the second most important factor in the location of ancient Chinese capitals. 'The major roles of the capital are in sacrifices and military' (Hou, 1989). In the various dynasties, the national capital had invariably been the place where a huge army had been concentrated. In early Tang Dynasty, the state had a total of 634 army units (*fu*). Within the administrative area of the capital alone were 261 units, while the capital city itself had 125 units. In the Wanle reign of the Ming Dynasty, the whole country had an army of 1.259 million, of which 826 000 were stationed in the capital city region. To keep such a large army meant a heavy burden on the country. Besides, the army could only be effectively deployed if the capital lay in a defensible strategic location. Xian is a good example of a strategic location. As early as the Qin Dynasty, a famous strategist had said that it was 'fortress-like' on four sides. The Guan Zhong Plain on which Xian is located is a basin-like structure. There are high mountains with strategic passes on the north, west and south sides, forming effective physical barriers to any attack from these directions. Yet in the Warring States (475–221 BC) and Han Dynasty (206 BC–220 AD), militant lords were only found in the east. Even on this side there is the famous strategic pass, Xiangu, which provided effective and easy defence from threats from the east while it facilitated the emperor's choice of the most opportune time for marching eastward to subdue any rebellious lord. Beijing offers the second best example as a defence location (Shi, 1986b, 8–9). Yet the defence factor ought not be mistaken as a chief function of the wall or of the city itself, as has been said in Chapter 1. The defence of the national capital lies mainly in numerous defence positions outside the city, yet within the strategic nodal region of the capital. Thus the defence consideration loomed largely as a factor in location rather than a real function of the capital city.

Harmonious human relationships as a factor apply more practically as the choice of the home town of the founding emperor or the base from which he had developed his power. It also means avoiding the choice of the capital of the defeated former dynasty as it represents a bad omen. The choice of the location of the national capital of Zhou after subduing the Shang Dynasty, and that of the Qin Dynasty after unifying China, both indicate a favouring of the home base. In the debate on where the capital should be located in the early years of the Ming Dynasty, the founder emperor's birth place had been strongly supported. The choice of Beijing by Hung Wu in 1421 was also attributable to that city being his power base. Clearly, the bad omen of the capital of a defeated dynasty was usually the reason for founder emperors finding a new location, in addition to the destruction to the old capital that usually accompanied the final fall of the ailing empire. The retention of Beijing as the national capital when the Qing succeeded the Ming Dynasty is a significant exception. Another expression of the principle lies in the ceremonial ritual in the process of selecting the national capital. Divination by tortoise shell signifies the choice of a prosperous location and the will of Heaven. Of course these also underlie the mandate of Heaven to the sovereign: as long as the mandate of Heaven is there, the place would become prosperous with the flow of *de* from the Son of Heaven, and in selecting the national capital, the stress should be on *de*, i.e. its harmonious quality, rather than on *xian*, i.e. its defensible quality. The ritual of divination has therefore bestowed a sense of mysticism as well as holiness onto a selected capital location, beside the force emanating from the decision of an autocrat (Hou, 1989, 49).

While the dynasties succeeded one another and the realm of the emperor was extended, the economic centre of China also changed with time, as did the source of its external threat in national defence. In the Zhou and early Han dynasties, the three principles could be said to be largely in congruence over Changan (or present day Xian) in the Guan Zhong Plain as the ideal location of the national capital. Then the plain was fertile and productive, and was the actual economic centre of the Zhou realm. Then too, the economic centre, political centre and cultural centre could all be combined in one place, the national capital, Xian or

Changan (see Figure 2.1). Yet the situation changed after the Western Han Dynasty (206 BC–25 AD). The economic focus of China had gradually moved eastwards to the lower Huanghe Basin and then southwards to the Yangtze Basin. But politics and defence dictated the persistent choice of the national capital in the northern part of the country. The divorce between the political and economic foci of China has obviously been a favorite topic for comment in studies of ancient capitals of China. For centuries, the Chinese dynasties resorted to a number of measures to strengthen the economic viability of the national capital which was not located at the economic focus of the country. The first was the dual and multiple capitals system mentioned earlier. In addition, there was forced relocation of rich and powerful families from other parts of the country to boost the capital city's economic significance as well as its population size, e.g. in the Qin Dynasty. Thirdly, canals were built for long-distance transport of grain, cloth, salt and other basic materials from the economically prosperous region to the capital region for supporting the huge army and capital city population. Lastly there were schemes of irrigation, techniques in cropping and other agriculture improvements to promote agricultural productivity of the capital city region, and hence to raise its level of self-sufficiency.

Although seemingly unrelated to present-day Beijing, such locational principles and measures to redress the divergence between the political and economic centres are reflected in the way the national capital of the People's Republic of China has been planned and run since 1949. We shall turn to the details in relevant chapters. Meanwhile let us examine the locus of the Chinese national capital as it shifted in response to historical and natural changes on the Chinese earth since the Zhou Dynasty.

Locus of shifting Chinese capitals

Ye (1988) divides the history of changing Chinese national capitals into four phases. This is a useful approach in bringing out the factors behind the shifting location of Chinese capitals, leading to better apprehension of the present location and significance of the current national capital – Beijing.

Phase of mobile capitals

For the Xia (23–18 century BC) and Shang Dynasty (18–12 century BC) of early Chinese history, there is a lack of written and believable record.

Recently, historical digs unearthed a Xia palace and a Shang capital of a feudal lord. They are rudimentary structures erected on pounded earth platforms. The buildings are of orderly layout with the main gate facing south. They combined a thatched roof with wooden walls and pillars. In the 472 years of the Xia Dynasty, available records show that the national capital moved seven times. The Shang Dynasty was a period of frequent shifts as well: known records indicate 13 changes in the location of the national capital. Available evidence of the national capitals of these early Chinese dynasties is limited to the 'Yin Destitute', a location made up of foundation remnants of some 50 palatial buildings with an encircling wall. The locale has about 24 sq km. The largest structure has an area of about 400 sq m on a pounded earth platform of about 2 m high.

Phase of emergent capitals

The Zhou Dynasty was founded in 1122 BC after Wu Huang had subdued the Shang Dynasty. After that Zhou's capital was located at Gao (present-day Changan county) and remained there for 352 years until Ping Huang moved to Luo in 770 BC, i.e. the start of the Eastern Zhou (or Chunqiu, 770–476 BC). City Luo followed very much the standards laid down by *Zhou Li*. The city took on a square shape. Each side had three gates, giving a total of twelve gates. Each gate had three doorways which were 20 paces wide. The palace was at the centre of the city. The Ancestral Temple was on its left and the Altar of Grains and Soils on its right. The sovereign's administrative quarter was in the southern side of the palace while the market was relegated to its north. The palace city had an entrance of five gates. Inside there were six residential chambers (see Figure 1.3). With the falling power of the Zhou emperor, the lords established their own small kingdoms. This later period of the Zhou Dynasty was described as the Period of the Warring States (475–221 BC) which lasted until Qin Shi Huang united China again in the second century BC. At the height of the Warring States, there were 140 states and it was a busy time for the building of capitals. In this period too, trade and industry flourished. Whereas the traditional Zhou capital was an administrative city, now many of the lords' capitals had flourishing trading and handicraft quarters.

Phase of development

This period lasted from the Qin Dynasty (221 BC) to the end of the Tang Dynasty (907 AD). Qin chose as its capital Xianyang (next to Changan) in 350 BC until its downfall in 206 BC. It served as a national capital, however, only for 15 years from 221 BC. Xianyang was a huge but loosely organized city. The main city was 45 sq km, yet its palatial buildings and royal gardens extended to a wide area of several hundred sq km. The whole city was composed of two parts, the old city and the palaces of the six states. The latter were gradually added to the old city by building a similar palace whenever one rival state had been conquered by the Qin army. Thus, the first planned national capital city of a reunited China was only to be built in the Han Dynasty.

The Han Dynasty was set up in 202 BC. In 8–24 AD it suffered a brief lapse. From 202 BC to 24 AD (i.e. Western Han), the national capital was at Changan, on a small terrace next to the ruins of Xianyang. The walls of the city measured 5940 m, 6250 m, 4550 m and 5950 m. Each wall had three gates and each gate had three doorways. Inside the walls, there were eight north–south and nine east–west main roads. Yet the palace was not at the centre; instead it was moved close to the northern wall, while the market place was located to its southern side. In spite of such differences from the Zhou rule, there were still the ceremonial buildings, the Ming T'ang and the Pi Yong, built in the southern suburb.

In 25 AD Guang Wu Di (*di* = King) moved the national capital to Luoyang (Eastern Han). In 190 AD Zen Di again moved to Xuzhou. Until the end of the Han Dynasty (220) Changan and Luoyang served as the dual capitals of the country.

The Han Dynasty was followed by a long period of disturbances in China (220–589) in which the dynasties of the Han Chinese were so weakened by nomadic tribes from the north and north–east that China was split up into many northern and southern independent states. Many of the northern states were set up by minority races who compelled the Han race to retreat southwards. A unified China reappeared only with the founding of the Sui Dynasty in 581. The new national capital of Sui started to be constructed in 582, just a short distance to the south-west of Changan of the Han Dynasty. The new city was named Da Xing. Soon the Tang Dynasty succeeded Sui, but the national capital was retained and renamed Changan.

The national capital of the two dynasties followed closely the *Zhou Li* specifications. The outer wall had twelve gates, with three on each side. The city was generally square in shape. It too had the relevant ceremonial buildings in the traditional orientation and location with respect to the palace city, such as the Ancestral Temple, the Altar of Grains and Soils, the Ming T'ang and the Pi Yong. There were two marked departures, however. The palace was tucked into the northern wall, and the market – indeed there were two in the city – moved to more southerly positions than was laid down by the classics (Figure 2.2). The

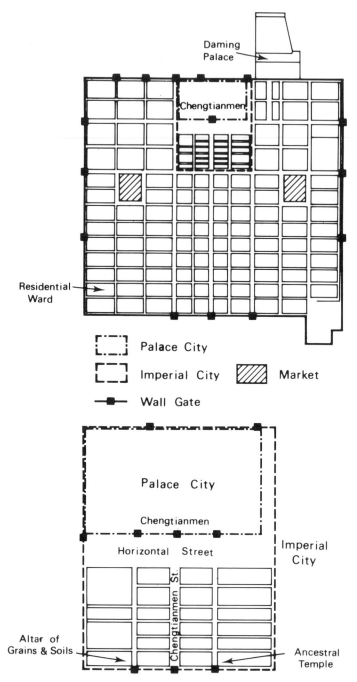

Figure 2.2   Plan of Changan in Tang Dynasty. Source: Hou, 1979

city had three walls: an outer wall, then the wall of the imperial city, and lastly the wall of the palace city. The latter was located at the central part close to the northern outer wall, while the palace city was south of it. Within the city were 108 enclosed neighbourhoods, each having four gates. The markets were located on the east and west sides outside the imperial city, each occupying an area equivalent to two neighbourhoods. Changan of Tang Dynasty had only minor changes, particularly changes in names of some palace buildings. The palaces outside the northern outer wall were notable Tang additions.

Both the Sui and Tang dynasties adopted the dual capitals system. They retained Luoyang as the Eastern Capital or New Capital as a means to control more effectively the Guan Dong area (Lower Huanghe Basin) and the Yangtze River Basin, the main source of food supply to the national capital.

Phase of maturity

In the four dynasties of Song, Yuan, Ming and Qing, the layout of the national capital conformed more with *Zhou Li*, as the palace city moved back to the central position of the capital city, the outer wall took on a square shape, while the main buildings followed rigid rules in their layout. Yet there was also one significant new development: the enclosed neighbourhood or ward system gave way to a pattern of open streets, and the nightly curfew was abandoned. Commerce and services were no longer confined to the markets under rigid official regulation. Instead they were freely located along major roads and road junctions where economic sense dictated.

The national capital of North Song (960–1127) was Kaifeng on the confluence of a number of navigable rivers adjoining the Huanghe. These rivers and a number of canals built since the Sui Dynasty made it the gateway of water transport between the Huanghe (*he* = river) Valley and the Huai He Valley in the south. Northern Song inherited it as a national capital from the three last states of the Five Dynasties period (907–960). In the early years of the Song Dynasty there was the intention to move the national capital to Guan Zhong, in the neighbourhood of Changan. That did not materialize because of the high degree of dependence on food supply from southern China; Kaifeng was located at a more convenient point for such traffic. The city was roughly square (the outer walls measured 6600 m, 5900 m, 6990 m and 6940 m). It had twelve gates, three in the south wall, two in the east wall, three in the west wall and four in the north wall. The palace city was at the centre, surrounded by the imperial city. The main gate was the south gate which led to the main entrance of the palace city by the imperial way, the widest road in the city and its central axis. In Kaifeng, for the first time there was no physical divide of the residential quarters. Enclosed wards and centralized commercial activities in the market from the Zhou Dynasty were gone. Business streets appeared and the city became more prosperous and lively with increased trade and less control of the residents. Trade and industry even spilled over the walls. The size of Kaifeng grew to 1.3 million people at its peak.

When Jin subdued North Song (1115) there were plans to set up its capital at Yanjing (present-day Beijing). The new capital was completed and officiated in 1153. Next to the same site, Kubilie Khan started the construction of his new national capital in 1267. The new city was named the Grand Capital – Da Du. Although the new imperial house was Mongolian, it followed closely the Han culture and ways of administration. It was the philosophy of the Great Khan that in order to administer China well, the new government must follow Han ways. He had appointed a number of Han Chinese as his key ministers, particularly Liu Bing Chong who was entrusted with the planning and construction of the new capital. The layout of Da Du was one step further than Changan of the Tang Dynasty in closely following the classical specifications.

Tai Zu set up the Ming Dynasty in 1368 and the Manchus from northeast China overwhelmed the Ming Dynasty in 1661. Both dynasties used Beiping (present-day Beijing) as their capital. Ming Beiping was largely built on the foundation of Da Du, whereas the Manchu dynasty, Qing, made even less changes to the Ming city. We shall discuss Beijing in more detail in the next chapter.

The choice of Beiping by the Mongols was clearly one of combining the consideration of relative proximity to their home base in Mongolia and the convenience offered by the site for quick advances to the Guan Zhong and Jiang Nan areas inside China proper. It thus offered advantages both to defensive and offensive desires. From the Nan-bei Dynasties onwards (420–589), the external threat to the Chinese central government shifted mainly to the north-east, the Mongols and Manchus. Therefore for national defence purposes, from the Tang Dynasty onwards, the central government always maintained a strong garrison in the strategic position of the Beiping area. Siting the national capital there offered the advantage of effective control of the garrison and minimized the cost involved in maintaining the capital and the huge army separately. Water transport of grains and other supplies from southern China was further improved by the digging of the Grand Canal which terminated at Da Du.

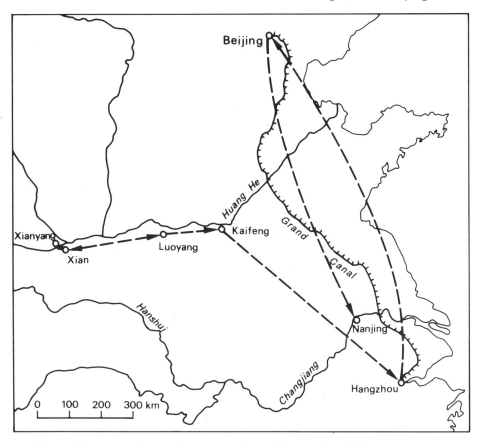

Figure 2.3   Locus of the shifting national capital. Source: Ye, 1988

Ye (1988) has plotted the locus of the national capital in the major dynasties, as shown in Figure 2.3. The two southward shifts to Nanjing (*jing* = capital) and Hangzhou took place when the Han Chinese controlled only the southern part of China. At that time, the northern dynasties still had their capitals in traditional capitals such as Changan and Luoyang, later including Kaifeng and Beiping (or Beijing). In general, the map represents a clear eastward trend. Tam (1982), based on the general location of the national capitals, has categorized the history of China into two periods. The Zhong Yuan Period includes locations of the national capital at Changan, Luoyang and Kaifeng, all of which are within the Zhong Yuan area. The second period is the Period of Eastward Coastal Shift. Hangzhou, Nanjing and Beijing are all to the east of the capitals of the former period and are very close to the sea. Liu

(1983) provides an even more detailed four-period subdivision with indicator capital sites, i.e.:

1. Guan Zhong Period: Fenggao, Xianyang, Changan.
2. Guan Dong Period: Luoyang, Kaifeng.
3. Northern Period: Beijing.
4. Southern Period: Nanjing.

The shifting capitals were in fact underlined by the changing location of the economic focus of China as well as the different sources of external threat in defence. During the Shang Dynasty the middle and lower basins of the Huanghe, the so-called Zhong Yuan area, was the most developed agricultural area of the country and it too was reasonably central to the realm of Han rule at that time (Figure 2.1). Control of this area would effectively mean control of the whole of China. After the collapse of a unified China at the end of Western Jin (316), massive immigration of Chinese into south China helped development there. In the Sui and Tang Dynasties, south China had become China's economic centre, and a huge volume of grain was shipped from there annually to maintain Changan and its garrison. From the Five Dynasties to North Song (907–1127) the economic north–south tilt became more obvious. The national capital moved eastwards to Kaifeng in order to shorten the distance of grain transport and to maintain effective command over it. Zhong Yuan, being still reachable by water transport, retained its pre-eminence as the location of the national capital for another 200 years. Yet chaos of the period after the retreat of the Song Dynasty to south China put Zhong Yuan into disarray in transport and political order. After that the national capital alternated between the choice of a southern location (Nanjing or Hangzhou) and a northern location (Beijing) and did not occur in the Zhong Yuan area again. Of the few choices in the last 800 years, Beijing had always been the choice of a stable, unified China, whereas the southern capitals represented a weak and retreating government in defence of an ailing dynasty, with the exception of the early Ming.

Geography of Beijing

Beijing lies on the northern edge of the North China Plain, at about longitude 114–116°E, and latitude 39–40°N. It is flanked on the north and west by the Jundu Shan and Xi Shan, rising to about 2000 m. These are lofty extensions of the Taiheng Shan, forming an effective physical

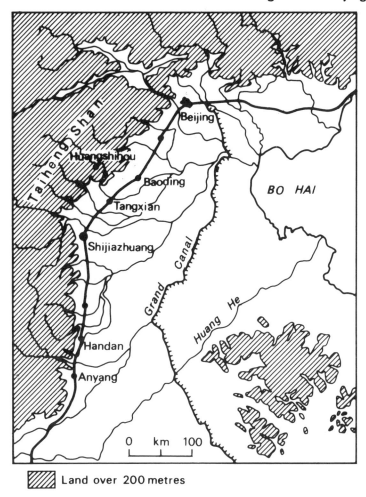

Figure 2.4   Beijing's strategic location. Source: Hou, 1982

barrier. This mountainous area averages over 1000 m and descends into a foothill area and then to the small Beijing plain (Figure 2.4).

The entire Beijing area is criss-crossed by over 40 large and small streams. Among them Yongding He, Chaobai He, Da Yunhe and Juma He are the larger ones. The small plain on which the city is located was also known as Beijing Wan (*wan* = bay), as it was a shallow bay 2–3 million years ago. The bay was filled by sediments brought down by the Yongding He and the Chaobai He. About 3000 years ago, when City Ji was first founded, the plain was largely marshy. At that time, passage from the North China Plain to the Beijing Plain was only convenient via a narrow strip of foothills of the Taiheng Shan, i.e. the eastern edge of the Xi Shan. As the passage was cut by a number of torrential rivers that debouched onto the plain creating a number of alluvial fans, safe passages were offered at a number of crossings adjoining nearby fans. One of these was located at Yongding He; it offered a strategic crossing into the plain and played an important role in Beijing's rise to eminence as a crossroads and important city in the Warring States Period.

Access to the Beijing Plain from the vast North-east China (Manchurian) Plain and from the steppes of Mongolia was possible only via three ancient mountain passes. They are the Nankou in the south, the Gubeikou in the north and the Shanhaiguan in the east (Figure 2.5). Thus from the North China Plain advancing towards north-east China or Mongolia, the critical nodal point was at Beijing. From there one could follow the directions of the three passes to reach the vast areas beyond the bordering mountains in the west and north. In reverse, advancing from these two outer regions of China into the North China Plain, the Zhong Yuan and even further to south China, Beijing also proved to be the confluence point. So Beijing was not only strategically significant when China's economic focus moved east and south, and when major external threats came from these two north and north-east outer regions, it was also boosted by its physical geographical qualities on the most convenient passage that linked up these routes. The Marco Polo Bridge in the western suburb of present-day Beijing marks this confluence point to which the city owes its significance. Of course, to avoid danger of flooding, the actual city was some distance away from that ancient crossing (Hou, 1982).

Through long periods of improvement the Beijing Plain, which is made up of the alluvial fans, formed a gentle and fertile agricultural area. Located within the semi-humid warm temperate zone, it has an average 680 mm annual precipitation and a mean annual temperature of 11.8°C, with more than six months frost free. Thus both its moisture and heat conditions favour agriculture, much more so than in the rest of the North China Plain. Local production was supplemented by canal transport of grain and other food supplies from south China. The numerous rivers in the plain facilitated this and the Grand Canal served for more than 800 years as the main conduit between the basins of Yangtze and Huai He and Beijing.

Rise in strategic importance

Economic consideration alone would not qualify Beijing as the national capital of China. By the Yuan Dynasty, Jiang Nan (the Yangtze Basin)

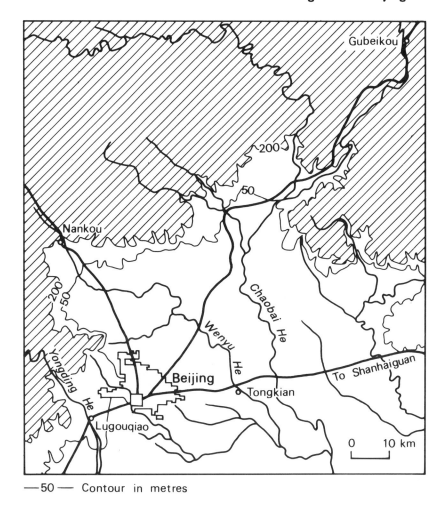

—50— Contour in metres

Figure 2.5 Beijing as a major transport node. Source: Hou, 1982

had clearly become the economic focus of the country. The Yuan emperor's choice of Beijing was based more on strategic considerations.

Of course, as a capital city region, the Beijing region does possess certain qualities to add onto its strategic position to warrant its significance. Beijing's first fame was derived in the Warring States (475–221 BC) when it served as the capital of the State of Yan, then already grown into one of the seven powers. At that time, the Beijing Plain had developed into a prosperous agricultural region producing three types of grain, rice, maize and millet, and was an important fishery and salt-producing area. Animal husbandry and cultivation of fruit trees in the foothills were also noted to be widespread in old records. The city of Ji was ranked as one of the richest cities in China, and reckoned as comparable to the Zhou capital of Luoyang and the capitals of the other powerful states of Qi, Zhou and Chu. It too was a transport node in north China.

In the unified China of the Qin Dynasty, City Ji served as an important gateway between the North China Plain and the north and north-eastern outer regions of the empire. The Qin emperor constructed major carriageways to all parts of the country, one of which reached Ji, linking it with the national capital, thus promoting trade between the Han people and the nomadic minorities in the North and North-east. The Han historian Sima Qian in his *Book of History* wrote of Ji: 'Yan was a metropolis between the sea and Guan Zhong. It linked the states of Qi and Zhou in the south and confronted the Mongols in the north . . . It was rich in salt, fish, dates and maize. Its northern neighbours included many other minorities such as the Koreans etc.'

The use of iron-cast implements further enhanced the agricultural productivity of the Beijing Plain in the Han Dynasty. It then thrived as a booming border trading city with well-developed crafts. The city was renamed Youzhou in the Tang Dynasty, and its agricultural land was further extended. Famous silk items from its handicrafts became state tributes. Mining of iron ore and iron foundry were well-known local industries. It also served as a strategic stronghold against the potential military threat from the minorities.

The rise to power of Qidan at the end of the Tang Dynasty in northern China raised the historical importance of Beijing. The leader of Qidan proclaimed himself emperor of a new dynasty, Liao (907–1125), and Beijing became its first major target of military acquisition. Initially Qidan's men looted the city and used the population as a foundation for developing agriculture in their home territory. Soon with their growth in power, Beijing was turned into Liao dynasty's economic focus with its developed handicrafts, and was revived as an important nodal position in trade. Finally, it was made the southern capital of Liao. When Jin (1115–1234) subdued Liao, Beijing was further upgraded to the national capital. The adoption of Beijing was a clear political and economic move on the part of Jin. The old capital Shangjing was located in the economically backward Songhua River Basin in north-east China. To supply the needs of its expanded bureaucracy and army, the new empire had therefore no other choice but to rely on the productive North China Plain. Relocating the capital to Beijing (renamed Zhongdu at the time) minimized the cost of long-distance transport to feed the expanded Jin bureaucracy. Thus although Beijing was never at the economic focus of China, the productivity of its immediate environs as well as its proximity to the much more prosperous North China Plain were an important economic background for its gradual emergence as a political centre of China, when military power and hence political power gradually shifted to the minorities in the north and north-eastern parts of the country.

The military and strategic significance of Beijing during the Liao, Jin and Yuan dynasties has been noted by Shi (1986b). The three major passes through Yan Shan, plus the roads that led southwards to the North China Plain, made Beijing of paramount importance in the reign of these dynasties in linking them with their home base while offering a convenient forward control base to the China that lay to the city's southward direction. The land routes leading off from Beijing to southern China did not diminish in significance in the Ming Dynasty, while the passes in Yan Shan still played a decisive role in the fate of the dynasty. Beijing, at the confluence of these Yan Shan passes and the starting point of routes leading to China proper, had been a strategic focus of the dynasty *vis-à-vis* its opponents from the Qin Dynasty until the end of Tang dynasty, for about 1000 years. When the political power of the ruling family in Zhong Yuan was strong, Beijing was used as the launching pad for their military expeditions into north-east China. When such power was weakened by peasant revolution, Beijing served as a strategic defence fortress against invasions from minorities that came from such outer regions of China, as it was the gateway from these areas into the North China Plain. The city therefore marked a divide between these two opposing military forces and became their bone of contention.

By the end of the Tang Dynasty, Qidan had captured Beijing and used it as the southern capital. The 16 provinces of Yan Yun on the North China Plain were also captured and started a new chapter for Beijing. The new Qidan dynasty, Liao, marked a massive onslaught on China by the northern minorities. Zhong Yuan was then for the first time under the military might of the northern minorities. Beijing naturally became the headquarters for the new rule in North China, as well as the base for organizing and directing further southern expeditions by these northern forces. Thus in the history of Beijing, the founding of the Southern Capital by Liao and the Middle Capital by Jin were significant landmarks, pointing to the process whereby the military strategic centre on the northern edge of the North China Plain was moving towards becoming the political centre of China as well. As Beijing was rising in importance, Changan was on the decline. In North Song, the Chinese capital moved to Kaifeng to counteract the advance of the Liao force from Beijing. When Jin ruled the northern half of China with Beijing as the capital, South Song (1127–1279) sought refuge in South China with

Hangzhou as capital. Yuan's success over Jin and then South Song finally turned Beijing into the national capital of China.

The emergence of Beijing may thus be attributable to the rise in power of the minorities in the north and north-east of China. The mixing of these people with the dominant Han race of different economic and cultural backgrounds favoured Beijing as the meeting point in military, cultural and administrative considerations. Since Jin (1115) Beijing had been the capital of dynasties set up by these minorities. Ming was the only exception. However, even for Ming, the economic, military and cultural circumstances were such that to control the north-east was strategic in maintaining stability of the empire. In such a regard, the city played a key role in integrating the northern and north-eastern outer regions and their minorities into the family of the Chinese races and in broadening the territory of China.

Beijing before the Ming Dynasty

Beijing first acquired its status as the capital of a dynasty in Liao (907–1125) but then it was only one of the five capitals of the dynasty, the Southern Capital or Yan Jing. Before Liao, the city was known as Yanzhou or Jicheng (*cheng* = city). In Song times, it was called Yan Shan Fu. Later in the Jin Dynasty, its name changed to Zhong Du (Middle Capital) and to Da Du (Grand Capital) in the Yuan Dynasty. In early Ming, it was Beiping and later renamed Beijing (Northern Capital) after it was made the national capital. The Qing Dynasty retained the name of Beijing. The actual site of the city and its layout changed substantially during the Liao, Jin and Yuan dynasties. From Ming onwards, the city was more or less stable in layout as well as in its key architecture.

Besides serving as the capital of the State of Yan, the city was never a national capital before the Liao Dynasty. It then functioned mainly as a border city and a military stronghold and was thus designed to meet such requirements in its city plan. The city was then not very big in size. According to records in the late Tang Dynasty, it measured nine *li* north–south, seven *li* east–west with ten gates. It was largely populated by the army and its dependants (Yu, 1989, 140–41).

The declining Tang Dynasty opened up a period of chaos. In less than half a century, five very weak dynasties succeeded each other in turn, a period called the Five Dynasties (907–960). The minorities in north-east China seized the opportunity to strengthen themselves, and exerted their military might on the Tang Dynasty. The route that they took to implement their military and political ambitions was to attack Beijing, the gateway to Zhong Yuan. The Qidan occupied Beijing in 936 and set up the Liao Dynasty. These people came from the upper reaches of the Liao River in Manchuria and led a nomadic life. With the help of a Chinese general, Liao easily obtained a large tract of land in the north-eastern part of the North China Plain with Datong and Beijing as its twin centres. The choice of Beijing in 938 as one of the five capitals was then obvious. The city served as the administrative headquarters for the newly acquired, economically advanced and densely populated Chinese territory. It too served as the bastion for launching further attacks on the ailing Chinese empire. Of the five Liao capitals, the South Capital or Beijing was the largest. It was roughly square in shape with a parameter of 36 *li*. The palace city lay in the centre, with the Ancestral Hall to its left and the Altar of Grains and Soils to its right, the market to its north and the administrative quarter to its front – a spatial arrangement clearly dictated by the principles developed by the Han people. However, there was evidence of blending of the Liao minority culture in the practical functioning of the city and in the principal décor of its major palaces. Of the four gates of the imperial city, although the main gate was the south gate, only the east gate was kept open, a reflection of the Liao culture's worshipping of the eastern direction and a constant need for defence. The main buildings of the palace were also decorated with draperies that oriented towards the east (Yu, 1989, 136–7).

When the Liao Dynasty set up its South Capital at Beijing and was competing with North Song for power in the North China Plain, another minority group, the later Manchus, Nu Zhen was gaining strength militarily in the Songhua River Basin in Manchuria. After a major victory over Liao, it established itself as the Jin Dynasty in 1115. In 1118 it allied with North Song for a wholesale attack on Liao and agreed to divide the spoils along the Great Wall when they succeeded in smashing Liao. In 1123, Nu Zhen inflicted a fatal attack on Liao, captured, looted and forced resettlement of over 30 000 households from Beijing into the Songhua Basin. Three years later, the Jin army broke into Kaifeng and ended the North Song Dynasty. It thus established complete control over the North China Plain, extending to the Qin Ling in the west and the Huaihe Basin in the south. In North China there was a longer period of peace under Jin (1115–1234). The Jin empire ordered the setting up of a new national capital on the former Yan Jing of Liao and renamed it Zhong Jing, Zhongdu or Middle Capital. This marked the start of Beijing as the national capital of a major dynasty.

The new capital of Jin was planned by Han officials and fashioned after Kaifeng (Ciu and Yang, 1989, 297). Construction started in 1250 and was completed in 1252. It took a square shape with the four outer walls measuring roughly eight *li* each and each with three gates. The imperial city was located to the south-west portion. It had four gates and measured about nine *li* in parameter. The palace city was roughly at the centre with the main gate in the south wall. The basic traditional Chinese layout of the market at the back, administrative quarter in the front, Ancestral Temple to the left and Altar of Grains and Soils to the right was rigidly followed. The administrative offices lay on the two sides of the Imperial Way south of the palace city, called the Square of the Character *ding*, in the same manner as the capitals of the Tang and North Song dynasties.

In two ways, Zhong Jing of the Jin Dynasty may be viewed as an important transition in the development of the structure and function of the Chinese national capital. First, although the market was located in the northern part of the city, commercial activities were no longer confined to that part of the city alone. The enclosed residential wards were largely turned into open streets, except for the central part of the old city. It marked a transition to a completely open street arrangement and the abolition of the ward system in the Yuan and earlier dynasties. Secondly, the city had not yet relinquished its border military strong-hold function and design. At each corner of the imperial city there was a 'citilet', effectively a military bastion for defence purposes. These were linked to the imperial city by walled passages. Thus the design of Zhong Jing combined elements of the traditional Chinese national capital concepts and the requirements of a military stronghold (Yu, 1989, 132).

The rise to power of the Mongols under Ginsi Khan soon led to the demise of Jin. In 1211 the Mongols attacked Beijing, and the Jin Dynasty was forced to move its capital to Kaifeng. Twenty years later, the Mongols overran Beijing. In 1227 and 1234 they wiped out the other major states in North China, i.e. the West Xia Dynasty and the Jin Dynasty. Kubilie Khan succeeded his grandfather as the Great Khan in 1259. The next year he decided to set up a permanent national capital of all China at Beijing. In 1271 the Yuan Dynasty was formally proclaimed and South Song was wiped out by 1279. Once again there was a unified China, and Beijing, which then was given the new name Da Du (Grand Capital), became the national capital of all China for the first time.

Da Du was built next to the ruin of Zhong Jing. The military and political success of Kubilie Khan reflected the coalition of part of the Mongol bureaucracy and the major landlord class of the Han Chinese. He relied mainly on Han officials to set up his imperial dynastic ruling system based largely on sinicization. The down-grading of the former capital in Mongolia to a supplementary capital status and the choice of Beijing as the Grand Capital was part of the attempt. Sinicization strengthened Kubilie Khan's centralization of power, and the adoption of Confucian and Taoist principles not only legitimized his rule but also helped him to stabilize his control over the bureaucracy and the country.

It was thus not surprising that he changed the dynastic name to Yuan, taking the meaning from the *Book of Change* (*Yi Jing*) as grandness. The design of the new capital too was part of this scheme of sinicization and legitimization of his rule. Therefore, although Kubilie Khan came from a minority race his new capital followed much more closely the scriptures of *Zhou Li* than even the great dynasties of Han and Tang of the predominant Han Chinese. Of course, the flatness of the small Beijing Plain facilitated the city's layout accordingly.

The system of administration of Yuan and the design of its capital were the responsibility of the same small group of Han Chinese who were known Confucians, particularly Ye Lu Zhu and Liu Bing Zhong. They assisted the Great Khan in setting up legislation, rituals and the system of civil service, using principles from Confucianism and Taoism, and they too laid out the new city (Wang, 1960, 65).

The plan of Da Du rigidly followed *Zhou Li*. It had three walls. The outer wall measured a total of 60 *li* and was slightly rectangular, with 11 gates. The imperial city lay in the south inside the outer wall. It had a parameter of 20 *li*. The Ancestral Hall was on the left, and the Altar of Grains and Soils on the right within the imperial city. In the northern portion there were the bell and drum towers. The palace city in the middle was also slightly rectangular with a wall of nine *li*, and six gates. The main gate, the south gate, was the Gate of Heavenly Worship. The main palaces were made up of the Da Ming Gong (*gong* = palace) and Yanchun Ge. Da Ming Gong was where coronations and major state ceremonies took place.

The layout followed a well-defined central point, the Central Tower, and the north–south central axis. In the southern part of the imperial city, on the two sides of the central axis, were marshalled the main government offices after the fashion of Kaifeng. These buildings, as well as the palace buildings, were laid in an organized way along or on the two sides of this axis. The front of the palace city was used for royal audiences and day-to-day administration, while the rear part was for royal residences.

Within the city were nine north–south and east–west main arteries. The central artery passed through the axis of the palace city and reached the Central Tower in the imperial city, the geographical centre of Da Du. The residential quarters were divided into 50 wards. Construction started in 1267 and was completed about 25 years later in 1293.

Besides following the specifications of *Zhou Li*, Da Du also applied many names and labels to its main architecture, as well as the division of its wards to reflect the cosmological symbolism of Confucianism and Taoism. For example, the naming of the main gates was based on the five directions and the five elements, e.g. east symbolizes the quality of benevolence and west symbolizes righteousness; the main south gate Li Zheng (meaning bright and central) took its meaning both from the south direction and a quotation from the *Book of Change*: 'The sun and the moon shine in the sky (Li Zheng Gate)'. The number of wards was set at 50, also a reflection of a quotation from the same source: 'Fifty is the number for great prosperity'. The name of the main hall in the palace city, Da Ming Gong, was equally fashioned after the Confucian classic, *Da Xue*: 'the essence of great learning lies in a clear review of one's inborn virtue'. The eleven gates in the walls were also taken as symbolic of Ne Zha, a legendary god with three heads, six arms and two feet. The three heads were the gates in the south wall, the arms were the six gates on the east and west walls, while the two feet were those gates in the north wall. Ne Zha was said to be impregnable. As the northern wall had fewer gates and no central gate in the middle, the palace city was not exposed to the inauspicious north wind. This way the auspicious ethers of the city would be better preserved (Wang, 1960; Yu, 1989; Chen, 1982; Ciu and Yang, 1989).

In Da Du there were further developments in the urban structure compared to Zhong Jing. The residential wards were completely open streets. The ward system existed in name rather than in practice. There were two markets, one in the north in the area of the drum and bell towers and the other to the west of the imperial city. Yet they were developed out of the pattern of water transport more than official sanction.

In spite of rigid adherence to *Zhou Li* and the established tradition of symbolism, we can still observe Mongolian touches. In the Chinese tradition, of the five colours red represents gaiety and was used as the colour for walls in royal palaces. Yet in Da Du the palace walls were coloured white, the colour for the Mongolian tent. In Da Ming Gong, there were thrones for the emperor and the empress, and both were seated for major state ceremonies, a practice not found in Chinese tradition. On the terraces of the Da Ming Gong the Great Khan deliberately planted some desert grass, a reminder to future generations of their desert origin. Other nomadic styles, such as the carpet and drapery decorations of the palaces, and a large and generally uninhabited northern part of the city where Mongolian tents for the army were often seen, may also be noted (Chen, 1982).

Conclusion

The choice of Beijing as the national capital of China viewed historically reflected not only the consistent Chinese considerations of centrality and maintenance of a harmonious relationship between man and the universe, but also the economic and ethnic processes of spatial developments that exhibited a marked trend of eastward and southward expansion in the case of the former and a north and north-eastward extension in the case of the latter. These developments made it impossible to locate the national capital at the economic centre of the nation as it used to be before the Sui Dynasty. The convergence of factors of economics, the military and culture had gradually given way to a divergence of these factors, particularly the separation of the political and military centre from the economic focus of the country. Such a separation was, as a rule, made good by large-scale, ingenious means of canal transport to maintain the huge army and the bureaucracy at the national capital.

Thus the spatial processes in the history of China seem to have increasingly stressed the importance of the factor of military defence in the location of the national capital. This is seen both for the strong and weak dynasties. In the former, the choice was usually one of the strategic sites in north China, whereas in the latter case it was a retreat to a defensible site in south China. Although in the classics, the principle of virtuous rule (*de*) of the emperor was emphasized as a better defence of the capital than a strategic site, in practice military considerations were given the upper hand. Yet military considerations should be broadly interpreted as the strategic position of the capital city region rather than a defensible or strategic site. As noted in Chapter 1, the defence of the capital usually lay in the outer, physically strong positions of the region in which the capital was sited.

The gradual progression of such spatial processes in favour of Beijing's emergence as the national capital has been the main theme of this chapter. In the next we shall examine the internal structure of the city and its wider location in some detail during the Ming and Qing dynasties.

3

Beijing of the Ming and Qing periods (pre-1949)

Choice of Beijing

In 1368, the Ming army inflicted a major defeat on the Yuan army and occupied Da Du. The city's name was then changed to Beiping Fu and Tai Zu's fourth son, Prince of Yan, was put in command of a strong garrison there. In 1398, the first Ming emperor, Tai Zu, died. His eldest grandson succeeded him. The young emperor wanted to strip military power from the various princes put up by his grandfather to control various sections of the huge army. This attempt to centralize military power and control of the country was met with stern opposition from the princes. Led by Prince of Yan, they defeated the young emperor in 1402. The latter then abdicated in favour of Prince of Yan, his uncle, who thus declared himself the new emperor, Ming Cheng Zu, and called his reign Yong-le. Cheng Zu was a well-known soldier and had been stationed at Beiping for over 30 years. He naturally preferred his own power base, Beiping, as his new capital. However, since his father had chosen Nanjing and had built there a grand capital, it was not possible to engage the country on yet another lavish capital building project immediately.

Beiping had therefore to be transformed into the national capital by three carefully planned steps that spanned a period of more than 20 years. The first took place in 1403 when the new emperor changed the province of his old fief, Beiping, into the Northern Capital, Beijing. The second step came after 1406 when the Grand Canal had been opened for five years, when massive amounts of men and materials had moved north and the emperor was residing there in person. To disguise his project he organized a full court discussion on the construction of a new capital at Beijing. His chief ministers jointly petitioned that Beijing was the place from which the emperor rose to power. So with the request of the full court, Cheng Zu ordered an immediate start on the construction of the new capital. In fact, prior to 1406, the emperor had resettled a huge number of rich families from Nanjing, Suzhou and 10 other rich southern prefectures into Beijing. Construction then engaged more than 300 000 workers. From 1409, in the name of 'northern tours', the emperor stationed himself in Beijing, making the new capital his personal project. The third step came in 1420 when work on the new palace, the Altar of Grains and Soils and the Ancestral Temple was completed. From that time onwards, Beijing was officially declared the national capital (Jing-shi), the first Ming capital was then renamed Nanjing (Southern Capital) and hence lost the status of Jing-shi (Farmer, 1976; Ye, 1987; Li, 1981, Ciu and Yang, 1989).

The choice of Beijing by Cheng Zu was thus owing to considerations based on geography, history, politics, the military and concerns over the minority races. The Mongol lords were still strong in early Ming. Cheng Zu wanted to continue his persistent expeditions to root them out. At that time Beijing was also said to be the focal point of the nine frontiers that stretched from the Yalu River in the east, reaching Jia Yu Guan in the west. These were the frontiers with Liaodong, Shenfu, Datong, Yensu, Ningxia, Gansu, Jizhou, Taiyuan and Kuyuan. Beijing was strategically located for combating incursions from hostile minorities and for protecting the empire. As Beijing had been his long-established power base since he was Prince of Yan, Cheng Zu had also cultivated it as his political headquarters. In the entire Ming Dynasty, the strongest line of defence of the empire remained along the line marked by the Great Wall where a huge army was marshalled and Beijing acted as its headquarters. Since 1420 it had been the national capital of the Ming Dynasty, except for a brief period when this was only in name and not in practice, 1425–1439.

In the late sixteenth and early seventeenth centuries, the Manchus (formerly called Nu Zhen) rose in power in north-east China. In 1639 they founded a new dynasty, the Qing Dynasty. The choice of the character Qing was based on the yin–yang theory in which the five elements are believed to be in a constant cycle of mutual interaction. Of the five elements 'water' is the element that subdues 'fire'. The 'Ming' character of the Ming Dynasty was symbolic of fire, whereas the character Qing was symbolic of water. The Manchus were much influenced by the Taoists. For these reasons and for similar strategic and 'home-base' considerations as the Mongolians, the Manchus retained Beijing as the capital when they overwhelmed the South Ming Dynasty in 1661.

Thus from 1420 to 1911, Beijing was the capital of the Chinese empire. From 1912 onwards, until 1949 when the People's Republic of China was born, the capital of Nationalist China shifted several times. Since 1949, it has moved back to Beijing again. Up to the present, for almost 570 years it has been the national capital of China.

Beijing in the Ming Dynasty

The new national capital comprised the Outer City, the Inner City, the Imperial City (Huang Cheng) and the Palace City (Zijincheng, or Forbidden City).

The Inner City

The Inner City followed much of the outer city of the Yuan capital. It had a circumference of 40 *li*, measured 6650 m east–west and 5350 m north–south, and had nine gates. The names of the nine gates were retained in the Qing Dynasty. During Ming times the type of traffic through each gate was strictly controlled. Zheng Yang Men was for use by the emperor and palatial carriages. Chong Wen Men was for wine traffic, as there were many breweries outside that gate. Chao Yang Men was mainly for grain traffic as grain from south China came to Tong-zhou through the North Canal, and thence by road to Chao Yang Men where the main warehouses were located. Timber came via the canal and through Dong Zhi Men. An Ding Men was for the daily flow of night-soil as there were three major night-soil pans outside that gate where the stuff would be dried for sale to farmers. De Sheng Men was the auspicious gate for the military. Soldiers marched out to battle through it. Xi Zhi Men was used for royal water carts that brought in water from the Yu Chuen Mountain. Fu Cheng Men was for coal traffic and Xuan Wu Men was the gate where condemned prisoners were taken out to the Cai Shi Kou Market for execution.

The general layout of the Inner City and the orientation of the gates and their relationship with the Yuan capital can be seen in Figure 3.1. The former northern tract of the Yuan capital was then relatively empty. For efficiency in defence, the Prince of Yan moved the northern wall five *li* (2.5 km) to the south. In the later construction of the new capital, the south wall was also extended southwards for two *li* to accommodate the enlarged Palace City and the new locations of the Altar of Grains and Soils and the Ancestral Temple. On the spot of the Central Terrace of Yuan, the former geographic centre of the city, a drum and a bell tower were built. They became the northern end of a new central axis of Beijing.

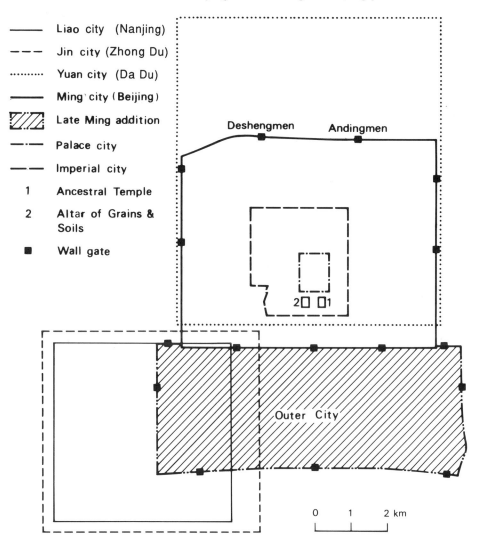

Figure 3.1   Beijing developments from Jin to Ming Dynasty. Source: Farmer, 1976

The Imperial City

The Imperial City had a wall of 18 *li*. It accommodated the two ceremonial buildings, the Ancestral Temple and the Altar of Grains and Soils and was the central military and administrative headquarters. The central ministries were marshalled on the two sides of a long open passage leading from Da Ming Men, to Wu Men (main gate of Palace City) (see Figure 3.2). The Imperial City had an interesting extension south of its main gate, Tian An Men or Cheng Tian Men in Ming Dynasty. This took the form of a walled enclosure in the shape of a Chinese character *ding* or the English letter 'T'. It opened to the south at the Da Ming Men (or Da Qing Men in Qing Dynasty). Along the perimeter of the vertical stroke of the letter 'T' were marshalled many offices, collectively known as 'the Gallery of One Thousand Paces' since Tang Dynasty. In addition to its administrative role, this huge open square enhanced the preponderant feeling of the main gate into the Imperial City, which when advanced further would be the Wu Men, main gate of the residence and office of the Son of Heaven. According to *Zhou Li* the sovereign's palace should have five entrance gates. The square helped to conform with such a rule. Elsewhere were palaces for the emperor's mother, the princes, residences of high-level officials, and imperial gardens (Tai Ji Chi Ping, Coal Hill). The present day Huangfujin, the commercial core of Beijing, was the location of the residences of 10 princes. Thus the Imperial City was heavily guarded and in general lacking in commercial activities. Moving the south wall of the Inner City further south enabled the Imperial City to expand southwards as well. The Yuan royal garden, Tai Chi Pond, was expanded southwards. In addition to Bei Hai and Zhong Hai, another pond the Nan Hai was now added. They remain until today as the 'three seas' (San Hai). The mud obtained from there plus that yielded by creating a deep moat for the Palace City was dumped north of the northern gate of the Palace City to form the Coal Hill or Hill of Longevity (Wan Sui Shan). The hill stood 70 m. high. It was located at the central axis of the city, as well as forming its new geographic centre (see Figure 3.2).

The Outer City

The Outer City was a later addition of 1553. When Yuan built Da Du, some of the former residents of the Jin capital were unable to find residence in the new capital. They set themselves up outside the city in the direction of the old Jin capital. Hence, outside the southern part of Da Du a busy settlement had already developed unbounded by a wall. In early Ming, this area continued as a prosperous area of commerce and handicrafts and of growing population density. In the construction of the new capital, Cheng Zu built two major ceremonial structures to the far south of the area, i.e. Tian Tan (Altar of Heaven) and the Altar of Rivers and Mountains. The new wall of 1553 enclosed this southward

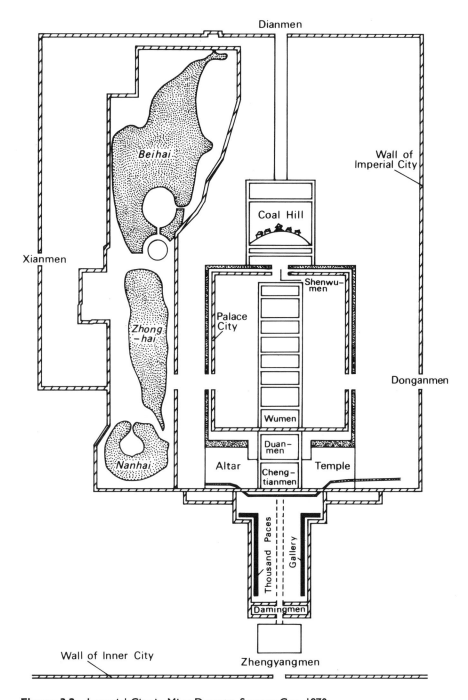

Figure 3.2 Imperial City in Ming Dynasty. Source: Cao, 1970

extension of the city to form the Outer City (sometimes called Wai Luo Cheng). The purpose was clearly one of defence. According to the plan, the outer wall should circumscribe the whole city and had a total length of 120 *li*. Owing to a shortage of funds, only the southern outer area was enclosed. The reduced outer wall had a length of 28 *li*. It thus provided Beijing with an untraditional shape in the form of the Chinese character *lu*, in contrast to most Chinese cities which are either rectangular or square (see Figure 3.1).

The Palace City

In Chinese the Palace City was known as Zi Jin Cheng (literally Purple Forbidden City), so it was also commonly known in English as the Forbidden City. It remains so named and its form and layout have also persisted without substantial change up to the present. There had been some change of names in the Ming and Qing dynasties, but otherwise there was no visible change throughout its long history since completion in 1420.

The city was located at the centre of the Inner City of Beijing with a wall 10 m high and adorned by four beautiful corner watch towers. The six *li* long wall had a deep, stone-paved moat. The city was flanked by Coal Hill in the north, the highest point of Beijing. Approaching northwards from Chao Yang Men, the main south gate of the Inner City, one would gradually face Cheng Tian Men, the main south gate of the Imperial City. Wu Men was its main south gate. The other three gates to the north, east and west were named after the cardinal points (see Figure 3.2).

There was a total area of 720 000 sq m within the city, of which 150 000 sq m was built-up area, with 9999.5 individual building units. The major buildings were all located on carefully planned and rank-ordered platforms along the central axis of the entire city. Figure 3.3 shows details of its plan and the layout of its important buildings. Six buildings formed the core of the Palace City and were so designed and located to symbolize the status of the Son of Heaven, his mandate to rule, as well as the old belief that he should be like the sage kings, to administer the country in such a way that the *yin* and *yang* ethers interacted smoothly and that all people observed the sacrifices and rituals accordingly. These six buildings were the Three Big Halls of the Main and Inner Courts, and the Three Halls of the Imperial Chamber (see Figure 3.3). They were all set on the central axis, whereas the former formed the core of the Palace City. Huang Ji Dian was the Throne Hall in which major state ceremonies such as the coronation, the emperor's

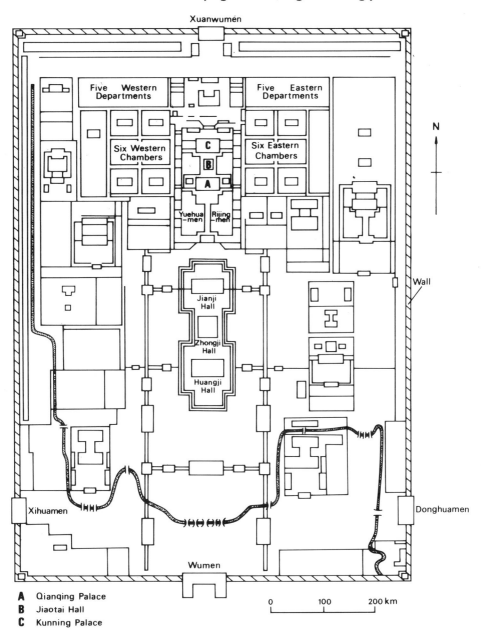

Figure 3.3 The Palace City in Ming Dynasty. Source: Ye, 1987

birthday celebrations and the initiation of military expeditions, and the full court took place. It was the tallest hall in the whole Palace City with a 35 m high roof. Hanging from the centre of the main roof was the Mirror of Huang Te. It was enshrined by emperors from one generation to another as a symbol of the orthodoxy of their rule. Underneath the mirror, slightly to the northern central part of the hall, was the carved dragon-design throne.

At the back of Huang Ji Dian was Zhong Ji Dian. The emperor took a rest there and received his cabinet and ritual officers before he proceeded to the Throne Hall during all major state ceremonies. Jian Ji Dian was further to the north, where the emperor offered annual feasts to foreign convoys and ambassadors. The highest-level civil examinations also took place in this hall. The main hall, Huang Ji Dian, was the largest and tallest. All three halls were sited on the same three-layered marble platform, 8.13 m high (Yu, 1990). The Three Big Halls constituted the official business quarter of state. Lesser buildings on the sides of these halls were places where the emperor received ministers and where royal orders and proclamations were drafted and copied. Behind were the halls of the Royal Chamber. Qian Qing Gong, the largest in the south, was where the emperor gave audience to foreign dignitaries and discussed state affairs with trusted ministers. The small hall in the middle was where the royal seals were stored. It was also used as the room for the first night of the imperial wedding. Behind it was the Kun Ning Gong, the official residence of the empress. As Qian Qing Gong was used for royal business as well, in some literature these three halls have been wrongly labelled as the Inner Court (e.g. Ciu and Yang, 1989).

Beyond Kun Ning Men to the north was the royal harem where the emperor's concubines lived, and the imperial garden, the only patch of green of the Palace City. In the plan, the living quarters were divided along the central axis into the six eastern palaces and the six western palaces (Dong Liu Gong and Xi Liu Gong). Each subdivision was enclosed by a wall and thus this rear part of the Palace City was clearly separated from the front part that was devoted largely to state business.

Concepts of layout

Zhou Li

The oldest and most authoritative document that governed the layout of the Chinese capital in traditional China was the *Zhou Li*. Most of its rules and details had been followed from the Zhou Dynasty to the Qing Dynasty, with minor exceptions in the Qin and Han dynasties, and some modifications of those capitals established in southern China mainly due to constraints of relief. Of course, development of society in economics, such as trade and handicrafts, also had increasingly demanded new modifications of the old model. Indeed, we can easily cite examples, such as the changed location of the market and, for that matter, the growing size of commercial and handicrafts activities in later dynasties, which finally breached the old practice of concentrating such activities in designated wards. The open street system which replaced the closed ward system also reflected such new developments. However, the layout of the Palace City, and most parts of the Imperial City, had followed very closely the specifications of *Zhou Li* down to Beijing of the Qing Dynasty.

Besides the standards of *Zhou Li*, the main elements of the Chinese world view that are contained in the *Book of Change*, in the theory of *yin–yang*, the five elements and the five directions, as well as the older concepts of the behaviour of the sage kings, had given the Chinese model city layout additional symbolism, in the naming of the key palace buildings, the major gates and detailed layout of key building groups, particularly of the palace city and the ceremonial buildings, i.e. the various buildings for sacrifices. In addition, the quasi-science, *feng shui*, that has developed since the Western Jin Dynasty, also had its impact on later national capitals, in the form of their layout as well as in naming of gates and buildings.

We have referred to the relevant parts of *Zhou Li* in Chapter 1 on the details of the model capital layout. Yet that passage itself did not give reasons as to why such a layout had been specified. In the most detailed study of *Kao Gong Ji*, the part of *Zhou Li* on the topic, Ho (1985) presented two main explanations. First, *Kao Gong Ji* wanted to use the layout of the national capital to strengthen the use of rites in the building of cities, hence the maintenance of law and orderliness, the main purpose of the rites. The rigid layout, its orderliness, and the rank principle used for the positioning, size and height of the key buildings were the methods used. As cities of the country were divided into three hierarchical levels, similar rules had indeed been specified for all cities relevant to their rank status. Thus a clear and effective objective for upholding the rites as the mainstay of governance was effectively implemented through such control over urbanization. Secondly, the detailed appropriation of land within the city wall and the size of the city, according to Ho (1985), were much related to the system of *jing tian* (literally well-field), in which the land was carved into nine equal squares out of a big square plot. In the Zhou Dynasty, that was how land tenure and the land tax were arranged. Cities too depended for their food and military subscription on eight surrounding tracks of 'suburban districts'. This integration between the city and country was believed by Ho to be the reason that in *Kao Gong Ji* the national capital had to have walls of nine *li* each.

Yet Ho's explanations are superficial. The *jing tian* system might have some relevance in the Zhou Dynasty, yet the concepts behind *Kao Gong Ji's* rules were much older. We believe it was more likely that the nine divisions of the capital city, with the palace in the centre as one of the nine units, came from the Ming T'ang. The earliest design of the Ming T'ang was attributed to Fu Xi in the shape of an octagon, following his famous eight *gua*. The central part was where the sage king positioned himself for watching the sky and for mediation with Heaven. The eight surrounding parts of the big room were for making sacrifices at different seasons. The location of the Altar of Grains and Soils and the Ancestral Temple, as well as the southward orientation of the main buildings of the palace city and southern location of the ministries, cannot be adequately explained by just saying that they reinforced the concept of the superiority of the sovereign (Ho, 1985, 59). Rather, they streamed from the concepts of the behaviour and role of the sage king in legendary China, and the ideal behaviour of any future emperor who claimed the mandate of heaven in a clearly defined Chinese world view of the interaction of the worlds of man and the universe. Ho (1985), however, has produced a marvellous piece of study, reconstructed details of the *Kao Gong Ji* model, and very successfully demonstrated through actual drawings the characteristics of the national capital model, which we shall present in a later section.

Cosmology

Hse (1980) used Chinese cosmology derived from the traditional Chinese world view to explain the layout of the national capital as exemplified by the Palace City and the Imperial City of Beijing in the Ming Dynasty. In Chinese traditional cosmology, the planets of the universe were seen organized into three 'constellations' (*heng*), and 28 'groupings' (*su*). The three constellations were the Tai Wei Heng, Zi Wei Heng and Tian Shi Heng. Zi Wei Heng was regarded as the throne of God on High. As the emperor was Son of Heaven, his residence and main office were taken to symbolize the throne of God on High and had thus been called the Zi Gong, or Tzi Wei Gong. In general, the name of the Palace City had been referred to as the Zi Jin

Cheng since the North Song Dynasty. The first reference to the Palace City being fashioned after Zi Wei Heng was in the Qin Dynasty, a much earlier date. The emperor's main court and his residence were thus seen as located at the centre of the universe, and it was there too that the *yin* and *yang* were duly represented by the Qian Qing Gong (Palace of Pure *Yang*, the official bedroom of the emperor) and Kun Ning Gong (Palace of Pacific *Yin*, official bedroom of the empress). Between the two was the Jiao Tai Tien (Hall of Intercourse) where the *yin* and *yang* interacted, and this was the bedroom for the emperor and empress on their wedding night. Around this core of the Palace City were arranged two gates to symbolize the sun (Ri Jing Men) and the moon (Yuet Hua Men) (see Figures 3.3 and 3.4). Also encircling the Zi Wei Heng were the 12 palaces of royal concubines to symbolize the 12 daily time divisions. The departments further to the north-east and north-west represented the other stars that huddled at the foot of God on High. South of the main court of the emperor skirted a curved water-course, Jin Sui He, which symbolized the Milky Way (Figure 3.3). The layout clearly matched what was said in Chapter 1, that the capital of the sovereign should be where 'Heaven and Earth are in perfect accord, where the four seasons come together, where the winds and rains gather, where the forces of *yin* and *yang* are harmonized'.

To the south of the Palace City, between Wu Men and Duan Men, the space was taken to be the Tai Wei Heng. South of this constellation were two stars which formed an opening like a gate. This opening was called Duan Men, where God on High would pass through. Thus before Wu Men there was an additional gate, Duan Men, to represent this cosmological element. The main gate to the Palace City, Wu Men, clearly bore the symbolism of the noonday sun, to mean the bright and almighty power of the sovereign.

The last constellation, Tian Shi Heng, consisted of 22 stars. They were said to symbolize trade and market. It was located further south, between Da Ming Men (or Da Qing Men) and Zheng Yang Men, in the present-day Qian Men area (see Figure 3.4).

Finally, Tian An Men was regarded as a group of five stars called Tian Sui that symbolized order and rituals, a location for political announcement and proclamation of rules and rituals. The gate and the four carved dragon stone pillars (the Hua Biao) were taken to represent these stars in their location as well as function.

Hse's cosmological interpretation has been based on gradual developments, as evidenced by relevant literature that sprang from the Qin Dynasty to Ming Dynasty. It has been a very useful addition to the evolution of the model of the classical traditional Chinese capital.

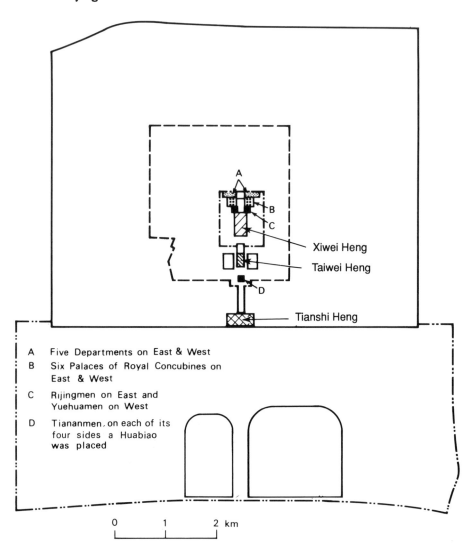

Xiwei Heng

Taiwei Heng

Tianshi Heng

A   Five Departments on East & West
B   Six Palaces of Royal Concubines on
    East & West
C   Rijingmen on East and
    Yuehuamen on West
D   Tiananmen, on each of its
    four sides a Huabiao
    was placed

0   1   2 km

Figure 3.4   Cosmology of the Palace City and Imperial City. Source: Hse, 1980

Feng shui

Feng shui (or Chinese geomancy) is a quasi-science on the siting of cities, houses and graves in traditional China developed out of the theories of *yin–yang* and the five elements and the overall Chinese concept of the overlapping and interaction of the worlds of man and nature. It is believed that there existed an environmental cycle due to the interaction of the *yin* and *yang* ethers. The latter produced the vital gas that passes through the stages of wind, cloud and rain. The vital gas brings good health and luck to all living things and thus, where the vital gas emerges, it makes the locale auspicious and potent. The first master and classics of *feng shui* appeared in the Western Jin Dynasty. Very briefly, the choice of an auspicious site depends on three main considerations. First, the surrounding land forms must be considered. An auspicious site needs to be sheltered by hills or mountains at the back, particularly from the cold north winds or from the inauspicious northward direction. Secondly, there must be water courses nearby for an auspicious site. The water should be slow flowing and with many curves. Thirdly, the soil should be fine in texture and firm in structure. The most desirable soil colour is yellow (Yoon, 1985).

Yu (1990) thinks that *feng shui*'s impact on Chinese city planning goes beyond siting considerations. Using Beijing as example, he indicated the general characteristics of an auspicious site as Yoon has explained. Beijing's location is clearly auspicious from the *feng shui* point of view as it is well protected by lofty mountains to its west, north and north-east in a horseshoe shape. In front of it are nine winding streams in a vast curved coastal plain. In classical *feng shui* interpretation this is a site full of the vital gas which gathers and stays there. Yet in the detailed layout of Beijing, *feng shui* has its significant influence as well, which Yu described as in three main forms:

a. *Cosmological symbolism.* The Palace City was at the meeting point of the east–west and north–south axes. The Zi Wei colour it used represents the Pole Star, taken to be the centre of the universe. The centre of the Palace City was Tai He Dian (Huang Ji Dian in Ming), its centre again was the throne. The nine steps of the throne platform symbolize the nine layers of Heaven. It was thus the centre of man's world as well as the universe. It must be the place where *yin* and *yang* are in balance, the vital gas at its strongest and the natural potency at its greatest.

b. *Balance of yin–yang and regularity of arrangement.* Yin–yang must be in balance and so are the left- and right-hand elements. This can be easily witnessed by the balance in location between the Altar of Heaven in the south and Altar of Earth in the North; the Altar of the Moon in the east and the Altar of the Sun in the west. The Altar of Grains and Soils in the right was equally balanced by the Ancestral Temple in the left. The *yin* elements (moon, ancestral temple, etc.) are all in the left, whereas the *yang* elements are all to the right. So are the relative locations of the male and female elements, and the office and residence of all palatial matters, in a south–north balance. In between the balances lies the most auspicious point, which was the Throne Hall or Tai He Dian. Thus the balance of *yin–yang* was expressed in the form of left-right arrangement along a central axis of most of the important buildings, whereas the most important ones were located along the axis itself, at the mid-points of the left–right balanced pairs, and the hierarchy of these buildings took a general south–north rank decline relative to the most auspicious centre, the Tai He Dian (Throne Hall).

c. *Quadruple division of the world and the five directions.* This concept says that the world was made up of four parts, each represented by one cardinal point and one guardian god, i.e. the Green Dragon for the east, White Tiger for the west, the Scarlet Bird for the south and Xuan Wu (a tortoise-like creature) for the north. These parts of the world plus the central position form the five directions. These concepts were often reflected in the geometrical shape of the base of architecture, i.e. round symbolizes Heaven and square symbolizes Earth, as well as in the naming of streets, gates and in the décors of roofs.

Other Confucian and Taoist Concepts

In this chapter, previous reference has been made to the symbolism of major Confucian and Taoist ideals in the naming of important palatial buildings. For example, in Da Du in the Yuan Dynasty, the Throne Hall was called Da Ming, taking its meaning from one of the Confucian classical principles. The names of the three audience halls, Fong Tian, Hua Gai and Jin Shen, also contained a great deal of symbolism. Fong Tian means 'with the mandate of Heaven'; 'Hua Gai' refers to the five-coloured cloud that protected Huang De while he was at battle and obviously means heavenly protection. 'Jin Shen' means to observe one's own rules. Confucius believed that the sage kings ruled the country well because they disciplined themselves well. In the Qing Dynasty the names of these halls changed, yet they bore two common and significant Chinese characters, *zhong* and *he*. These two were taken from yet another classic quotation: 'the mainstay of the universal order is centrality (*zhong*); the main rule for the world is harmony (*he*)'. Such has been a tradition in the naming of major halls and gates of the Palace City from Tang to the Qing Dynasty, which clearly underlines the common use of names to symbolize the mandate of Heaven and the way the country was to be ruled, as emanated from Confucianism.

However, these diverse sources have been intimately blended into one, the model layout of the Chinese national capital, as we shall examine further in the coming paragraphs.

Layout of the ideal capital

Ho (1985), in his detailed study of *Kao Gong Ji*, concluded that the main rules for the layout of the ideal capital are as follows:

1. The wall was square and was nine *li* long on each side, with three gates each.
2. Within the city were nine north–south and nine east–west trunk roads; the north–south trunks were each nine chariots wide.
3. The Ancestral Hall was on the left while the Altar of Grains and Soils was on the right.
4. Inside the inner part of the palace city, beyond the royal courts, were nine buildings for the nine female palatial officers; outside the royal courts were nine buildings for the nine ministers.

Rule (1) fixed the shape and size of the city as well as the number of gates it had. Rule (2) specified the main road network. Rules (2), (3) and (4) taken together further fixed the structure of the city, as follows:

a. The Palace city is to be the centre of the Imperial City. Its north–south axis was the capital's planning axis. This line starts from the south gate of the Imperial City, passes through the Outer Court, the Palace City, then the market to reach the main north gate of the Imperial City. The major gates, courts, royal residences and the market, which are all important functional and symbolic elements of the Imperial City are arranged in rank order along it in a south–north manner (see Figure 3.5).
b. The road network of the Imperial city focuses on the Palace City which forms the heart of the whole Imperial City. Similar to the main arteries of a human body, these roads link the Palace City with all parts of the Imperial City and, through its wall gates, to the entire empire beyond. The road network in a chessboard style has also reinforced the centrality of the Palace City and the central axis of the whole city (see Figure 3.6).
c. The outer court is located in front of the Palace City. The Ancestral Temple and Altar of Grains and Soils are placed on the left and right of the central axis. As the outer court was for royal business much more directly related to the public, e.g. proclamation of royal

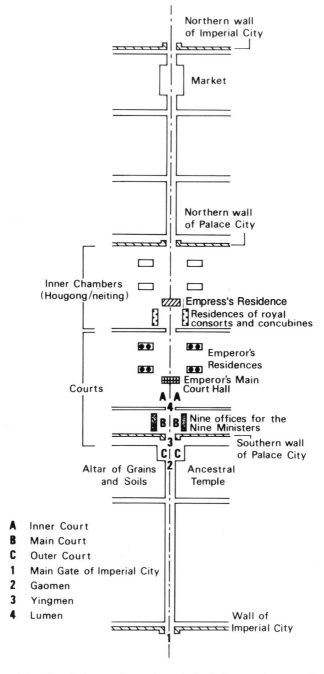

Figure 3.5 The ideal central axis through the Palace and Imperial City

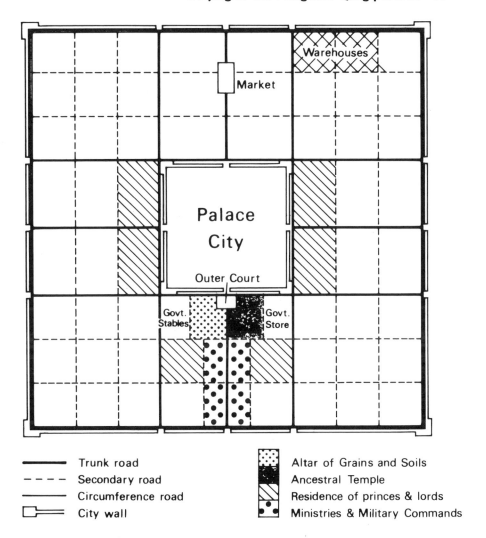

——— Trunk road	Altar of Grains and Soils
- - - - Secondary road	Ancestral Temple
——— Circumference road	Residence of princes & lords
City wall	Ministries & Military Commands

Figure 3.6 The ideal layout of the Palace and Imperial City. Source: Ho, 1985

decrees, final royal decisions on death sentences, holding of 'public enquiries', and ceremonies related to the Ancestral Temple such as presentation of captives from battle, its location outside the Palace City is reasonable. Similarly, the sacrifices and rituals related to the Temple and Altar had direct meaning to people of the country at large and served as examples for them to follow. They too were the key links and services provided to the people and Heaven by the sovereign. Further south, lined on the two sides of the central axis, are the offices of the various civil ministries and departments on the left and military offices on the right (see Figure 3.6).

d. Within the Palace City, the layout is governed by two functional considerations: the administrative responsibility of the sovereign and his private life. This has been specified by the arrangement of 'Qian Chao Hou Gong' (administration in the front and residence at the back). The delineations of these functional zones are by means of two gates: to the north of Lu Men is the emperor's residence, to its south is the main court. The nine ministers and their nine offices are in between the Lu Men and Ying Men.

The above reconstruction of the detailed layout of the national capital, based on *Kao Gong Ji* and other records by Ho, still has some gaps. The most obvious one is whether the main residential chamber of the sovereign is to be considered as part of the 'administrative quarter'. It lies clearly within the southern half of the Palace City, though it is to the north of the Lu Men. Ho also placed various functional zones within the palace wall. General workshops are to the north-west corner and workshops for the *hou gong*, or queens, royal concubines and ladies, are to the north-east, palaces for the crown prince and other princes are to the east and south-east. The royal kitchen and stores and 'internal' officers are to the west.

With such arrangements, Ho worked out the area of each of the main functional zones as shown in Table 3.1.

Outside the Palace City, with the exceptions of the Temple, the Altar, the Outer Court, the central military and civil administrative offices and the market, the locations of which have been clearly specified, *Kao Gong Ji* has not provided any guidelines on the location and orientation of other functions. Working on other records, and following the general philosophy of *Kao Gong Ji*, Ho produced a rough indication for land use to be found within the rest of the capital city. In Figure 3.6, we can see that to the left and right of the Temple and the Altar are the government stores and the government stables. General warehouses are found to the north-eastern part of the city close to the northern wall and the market. Residences of relatives of the royal family and chief ministers and lords are next to the Palace City, whereas other residences of the public are scattered throughout the city, following a strict social rank order.

Before the Sui Dynasty, the national capital had no Imperial City and only two walls, i.e. the wall of the Palace City and that of the whole city, later called the Outer City; in the case of Beijing in the Ming and Qing dynasties, we call it the Inner City in this chapter. The Da Xing Cheng of Sui Dynasty started the system of the Imperial City by enclosing the

Table 3.1   Functional zones within the ideal palace city

Zone	% of total area
Administrative	4.45
Emperor's Residence	12.23
Empress's Residence	16.67
Princes' Residence	22.22
Palatial Officers' Quarters	3.70
Stores	7.40
Kitchens	11.11
Workshops to serve *hou gong*	11.11
Other workshops	11.11

Source: Ho, 1985.

Palace City with a further wall, which put within it the Temple, the Altar, the central bureaucracy and the royal gardens and lesser palaces that had spilled over from the Palace City. This new development was interpreted by Ho (1985) as further segregation of the sovereign from the populace and an intensification of the differences of the social ranks.

To draw a brief conclusion from this section, it is obvious that in *Kao Gong Ji* the planning of the national capital, in essence, is the planning of the Palace City and its complementary ritual ceremonial buildings and administrative quarters; the other functional zones are of much less significance and they are there to provide the necessary service and support to the Palace City. Even the market has been regarded by Ho as basically a 'palace market' for servicing needs derived from the presence of the royal family and its appendages, rather than a genuine reflection of the trading and commercial roles of a natural city. Another point to be stressed is that *Zhou Li* has clearly specified three levels of capitals: national (i.e. the sovereign's), regional (the capitals of lords and princes), local (the capitals of the chief ministers). It too has stated similar principles for their layout and specified a hierachical order of standards regarding the length of their walls, the height of their gates and the measurements of their palaces, and the roles of their ancestral temples and altars of grains and soils. Thus the cities and the city system of China had a well-ordered doctrine in their detailed design that comes mainly from *Kao Gong Ji*.

Later developments of ideas and concepts, and the new roles of cities, particularly their increasing trading and handicraft activities and greater population size, had obviously made it necessary to evolve in such a way that the *Kao Gong Ji* model could not be totally replicated. In addition, new interpretations of the *Kao Gong Ji* specifications had also caused changes in the layout. These new departures may be observed from Beijing of the Ming and Qing Dynasties, the last living example of the design of the traditional Chinese national capital.

The cultural root of old Beijing

The old city of present-day Beijing, in spite of the disappearance of its walls and most of the gates, still provides the visitor with the most vivid illustration of the persistent Chinese world view regarding how cities were laid out and what role they played in the long history of China.

The almost intact form of the Beijing that has come down from the Ming and Qing Dynasties has incorporated all the previous key principles. Indeed, the planners had even developed these ideas to achieve a better and coherent layout consistent with the classical rules of *Zhou Li* than any previous national capital. Let us pick up the main points with reference to Figure 3.7.

The location of the Palace City, almost at the centre of the city, is obvious. The location of the Ancestral Temple and the Altar of Grains and Soils followed rigidly the specification of *Zhou Li*, and are respectively tothe left and right in front of the Palace City. In Yuan Da Du, these were to the left- and right-hand side of the Palace City, not in front of it. The Ming Dynasty relocation put these buildings in more auspicious locations in the south of the Palace City. At such locations they helped to strengthen the importance of the central axis and the 'southern palace' of the sovereign, the Tai Wei Heng, according to Chinese cosmology.

In the general layout, we can also observe that several important *feng shui* principles had been incorporated. The Coal Hill was an artificial creation made by dumping the mud dug from the site to yield the Nan Hai and for the creation of a deep moat around the Palace City. This 70 m high artificial hill served two *feng shui* purposes. First, it supressed the bad omen of a former defeated dynasty, the Yuan Dynasty, as the hill sits right on the Throne Hall, Da Ming Dian of Da Du, such that there would be no chance for the revival of the former dynasty. Secondly, it provides a *zhen shan* (protective mountain) for the Palace City. According to *feng shui* principles, an auspicious site should be on the slope or protected by a mountain on its northern side. The Coal Hill serves such vital purposes for the new ruling house of Ming. Coal Hill's significance is further amplified by being planned as the geographic centre of the national capital. Figure 3.7 has illustrated this, remembering the fact that the 'Inner City' of Ming and Qing Beijing are in fact the 'outer city' of other national capitals, whereas its 'outer city' is simply an 'outer' adjunct by general Chinese rule. In fact the *feng shui* concept of a *zhen shan* to the north of the capital came first when the Jin Dynasty built

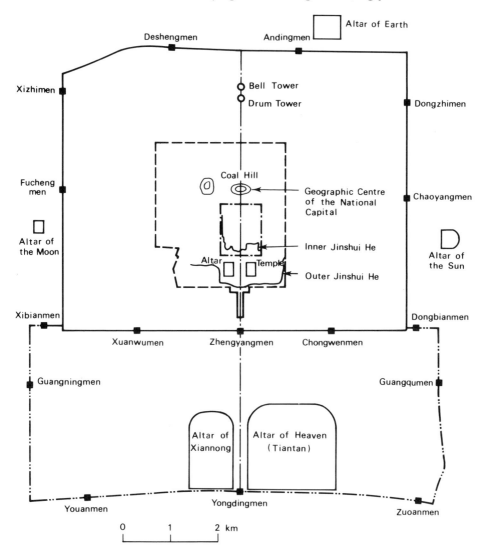

Figure 3.7 Principal elements in the layout of traditional Beijing (Ming and Qing Dynasties)

its Zhong Du. The small island to the west of Coal Hill was the *zhen shan* which still remains, though Zhong Du had vanished completely.

The omission of the central gate in the northern wall of the city, and thus the reduction of the number of gates on the wall from 12 to 11, underlines yet another modification of the *Zhou Li* rules to accommodate later concepts of *feng shui* and Taoism. As previously said, the 11 gates and their orientations represent the body of Ne Zha, a Taoist god that is regarded as impregnable. Elimination of the central gate in the northern wall also helps to keep the vital gas or auspicious ethers within the city which emerge through the interaction of *yin* and *yang* in the Palace City, and minimizes the inauspicious influence of the northern winds.

Further *feng shui* principles are represented by the two curving streams through the southern part of the Palace City and the Imperial City. The Inner Jin Sui He had been an old-established element within the Palace City since Qin Dynasty to symbolize the Milky Way, hence the city being the court of the Son of Heaven. Yet such streams are also regarded as one of the three vital factors for an auspicious site in *feng shui*. In addition, the new moat that was added to the wall of the Palace City, according to this author, takes its meaning from the circuit of water, the Pi Yong around the Ming T'ang. It represents the smooth flow of the benevolent effect of the sovereign's rule. Very obviously, the moat has little defence purpose as it is again walled on the outside by the Imperial City which too has a moat.

In the overall layout, the Ming design had enhanced the centrality of the central axis, not just by the creation of Coal Hill, but equally by building the bell tower and drum tower, and by extending the Imperial Way to the Altar of Xian Nong and Altar of Heaven in the southern suburb. In its total extended length of 8 km, the concepts crucial to the notion of centrality, i.e. concentration, orderliness, and balance, have been intensified. The Palace City as the Son of Heaven's residence thus stood out more prominently. The same effect has been promoted by the location of the Altar of Heaven, Altar of Earth, Altar of the Sun and the Altar of the Moon. These altars are at their right cosmological positions regarding the cardinal points, i.e. the sun in the east, the moon in the west, heaven on top (south) and earth at the bottom (north). However, they spelled out one thing, that the sovereign, being mandated by Heaven, is at the centre.

In the detailed layout of the Palace City, particularly in the arrangement of 'Qian Chao Hou Gong', in the location and delegation of functions of the three Big Halls, and in the ordering of the main palatial gates, Beijing of the Ming and Qing dynasties has achieved what former designs failed to bring out: the essence of the rules of the *Zhou Li*. In the Ming design, the Three Big Halls that formed the Main Court and the Inner Court have been put into one core group. This group of buildings was set on a three-layered marble platform which gave them a ground elevation above all palatial buildings. The main hall, the Throne Hall (Fung Tian, Huang Ji, Tai He) has the tallest roof height within the Palace City. Location-wise the core group is set right at the central part of the city. These arrangements are very different from Ho's reconstruction shown in Figure 3.5. Thus to the two internal courts, i.e. the Zhi Chao (Main Court) and Ying Chao (Inner Court), had been added the Hua Gai Dian (Zhong Ji, or Zhong He), and these are not separated by the Ying Men. Clearly, the Ming arrangement had been an improvement, and the addition of the middle hall made it more reasonable in providing a preparatory place on the same platform before the emperor proceeded to the grand ceremonies in the Throne Hall. Without the separation of Ying Men, the functions of the two inner courts were also better integrated.

A second improvement was the complete separation of the emperor's residence from his places for official business, in the form of the Three Halls of the Inner Palace. In fact, this quarter marks a transitional zone within the Palace City. If the Three Big Halls and all the buildings in front of it represent the public life of the emperor, then those encircling and behind the Three Halls of the Inner Palace represent his private life, or *hou gong* (Inner Palace). In the *yin–yang* theory, the former is positive, male or *yang*, the latter part is negative, passive, female or *yin*. The transitional zone is where the *yin* and *yang* portions of the Palace City interact along the central axis. Detailed examination of Figure 3.3 shows that the Three Halls are, from south to north, Qian Qing Gong (Palace of Pure *Yang*), Jiao Tai Dian (Hall of Intercourse) and Kun Ning Gong (Palace of Pacific *Yin*). Qian Qing Gong is the official residence of the emperor (he represents *yang*, or pure *yang*), whereas the Kun Ning Gong is the official residence of the empress (pure *yin*). The bedroom for the emperor's wedding was Jiao Tai Dian, a place for the interaction of *yin* and *yang*. In such a way, the traditional conceptual symbolism so much underlying the design of the national capital has been effectively borne out: the auspicious place for the smooth process of nature, i.e. interaction of the *yin* and *yang* ethers. Separating the emperor's residence from the inner court (Ying Chao) showed a marked improvement in adherence to the original ideas of *Zhou Li* than Ho's reconstruction. Of course, the Ming design had also clearly brought in new ideas of Chinese cosmology which *Zhou Li* had not detailed. This has been presented in previous paragraphs and illustrated in Figure 3.4.

The Outer Court, according to *Zhou Li* (as interpreted by Ho, see Figure 3.5), should be between the Gao Men (Duan Men in Ming and Qing) and the Ying Men (Wu Men in Ming and Qing). That space was too small. In the Ming design, it was located further south to the enlarged 'T'-shaped square outside the Cheng Tian Men (Tian An Men). The new arrangement allowed the main gates of the Ancestral Temple and the Altar of Grains and Soils to face south, the auspicious direction, instead of facing each other across the central axis. It too increased the solitude and depth of the Imperial Way on this stretch of the central axis in the approach to Wu Men, the main gate of the Palace City (see Figure 3.2). This development is also consistent with the evolution of the Imperial City into more or less part of the Forbidden City or Palace City, and better integration of the Outer Court with offices of the central civic and military headquarters.

In the 500 years of the Ming and Qing dynasties, the above general layout and functions of the Palace and Imperial City had remained largely unchanged. The national capital was in fact dominated by the Palace City. The Imperial City was merely its outgrowth. The road network also served the Palace and Imperial City, bolstering this core's centrality and connectivity with all parts of the national capital and the realm of the sovereign beyond, though it made little economic and transport sense as a network for intra-urban movements of people and goods.

The predominant political and military role of the national capital could also be seen in the size of its population, population composition and their economic activities. In Liao, Jin and Yuan dynasties, the city was dominated by the ruling minorities who filled most posts in the civil and military wings of the administration. In Ming, though the House was Han, the Inner City was still largely populated by the nobles, lords and high-ranking officials, military personnel and their dependants. The commoners, tradesmen and craftsmen were largely found in the Outer City. Chen (1977), quoting from historical records, indicated that in Yuan Dynasty at 1270, the population of the national capital was 410 350. In early Ming, at 1491 before the outer city wall was built, it had a population of 669 033. In 1579, after the outer wall was built, the population increased only slightly to 706 861. The last figure had seemingly been reasonably steady from early to middle Qing Dynasty. Considering the large bureaucracy and the need to station a huge army there, there was little left behind in terms of manpower for developing 'city-forming' activities. We can substantiate this point by a brief review of Beijing's population in the Qing Dynasty.

As a minority race, the Qing Dynasty had all the reasons to make the national capital a community of the ruling house, and tried as much as possible to exclude the Han Chinese. This was achieved by a system of the Eight Banners that combined military service with strict population registration and residence control in favour of the Manchus.

In 1645, when the Qing army moved into the Beijing area, the large army of the Eight Banners, together with their dependants and servants, was estimated to be about 950 000 strong. With the exception of about 100 000 soldiers who continued their military expedition further south, most settled in an area of about 500 *li* around the capital city region.

Within the national capital itself, it was estimated that about 240 000 Manchus had settled. At that time, the number of Han Chinese within the present-day Beijing city area had dropped to only about 600 000, a consequence of repeated natural hazards and war, whereas those within the Yuan city only numbered around 80 000 in late Ming. When the Qing army and court moved into the city in 1648, there were orders to evacuate all Han Chinese from the Inner City, except those related to the service of the bureaucracy, and monks in temples and monasteries. Han Chinese had to move into the Outer City. There were further decrees in 1755 that the 59 hotels within the Inner City had to relocate into the Outer City. At the same time, there were restrictions on members of the Eight Banners residing elsewhere than within the Inner City, except two bands of soldiers that had to be stationed in the Outer City for security and control purposes. Orders on 'demarcation of land' within the capital for various sections of the Eight Banners and the Qing royal house were proclaimed.

Racial segregation in the Qing Dynasty had thus forced a new element into the nature of the national capital and had reinforced the traditional notion that it served the purposes of political and administrative control of the sovereign. Until the last years of the reign of Qian Long (1781), there were thus in official records almost no Han Chinese within the Inner City. In 1647 there were 315 000 Manchus; and 393 000 in 1671; 496 000 in 1781. Those few that were found there were either servants of the Manchus or petty traders providing the necessary services, and they were all subsumed under the respective sections of the Eight Banners. Until the end of the Qing Dynasty Manchus, both males and females, had to be registered under the respective Banners. The men served as soldiers at call, except those who were officials of the third rank or above. The Eight Banners served the main purpose of protecting the Forbidden City and the Imperial City. The civil offices and warehouses were guarded by the cavalry of the Banners. Within the Inner City the Eight Banners, which combined the army and its attached dependants, were distributed as follows: the Banner of the Yellow Edge was stationed inside An Ding Men; the Yellow Banner inside De Sheng Men; the White Banner inside Dong Zhi Men; the Banner of White Edge inside Chao Yang Men; the Blue Banner inside Chong Wen Men; the Banner of Blue Edge inside Xuan Wu Men; the Red Banner inside Xi Zhi Men; and the Banner of Red Edge inside Fu Cheng Men. Even high-level Han officials were banished from the Inner City (Hon, 1984; Li, 1981).

The strict racial restrictions of the dynasty were only relaxed in the late nineteenth century when the young emperor of the Hundred Days Reform took over control. Thus the Inner City was almost exclusively populated by the Manchus for as many as 250 years. Even in 1910, there were 344 000 Manchus compared to 105 000 Hans. In the suburbs, which provided the income of the Eight Banners through ownership of land and a means for absorption of excess Manchus from the Inner City, the Manchus also predominated. For example, there were 85 000 Manchus in 1657 and 225 000 in 1910, compared to 36 000 and 83 400 Hans respectively. In the Outer City, except for less than 10 000 Manchu soldiers, the residents were Han Chinese. Due to forced relocation of the hotels and all Han Chinese residents into the Outer City, as well as increasing numbers of Han Mandarins and their dependants, and the constant and large number of Han scholars taking part in the civil examinations who needed to stay within the capital for months, the Outer City had become a busy place for commerce, trade, recreation and culture, especially the area immediately outside Zheng Yang Men (present-day Qian Men) (Li, 1981). However, even for the Outer City, the population and its function were largely dependent on the national capital as the political and administrative centre of the country. The total population there, including the Manchu soldiers and their dependants, numbered 145 390 in 1647, 158 925 in 1711, 184 092 in 1781 and 281 360 in 1910. These people provided it with support services rather than being drawn into it by pure economics of trade and commerce.

The slow and almost stagnant population growth of the Outer City reflected the very nature of its role, as well as the rigid population migration measures of the Qing Government to keep its population within limits, in view of both the burden of supplies as well as security. All retired Han officials had to return to their home villages and were not allowed to stay behind in Beijing. All people without a justifiable cause (e.g. to sit for civil examinations, to come for trade, and to come for news of official appointments) were banished from the city (Hon, 1984). We have no reliable statistics on the economic activities of the population of the city for the Qing Dynasty. Yet figures available for 1911, the first year of the Republic of China (last year of the Qing Dynasty), indicated that it was still largely a place of service industries, i.e. 56.4% of the population was unemployed, 28.7% in the tertiary sector, 2.5% in the secondary sector, and 12.4% in the primary sector. The total population of Beijing, all told, increased very slowly from 580 000 in 1647 to 822 625 in 1711, only reaching about one million (1 039 360) in 1910 (Hon, 1984).

In conclusion, Beijing by the end of the Qing Dynasty had remained very much a traditional Chinese national capital, functioning mainly as the headquarters of the ruling imperial house, and the symbol of its mandate of rule from Heaven. The layout of the city, its major architecture, as well as its day-to-day business were subconsciously interwoven together by the long stream of Chinese history based on the Chinese world view of the interaction of the two worlds of man and nature and how the sovereign, as Son of Heaven, should behave to achieve the balance of the two worlds and to invoke blessing from Heaven, such that there would be good harvest and good order in his reign, and happiness and stability among and between the ruled and the ruler.

4

Beijing under socialism: planning history and its role

Beijing as the PRC capital

The transition of Beijing from a traditional Chinese national capital into a Chinese socialist national capital was short, and is not as turbulent as one might expect considering the swift turn of events in China both from the political and military points of view. Although Beijing had the earliest taste of Western modern inventions compared to other Chinese cities, it was the last to actually go 'modern'. The ruins of the Yuan Ming Yuan (Garden of All Gardens) in its suburbs testified to the adoption of Western architecture long before the Opium War of the mid-nineteenth century. The steamboat which still remains today in the Summer Palace was the first steamboat ever imported into China. So was the electricity plant of the Summer Palace, the first modern infra-structure of its kind in Chinese cities. In spite of all these early Western toys, the national capital had been little influenced before 1949 by the growing impact of Western commercialism and industrialization and their consequent results for the changing Chinese city form.

The Treaty of Nanjing of 1842 forced the opening of five Treaty Ports in China. Together with later treaties signed with foreign powers, this imposed on the traditional Chinese city hierarchy new occidental elements in city functions, city form and the style of architecture. In the Book *History of Chinese City Construction* (1987), the authors have discerned two types of new cities emerging in China in the modern era. The first type were those cities that had experienced major changes due to invasion of imperialists, foreign capital or a rise in indigenous bourgeois, or brand new cities created by one or a combination of these forces. Qingdao, Harbin, Shanghai and Tianjin are examples. The second type were well-established feudal cities of traditional China that had undergone some changes as a result of the above-mentioned new forces. The most prominent were those that had foreign concessions or foreign settlements. In addition, many coastal cities that were forced to open to Western trade and industrialism, such as Wuxi, Nantong, Nanjing and Ningbo. Although the authors of the book included Beijing as a sub-category under 'feudal administrative centres', Beijing had largely remained unchanged, save for the foreign quarters of the embassies and of foreign troops.

Indeed, the 'closedness' of Beijing was maintained very much up to the Hundred Days Reform (1898), after which there was some slow movement in the direction of allowing Han Chinese residence in the Inner City and development of modern industries and modern infra-structure. These were, however, trivial compared to huge modern industrial–commercial centres that had taken root along the Chinese coast, e.g. in Shanghai and Tianjin.

The Fall of the Qing Dynasty in 1911 did not bring positive changes to Beijing either. Instead, the city had been for some years the rival ground for political ambitions of the war lords. It even lost its national capital status in 1927 when the Kuomintang (Nationalist Party) government chose Nanjing as the national capital and Beijing was renamed Beiping. Under the threat of the Japanese, the city of Beiping further declined in population and economy. From 1937, it was under Japanese occupation until 1945.

Two observable changes in Beijing since the late Qing Dynasty are: the appearance of the foreign quarters to the south-east of Tian An Men which accommodated the foreign embassies, banks, Western offices, clubs, hospitals, hotels and military garrisons; the construction of a number of Western churches, schools and hospitals in the city. Most often, the latter buildings were congregated together in one district. During the Nationalist government period Western architecture, such as the Senate and House of Commons and a number of municipal offices, public libraries and Western-style universities, was also constructed. Yet Beiping remained very much a consumer city, living still very much on its administrative and military roles, although in a slightly different fashion to before. Indeed, the last Qing emperor, Pu Yi, remained the master of the Forbidden City until he was driven out by General Feng in 1924.

The period of Beijing's stalemate and uncertainty about its status and role ended in 1949, when a new government of a unified China emerged. Beijing was made the national capital of the People's Republic of China (PRC). Its role as the political centre of the whole of China was effectively reaffirmed. What is more significant is that the PRC govern-ment subscribed to a very different ideology to the traditional Chinese world view or the Western capitalist ideas that had already taken root in new Chinese cities like Shanghai, and which had already transformed some traditional Chinese cities like Nanjing.

In this chapter we shall describe the socialist planning principles that have a bearing on Beijing's rebirth as a major city in China and the history of the city's planning since 1949, to reflect the new influence of socialist ideas on the function and form of the city.

Socialist planning: theory and practice

The success of the Chinese Communists (CCP) owed much to Soviet support. The CCP's political inclination was also obvious. The confrontation between the USSR and the USA in Asia over China and Korea and in Europe had also started the cold war. Amid all this, the PRC had little choice but to rely on the USSR for military and economic support. Thus when they took power in 1949, the CCP immediately embarked on an economic recovery programme to tackle inflation and to rehabilitate the crippled industries which had resulted from the preceding long years of war. Following the success of this reconstruction period in 1952, China implemented its first Five Year Plan in 1953. Guided by the slogan 'Learn Everything from the Soviet Union', the key objective was rapid industrialization with priority to heavy industry, following the model of Soviet construction methods and the accompanying administrative structure. As the CCP had little knowledge and experience in the building and planning of cities, they resorted to the Soviet model for this also and sought assistance from Soviet experts. Although a rift between the USSR and China occurred in the early 1960s, Soviet influence on Chinese city planning remained strong, even up to the present. As the national capital, Beijing may be taken as an outstanding example in this regard. Indeed, the purpose of this book is to investigate how far the pre-1949 traditions and the post-1949 socialist ideas have affected the present-day urban role and urban form of Beijing. It is therefore apposite first to briefly outline the characteristics of the 'socialist city' as it had evolved since the 1917 revolution in Russia, in the USSR and the East European countries, before the post-1949 transformation of Beijing is discussed.

City planning in Russia had the longest history of modern town planning in Eastern Europe. Peter I introduced European town planning concepts through the construction of a new city, St Petersburg, in the early eighteenth century. Town planning was more actively pursued with the formation of the Commission for the Masonry Construction of St Petersburg and Moscow in the reign of Catherine II (1762–96).

Besides dealing with St Petersburg and Moscow, the Commission had prepared more than 400 other town plans. The scale of endeavour was regarded as unparalleled in Europe or America (Bater, 1980, ch. 2). In the late nineteenth century, the Commission's work was taken over by the Technical Building Committee of the Ministry of Internal Affairs.

Russian town planning in the mid-eighteenth to early twentieth centuries had already developed a number of characteristics, some of which had continual influence on Soviet town planning after 1917. Briefly, the town plan is largely geometric, with emphasis on the city centre. During Peter's time the cityscape was usually dominated by a single central building. A century later, the usual design of the town centre featured an architecturally harmonious façade surrounding a central square with one or more thoroughfares providing accessibility. The softening or 'greening' of the cityscape through generous provision of open space in the form of parks to exploit site characteristics forms yet another planning characteristic. Geometry and symmetry of the plan layout were other obvious features. Land-use segregation to separate industries from residences as well as the enforcement of social class segregation became yet another integral part of the town plan. In the early twentieth century, under the influence of Howard's garden city concept, the creation of small satellite towns for relieving the pressures of congestion and the deteriorating environment in cities became a newly added element of many town plans.

The Bolshevik revolution that led to the formation of the socialist USSR meant a new page for town planning not only for former Czarist Russia, but also all forthcoming socialist states in Eastern Europe and other parts of the world, China included. The USSR did retain, perhaps subconsciously, some of the elements of town planning in the pre-1917 years, but under the new ideology and the new society it vigorously espoused, a new form of city, both in physical and in functional terms, seemed inevitable (Bater, 1980, 21).

Nature of the socialist city

Certainly we can point to many overt features which distinguish socialist cities from Western cities, or differentiate them from what they were in the pre-revolution days. New names were given to streets to commemorate heroes of the revolution and there were new statues for similar purposes in major squares or public spaces. Some mentioned functional adaptation of the urban fabric to the new society, such as churches being turned into kindergartens, or middle-class town houses into multi-occupier flatlets after their ownership had been 'municipalized'. Yet the greatest change lay within the general transformation of cities from the perspective of Marxism. First, this involved a macro principle of equity. This, is the overall political–ideological principle guiding the socialist character of urban development. It is to be pursued at two levels. One is the attempt to reduce the gap between the proletariat and the peasantry, i.e. between town and country. In the USSR this role had been stated, yet how it was to be pursued had never been clear (though it was at one time vigorously pursued in the PRC). Second is the equal provision of all items of consumption within the city:

> The ideological objective of equity is to provide equal opportunities for all people through the socialist control and allocation of highly equalized living conditions or public-consumption goods. Irrespective of location, ethnicity, skills, or income, all people should have access to the same standards or norms in housing, transport, education, medical care, and cultural and recreational facilities. (Hamilton, 1979, 200)

The second macro principle is that the socialist city had to provide the physical environment for the fulfilment of the economic plans of socialist construction. They were subject to the major forces in the economic milieu of the socialist state as reflected by the investment policies of various economic plans, which persistently underlined (*a*) the predominance of 'production' activities (i.e. industry, construction, transport and communication) over non-productive activities (i.e. wholesale and retailing, storage, finance, insurance, housing, municipal services, catering, medical and defence), (*b*) the key role of the secondary sector and (*c*) restricted growth and development in the retailing of consumer goods. Such investment bias had distorted the role of the Soviet city and imbued it with a unique occupational composition. By the 1970s cities of the communist countries were still, on average, registering 50% or more of their employed people in the secondary sector, while trade occupied between 11 and 12%. The last macro principle is the abolition of the price mechanism in the allocation of urban land, and its greatly restricted role in urban transport and urban housing. Theoretically, this should create for state investors in economic and welfare sectors and for city councils a wide range of site options open on economic grounds for development, and hence enhance the possibility for more decisive weight to be given to town planning concepts and welfare criteria in selecting the type of functions and the scale of land use. In practice, dysfunctioning of the price mechanism meant grossly inefficient use of urban land, and a homogeneous city of prefabricated housing with poor services.

The 10 general planning principles

Based on the 1935 General Plan of Moscow, Bater (1980) has listed 10 general planning principles which succinctly outline the main ideas and purposes behind socialist town planning:

1. To limit the size of the city. This implies that urban growth must somehow be monitored and controlled.
2. State control of housing. A 1922 sanitary minimum of 9 sq m of living space per inhabitant was adopted; in fact it served as the maximum allocation. Private housing in the long run would be abolished.
3. Planned development of residential areas, based on the three levels of organization, i.e. the superblock, the *mikrorayon* (residential district) and the residential complex; each was to be provided with the necessary day-to-day shopping and recreational facilities.
4. Spatial equality in the distribution of items of collective consumption such as consumer and cultural services.
5. Limiting journey to work for large cities to 40 minutes, mostly by means of public modes.
6. Stringent land-use zoning to ensure that housing and employment should not be far from each other, yet should be adequately separated to avoid the bad effects of environmental pollution.
7. Rationalized traffic flow to ensure heavy flow within designated streets to minimize congestion and noise.
8. Extensive green space.
9. Symbolism of the central city. It was to be the nucleus of the social and political life of the city. The objective was to have the resultant ensembles of architecture and squares to reflect the glory of the socialist state.
10. Town planning was to be an integral part of national planning, i.e. the general principle governing locational decisions was that industrial development should be directed away from large cities and existing agglomerations to less industrialized, rural or minority group regions.

In so far as the planning of the Soviet city is concerned, these principles figured prominently and it was their near universal application which had helped to standardize individual parts of all Soviet cities.

Spatial form

The spatial forms of the Soviet cities were much influenced by the ideas of three planners: Milyutin, Ladoviskiy and Strumilin. Milyutin (1974) in the late 1920s, through the design of Sotsgorod, propounded his ideal form of the city for achieving the socialists' objectives. This is the so-called 'linear-city'. It comprised parallel belts of housing with services, and industrial plants separated by a green 'sanitary' zone. Parks and water bodies were to be to the windward and industrial zones to leeward of the residential areas. In 1932, Ladoviskiy proposed a new 'trident-like' version of Milyutin's parallel-belt idea to guide the allocation of functions among zones and sectors within the ring-radial pattern of expansion of Moscow. The *mikrorayon* or 'micro-district' of Strumilin (1961) provided a form of communal living embodying the socialist principle of equity, and the urban-spatial framework for such living, being a self-contained community of residential quarters, dormitories, communal eating and recreation places, kindergartens, school and local medical facilities, shopping and other service provision. Each *mikrorayon* would be linked through locational proximity and through employment of its residents in an industrial plant or other major activities. These three spatial ideas formed the basis of socialist urban planning.

Ian Hamilton, summarizing 30 years of operation of the urban dynamics and urban planning process in the USSR and East European countries, generated a description of the typical socialist city:

> That city comprises several quite distinctive zones which may be portrayed in model form [see Figure 4.1]. These zones are clearly evident in townscape throughout the region, irrespective of city size or location. Nonetheless, in reality, the relative scale and importance of each zone does vary from city to city. When travelling out from the city centre one can observe the following zones: (1) the historic medieval or renaissance core; (2) inner commercial, housing, and industrial areas from the capitalist period; (3) a zone of socialist transition or renewal, where modern construction is partially and progressively replacing inherited urban or relict-village features; (4) socialist housing of the 1950s; (5) integrated socialist neighbourhoods and residential districts of the 1960s and 1970s; (6) open or planted 'isolation belts'; (7) industrial or related zones; and (8) open countryside, forest, or hills, including tourist complexes. Broadly speaking, outward expansion of city areas yields a concentric-zonal pattern, successive stages of building being readily recognizable in architectural styles and skylines. This pattern tends to 'overlay' a more sectoral or 'wedge-like' distribution of functional zones associated with particular site qualities, historic traditions, and major transport arteries. Fundamentally distinct, however, are the pre-socialist inner and socialist outer urban areas. (Hamilton, 1979, 227)

Of course, other than these spatial characteristics the typical socialist city had been seen as having a high density yet with a flatter population density gradient than Western capitalist cities. The generally homogeneous social structure and monotonous architecture had often been noted,

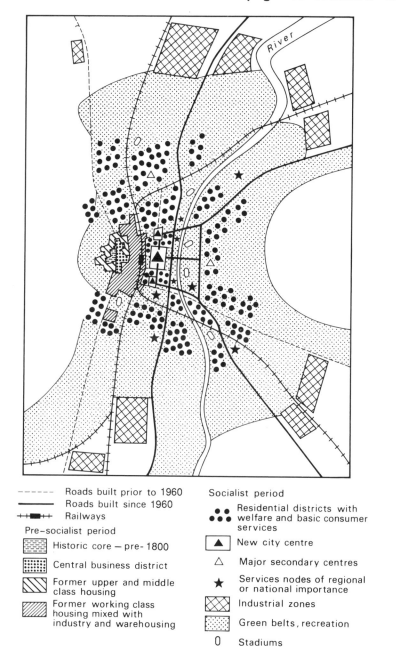

------ Roads built prior to 1960
——— Roads built since 1960
+++■+++ Railways

Pre-socialist period

Historic core — pre- 1800

Central business district

Former upper and middle class housing

Former working class housing mixed with industry and warehousing

Socialist period

● ●
● ● ● Residential districts with welfare and basic consumer services
● ● ●

▲ New city centre

△ Major secondary centres

★ Services nodes of regional or national importance

Industrial zones

Green belts, recreation

0 Stadiums

Figure 4.1   A model of the growth of an East European socialist city. Source: French and Hamilton, 1979

as had more generous provision of open space and the use of green separation belts between industrial and residential districts. In addition, there was the concept of urban agglomeration or city-region planning. The agglomerations are often mono-centric, being focused on one major city, a poly-functional centre, with satellite dormitory and industrial towns linked to it and lying within a radius of 50 to 80 km. The outlying members of the agglomeration served to steer the growth of industry, research and development, and population away from the main centre to areas often beyond the green belt (French and Hamilton, 1979).

City plans and implementation

The Soviet system of public ownership should definitely provide a clear advantage for town planning. Central planning of the economy should offer an edge for rational allocation and use of resources. As an integral component of planning at the local, regional and national level, town planning should share all these advantages; yet, in practice, central planning decisions and hence resources had been made, channelled and implemented through ministries. Given the fulfilment of centrally planned production quotas as the basic criteria for judging success, individual ministries tended to spawn autarchic empires in which the welfare of the economy was sacrificed to individual ministerial objectives. Another casualty of the approach was the lack of effective cooperation and coordination. All too often narrow departmental interests took precedence over integration, sectoral and spatial.

As town planning operated in the lower echelon of decision making of the Soviet system, the town planners' difficulties were clear. Many enterprises and departments in the city did not fall under the town planners' or even the city's jurisdiction. The planners were either unaware of or unable to influence them. Thus it was common that major components of urban water and sewage systems belonged to different ministries and a large proportion of urban housing remained outside the control of the municipality, to the extent that the municipal government was unable to control events and could only struggle with difficulty in *ad hoc* planning to patch up imminent problems (Bater, 1980).

In theory, the basic development determining the ultimate spatial organization of the Soviet city was the general plan. What went on in the city could not be divorced from it. In practice, as the city Soviet was not 'master of its own house', a multiplicity of ownership of essential facilities rendered having reality conform to the general plan exceedingly difficult. Ministries and departments seeking to fulfil their branch plans as fast as possible built not only production facilities but also housing, nurseries, kindergartens, recreational facilities, their own educational institutions, etc. The result was a burgeoning sector not subordinate to city agencies but developed under different branch programmes. For example, in Moscow and Leningrad, 30 to 40% of the housing stock did not belong to the local Soviets. In Leningrad in 1976, the 'branch' sector accounted for 22% of all hospital beds, 35% of the physicians, 36% of the places for day nurseries, 47% of the seats in cinemas and 51% of the hotel rooms (Bater, 1980, 131–2).

Under such a system, the development of a city was dependent on its administrative status, or the attention it was able to attract from the central government. Central planning decisions shaped the growth, stagnation or alteration of a city's function, infrastructure and population dynamics. They too determined the degree of autonomy and authority that city councils might be permitted to have. Higher administrative status endowed a city with greater ability to attract and to exert local planning controls over centralized investments (Hamilton, 1979, 201–2).

To what extent have the Socialist urban dynamics and urban planning process applied to the PRC? In particular, as the national capital of the PRC, how has Beijing been affected by the experiences of these processes in the East European socialist countries? What follow will first be a brief review of the history of planning of post-1949 Beijing and then a discussion on its planning mechanism and the main shifts in planning goals.

History of planning in post-1949 Beijing

In 1949 when the city was liberated, within the 62 sq km of the inner and outer city (i.e. within the wall) lived 1.4 million people, with an average density of 22 000 per/sq km. In the Palace and Imperial City, as well as the south-eastern and south-western corners of the outer city, there were very few people. Thus most of the population congregated in an area of roughly 52 sq km, in which were located 1 002 000 houses, mostly single-storey Chinese houses. Of the working population, only about 4% were in industries, with a large number unemployed.

In 1949, the city government proclaimed the guiding principle for urban construction of the city as 'to serve the masses, to serve production and to serve the Central Government', and requested immediate action to improve the provision of piped water, the sewage system, sanitation and to clear the rubbish and night-soil, and to use paid labour as surrogate for unemployment benefits to mobilize people to mend and construct roads and clear waterways and ponds. In May 1949, the

Beijing Municipal Town Planning Commission was formed and was charged with the planning of the city. As the PRC government was inexperienced in town planning and there were very few qualified professionals around, i.e. only 15 architects in Beijing, it was logical that outside expertise was to be relied on. In September of the same year, the city government invited a Soviet expert team to Beijing to assist the Commission in planning for the city. Thus, modern town planning on China's centuries-old national capital started under the sway of Soviet planning concepts and methodology. The history of Beijing's planning process may be broadly divided into four phases, each marked by a new general plan (or modified general plan) and important political events that impinged on the function of the city and its planning and construction activities. The four phases are: (1) 1949–57, (2) 1958–65, (3) 1966–76 and (4) 1977–92.

1949–57, phase of early construction

The main effort of the municipal government in the early years of 1949–52 was to revive and improve the normal municipal functions and facilities. In all, ten major jobs had been achieved. These included the clearing of heaps of night-soil, repairing the defunct water plant and extending the piped water system so that 95% of the citizens could be supplied with water.

Formal planning started when the first team of Russian experts arrived in September 1949 to assist in Beijing's planning. At least five different draft general outline plans, excluding that prepared by the Russians, were presented for consideration by the Municipal Planning Commission (Beijing Construction History, 1987). These plans, including the Russians', concurred on three main points. First, the city should be developed into a major industrial centre, besides serving as the administrative centre of the country. Second, there should be a strict limit on the future size of the city. Based on the experience of Moscow and the recommendation of Russian experts, the limit was set at 4 million persons. Third, in the city's layout, a network of ring roads supplemented by radial roads from the city centre and discrete functional zoning were agreed on. Based on the prevailing wind directions, industrial areas were to be located to the south and east of the city, while Xi Shan was designated the scenic and sanatorium zone. Next to it was to be the area for institutions of higher education. Residential quarters were, in principle, located near the concentrations of employment. The greatest divergence between the draft plans happened on the issue of where to put the administrative centre. One group, led by famous local architect Liang, argued that the old city was already so congested that there was no sufficient space there for accommodating this function and its conceivable future expansion. The better site was to be outside the old city to the west of its wall, filling the gap between the west wall and the new city in the western suburb that was started by the Japanese and as yet not completed. Liang's arguments included also the need to preserve the Imperial City intact. The other group was led vigorously by the Russians who insisted that time and cost considerations dictated the use of all available empty space and the demolition of old and dilapidated structures in and around the southern part of the Imperial City for the headquarters of the national administration, i.e. Zhong Hai, Nan Hai, along Changan Avenue, around Tian An Men Square, and between Dongdan and Chongwenmen.

By the spring of 1953, the Commission had produced two alternative plans for the municipal government's consideration. Both alternatives assumed the location of the administrative centre within the old city. Other common elements included: a 20-year plan horizon; ultimate population limit of 4.5 million persons; an urban land area of 500 sq km with an average population density of 90 persons per hectare, the same as Moscow; industrial zones dispersed in the suburbs; new residential areas between the old city and the industrial zones; separation of these zones by green belts; a pattern of ring roads supplemented by radial sub-arteries. Construction of the major industrial zones and zones for higher education and sanatoria and new accommodation for the central government had indeed gone ahead according to these principles. Thus although no formal general plan was approved by then, in practice the central administration had been moved from Xi Shan to the areas mentioned above and a number of planning features typical of Soviet cities had been adopted.

From 1953, the PRC extended its planned development after having successfully concluded its phase of 'post-war reconstruction', and the First Five Year Plan was announced (1953–57). As the national capital, Beijing entered into large-scale construction and the number of central ministries increased and the population shot up rapidly. The demand for all types of buildings and housing rapidly multiplied and application for land grants became a flood tide. The municipal government felt an urgent need for a general plan to guide these developments. In March 1953, another team of Soviet town planners and construction experts was invited and arrived to assist in the formulation of the general plan.

In summer 1953, the municipal government set up a Planning Committee to work with the Russians to generate a new general plan on the basis of the two alternatives presented in March. In November that year, a new draft general plan was produced, entitled the '1953 Plan', or

'Draft Plan on Reconstructing and Expanding Beijing Municipality'. The new plan had inherited much of the planning principles and methods of the USSR. It proclaimed six planning principles for Beijing:

1. The central part of the city should become the location of the central government. It is to be the centre of the city as well as the focus of the whole country.
2. The capital should be the country's political, economic and cultural hub; it is especially important for it to be the nation's large industrial base and centre of technology and science.
3. The city should be developed into a socialist city suitable for communal life under socialism.
4. The major danger is an extreme respect for old architecture, such that it constricts our perspective of development.
5. Beijing lacks sufficient water resources, and is plagued by wind and sand. Such environmental conditions have to be altered. That too will provide better conditions for the development of industry.
6. In reforming the road network, the existing situation should be adhered to as much as possible.

In addition, in its 20-year plan horizon, the ultimate population was raised to 5 million, and the planned urban area to 600 sq km. For planning the residential areas, the concept of 'residential complex' was adopted and each modified to a site of 9–15 hectares to suit Beijing's situation. Average blocks were to have four or five storeys, with those around open spaces or squares to attain seven, eight or more storeys. In the east, south, west and north-east suburbs huge industrial zones were to be developed. The higher education and sanatorium zones were also clearly defined. The plan confirmed the ring-road network and the supplementary radial arteries and laid down standard widths for the various classes of roads, i.e. main trunk roads were to be at least 100 m, radial arteries no less than 80 m, ring roads 60–90 m and secondary roads about 40 m wide.

The draft plan was disputed by the National Planning Committee on four main counts. It did not support the idea that Beijing should become a major industrial base. Instead it suggested the city should develop precision machinery, textiles and other light industries. It was felt that the ultimate population of the city should not exceed 4 million. The provision of land for residences and the width of roads were regarded to be too generous and wasteful of land resources. Higher education institutions should not be congregated into one zone. Instead such institutions should be dispersed such that students can be in closer touch with society, which would cut down construction cost, improve the scenic beauty of the city and make life more convenient for students and staff.

The municipal government countered the ideas of the National Planning Committee in two further reports to the central government, insisting on its original plan (slightly modified and renamed 'the 1954 Plan') and urging the central government to come to an early decision. In particular, the reports emphasized the following:

> The capital is our country's political centre, cultural centre and science and art centre. At the same time it should, and must be a major industrial city. If we do not develop major industries in Beijing, and only develop central ministries and institutes of higher learning, then our capital can only be an extremely high level consumptive city, without the huge base of a modern industrial proletariat. This will not be suitable for the city's status as the national capital. Besides, it is not convenient for the central ministries to absorb production experiences directly and hence impair their ability to direct the rest of the country. It too impairs the combination of research and production. (Beijing Construction History, 1987).

The central government refrained from making a decision. Another Soviet expert team was then invited to come in 1955 for further study. Despite the lack of official sanction, the 1953 plan was indeed implemented during the First Five Year Plan period. A wide range of industries took root in the new industrial suburbs, boosting industrial gross output 1.6 times in 1953–57. A total of 50 big factories were built, with a total floor space of 1.87 million sq m. Within the higher education zone, institutions of higher education increased to 31 (compared to 15 in 1949) and the number of students rose by 4.7 fold. In those five years a total of 1.02 million sq m of higher education institutions and 340 000 sq m of research institutions were built. The central administrative quarters and the foreign embassy areas also gradually took shape in the city centre. Along the trunk road from Chaoyangmen to Fuchengmen were new office blocks of the Ministries of Culture, Metallurgy, Geology, the Design Department of the Ministry of Forestry and the Workers' Press, etc. From Xidan to Huangfujin were new offices of the Central Organization Bureau, People's Daily and the office of the Central Committee of Beijing Municipality. The Ministry of Defence was located to the west of Bei Hai. In the western suburb, in Sanlihe, were offices of the National Planning Committee, the Ministries of Machinery Industry, and Finance. In Baiwanzhuang were the Ministry of Construction and the departments of foreign trade. The municipal construction bureau was located on the Nanlishi Road. In the five-year period, a total of 2.25 million sq m of office buildings were completed. The new embassy area was constructed between the Altar of the Sun and Jianguomen.

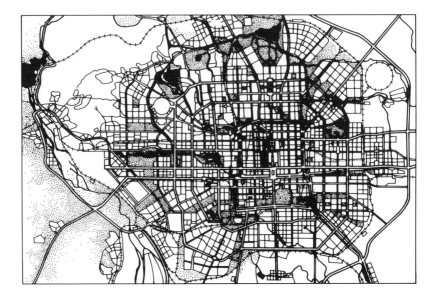

Figure 4.2   The 1957 Preliminary General Plan

In April 1955, the team of nine Soviet experts arrived. They had all participated in the planning and reconstruction of Moscow. Beijing Municipality formed a special Office of Experts to work under the Soviet experts and formed a new Town Planning Committee whose members were those of the Office of Experts. On the basis of the 1954 plan, a 'Preliminary Version of the General Plan of Beijing' was completed in 1957. The new plan emphasized the Soviet experience and its combination with Beijing's local circumstances. The plan was submitted to the central government for approval in June 1958 (see Figure 4.2).

The 1957 Plan further emphasized the development of big industries in Beijing. In the First Five Year Plan period, for national defence reasons, only 10 factories were added to the city and there were still debates on the suitability of Beijing for the development of major industries. In 1956, when Mao's famous article 'On the Ten Relations' was tabled at the Poliburo meeting, the way was cleared for Beijing's development as the nation's major industrial centre. The new plan thus requested the 'rapid construction of the city into a modern industrial base and a centre for science and technology' and claimed that 'on such basis, the city's population should not be small'. Thus the plan envisaged an extension of the planned area to 8860 sq km, though the planned urban area was maintained at 600 sq km, and the urban area population was raised to the ultimate 5–6 million. For the entire city, an ultimate population (in 50 years' time) was targeted at 10 million or more. In addition to the existing planned industrial areas, a large new chemical industry zone was added to the south-eastern suburb, and two smaller industrial zones in Fengtai and Qinghe.

On housing, the plan projected an annual demolition of 1 million sq m of dilapidated housing and building 2 million new houses in the old city so that reconstruction of the old city could be completed in 10 years. It also stressed again that new housing must be at least 4–5 storeys high. Along main streets and centres they could be 10 or more storeys tall. Housing construction had to be centrally planned, designed, funded, constructed, managed and allocated, and so were other buildings.

Following the Russian example, the plan clearly raised the planning principle that 'housing and work places are to be close to each other to minimize people's commuting time and decrease the traffic volume of the city'. Residential districts were to be based on the 'small district' as the basic unit which had 30–60 hectares of site and housed 10 000– 20 000. It replaced the smaller 'residential complex' of the 1953 plan. This allowed the 'small district' to be supplied with primary and secondary schools, kindergartens, shops and other public service facilities. The plan established four ring-roads within the urban area and three outer ring-roads. From the central area would radiate 18 radial arteries. The trunk roads were to be 100–110 m, municipal arteries 60–100 m, sub-arteries 40–50 m and minor roads 30–40 m wide.

In this early phase of town planning, the influence of the Soviet model was explicit. Not only were Soviet experts present in the major plan formation exercises, they 'supervised' them. A number of local objections to key planning decisions were defeated largely owing to the weight of the Soviet experts. Although Soviet experts were not seen to participate in Beijing's planning process after 1959, nonetheless the key concepts and standards adopted in the 1950–57 period held sway until the latest plans of 1982 and 1992.

1958–65, phase of the 'Great Leap'

In January 1958, the CCP raised a new political line, the 'Great Leap Forward'. The Beijing municipal government moved quickly in responding to this latest call and decided to develop Beijing into a modern industrial base as fast as possible. The June 1958 plan was drastically modified in September 1958 and reflected the new ultra-leftist mood of the time. In its preamble, it stressed the guiding principle of rapid transition towards communism and strived for ways to eliminate the three contradictions, i.e. town–country, manual labour–mental labour, and industry–agriculture. The main ideas involved in the new institution, the People's Commune, were also written into the plan, i.e.:

> Urban construction's main purpose is to serve industrial and agricultural production, especially for increasing the capital's industrialization, industrialization of the people's communes, factorization of agriculture, for uniting the workers, the peasants, the traders, the academics and the soldiers, and for providing conditions for gradual elimination of the serious differences between industry and agriculture, town and country and manual labour and mental labour.

Based on this new concept, the Soviet model of the urban structure was modified to a new format, the 'dispersed constellations'. The old Soviet concept of discrete segregation of various land uses, particularly residential, industrial and educational, was disputed. Some degree of concentration was accepted, yet it was also acknowledged that putting factories into areas primarily for residential and educational purposes would facilitate convenience and complementarity of the functions. The revised plan subdivided the city into a number of 'constellations' and used extensive 'green belts' to separate them. In addition it extended the planning area from 8860 to 16 800 sq km and the population of the planned urban area was reduced to 3.5 million. The principle of turning the city into a big garden was expounded with new requirements that 40% of the central district and 60% of the suburbs should be devoted to green space. Within the green belts cultivation of farm crops should also be emphasized, so that the urban areas would not only possess industrial but also agricultural functions, making the city a new entity of mixed industrial–agricultural uses. In the residential uses, the principles of communal life of the People's Commune were adopted. A few neighbourhoods were designed to facilitate communal living, such as communal kitchens and mess halls. Young children were assumed to be 100% looked after by day-care centres, all students were fully boarded and industrial uses were included in residential neighbourhoods. The plan was accepted by the Central Committee of the CCP and formed the basis for development until the Cultural Revolution.

Within that period six major heavy and light industrial areas were developed and Beijing became a broadly comprehensive industrial base of China by 1960, with almost all types of industries of the whole country represented. Some of the ultra-left principles produced negative effects. For example, a number of harmful factories were set up within residential zones, the central area and the educational zone, causing much pollution and traffic problems. Yet the reduction of the population target for the urban area and the introduction of the 'greening' movement, as well as the new 'dispersed constellations' layout, had positively contributed to improving the land reserve and ecological balance of the city. Within the period, the reconstruction of Tian An Men Square and the completion of the '10 major building structures' were other big events for commemorating the 10th anniversary of the PRC. In the former, the Russian influence was felt as well. Under their supervision 11 drafts had been proposed in addition to other suggestions by local planners and architects.

In 1959–61 China suffered from the excesses of the Great Leap Forward campaign and added problems of natural disasters and the withdrawal of Russian aid. About 1200 Soviet experts were called back by the USSR without prior notice and many major industrial and construction projects came to a standstill. Like the rest of the country, Beijing cut back on many of its major development and construction projects. In 1961–65, the population of the urban areas declined by 420 000, as part of the retrenchment policy. Most of this took place in 1961 and 1962. In 1962, the Town Planning Bureau completed a year-long review of the planning processes and experience of the 13 years since 1949. The review raised six main points:

1. There was an overconcentration of factories within the urban area. There they occupied too much land and were located in an unplanned manner, causing congested land use, insufficient water supply and chaotic traffic problems.
2. Metallurgical and chemical industries were causing serious pollution to the city.
3. Many factories had taken up land for residential use causing an imbalance between housing and employment. Within the residential areas, service provisions were insufficient.
4. Construction lacked coordination and unified planning, design and management. This slowed down the overall pace of construction and produced little positive contribution to renewal of the old areas.
5. There had been an overextended programme of satellite town construction. Under the Great Leap Forward in 1958, 37 townships in the outer suburbs were planned as satellite towns for accommodating 113 planned major industrial projects. Due to the retrenchment, only 60 such projects were actually implemented and they were scattered over 31 satellite towns. Thus these townships were neither efficient nor self-contained, as the actual development was insufficient to warrant a full range of support facilities, leaving already developed projects and their accompanying workers stranded.

Table 4.1 Ratio between basic infrastructure investment
and total municipal capital investment 1952–60

Year	Ratio (%)
1952	18.4
1953	9.8
1954	5.7
1955	6.2
1956	8.2
1957	6.3
1958	5.7
1959	7.1
	(including 10th anniversary projects)
1960	4.8

Source: Compiled from Beijing Construction History, 1987,
p. 291.

6. There was a growing discrepancy between investment in basic
   infrastructure such as water supply, roads and transport and
   communications and the city's total capital investment, thus the
   infrastructure of the city was gradually falling behind overall urban
   development, creating serious problems of shortages (Table 4.1).

In addition to the six problems, the review raised criticism about the
autarchy of the central ministries and departments, and the lack of
sufficient power and control of the municipality, which caused serious
shortages in infrastructure and major land-use deviations from the
general plan. It proposed a system of unified planning and allocation for
building construction and strict control by the central government on
placing further development projects and personnel by all central
ministries and departments into the capital.

In 1958–60, 2.94 million sq m of factory space was built, the highest
level since 1949. Total gross industrial output reached Yn9.34 billion in
1960. Industrial sites of the urban area were basically saturated. In
addition, 796 000 sq m, 1.22 million sq m and 3.63 million sq m of floor
space respectively were built for science and research, higher education
and residence. In the later years of 1961–65, in comparison, only a total
of 10.56 million sq m of space were built for all uses, or, on an annual
basis, an equivalent of only 55% of that completed in 1958–60.
Investment in basic infrastructure in the latter period also averaged
only Yn16 million compared to the average of Yn99 million annually in
1958–60.

1966–76, phase of the Cultural Revolution

May 1966 to October 1976 was officially regarded as the period of Cultural Revolution, during which Beijing suffered another wave of ultra-leftist influence. In January 1967, the city's general plan was suspended and between 1968 and 1972 the Town Planning Bureau was dismantled. Beijing was thus plunged into a period of planning anarchy. Urban development was in the form of almost absolute autarchy of the central ministries and other departments. In the government announcement suspending the application of the general plan, only a few vague guidelines were mentioned and left to the interpretation of individual offices and enterprises. These were: (*a*) new construction in important thoroughfares such as Changan Avenue should stop until there was a new plan; (*b*) developments within the urban area should seek whatever spatial gaps existed to avoid demolition of residences; (*c*) there will not be any new residential districts; and (*d*) to adopt minimum standards in construction.

The chaos resulting from the general situation of anarchy had led to haphazard growth of dangerous factories within residential zones and the blind location of many buildings right on basic infrastructural lines, as well as completion of several hundred thousand sq m of substandard housing, the erosion of the green and open space and harm done to cultural relics.

In 1971 Wan Li became the new mayor. Under him there was a call for a new general plan and the formation of the Town Planning Lead Group in 1972. By December 1972 the Town Planning Bureau was revived and a new general plan was completed by October 1973. The new draft plan laid emphasis on solving the city's water shortage and pollution problems and called for the prohibition of new factories within the urban areas and suburbs, and no 'polluting factories' at all for the entire city. Renewal of the old areas and development of a number of small townships in the outer suburbs in association with spatial restructuring of industries had also been suggested. Yet the draft plan was shelved by the municipal government and was not even discussed.

In December 1974, the municipal government prepared two further documents for the State Council and the Central Committee of the CCP, obliquely reflecting its concern over insufficient investment in housing and basic urban infrastructure, and suggesting a general stoppage, or a great reduction in the pace of the construction of 'production space' in favour of housing and facilities for decent urban living. In its reply in 1975, the State Council instructed that urban construction and the development of the capital should be put under the unified control of the municipality, and that in the process of construction there should be a balance between 'productive' and 'consumptive' elements. The State Council also allocated an annual sum of Yn120 million and a related amount of materials for improving the urban basic infrastructure in the Fifth Five Year Plan.

The Cultural Revolution period was the lowest point in Beijing's urban development. In 1966–76, total building construction was 18.11 million sq m, or 1.64 million sq m annually. In the 11 years, an annual Yn26 million was invested in urban basic infrastructure, about 2.9% of the total capital investment of the municipality. Thus the situation of inadequacy of Beijing had been made much worse.

1977–92, phase of liberalization and enlightenment

In October 1976 the 'Gang of Four', which represented the ultra-leftist fraction of the CCP, was toppled by a coup. A two-year transition under Hua Kuo-feng was soon succeeded in 1978 by new reforms and the 'open door' policies of Deng Xiao-ping. The new Central Committee of the CCP pointed out the need to eradicate the long-held mistakes of the ultra-leftist inclination and insisted that economic construction must conform with China's circumstances as well as the economic and natural forces. In April 1980, the Central Committee issued an important directive regarding the role of the capital. Beijing was to be the political centre of the nation, and the centre for China's dealings with foreign countries. It should be developed into one of the best cities of the world in the following areas: (*a*) social order and morality; (*b*) cleanliness and hygiene; (*c*) culture, technology and level of education and (*d*) economic prosperity, convenience and stability.

In November 1981, a new Beijing Town Planning Commission was set up with the mayor as the chairman. Under the Commission a new draft general plan was completed in 1982 and was approved by the State Council in late 1982 (Figure 4.3). In the new plan, a number of planning principles were defined:

1. The nature of Beijing. This is the most important change compared to previous plans. The capital was defined as the 'political and cultural centre' of the nation, and there was no mention of it being an 'economic centre' nor a 'modern industrial centre'. The plan severely criticized the former planning emphasis on Beijing's industrial role and indiscriminate development of the entire range of industries without regard to the city's natural resources and environmental quality.

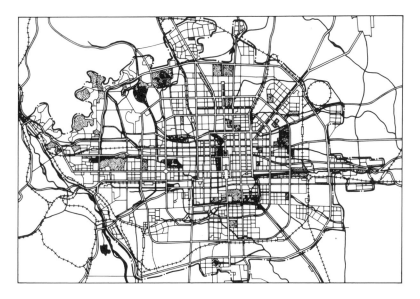

Figure 4.3   The 1982 General Plan

2. The plan reaffirmed the need to constrain the population of the city to 10 million.
3. It stressed the importance of 'greening' the city and the need to protect and conserve the natural environment.
4. A spatial programme for the restructuring of the city was laid out which included redeveloping the old centre, improving the infrastructure of the suburban areas and actively promoting the growth of the outer suburbs. The city region would take the 'mother–children pattern' of development by fostering the growth of satellites around the central city, yet the mono-centric ring pattern of growth was rejected with the continued adoption of the 'dispersed constellations' pattern of the urban areas.
5. More stringent requirements were laid on the conservation and preservation of the cultural and historical heritage of the city.
6. The plan clearly specified the need for a ratio between housing and related services and established the 'residential district' as the basic unit in the planning of residential areas. The ratio is targeted at 7:3 by the year 2000 and the per capita living space would be raised from 5 to 9 sq m.
7. It proposed five measures for plan implementation, i.e. rule of law; to reinforce the leadership of the municipality; administrative reform to achieve unified planning and development in the redevelopment

of the city centre and development of the satellite and lesser town-ships; phased implementation of the general plan; and concurrence with the local district authority, e.g. the lowest-level residential districts should conform with the street offices for implementing the management and planning details of the plan.

The 1982 plan reiterated the need to limit the city's population to 10 million and its urban area population to 4 million. The planned urban area was restricted to 750 sq km, an increase from the 1973 plan. Indeed development in Beijing was hectic from 1978 on. The plan reflected some of the new trends that were already rapidly unfolding as a result of the new era of economics and reforms. In 1977–83, a total of 23.5 million sq m of houses were constructed, or equivalent to 46% of the stock built after 1949. This new addition raised the per capita living space in Beijing from 4.57 to 5.68 sq m in 1979–83. Floor space for services, i.e. commerce, culture, medical and health and other services, totalled 4.06 million sq m. These 'consumptive' floor areas comprised about 70% of all floor space built in the period, reaching the planned target of a reasonable balance between 'consumptive' and 'productive' construction. Investment in basic infrastructure also increased to 6.56% of total capital investment, reversing its previous trend of declining input.

In July 1983, in approving the 1982 Draft Plan, the Central Committee of the CCP and the State Council further specified that all urban construction and activities within Beijing should pay due respect to its role as the socialist capital, and the nation's political and cultural centre. They also announced the formation of the Capital Planning and Con-struction Commission, whose role is to vet the city's general plan and its annual implementation plans, to draft relevant legislation for the construction and management of the implementation of the general plan and to resolve conflicts between related parties. The Commission has as its members representatives from the municipal government, National Planning Commission, National Economic Commission, Town and Country Environmental Protection Ministry, Finance Ministry, Admin-istrative Office of the State Council, Office of the Central Military Committee, General Department of the People's Liberation Army, National Civil Administrative Office, and the Central Administrative Office of the CCP. The chairman is the mayor of Beijing. The scale of industrial development was to be strictly restricted according to the same document, which also instructed rapid development of commerce and service activities to promote the capital's economy and to solve its employment problem. The state should assist Beijing in finance and materials and these should be incorporated into the long-term and annual plans of the National Planning Commission.

The 1982 plan was further revised to reflect the increasing trend of economic transformation, liberalization of the government and internationalization of Beijing as the capital of the PRC which is rapidly developing economically and is more and more integrated with the world market and the international community. The revised draft plan as at the end of 1991 underlined four main planning principles adopted in 1982, viz.:

1. The capital's nature should be the political and cultural centre of the nation.
2. Strict adherence to the 'dispersed constellations' pattern of layout.
3. Strict control over the size of its population and development area.
4. Restrict the economy sectorally and spatially so that it befits the capital's nature.

The plan suggested that effort should be made to limit the city's population to 11.4 million, with an extra 1.8 million mobile population by the year 2000, and respectively 12.2 million and 2.2 million by 2010. In the planned urban areas the population targets are 5.8 million and 6.2 million for those target years. The planned urban areas will be 1000 sq km; 600 sq km are within the planned urban districts, 300 sq km form their green belts, and another 100 sq km are located in the townships of the outer suburbs. Other details of the plan specified electronics and motor vehicle manufacture as the city's preferred industries, followed by machinery, textiles and electrical engineering industries. Energy- and water-intensive and polluting industries would be subject to significant reform. The city's GDP is projected to grow 5.5–7% in 1990–2000, and then 5–6% in 2000–10. There is projected change in the sectoral composition, as the primary sector contribution is expected to decline from 8.8% contribution to 6% in 2000, and then 4% in 2010. For the secondary and tertiary sectors, the respective figures are: 52.4%, 49% and 41%; 38.8%, 45% and 55%. Thus there is expected to be a shift towards the tertiary sector as the mainstay of the economy. As a consequence of that expected transformation, the plan proposes the setting up of a Central Business District to straddle the eastern suburb and Chaoyangmen, for finance, insurance, domestic and foreign trading, communication, consultancy and business and cultural service activities (Beijing Municipality, 1991).

The Soviet influence

The historical development of urban planning and its implementation in post-1949 Beijing, as presented above, have vividly demonstrated the clear influence of the ideas of socialism and the experiences, concepts and planning standards that had developed in the USSR. Some of these have found long-standing acceptance by the PRC authority and planners, and they have since also been so much integrated with Chinese city construction and city planning that they can be regarded now as part of the characteristics of the contemporary Chinese city and Chinese urban planning.

As previously discussed, active involvement of Soviet planners in Beijing's planning process took place in 1949–57. During that period, three batches of Soviet experts on town planning and urban construction were invited to take part officially in the planning of Beijing. The first batch arrived in September 1949. They laid down the main planning principles and key planning standards of the city. In addition, they participated in the key decision in locating the central bureaucracy and were successful in pushing through their ideas which were adopted and implemented. The second batch came in April 1953 and were instrumental in the formulation of the 1954 General Plan. The last batch came in 1955. They assisted in the formulation of the 1957 Draft Plan which later became the 1958 General Plan. They also actively participated in the redevelopment of Tian An Men Square. It was reported that they had put up a total of 11 plans for the square, yet how much they had influenced its final plan is not known. In this section, we attempt to outline the key Soviet ideas and methodologies which had been adopted by the Chinese in their various planning exercises through an evaluation of the different general plans, as well as the key planning principles that they had proposed and accepted, in the form of formal incorporation into the general plans.

The 1949 Soviet expert team was responsible for two major planning events in Beijing in 1949–50. First, they swayed the decision of the Chinese to locate the bureaucracy of the central government within the old city, at the western and southern periphery of the Forbidden City. This was not an easy victory, as the best known and respected local experts, Mr Liang and Mr Chen, were strongly opposed to it and they had proposed and produced an alternative location in the western suburb. The Russians argued on economic grounds based on the experience of the redevelopment of Moscow. They quoted Moscow's experience that developing the new administrative headquarters within the old city would cost only 20–30% of the cost if the headquarters was to be constructed on virgin land in the western suburb. There was a similar proposal to set up a new city next to old Moscow, but this was rejected. They insisted that China needed to develop industries urgently and the savings from locating the administrative centre in the old city were indispensable and pragmatic. Finally, they claimed that Chairman

Mao had said that the central government would be located in the old city.

On major town planning principles, the team successfully pushed through the line that, as a socialist national capital, Beijing should develop its industries quickly. The primary purpose of this was to raise the proportion of its working class within the total population. The 1949 figure of 4% as compared to 25% in Moscow was regarded as grossly unreasonable. The city should therefore concentrate its effort on development of industries. In addition, development of industries would contribute to turning Beijing from a consumptive city to a productive city. Other reasons were also mentioned, such as providing the institutions of higher education, science and research with the convenience of combining learning and research with implementation, and the central ministries with direct experience in the running of productive enterprises. This main principle set the trend of development not only of Beijing, but also of all Chinese cities until the early 1980s.

The second Soviet principle that had been successfully engraved by the team on Beijing (and the whole of China) is that it is a characteristic of socialism to avoid excess concentration of population in big cities. Thus the size of the city, both in terms of population and its planning area, was to be strictly restricted. Planning measures as well as migration and population control measures were the main mechanisms for achieving such a goal.

Thirdly, the team clearly and strongly denied the applicability of Western planning principles and methodologies in planning Chinese cities and exhorted the relevance of the experience of the USSR to China (Beijing Construction History, 1987, 117).

Besides the general principles, the team also gave the Chinese a number of planning concepts and standards. Most of them went into the 1952 draft plans and some are still used today, i.e.:

1. Basic and non-basic population. This is to divide the urban population into two categories. The basic population are those employed in the central government, industries, and institutes of higher learning and research, etc. The non-basic population refers to the self-employed, workers in the municipal government, police, shopkeepers, traders, school teachers, etc. The normal ratio of the two is 1 to 1.
2. Areal standards for different land uses within the city:
    *   industries – 7 hectares per 1000 workers;
    *   residential use – 110 sq m per person;
    *   service activities – 4 hectares per 1000 employees;

- higher education use – 10 hectares per 1000 students plus 150 sq m per staff employee;
- city centre – 77 sq m per person;
- whole city – 147 sq m per person (higher than Moscow which was 120 sq m per person).

3. Housing: based on the experience of Moscow, five-storey blocks were seen as most economical.

In the 1954 Draft General Plan, further Soviet standards had been included in the planning of Beijing. In housing, the concept of 'big neighbourhoods' in the redevelopment of Moscow was adopted. Each was about 9–15 hectares in area. Residential land standard was confirmed at 75 sq m per person and the living floor space of 9 sq m per person was taken as the long-term (20-year) goal. Beijing also adopted an open/green space standard of 12–15 sq m per person, based on the general rule of 10–12 sq m per person then obtaining in the USSR. The plan also recommended combining all relevant departments to form a unified office for planning, design and construction, using Moscow's model.

In the 1958 General Plan, the preamble stated that the plan was formulated on the basis of combining the USSR's advanced experience and the circumstances of Beijing and represented an improvement on the 1954 plan. It reaffirmed that the plan put industry as its top priority, a point stressed by many Soviet experts. The new elements included the adoption of the city-region layout, in Chinese terminology the 'mother–children' city pattern, or central city-satellite spatial structure. It made use of satellite towns as a means of relieving congestion and lack of space for new development in the central city. In housing, the 9 sq m per person living floor space goal was maintained, and new housing should be 4–8 storeys high. In the layout of housing and relevant service provisions, the Soviet hierarchy of 'super-block', *mikrorayon* and 'residential complex' was modified to 'small districts', 'residential districts' and 'district'. The 'small districts' had a serving radius of 200–500 m, provided with basic low-order services such as small shops, primary schools and clinics. The 'residential districts' had a serving radius of 1–2 km, and were equipped with medium-order services such as central stores, middle schools and a commune hospital. The 'district' served an area of 3 km radius. It had higher-order facilities such as shopping centres, theatres and cinemas and a general hospital.

After 1960, the relationship between the USSR and PRC deteriorated and the former unilaterally withdrew all its 1200 experts from China. Since then, the planning of Beijing has been performed without direct participation of the Soviet experts. However, many of the key planning concepts have been maintained in the 1982 General Plan and even in its 1992 revision. Among these are the standards for housing provision, open/green space, organization of housing areas and their service provision, the 'mother–children' spatial pattern, discrete zoning for higher education and research, and the sanatorium area, stringent control on city size, etc. Some of the standards are complete duplicates of the Russian ones, but some have been modified, i.e. the residential units, to suit the higher population density and the tradition of more centralized services, particularly shopping facilities, in Chinese cities. Some standards are deliberately higher than the Russian, or even those of Moscow, such as those for open/green space, residential area and overall urban land area, with a clear view to boosting Beijing as the national capital of China. In this regard, the attitude towards preservation of the historic core and cultural relics of Beijing had represented a distinct difference in opinion between the Soviet experts and the local planners. The latter, though they lost to the former in the issue of where to locate the administrative centre, have been quite successful in holding down the height of buildings in the old city, and in the 1982 General Plan even succeeded in maintaining very stringent developmental control in the old city for the preservation of the historic buildings and sites of Beijing.

Conclusion: planning experience in Beijing

Table 4.2 outlines the main features of the four officially adopted and implemented general plans of Beijing (with the exception of the 1954 Plan which was implemented but not officially proclaimed). Three of these were formulated in the 1950s under very strong Soviet influence. The two decades between them and the 1982 plan were a period of dramatic political turmoil and planning anarchy, in which the ministerial vertical autarchical central planning system was allowed to work to its utmost in creating a mess for Beijing. The six main planning problems that the 1982 plan discussed and which we have outlined provide vivid substantiation for such a claim. Yet the breakdown of the town planning system in these two decades coincided with China's own experience of building socialism, and even an attempt at an early advance into communism on her own. Thus there had been unique and academically interesting new concepts such as the principles of people's communes in the planning of residential areas, and the ruralization of the city by extending green wedges into the city centre and the incorporation of farm activities in all the green belts, with added rural industrialization in the outer suburbs, all experimenting with the

Table 4.2 Key features of Beijing's general plan at different times

	1954	June 1958	September 1958	1982
A. Nature of the City				
Political/administrative	Centre of respect of whole country; communal living; socialist city	Political, cultural and education centre	Political, cultural and education centre	Political and cultural centre
			Eliminate the three 'contradictions', 'old Beijing is increasingly unsuited to socialism'	The nation's best city in technology, culture, education and morality
Economic	Strong industrial, technological and science centre	Modern industrial, technological and science centre	To serve industrial, agricultural production Rapidly developing into a modern industrial base	Suited and subservient to the nature of the capital
B. Physical size				
City territory (sq km)	–	8 700	17 200	16 800
Urban area (sq km)	60	–	640	750
Population:				
whole city (10 000)	500	1 000	1 000	1 000
urban area		600	350	400

	Discrete segregative zones	'Mother–children' pattern	'Dispersed constellation'	'Dispersed constellation' 'Mother–children' pattern
C. Spatial Structure				
D. Housing Basic planning unit	'Big neighbourhood', 9–15 hectares, 500 persons/hectare with relevant facilities and services		People's commune	'Residential district' 'Small district'
Predominant building height	4–5 storey; over 8	4–8; over 10 storey		5–6 storey; over 10 storey 10 000–12 000 sq m living space/hectare
Per capita living space	9 sq m/person	9 sq m/person	9 sq m/person	9 sq m/person (by year 2000)
E. Green and Open Space Central area			40% of total area	105 sq m/person (by year 2000) Total forestry cover 28% for whole city by year 2000
Outside			60% of total area	

Source: Compiled from Beijing Construction History, 1987.

possibility of a new form of town–country convergence. While there are some beneficial consequences in the form of lessening the overall population size of the urban areas and preserving more green and open space, this period of choas and ultra-leftism brought with it the harmful effect of chaotic land uses, low standard of building construction, and deteriorating basic urban infrastructure and slackening growth in general.

While the overriding Soviet interpretation of the socialist principle – that the capital should primarily be industrial, so that it can have a huge foundation of working proletariat – was only realized to be a mistake after three decades, that mistake still continues to haunt the planners of Beijing. It could not be reasonably corrected just by a new general plan without massive support in the form of municipal financial independence and resources, and a rearrangement of the tax system, in addition to drastic structural reform in the ministerial hierarchical decision process. It would perhaps take one or two more decades for Beijing's economy to be so restructured to suit the new role of the city.

The realization that the Soviet model might not exactly fit Beijing had appeared quite early. The National Planning Commission in 1954 had written strongly against Beijing going down the path of rapid industrial construction. It too pointed out that the standards for per capita living space and urban land of the USSR were not achievable in Beijing within its planning horizon. Indeed, it noted that they had not yet been achieved within the USSR itself after 30 years of socialist construction. The Commission also lashed out at local planners' overplanning regarding excessive width of the roads, overgenerous green and open space, and excessive residential land provision. These criticisms, though mentioned just as unreasoned pieces, point to our suspicion that in the minds of local planners, possibly more true if we say in the minds of their bosses, the top leadership of the country, there was the subconscious intention of 'specificity' in bolstering Beijing as the 'outstanding', the 'best', the 'glamorous', like the 'Pole Star' of the traditional Chinese national capital, to be respected and revered by all within China, i.e. an adherence to the traditional symbolism of the national capital. Mao's consent, or rather decision, to put the central government of the new regime within the old city may add weight to such a hypothesis. Mao's decision certainly weighed heavier than all academic and professional arguments that local planners Liang and Chen could put forward in 1950. The 1980 Directives of the Central Committee of the CCP on the nature and goals of development of Beijing yet again underlined the long traditions of the monarchs in feudalist China in upholding the national capital as the source of all inspiration for the entire realm, i.e. one of the best cities in the world and the best city in China, in social order and morality, in culture, technology and education, in cleanliness and hygiene, and lastly in economic prosperity, convenience and stability.

The post-1949 twists and turns of the series of general plans and the planning process obviously reflected the two main dynamics: the socialist movement which was both foreign and domestically imbued, and the traditional Chinese world view. Though it is not easy to disentangle events and point out the parts played by each in the present living city and its physical form, it is our research guide as well as the magnifying glass used when examining the nature and characteristics of Beijing in its post-1949 development. In the chapters to come, our attempt will be brought down to the sectoral level when we examine the various aspects of development of the city.

5

Urban and spatial growth

Administrative and territorial expansion

The first problem encountered in studies on contemporary Beijing is the definition of its territory. Due to statistical collection practices, administrative and historical reasons, the city means quite different things to different people. Hu (1992) has identified six territorial connotations of the term 'Beijing', or six different spatial concepts or extent of the city, i.e.:

1. Beijing City (Beijing Cheng) – referring to the city of the Ming and Qing dynasties, i.e. the area within the old wall.
2. Beijing Urban Area (Beijing Cheng Qu) – the four city districts laid out since the 1950s.
3. Beijing Planned Urban Area (Beijing Cheng Shi Gui Hua Qu) – including the four city districts and parts of the four suburban districts. Within this area of 750 sq km town planning rules are meant to be strictly enforced, and detailed development plans are to be made according to the 1982 General Plan. In the 1992 revised plan, it was extended to the entire four suburban districts (except parts of Fengtai), so that there is conformity with the administrative boundaries. The new expanded area of the planned urban area is roughly 1000 sq km.
4. Beijing Urban and Suburban Areas (Beijing Cheng Jin Jiao Qu) – the four city districts and the four suburban districts.
5. Beijing Urban and Fringe Areas – the urban and suburban areas plus the two outer suburban counties.
6. Beijing Municipality – embracing the four city districts, four suburban districts, two outer suburbs and eight Beijing-administered rural counties (see Figure 5.1 and Table 5.1).

Municipality
.... Urban & Fringe Areas
.... Urban & Suburban Areas
------ Urban Area (Cheng Qu)
——— Old City (Beijing Cheng)

Figure 5.1   Different spatial concepts of Beijing. Source: Hu, 1992

As Table 5.1 shows, almost 60% of the total population of 10 million (in 1988) was concentrated in the Beijing urban and suburban areas, which in effect can be viewed as the city. This represents an area of about 1400 sq km, which has a fairly high population density. For the four city districts, the density averaged 27 673 persons per sq km, whereas the suburbs averaged 2659 persons per sq km. The outer suburbs and the rural counties may be viewed as the rural adjunct to the city, as Sit (1985) mapped out, see Figure 5.2. Sit has characterized this spatial arrangement of the city as typical of Socialist China for very explicit ideological and economic purposes:

> As well as being a production and service centre, the Chinese City has been an agent for bridging the gap between town and country and integrating industry and agriculture. To facilitate the achievement of these goals, Chinese cities have extended their administrative boundaries to include a number of rural *xian* (counties). This extended outer ring constitutes the source of the city's grain and non-staple food supply. At the same time, within this outer ring, are the industries which have been transferred from the overcrowded inner city. (51–2)

Table 5.1   Administrative division of Beijing

District	Zhen (no.)	Area (sq km)	Permanent population* ('000s)	Population density (persons/sq km)
City Districts		87.1	241.0	27 673
East Districts		24.7	64.2	25 986
West City		30.0	77.0	25 663
Chongwen		15.9	42.7	26 884
Xuanwu		16.5	57.1	34 612
Suburbs		1 282.8	341.1	2 659
Chaoyang		470.8	122.1	2 593
Haidian		304.2	66.7	2 191
Shijingshan		81.8	27.4	3 351
Fengtai		426.0	124.9	2 933
Outer Suburbs	3	3 198.0	97.3	304
Mentougu		1 331.3	25.6	192
Fangshan	3	1 866.7	71.7	384
Rural Counties	10	12 239.9	321.8	263
Changping	3	1 430.0	40.1	280
Shunyi	1	980.0	50.1	511
Tongxian	1	870.0	56.1	645
Daxing		1 012.0	46.6	461
Pinggu	1	1 075.0	37.0	344
Huairou	1	2 557.3	24.7	97
Miyun	2	2 335.6	41.5	178
Yanqing	1	1 980.0	25.7	130
Whole City	13	16 807.8	1 001.2	596

* 1988 data.
Source: Beijing National Land Agency, 1990.

For Beijing, the entire municipality extended to a huge area of 16 800 sq km, about half the size of the entire Taiwan Province. Within it are large tracts of mountains and rural farm areas, and a rural population of about 4 million. The setting of the 'city region' not only facilitates the attainment of the unique combination of socialist and economic objectives in China's circumstances, it also allows the integration of economic and physical planning goals through regulated processes of land-use development and urbanization within it, as Sit (1985) states:

In many ways the concept of the city region represents an important step in the PRC towards manipulation of the process of urbanization. The city region provides the scope for better organizing the 'city' into a functioning, working and living entity, while eliminating the barriers between city and country . . . . The Chinese have not only transformed cities from centres of consumption to centres of production, but they have also pioneered the

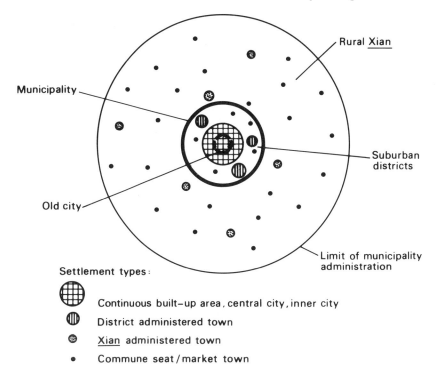

Figure 5.2   Spatial organization of the Chinese city. Source: Sit, 1985

search for a better delimitation of the city to include all of the territory under the operation of unitary functional systems based in the central city. By attaching to a municipality a large rural territory, a city is assured of a supply of food and water, a green belt for recreation, and a vast space to redress some of the problems arising from the over-concentration of people and activities in the central city. (55–56)

Of course, the extension of the territory of Beijing spanned a period of time and generally reflects the course of political changes and the accompanying interpretation of socialist ideals as they relate to city planning and economic organization. When Beijing was made the national capital in 1949, it had a territory of only 707 sq km and a total population of 1.56 million. Substantial expansion of territory took place after the adaptation of the Soviet idea that the national capital should have a large proletariat. In the First Five Year Plan (1953–57) there were some new industrial plants planned in Beijing. But the main leap in territorial expansion came after Mao's new policy as contained in 'On the Ten Contradictions' which wiped out worries on the strategic insecurity for industrial location in the coastal cities, and then the main boost of the Great Leap Forward in 1958. In 1956–59, Beijing's territory was more than tripled and its population about doubled.

In the past few years there have been suggestions of further extending the boundary of the city to a total of 23 000 sq km, mainly to include three counties of Hebei in the south and a large tract of land in the east to reach the western edge of Tianjin. The main purpose of the proposal is to raise the municipality's lowland from 6390 sq km to 12 000 sq km, or from 38% of its total area to 50%, thus to enable it to be self-sufficient in agricultural products (Wan, 1987), an ideal deep rooted in the Great Leap Forward and Cultural Revolution movements.

The physical environment

Location and nodality

Beijing lies between longitude 115°25′ E and 117°30′ E and latitude 39°28′–41°25′ N, on the north-western margin of the North China Plain. It measures roughly 160 km east–west and 170 km north–south. Although it is not the geographical centre of China, considering China's lowlands and its most convenient and most developed parts, i.e. the third of China that lies east of longitude 110° E, Beijing definitely is at a central commanding position (see Figure 5.3). It lies at the margin of China's two largest eastern lowland regions, the North-east China Plain and the combined North China Plain and Lower and Middle Plains of Yangtze. There are some lowlands in South China and Szechuan, but they are of lesser significance compared to the two former lowland regions. Such a commanding position in respect of the agricultural wealth and the dense population and developments that it engenders explained Beijing's importance in the Chinese empire during the Ming and Qing dynasties, besides the strategic role played in national defence against predominant minority threats at those times. The present-day economic centrality of Beijing has been maintained as the North-east continues to be China's significant agricultural and modern industrial base, while North China and East China too contain most of China's agricultural population and its heavy and light industries. A glance at the railway network and air flight network (both domestic and international) provides further substantiation for such a claim.

In 1981, China possessed 46 major railway lines, of which six originated from Beijing. These six lines had a total mileage of 7132 km, or 13.6% of the national mileage (Ditu Chuban She, 1984). These lines linked the city with all provinces and provincial capitals of China, with

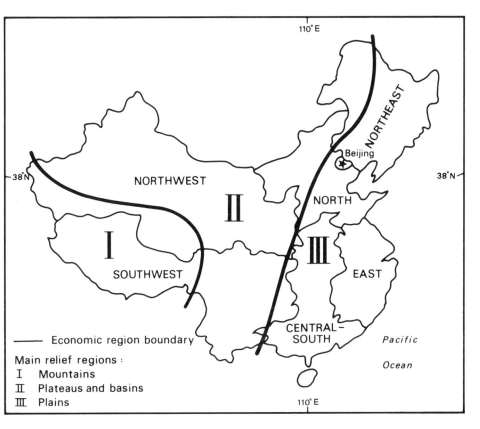

Figure 5.3   Location of Beijing

the exception of Xizhang and Taiwan. As the meeting point of several economic regions, Beijing serves as the nation's important railway cargo centre. Quite a large portion of industrial products from the North-east and the coastal provinces go through Beijing for markets in the interior. It also is the gateway for exporting coal from Shanxi and Inner Mongolia to the rest of the country. Thus the main characteristic of the railway cargo handled by the city is its preponderance in coal, timber, iron and steel. Over half its railway cargo are transhipments between the economic regions. Coal transport takes up about a third of the total freight volume; in addition to supplying the needs of the city, the bulk is destined for East China and Central South China. Timber comes mainly from the North-east and goes to North China. Grain transport forms another important freight item. Massive amounts of grain come from the Yangtze Basin, partly for the city and the rest for North-east and North

China to diversify their staple supply. In reverse, wheat, soya bean and other North-east food staples also pass through Beijing for southern China. Besides cargoes, Beijing is also the largest passenger rail centre of China. It is connected to 27 provinces of the country by passenger lines. Beijing station is the largest passenger rail station of the nation. In 1990, the city handled 50.95 million passengers and 4861 million ton/km freight cargo (Beijing Social and Economic Yearbook, 1991).

Of the major railways, the Beijing–Harbin line is the most heavily used. It handles iron and steel, coal, timber, oil, grains, cement and chemical fertilizers from the North-east, Tangshan and Tianjin for transhipment to Central South, South-west and North–west China. It is also the busiest passenger line in the whole country. The Beijing-Guangzhou line handles mainly grain from South China and cotton from North China. Besides iron ore and iron and steel, the Beijing–Taiyuan line, together with its supplementary and extended lines, serves to provide the most direct and cheapest outlet from coal mines in North-west China. The Beijing–Baotou line provides an outlet for the steppes and oilfields in North-west China and supplies it with light industrial goods from North China.

In terms of air transport, Beijing is also the focus of the country. Its airport handled 2.35 million or about 10% of total national air passengers in 1991, and is connected with more than 80 cities of the country. In 1990, China had 437 scheduled passenger routes, of which Beijing shared 74. In the same year, China had 44 international schedules, the majority of which were taken up by Beijing. Measured in flight mileage, Beijing ranks much higher. In 1990, the national total was 506 762 km; Beijing took 327 308 km, or 64%, underlining its importance as the air hub of China and as the international air centre of the country (China Statistical Yearbook, 1991; Beijing Social and Economic Yearbook, 1991).

Relief and climate

The main topographic characteristic of Beijing is that it is high on the north and west and slopes down to the south-east. The hilly areas comprise 62% of its area. They are the Northern Hills or Jundu Shan, composed largely of igneous rocks of the Yan Shan System (Figure 5.4). The western hills are locally called Xi Shan, a part of the Tai Heng Shan System, and are largely of sedimentary rocks. Medium height hilly areas of over 800 m make up 14% of the city's total area, rising to two highest peaks of 2303 (in the west) and 2334 m (in the north-west). Low hills of 200–800 m are more extensive, occupying 5700 sq km or 35% of the total area. Rolling hills, terraces and broad valleys of less than 200 m cover an

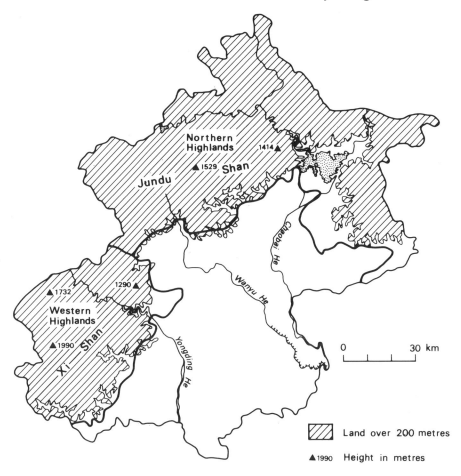

Figure 5.4   Relief regions of Beijing

area of about 2300 sq km. They are suitable for orchards and farm activities.

The lowlands in the south-east are less than 100 m high, mostly 30–50 m. They are composed of foothills, alluvial fans and flood plains. The last category covers 4000 sq km, or about a quarter of the city's area. It is the most intensively used area, particularly the plains of 30 m or above, providing suitable space for urban development and agriculture.

In terms of climate, Beijing lies on the eastern rim of the Eurasian land mass and belongs to the West Wind Belt. Although only 150 km from the sea, the sheltering effects of the Korean and Shangdong peninsulas have reduced the maritime influence, enhancing its character as a warm temperate continental monsoonal climate. The four seasons are quite distinct. Spring is marked by windy and dry conditions. Summer is hot and rainy. Autumn is fine and mild, while winter is dry and cold. Of the four seasons, spring and autumn are relatively short, and winter lasts for five months. In spring, strong winds from the north-west bring gusts of sand. The annual average temperature is 11.5°C, with an average precipitation of 630 mm, about 70% of which is concentrated in July–August. On the lowlands, the frost-free period is 190–195 days. Thus Beijing allows two crops in a year or three crops in every two years in most of its cultivatable parts.

In general, the city possesses a variety of relief types for primary activities and commands suitable soil, heat and water conditions for agricultural development to complement its large-scale urban growth.

Natural hazards

However, the city has been plagued by a number of natural hazards. First there are great fluctuations in precipitation leading to temporal and spatial occurrences of droughts and floods. Its 205-year average precipitation is 609.2 mm. In 1959 it registered a record high of 1400 mm, while in 1869 there was a record low of 242 mm. According to past records, there appeared to be a cycle of 42 years, in which 20.3 years pertain to 'drought' conditions and 21.3 years pertain to 'wet' conditions. Since the evaporation rate of the city is very high, annually 1842 mm, water shortage is paramount. The per capita water resource of the city is 274 cu m, ranking 100 among the 120 national capitals of the world. In the twentieth century, very dry years have occurred more frequently than before. In the past 20 years, it is estimated that there have been 40 billion cu m short of the average. The trend is obviously towards a drier condition. Yet flooding occurs between years of serious drought. Historically, serious floods that inflicted large-scale damage on the urban district were registered in 1470 and 1626. In more recent history, 1976 was the worst year. In Miyun, 287 mm of rain was recorded in a two-hour period causing the collapse of a dam of the reservoir and 104 dead. All told, in the past 500 years, floods that caused damage to the city occurred in 300 years. Historical records show that in a 10-year period, one will be a year of damaging drought, another will be of damaging floods. Only three years will be 'normal'. 50% of the period will tend to be either dry or pertaining to floods. Seasonal variation in rainfall has been previously noted, but added to this is the spatial variation between the hills and the lowlands. Limited water resources (annual maximum 6 billion cu m) had been a major factor in the decision of the city government to restrict growth of the city and its water-intensive industries. This will be discussed in later sections dealing with environment and future planning.

Hailstorms are frequent and are damaging occurrences to buildings and crops in Beijing. On average there are 28.1 days of hailstorms in a year. In 1971, there were 46 days. In a severe hailstorm in 1969, large hailstones of 6 mm diameter and weighing 2.5 kg were seen. In some suburban areas, the hailstones piled up to half a metre thick. They damaged 120 000 (8 sq km) mou of orchards and smashed two-thirds of the street lamps along Changan Avenue.

Yet the most terrifying hazards that threaten the city are earthquakes. On average, the city is disturbed twice in a year by quakes of the third grade or above, and once by a quake of the fourth grade or above. It is classified as an earthquake-prone area and buildings are required to be constructed to withstand shocks of the eighth grade. The earliest recorded major quake happened in 194 AD, a quake of grade 5.5. From then on until 1967 (over 1600 years), Beijing had registered quakes above grade 5.5 twelve times. In the latest Tangshan Quake of 1976, Beijing was 100–240 km from the epicentre where the quake intensity was graded 7.8. In Beijing, quake intensity of grade 5–7 was felt. In the suburbs, 393 137 houses were seriously damaged and 140 173 houses damaged. Within the city districts, 462 single-storey structures collapsed and 399 421 were damaged. Of the multi-storey structures, 2985 blocks and 43 factories were seriously damaged. Seismologists believe that 1484–1730 is the third period of active quakes in North China. After that there were 200 years of quietness. Since 1966, the area has entered a new phase of activity. Up to 1976, four quakes of grade 4–7 happened in the area (*Beijing Daily*, 27 July 1991; Beijing National Land Agency, 1990).

Urban growth

Measured in terms of built-up area and urban construction area, Beijing grew rapidly after it had attained the status of national capital in 1949. As the political, educational, scientific and research centre of the country, new constructions to meet the needs of the burgeoning new regime and relocation of former research institutes from Nanjing were rapidly unfolding in the city. These created a new political–administrative centre within the old city and a new education and research area in the western suburb. The decision to turn the city into a significant industrial base of the country commensurate with its role as the socialist national capital with a broad proletarian population added further impetus to its urban growth, especially since the First Five Year Plan started. The pace of growth and its spatial form were captured by a series of aerial photographs in 1951, 1959 and 1983. In 1949, the built-up area of the city and suburban districts was about 109 sq km, largely within the four city districts or the old city. By 1983, it extended to 371 sq km, an increase of 160 sq km, or more than three-fold. Yu (1986) produced an interesting analysis of the growth of the city based on this set of aerial photographs.

Growth in 1949–51 averaged 1.43 sq km per year. By 1951, the built-up area of the urban and suburban districts reached 111.87 sq km. The old city was largely built up, except the south-eastern and south-western corners of the outer city. Two patches in Fengtai and Nanyuan in the south and the burgeoning higher education and sanatorium district in the north-western suburb were also developing. Development was still mostly concentrated in the old city. New developments were limited, and mainly tended towards the west.

In 1952–59, Beijing was subject to a crash programme of industrialization with the dual purposes of turning it into a 'productive' city and a leading industrial base whose status was considered to befit a socialist national capital. Urban growth took the form of hectic growth of new industrial areas in the suburbs, with accompanying residential districts. In this period, the annual average increase of built-up area was 13.62 sq km. By December 1959, the total built-up area reached 220.81 sq km. Most notable additions were found in the eastern suburb, the western suburb and the north-western suburb. In the eastern suburb, constellations of factories of mechanical engineering, textiles and electronics were constructed, with an average annual increase of 1.4 sq km built-up area. In the western suburb, the Shijingshan industrial area quickly developed around the Capital Iron and Steel Works, the new iron and steel base of the city, with complementary industries in construction materials, electricity and mechanical engineering. In the area closer to the old city, new administrative offices and related staff quarters were multiplying quickly as well. In the 1950s, the higher education, research and sanatorium district was further developed, where eight major universities and the Academia Sinica were gradually set up. Within the period, the other districts grew slowly. Those in the south-west grew slowly largely because they form the water-catchment area of the city's water supply and were thus protected from development. The south-east suburb had many polluting industries and was not allowed to grow further. The spatial pattern of growth followed closely the direction of the general plans and was based on the concept of 'dispersed constellations'.

After 1960, Beijing's urban growth was much affected by political movements, especially by the Cultural Revolution. The former rule of

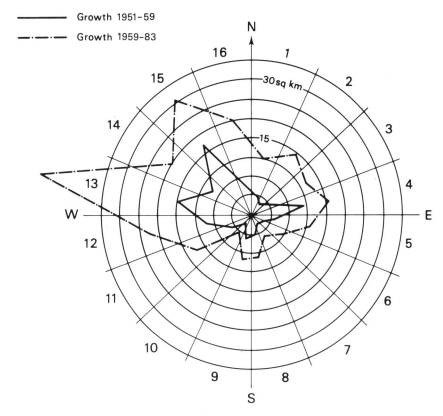

Figure 5.5 Increase in built-up areas in different periods for different parts of the city. Source: Yu, 1986

'dispersed constellations' separated by green barriers was unable to be implemented as the general plan was not enforced and the Municipal Planning Bureau was made defunct. This long period of anarchy led to the coalescence of the 'dispersed constellations' among themselves and with the central city. The overall pace of growth was much slackened, with an annual increase of 6.26 sq km. Rapid growth was only registered in the Shijingshan Iron and Steel Works area.

The spatial pattern of growth of the two phases from 1951 to 1983 is shown graphically in Figure 5.5. The predominance of the western orientation is obvious. It underlines the important pull of location decisions regarding major industries and institutions of administration, higher education and research on the direction of urban growth in Beijing. In the years before 1983, the average annual rate of growth of built-up area was 6.26 sq km. In the latest general plan, it is foreseen that the built-up area of the urban districts and the suburbs is to be restricted to 440 sq km by 2000. That is to say, the annual average growth rate has to be trimmed down to 4 sq km. There is therefore much need to economize on land, and to redirect growth to the outer suburban area of Beijing.

Urban land-use characteristics

From the previous sections of this chapter, it will be obvious that the Chinese had subjectively channelled growth into Beijing when they were capable of implementing their plans, basically within the urban districts and the suburban areas. They also had very early on, in the 1960s, expanded the jurisdiction of the city into an extended city region, thus putting under the municipality's control a large tract of basically rural and mountainous areas. The latter served mainly to combine country and city, agriculture and industry, manual labour and mental labour, as well as to make the city 'self-sufficient' in staple food, and non-staple food supply, in addition to providing a vast catchment area for the city's water supply facilities. Yet urban development had been very much restricted to the 'planned urban areas'. In 1986, these areas embraced 750 sq km and comprised the four urban districts, and a substantial part of the four suburban districts. Within roughly 4.5% of the municipality's total area were concentrated 82% of its total urban population, all the central and municipal government offices, 90% of the research and higher education institutions and 80% of industries administered both by the central and municipal authorities. In the vast areas that lie beyond, generally (not exactly) called the outer suburbs and that comprised 95% of the total area, there was only 950 000 urban population, yet it had close to 3.5 million farm population, i.e. an urbanization rate of just about 20%.

According to the Draft General Plan of 1982, actual urban land was 444 sq km in 1979 (Table 5.2), roughly 2.6% of the total area of the municipality. If we add to it land under roads, railways and airports, then the total amounted to 557 sq km, still only 3.3% of the entire territory of the municipality. The main land use of the municipality was agricultural. It took 8580 sq km or 51.0% of the total territory, of which about half was farmland. Rural settlements took 564 sq km or about the size of the urban land. About 40% of the municipality was barren hills and steep unused slopes. This last category lies mainly within the mountainous areas to the west, north and north-west.

The 1982 Draft General Plan assumes a 10 million population target for the entire city, 4 million population within the planned urban areas,

Table 5.2   Actual and planned land uses within Beijing

Use	Actual use in 1979		Planned use in 2000	
	sq km	%	sq km	%
1. Urban land	444	2.6	740	4.0
Planned urban areas	340		440	
Townships and industrial and mining centres	104		300	
2. Transport and municipal land use in other suburbs	117	0.7	165	0.9
Roads	77		113	
Railway	32		42	
Airports	8		10	
3. Rivers, ponds and reservoirs	1 000	5.9	1 200	6.7
4. Agricultural land	8 580	51.0	13 651	75.5
Farmland	4 269		3 867	
(of which vegetables)	(253)		(267)	
Woodland	1 287		} 7 933	
Orchards	1 027			
Market towns and villages	564		585	
Others	1 433		1 266	
5. Others	6 668	39.2	2 317	12.8
Bare hills suitable for afforestation	4 353		–	
Rocky and slope surface unsuitable for afforestation	2 315		2 317	
Grand total	16 809	100.0	18 073	100.0

Source: Compiled from 1982 Draft General Plan of Beijing.

and that total urban land would expand to 740 sq km in the year 2000, i.e. by a hefty 67%. Land for transport and municipal uses in the outer suburbs also would increase to 165 sq km, i.e. by 41%. However, there would only be a very slight increase in the area covered by rural settlements, i.e. 3.7%. Of the 296 sq km increase of urban land, most would expect to take place within townships outside the planned urban areas, i.e. in the satellite towns. There would be an almost three-fold increase of land under this subcategory. Expansion of the planned urban areas would be in the order of about 100 sq km which would take place largely within the 'dispersed constellations'. Table 5.3 shows more precisely the distribution of urban land in the various parts of the municipality. The central mass of the planned urban areas which constitutes largely of the central city will reach its limit by the year 2000, i.e. about 290 sq km of built-up area. The 'peripheral constellations' or

Table 5.3 Planned urban expansion in Beijing 2000–10

	Total area (sq km)	Built-up area (sq km)					Urban population (in 10 thousands)		
		1979 Actual	1982 Draft	1983 Plan	1986 Draft	2010 Plan	1980	2000	2010
Planned urban areas									
Central mass	287	205	285	287	287	290	346	460	350
Peripheral constellations	135	135	155	198	218	220	72	140	200
Farm land + green belt	328	–	–	–	–	100	–	–	100
Subtotal	750	340	440	485	505	610	418	600	650
Urban districts	87	62	62						
Suburban districts	1 283	143	223						
Outer suburb									
Townships and major industrial plants	104	104	300		190	290	92	160*	205*
Other urban infrastructure	117	117	165		?†	?	–	–	–
Rural area	15 217	(564)	(585)		(?)	(?)	–	–	–
Subtotal	15 438	221	465		?	?		160	205
Grand total	16 808	560	905		?	?	510	760	855

* includes some rural population
† ? = data not available
Source: Compiled from various unpublished official planning reports.

'dispersed constellations' will still have new capacity to expand, taking mainly adjacent green belts and engulfing rural land in their outer rims. According to the 1992 version of the General Plan, the total built-up area of these 'constellations' will increase from 135 sq km in 1979 to 220 sq km in 2010. Within the green belt of the planned urban areas, another 100 sq km would be converted to townships.

We may draw two observations from the above analysis. First, Beijing's urban growth before 1980 had been one of concentration within the central mass of the planned urban areas (which may be compared to the central city). Since then, the logical trend would be one of dispersion to the outer rim of the planned urban areas. Such a dispersion had been planned ever since 1957 with the designation and construction of a number of satellite towns and new industrial areas. Yet this early attempt was not very successful. Lack of efficient public transport as well as the inability of the municipality to implement the General Plan were the main reasons. The post-1980 re-emphasis on dispersion may be more appropriately interpreted as yet another round of concentration, or 'filling the gap' of the enlarged central city. As the central mass will be completely saturated by 2000, extension of the built-up area into the peripheral constellations and the green belt is in fact a 'compaction' process and not genuine dispersion. Thus the planners of Beijing may be seen as committing the same mistake as those in the 1960–80 period to which they claim to be averse. Indeed, our second observation reinforces this last point: the vast areas in the outer suburbs would be little urbanized. According to the 1992 General Plan, there will only be 290 sq km of urban land and an urban population of 2.3 million by 2010. Even this amount of urban growth will hinge on the mass rail transport which the latest plan provides and it is still doubtful whether it will be successfully implemented.

Sufficient data available for 1949, 1979 and 2000 (planned) allow us to go a little deeper in examining the quality of urban growth, through analysing the increases and planned increases of various categories of urban land (Table 5.4). Of the total increase in urban building land, the majority went to productive uses of 'industry', 'warehouses', 'special work area' (offices, research institutes and universities), 'commerce, service, culture and health, etc.' In 1979, these uses took 67% or 159 sq km of all building land. Among them, industrial land figured promi-nently, and took 55 sq km or 16.2% of all building land. In comparison, the percentage was 10.7% in Paris and 9.6% in Tokyo. In contrast, residential land accounted for 22.5% in Beijing, whereas figures were 32.8% in London and 41.4% in Paris for the comparable year. The acute imbalance between growth of 'living space' and 'working space', or what the Chinese called the 'flesh' and 'bone', was obvious. It declined

Table 5.4 Distribution of uses within the planned urban area, 1949, 1979 and 2000 (planned)

	1949[+]			1979[+]			2000[+]		
	sq km	%	sq m/person	sq km	%	sq m/person	sq km	%	sq m/person
Building land	57.3	52.6	36.7	236	69.3	58.1	275	62.5	68.7
Industrial	7.2	6.6	4.6	55	16.2	13.5	55	12.5	13.7
Warehouses	19.3	17.7	–	16	4.7	3.9	16	3.6	4.0
Special Work Area				81	23.8	20.0	86	19.6	21.5
Commerce, Services, Culture, Health, etc.				7	2.1	1.7	10	2.3	2.5
Residential	30.8	28.3	18.1	77	22.5	19.0	108	24.5	27.0
Municipal use	47.1[*]	43.3	30.1	74	21.8	18.2	108	24.5	27.0
Roads, squares	12.0	11.0	7.6	24	7.1	5.9	43	9.8	10.7
Rivers, ponds	23.0[*]	21.1	14.7	23	6.8	5.7	31	7.0	7.7
External transport	12.1[*]	11.1	–	19	5.6	4.7	23	5.2	5.8
Municipal depot				8	2.3	1.9	11	2.5	2.8
Green space, public sports	4.6	4.2	2.6	30	8.8	7.4	57	13.0	14.3
Green space	4.6	4.2	2.6	28	8.2	6.9	52	11.6	13.0
Public sports	0.0	0.0	–	2	0.6	0.5	5	1.2	1.3
Grand total	108.9	100.0	68.4	340	100.0	63.7	440	100.0	110.0

[*] 1949 figures are not complete. These have been deduced from the total and the assumed 23 sq km of rivers and ponds

[+] Assumed population: 1949, 1.56 million; 1979, 4.06 million; 2000, 4 million

Source: 1982 Draft General Plan; Zhou Yu Zhen, 1987 (unpublished).

from a ratio of 1.55 to 1 in 1949 to 0.61 to 1 in 1979. In addition, of the 'bone' land uses, the proportion that went to 'commerce, service, culture, etc.', i.e. the 'soft' functions rather than the 'hard' production functions, was dismally small. There were only 7 sq km of such uses in 1979. On top of the imbalance between the 'flesh' and the 'bone' in building land, green space per capita was only 6.9 sq m per person, much lower than figures for major cities in the West, such as 19.2 sq m in New York, 22.8 sq m in London and 24.7 sq m in Paris.

However, attempts to redress the situation may be reflected in targets set for urban land-use development up to the year 2000. There is a planned increase of the per capita urban land within the planned urban area from 63.7 sq m to 110 sq m, an increase of 72.6%. Industrial and warehouse land will be held constant in 1979–2000, but there will be substantial growth of residential land, pushing the 1979 figure of 77 sq km to 108 sq km in 2000. Increase will also be registered in the 'special work area', i.e. mainly offices, research institutions and universities, as these uses are needed for the city to fulfil its role as national capital, and as the political, cultural and education centre of the country.

There will also be a significant increase of land under municipal use and green space to improve the urban infrastructure and the general urban environment. Although still lower than figures quoted for London, New York and Paris previously, the target for 2000 of 13 sq m of green space per capita would be a great achievement compared to its 1979 situation of 6.9 sq m. As a Third World city, Beijing may not be directly comparable to the capitals of the advanced developed nations of the West even by the year 2000. Nevertheless, the latest planning targets show that the authority there has grasped the problems of overconcentration in 'productive' land uses while grossly neglecting the building of sufficient housing and a reasonably pleasant urban environment for its citizenry. The data in Table 5.4 also show that, whereas we may criticize the existence of the imbalance of 'flesh' and 'bone', there had been clear positive development of the city in 1949–79 in expanding the building land and extension of municipal uses, a feat seldom encountered in other Third World cities. Of course, the low standard was caused also by the rapid increase in population, an issue with which the city tried hard to grapple, but so far with little success. This situation may be further illustrated by the amount and distribution of floor space in 1949–82. In that period, a total of 97 million sq m of new floor space was added to the city, more than four times that which existed in 1949. Of the various categories of use, the increases of floor space in the period were: industrial, 1000%; residential, 300%; educational 620%; medical and health, 580%; cultural 320%; commercial and services 240%; while the increase in population was 200%.

Spatial characteristics

The development of Beijing after 1949 initially took the form of compaction. New offices and residences to accommodate the first batch of central administrative functions were built in the empty space resulting from the demolition of dilapidated old houses within the old city. Yet most of the old city was untouched. Soon significant new construction took place in its periphery, i.e. within the suburbs, or within and around the third urban ring-road that encloses 158 sq km of the inner city. Such works begun in the First Five Year Plan period comprised six new areas of diverse functions. Based on the prevailing wind directions, major water courses and existing developments, these new extensions were laid out and constructed in a planned fashion. In the eastern and western suburbs, two industrial areas were developed. In the western suburb, based on the existing iron works, the Shijingshan Iron and Steel Area was formed and became the heavy industrial base of the city. New higher learning institutions and the Academia Sinica were added to Beijing University and Qinghua University to boost the north-western suburb as the new district for higher education, technology and research in addition to its sanatorium role. On the former site of the Japanese planned new city in the western suburb, new offices for the central administration began to congregate into a new office area. In addition, two foreign legation quarters were added to the eastern suburb. Thus six nearby suburban areas were gradually built up in a planned manner to cater for the new functions of the national capital.

This manner of growth can be described as peripheral accretion, as has also been witnessed in other very large cities in China at the time (Sit, 1985). The old city, together with the six suburban extensions of built-up areas, formed the central mass which we have earlier referred to and shown in Table 5.3. This central mass was limited to the old city of 62.5 sq km in 1949. By 1979, it had extended to cover a built-up area of 205 sq km. It not only contained much of the physical growth of the city in built-up area (about 62% since 1949), but also much of its added urban population (76%), and accommodated much of the new adminis-trative, higher education, research and development, cultural and medical and health functions. The extent of the central mass is shown in Figure 5.6. It covered a total area of 287 sq km and was largely built up (71.4%) by 1979. Detailed spatial expression of the compaction and peripheral accretion processes have also been mapped out in Figure 5.7.

While the central mass was extending outwards, construction of ten 'dispersed constellations' started. They were actively pursued since the promulgation of the 1958 General Plan as one of the major urban spatial development strategies of the city. Six of them were sited on existing

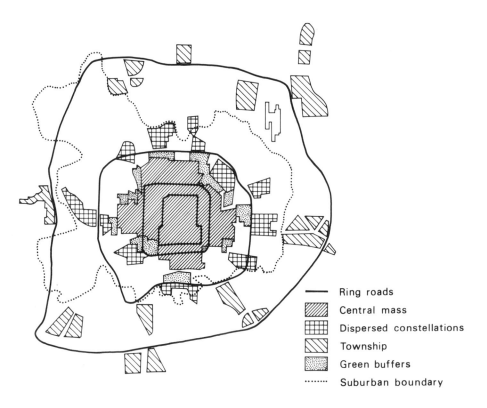

Figure 5.6   The central mass and the 'dispersed constellations' of the central city in Beijing. Source: Wang, 1991

small townships (*zhen*), i.e. Qinghe, Xiyuan, Shijingshan, Fengtai, Lugouqiao and Nanyuan, and four were constructed on virgin land (or former farm land), i.e. Jizinqui, Dinfuzhuang, Fatou and Beiyuan. As part of the strategy of 'dispersed constellations', extensive green areas were zoned around the 10 constellations to act as buffers, such that the central mass would be restricted from growing further, to provide sufficient 'urban lung' to the central city for preserving the urban ecological environment as well as for conserving suburban vegetable fields. Expansion of the constellations would only be allowed in the direction away from the central mass. The locations and relationship between the central mass, the 'dispersed constellations' and the 10 green buffers are shown in Figures 5.6 and 5.7. The ten constellations took up 135 sq km of land, and accommodated about 600 000 persons in 1979. They, together with the central mass and 328 sq km of green buffers and

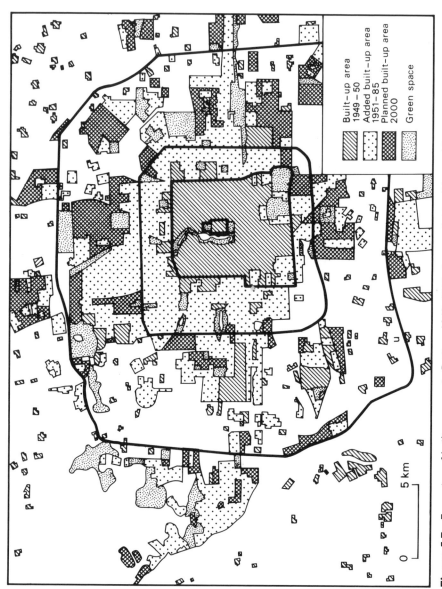

Figure 5.7 Expansion of built-up areas in Beijing, 1949–2000. Source: Beijing National Land Agency (1990)

farm land, constituted the planned urban areas of Beijing (Table 5.3). The latest (1992) General Plan envisaged continual growth of the 'dispersed constellations' to a total built-up area of 220 sq km. This means that the existing green belt and farm land of the planned urban areas would decline markedly as visible by comparing Figures 5.6 and 5.7. To avoid the central mass converging and blending with them, expansion of the constellations is to be directed towards the edge of the suburbs, with an extended boundary of the planned urban areas pushing further outwards to yield a total area of 1100 sq km. Thus the vehicle for further urban growth in Beijing, up to 2010, would still be peripheral accretion by expanding the outer edges of the constellations. By then the population of the central mass would have fallen back to its 1979 level of about 3.5 million, while that within the enlarged constellations would increase to about 2 million. All told, the central mass and the constellations will together accommodate 65% of the total urban population of 8.55 million at that time.

The 1958 General Plan adopted the Soviet concept of satellite towns in order to decentralize congestion of the inner city and to provide space for new, mainly industrial, development projects. The plan modified the Soviet model somewhat and relabelled it the 'mother–children' principle, i.e. these satellites are to be regarded as 'children' or outgrowth of the 'mother', the central city. Based on the ideals of town–country and farm-industry convergence, they were upheld as a step towards communism as well as helping to solve the congestion problems of the central city. Around 1965, owing to considerations of 'be prepared for war', a number of industrial plants were decentralized to these townships in the outer suburbs. This provided a second boost to the growth of satellite towns. The 1958 General Plan designated over 40 'children' or satellite urban centres. Yet the depression of the early 1960s left many of them undeveloped. Only 24 had been treated as satellites up to the 1980s. These include eight county seats, i.e. Changping, Miyun, Huairou, Shunyi, Pinggu, Yanqing, Fangshan and Tongzhen; eight townships, i.e. Mentougu, Huangcun, Yanshan, Liangxiang, Shahe, Nankou, Niunanshan and Changxindian; and eight industrial centres, i.e. Liulehe, Xinzhen, Lugezhuan, Zhoukoudian, Tianju, Anding, Kangzhuan and Nindou. These 24 satellites had a built-up area of 104 sq km. in 1979, and accommodated about 920,000 persons.

The concept of satellites has been a confused issue for some time, as many local officials treated all townships and industrial centres in the outer suburbs as satellites. In fact they differ markedly from rural central places of the outer suburbs in a number of ways. Functionally they are the product of the inner or central city, taking some of the functions from it, and provide a means for it to control its scale and size while maintaining healthy growth. Their development is largely planned and centralized and is funded by either the central government or municipality rather than based on local resources. The development also took place rapidly. In population, the satellites consist mainly of urban population decentralized from the inner city. They are used to urban living and demand high-level urban and municipal facilities. The satellites too are closely linked to the central city through convenient transport and communication such that they can perform their functions as well as satisfy the economic, cultural and other daily urban needs of their population, which are part and parcel of the urban population of the municipality. In the 1982 General Plan, in spite of lacking a clear redefinition of the satellites, only four satellites were singled out as major foci for development. By the 1992 General Plan, the concept of satellites was further clarified and only 14 out of the original 24 were labelled as satellites. Again four were singled out as immediate targets for active promotion. These four satellites are Fangshan, Tongzhen, Huangcun and Changping.

These four satellites had a total employed labour force of 81 000, an industrial output of Yn2.79 billion, 3.5 sq km of built-up area and 222 500 urban population in 1980, respectively these were 5%, 12%, 6.1% and 4.3% of the city's total. By 1990, their combined population had been doubled to 471 000 and built-up area extended to 76.5 sq km, an increase of 900%. Thus in 1980–90 growth in these largest satellites had been spectacular. Future growth potential of Tongzhen and Huangcun had been substantially upgraded in the 1992 General Plan. By 2050, the planned total population of the four satellites may reach 1.37 million.

Of the 14 satellites, two, Kangzhuang and Houshayu, would not become established until well after 2010, and four were still very small, i.e. with a population of less than 50 000 in 1990. A cautious approach to satellite development has thus been adopted, with concentrated effort in a small number of selected centres which are more suitable in terms of their location on major traffic routes, proximity to the inner city, readily available land for development as well as sufficient existing development. In the two decades of 1990–2010, the 14 satellites will expect to increase their population from 950 000 to 1.94 million, i.e. their share of the total urban population in the municipality will be raised from 14.8% in 1990 to 22.7% in 2010. The projected proportionate share for 2050 would be 35%. Thus it seems that meaningful decentralization of urban growth in the 'mother–children' pattern would only become a vigorous process in the twenty-first century.

Other than the satellites, the smaller urban centres may be regarded as central places providing comprehensive services to the surrounding rural hinterland. In the 1992 General Plan, of the 26 such centres projected in 2010, 22 are classified as 'comprehensive' in function, one as an administrative centre and three as tourism oriented. The situation is expected to remain the same in 2050. In other words, from the planners' point of view, urbanization and urban growth will be restricted to the 'dispersed constellations' and satellites for many years to come. Though the 1990 population figures are not available for these small central places, which we may still consider as urban centres, in 1980 they contained only 280 000 persons and their projected population in 2010 would only be 360 000.

Rural settlements are the last category of settlement in Beijing, and they differ markedly from urban settlements in function. They are the concentrated location of residence of the farm population. In the municipality, there are over 7000 such villages or rural settlements, occupying 778 sq km of land, the largest category of non-agricultural built-up area. In the suburbs, there are about 1000 such settlements which accounted for 17.3% of the rural population of Beijing in 1981. In the lowland part of the outer suburbs, there are about 4000 villages, accounting for 45% of the rural population. In the hilly areas of the outer suburbs, which took 62% of the entire area of the municipality, villages are far less dense and much smaller in size. There are about 2000 villages which accommodated 37.3% of the rural population. The existence of a vast and densely settled rural area within the municipality of Beijing is characteristic of the Chinese socialist city. The relationship between this part of Beijing and its urban core is an important pointer to the 'Chinese' and 'Chinese socialist' elements of Beijing and will be discussed shortly.

The entire urban system of Beijing is presented in Figure 5.8. It underlines the general peripheral accretion style of growth, though Chinese planners have couched it in terms of 'dispersed constellations' and 'mother–children' urban growth patterns.

The rural adjunct

As earlier paragraphs of this chapter indicate, Beijing, like most very large Chinese cities, has been given a huge rural adjunct under its jurisdiction in 1958 as an effort to combine agriculture with industry, rural living with urban living, mental labour with manual labour, and most importantly to maintain a high level of self-sufficiency of the city in terms of food supply. The rural adjunct had for two notable periods served as the principal area for rustication of urban cadres and intellectuals, as well as the destination for urban youths during the 'Shang-shan-xia-xiang' (up the hills and down to the villages) movement

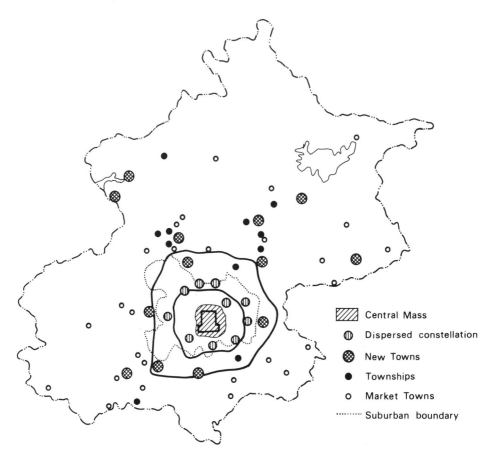

Figure 5.8 Urban system in Beijing, 2010 (total population 11.05–12.95 million).
Source: Wang, 1991

in the late 1950s and early 1960s and during the Cultural Revolution. Although since the end of the Cultural Revolution and the start of the new reforms in 1978 these political objectives of the rural adjunct have largely been phased out, it still provides the city population with much of its necessary food. It is a strange thing that a very large city of over 10 million can be self-sufficient and near self-sufficient in a large number of daily food items. Beijing is self-sufficient in fresh eggs, vegetables, ducks, milk and dry fruits and is almost self-sufficient in pork and honey. It also produces half its needs in chicken and aquatic products. Although the self-sufficiency rate for staple food (grain) is only 37%, the actual amount is substantially higher as these percentage figures exclude that produced for consumption by the farmers. For example, the actual production of grain in 1990 was 2 646 186 tonnes, and only 46.2% was sold as commercial goods; the larger bulk was consumed by the producers themselves. For other major items, the commercial goods rate was also less than 100%, reflecting some being consumed by the producers and not entered into trade, i.e. the rates are: 86.3% for vegetables, 95.6% for meat, 94.7% for fresh milk, 89.1% for fresh eggs and 88.9% for aquatic products.

Municipal self-sufficiency can be both beneficial as well as disadvantageous to Beijing. In a situation of lack of transport capacity, local sufficiency is a sure means to safeguard supply. A rural adjunct also provides an effective way of conserving land for future urban growth and of helping to improve the urban living environment by inserting green wedges of farmland into the otherwise continuously built-up urban mass. For the latter function, the most noticeable suburban land use is for vegetable fields which require to be close to the urban market because of the produce's high degree of perishability and the high intensity of daily traffic between the production bases and the market place, in a country where refrigeration and modern packaging for long-distance transport is either too costly or as yet undeveloped. There are about 400 000 mou (267 sq km) of vegetables in the city; about half, or 160 000 mou (107 sq km), lie within the suburban districts. Yet the suburban districts are the most productive and most heavily capitalized. They produce better quality vegetables and generate over 85% of the supplies needed by the city market. The suburban vegetable fields form an almost continuous green belt around the central urban mass (Figure 5.9). Yet urban peripheral accretion has been encroaching onto this area of best vegetable fields. The amount of area had dropped from 230 000 mou (154 sq km) to the level in 1990. It is now the policy of the municipal government to maintain the existing 160 000 mou (107 sq km) and to open up new production bases in the outer suburbs.

Conclusion

In this chapter we have attempted to outline Beijing's natural setting as well as to chart its post-1949 urban growth, examining the main underlying factors and characteristics as a basis for further deliberation on the various urban elements and to formulate our overall image of the city in the later chapters.

Location-wise Beijing is an inland city, yet it is not far from the coast or the major seaports in North China, i.e. Tianjin and Qinhuangdao. Its position on the focal point of eight major national railways and the

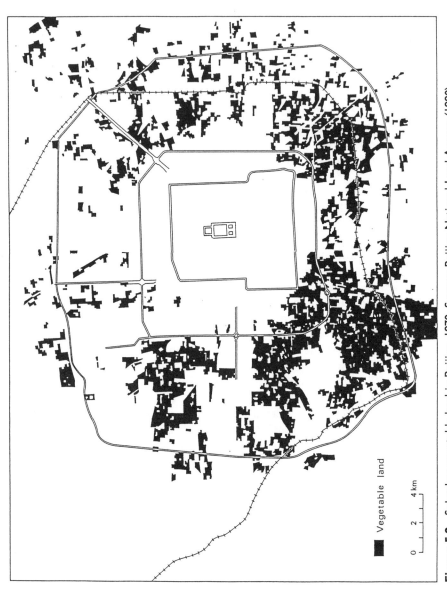

Figure 5.9 Suburban vegetable land in Beijing, 1970. Source: Beijing National Land Agency (1990)

converging edge of three of the six economic regions of China makes it very naturally a transport node and a transhipment centre in the northern half of the nation. These conditions definitely boost its economic and administrative significance in a country where the bulk of cargo and passenger traffic is carried by railways. Beijing is also the hub of the country in domestic and international air transport, a role developed out of both a good location and the dictate of it being the national capital.

Yet the natural environment, excepting a benign location, shows clear limits on the possible extent as well as the preferred nature of growth of the city in total population size and in its economy. Limited water resources and local fuel and other raw materials put a constraint on the growth of heavy industries that are intensive in water, energy and raw materials. As a location prone to a number of natural hazards, Beijing should cautiously plan its future growth in order to avoid major disasters, as happened in Tangshan some two decades ago.

Rapid expansion of the built-up areas, hence urban growth, in the past four decades has a lot to do with Beijing being the national capital. Both the Chinese tradition and Soviet socialist inclination are such that Beijing should be a sizeable city, preferably a 'number one city' as Hu (1990) has put it. He says that China has a 2000-year tradition that the national capital should be number one on all counts. Under the socialist system, the capital is also destined to be a city of composite functions. Under the dictate of central planning, the political centre functions as the coordinating centre of all economic sectors, therefore it has to possess a large amount of offices and activities in finance, insurance, post and communications, broadcasting, international negotiations, etc. Under the central planning system, the political centre can obtain resources much more easily than other cities and this too has fuelled its growth. Hu therefore believes that both the Chinese tradition and socialist ideas generated a peculiar socio-political background against which Beijing has developed into the 'number one centre' in seven major urban functions: political centre, economic management centre, communication centre, transport centre, tourist centre, cultural centre and international exchange centre. It is also second in rank as an industrial centre in China. Indeed, centralism is a common factor in the traditional Chinese world view and in socialism.

In order to make central control and coordination feasible, multiple functions covering the widest possible extent suited to the nation (rather than the locale of the capital) commanded much more attention than the carrying capacity and suitability of the local environment. Magnitude, in terms of the city bureaucracy and its economic sectors, is a necessary outcome of such a desire for centralism. In addition, the symbolism which so greatly affected the layout of the traditional Chinese capital played its role in the post-1949 PRC capital as well. As the capital of a socialist country with the proletariat as the ruling and exhalted class, the development of a sizeable industrial base in Beijing was deemed to be not only obvious but a must. The capital also had to be the leader in the political twists and turns of the nation in its tumultuous years of 1958–78. Such political events found expression in the planning ideas and actual urban development of the city. Thus we may compare the development of Beijing to a stage in the long stream of evolution of the traditional Chinese capital that started with a single thatched hut of the sage king, then to the Ming T'ang, and then to *Zhou Li Kao Gong Ji's* model of clearly delineate functions and functional zones of the national capital, each of which represents a convenient nearby living and symbolic example for the emperor to grasp as a show piece for duplication or observance in all cities in the rest of the country. Beijing in the PRC has been a new stage of such an evolution on the same trajectory of centralism, symbolism and top rank.

The other element in Beijing's urban development is what we have called the city-region concept. Though seemingly contradictory to the previous element of centralism, it is in essence complementary to it. The wholeness of the city and its economy is the basis for its security, and hence a precondition for it to be on its feet to 'centralize' and 'coordinate' the rest of the country. In implementation, it is the emphasis on self-sufficiency over the regional division of labour. This element is common to all Chinese cities, and may be found in the tradition of the Chinese city as we have discussed in Chapter 2. The traditional Chinese city had been compared to the centre of a nodal region in a rural hinterland. Such nodal regions formed a cellular structure over the Chinese space. Such an analogy seems to be true for China after 1949. In this regard the city resembles a closed system, looking inward within the city-region for solving most of its problems, such as congestion, water supply, food supply and industrial development. In the traditional rural-based economy of old China, this is easy to apprehend. In socialist modern China, the explanation may partly lie in tradition, partly in the general deficiency in inter-region and inter-city transport facilities, as well as in the hierarchical ministerial system that forces municipal governments to develop a lower-level, yet comprehensive municipally administered network of systems to maintain itself, both financially as well as in the necessary production and service for meeting its own demand.

On top of the long tradition of nodal regions, the city-region concept does have in it new connotations from the Chinese interpretation of socialism and the attempts to implement them within the framework of spatial arrangement. The attempt to combine town and country, agriculture and industry, and mental and manual labour, has been an important factor for adding to the Chinese city's jurisdiction a large rural adjunct to form the city-region.

In essence, however, the spatial process within the city-region in respect to urban growth has so far been limited largely to peripheral accretion, known to local planners and academics as 'spreading out the cake'. The crux of the 'dispersed constellations' approach is not to exceed a certain maximum urban growth over one area in order to avoid problems of congestion and other environmental issues. This is done by dispersion of growth around a number of centres, each forming a more or less self-contained unit with its own work places and complementary community and urban facilities. These 'dispersed constellations' and the central mass are to be clearly separated by green buffers of open space or vegetable fields. For over 30 years, the 'dispersed constellation' was upheld as the strategy of growth of the inner city. It has been criticized by Chen (1989) as an inflexible rule which does not reflect the economic dynamism of the city economy as it changes through time and in the context of changing official policy. It has also not paid heed to the pattern and mode of the transportation network in the Beijing area. Chen views the strategy as passive and increasingly facing difficulties as more and more of the surrounding green buffers fall to the encroachment of new developments and a unified urban mass of the inner city seems to be inevitable. A more realistic approach, suggested by Hu (1990, 1992) and Li and Liang (1989), is to decentralize some of Beijing's functions to other better suited cities, to take away some of the underlying economic (and political) fuel for its rapid growth and to set up a 'secondary capital' within the municipality as a counter-magnet to the present inner city. We shall take up this discussion in more detail in the concluding chapter.

The other spatial sub-process that has been repeatedly endorsed and emphasized by the series of general plans is the 'mother–children' pattern of inner/central city and satellites. Using the development of satellites to steer growth away from the inner city and avoid overcrowding and environmental problems has been an obvious tactic copied from the Soviet model. Yet the Chinese have been emphatic in word rather than in deed. This has to do with the lack of authority of the municipal government to implement the plan, the years of economic retrenchment that affected a large number of industrial plant development programmes in the Beijing area, and the over ambitious satellite programme in 1958–60. In 1958, 37 satellites were planned for the outer suburbs to accommodate 113 central government administered new industrial plants. Owing to the economic depression of 1959–62 and the withdrawal of Soviet aid and expertise, half the programmed new plants were cancelled. Only 61 new plants were constructed and they were scattered over 31 satellites. Thus not only was it uneconomical for these 31 new centres to meet the urban support demanded by these plants, there was also great inconvenience for their workers and dependants. Thus the three years of depression had effectively undermined the thrust of the satellites, and by 1992 the largest satellite only attained a population of about 90 000. Lack of impetus for growth had been the main trend for most of these new centres. By 1982, it was recognized that concentrated effort on a small number of satellites is a better alternative for satellite growth. A similar approach was endorsed in the 1992 General Plan. Despite this, the growth of satellites will take a long time, until 2050, to have some obvious impact on the decentralization of urban growth in Beijing.

Thus decentralization has been more tokenism than dynamic action. Concurrently, particularly during the Cultural Revolution period, a sub-process of compaction or 'filling the gap' was officially promoted. This, coupled with the demise of the planning office, led to mixed uses, caused much damage to later developments and frustrated all the good intentions of former and later general plans.

To sum up, although there were a series of general plans, there exists a large gap between the plans and actual implementation on the ground. What happened in Beijing in urban growth has more to do with the political inclination of the day and the system of central planning through the autarchy of the powerful industrial ministries. In general, the combination of the Chinese traditional world view and the new ideas of socialism has, albeit strangely, worked to produce a character of 'closedness' for the national capital. This inward-looking attitude espoused the strategy of self-sufficiency and even contributed to the attempt to minimize the three contradictions and the belief that the capital should be an all-round 'number one' city. Genuine decentralization, rational economic cooperation and division of labour, and structural transformation of the city's economy to befit its capital status and natural environment have not been even looked at within the context of the Beijing–Tangshan–Tianjin region, less so in the wider context of North China, or the economically advanced coastal region of the country. Turning from a 'closed system' approach to an 'open system' approach not only holds the key to problems generated by four decades of urban growth in Beijing, it may offer many more new opportunities for a better economy and a pleasant urban environment in future.

6

Economic development

Overall economic development

Total production and GNP

The record of growth of Beijing's economy in the post-1949 years has been graphically presented in Figure 6.1. Total social production had increased by 69 times in 1952–88 and national income by 49 times. Even if one takes away the influence of population growth, real growth, as measured by per capita national income, had increased by 30 times. The annual rates of growth of the two economic indicators in 1952–88 are respectively 10.1% for total social production and 9.6% for national income. Using the more commonly accepted Western indicator of GNP, the average annual rate is 11.6% for the same period. It is thus clear that by all these measurements, Beijing's economy had experienced sustained rapid growth since 1949. Yet this rapid growth was closely related to the much faster rate of growth of new investment and reinvestment in fixed assets, mainly in productive capital, which averaged a high annual rate of 14.7%. The growth in the total wage bill, as well as housing construction, significant indicators of the welfare of the people, was lagging a long distance behind. The average annual rate for these is respectively 5% and 9.5% only. The latter includes an annual increase of the labour force at 3%, otherwise it would be even smaller (*Forty Years of Beijing*, 1990). Inflation rates of retail goods and cost of living for the average worker are, however, much lower, at 2.3% and 2.2% annually. They are being held down substantially by subsidies from the municipal government which registered an annual increase of 11.7% for the period. From these macro data, we may infer a pattern of growth of the urban economy of Beijing: one of forced industrialization through a high level of savings, and artificially depressed consumption and rate of increase in real wages. Yet social morale and acceptance were ensured through

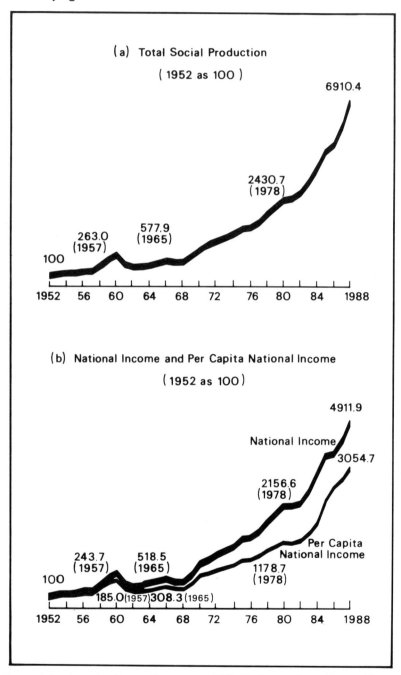

Figure 6.1   Growth of Beijing's economy, 1952–88. Source: Forty Years of Beijing (1990)

official subsidies on basic consumption items, leading to low inflation rates on retailing and daily consumer goods. Although there had been some increase in average income, it was slow. In 1957, it was annually Yn250; 1965, Yn252; 1978, Yn365; 1980, Yn501, and in 1991, Yn2877. Even in 1991 the figure was still very low, and thus we may view Beijing as a 'developing' area in such a respect (*Beijing Statistical Yearbook*, 1992).

Sectoral composition

The disproportionate share of industry in the economy has been illustrated in Table 6.1. Industry accounted for over 60% of total social production, with a peak in 1972 at 81.3%. In 1991, it still remained at the high level of 73.8%. Agriculture had fallen off rapidly in 1952–57, with the advent of forced industrialization. It was relatively reduced from 17.2% in 1952 to 8.5% in 1957. The low figures for transport and commerce at the 3–4% level in 1965–80 reflected the political movements of the Commune and the Cultural Revolution which de-emphasized the service sectors. They only started to recover after the new Open Policy of 1978 and are reflected in the new figures for 1991 in the table. Construction also suffered some decline during periods of intensive political activities, and recovered somewhat post-1978. The preponderance of industry has again been underlined by the relative shares of the secondary sector in GNP contribution throughout 1952–91. It rose sharply from 38.7% in 1952 to a peak of 71.1% in 1978, but has declined substantially since the late 1980s when growth of the tertiary sector as a means to broaden the economy and to ameliorate unemployment started to have its impact felt.

The relatively different policies on industry and the service and commerce sectors also have a lot to do with basic principles regarding the role of the socialist city. The post-1949 proclamation that Beijing should turn from a 'consumptive' city into a 'productive' city meant a two-pronged approach to transforming the city's economy in the early 1950s. Since 1949, over half the fixed capital investments of the city have gone to productive pursuits, of which industry accounted for the majority. In fact, in 1958–65, over 60% of total fixed investments went to productive projects, and industrial projects alone took over 40%. In 1966–75, i.e. the Cultural Revolution period, over 80% went to productive projects; industrial projects alone took 40–50%. Of the total fixed capital investments, central government funds were responsible for 59.6% for the entire period of 1949–78, i.e. before the start of economic reform and the Open Policy. In 1953–57, they were as high as 80.8%,

Table 6.1 Major sectoral growth indicators of Beijing, 1952–88 (proportionate share, %)

	1952	1957	1965	1975	1978	1980	1988	1991
Total Social Production:								
Agriculture	17.2	8.5	9.3	6.2	5.3	5.2	6.4	6.4
Industry	61.1	61.6	74.1	78.3	78.3	77.3	69.9	73.8
Construction	7.4	16.2	8.9	7.4	8.3	9.5	12.3	9.3
Transport	4.0	3.5	3.0	3.4	3.6	3.1	4.2	3.8
Commerce	10.3	10.2	4.7	4.7	4.5	4.9	7.2	6.7
GNP:								
Primary	22.2	10.6	12.5	6.6	5.2	4.3	9.0	8.1
Secondary	38.7	47.8	59.0	66.6	71.1	68.9	53.9	52.2
Industry	(34.1)	(37.8)	(52.7)	(61.7)	(64.5)	(62.5)	(46.2)	(43.8)
Construction	(4.6)	(10.0)	(6.3)	(4.9)	(6.6)	(6.4)	(7.7)	(8.6)
Tertiary	39.1	41.6	28.5	26.8	23.7	26.8	37.1	39.7
Transport, communication	(5.1)	(5.7)	(6.5)	(6.7)	(6.4)	(5.0)	(4.6)	(5.7)
Utilities	(2.8)	(0.6)	(0.7)	(1.4)	(0.6)	(1.4)	(0.9)	(1.1)
Commerce and restaurants	(15.6)	(15.2)	(7.7)	(7.5)	(7.6)	(7.9)	(9.5)	(8.5)
Finance	(0.5)	(0.5)	(0.2)	(0.1)	(1.7)	(4.6)	(10.3)	(12.3)
Services	(1.3)	(1.4)	(0.4)	(0.5)	(1.2)	(1.3)	(3.3)	(2.8)
Education, research, culture, medical and health	(6.5)	(11.6)	(8.3)	(6.4)	(3.8)	(4.2)	(5.5)	(5.9)
Administration	(5.2)	(5.0)	(3.6)	(2.7)	(1.6)	(1.6)	(2.2)	(2.5)
Others	(2.1)	(1.6)	(1.1)	(1.5)	(0.8)	(0.8)	(0.8)	(0.9)
Fixed Capital Investment:								
Agriculture	1.5	1.1	6.0	3.7	8.3	2.7	1.4	1.9
Light industry	9.0	6.0	11.5	5.4	5.4	11.0	8.7	} 34.1
Heavy industry	25.8	16.3	33.1	57.5	36.2	31.8	25.3	
Productive	49.5	55.0	65.2	84.4	67.4	55.7	40.5	46.4
Consumptive	50.5	45.0	34.8	15.6	32.6	44.3	59.5	53.6
(Housing)	(20.5)	(13.6)	(9.7)	(5.8)	(9.7)	(22.4)	(16.9)	(14.4)
Central government source	56.9	81.2	74.6	27.7	42.3	46.4	47.4	39.3
Municipal source	43.1	18.8	25.4	72.3	57.7	53.6	52.6	60.7

Source: Forty Years of Beijing, 1990; Beijing Statistical Yearbook, 1992.

and continued at 65–75% for the rest of the long period of 1958–70. Active central government funding, primarily in industrial investments, underlines the significance attached to Beijing as the socialist national capital of the proletariat. Such an impact on its urban economy has been obvious. Conversely, as the national capital, Beijing had set the example for the nation during the leftist movements in suppressing the 'consumptive roles' of the city. Until 1978, it was believed by Chinese leaders and planners that the tertiary sectors, particularly commerce and restaurants, finance, and services (see Table 6.1) do not add value. Instead, they are wasteful uses of resources and the government should transfer most of their manpower and assets to productive activities. Reduction of the total number of establishments and employment in commerce and restaurants, and services was achieved through the collectivization programme of 1955. In the Great Leap Forward of 1958–60 there were more massive reductions, i.e. in 1960 alone, within commerce, the number of establishments dropped by 78% and those employed by 22%. The relative contribution of these 'consumptive' activities had thus been greatly reduced and remained at very low levels in 1958–78, as reflected in Table 6.1.

The sectoral composition of Beijing's economy faithfully reflects the Chinese socialist perception of the time and was rapidly effected through central planning and administrative interventions in the urban economy.

Employment composition

The socialist transformation has led to a sequence of change in the employment composition of the city. At liberation in 1949, Beijing faced a grim situation of serious unemployment. In 1949–57, great efforts were made to revive the tattered economy and develop new activities to provide employment opportunities for about 270 000 unemployed. In addition to that, new employment had been created for 314 000 people who were resettled or attracted into the new national capital from the rest of the country. As seen in Table 6.2, total number employed in the city increased by about two-fold, i.e. a net increase of 778 338 jobs. Contributions to the increase came mainly from the sectors of industry (added 204 662 jobs), culture, education, etc. (added 128 632 jobs), construction (added 156 914 jobs), administration (added 120 832 jobs) and R & D (added 31 319 jobs). Not only was the unemployment problem eliminated, sizeable increases were registered in sectors that reflected the city as the national capital and its role as the political, cultural, education and technology centre of the nation, as well as it

Table 6.2 Employment structure of urban Beijing, 1949–88 (number of people)

	1949	1952	1957	1965	1975	1980	1990
Industry	156 317	247 174	360 979	546 567	1 115 449	1 378 070	1 608 233
Construction	6 960	117 167	163 874	169 013	207 421	329 240	555 943
Agriculture	1 234	2 857	9 331	68 114	51 287	49 212	82 026
Transport and communications	51 464	72 709	88 870	85 970	109 947	144 319	187 774
Commerce	91 940	118 140	142 834	126 349	196 465	283 173	469 567
Restaurants	16 773	20 394	19 789	14 382	26 620	44 851	72 798
Services	12 247	15 723	21 989	36 296	50 319	70 140	208 754
Supplies	–	–	–	16 137	16 259	22 975	44 205
Utilities	3 153	12 465	24 551	55 639	78 228	132 894	132 661
R & D	221	1 719	31 540	133 576	118 206	181 574	261 093
Culture, education etc.	31 014	65 114	159 637	243 716	273 121	359 639	538 659
Finance, insurance	3 608	6 282	9 043	8 071	7 590	16 207	41 594
Administration	58 468	103 886	179 300	253 869	127 930	185 464	345 790
Total	433 399	783 630	1 211 737	1 757 699	2 378 842	3 197 758	4 549 097

Source: Compiled from *Forty Years of Beijing, 1990; Beijing Statistical Yearbook,* 1991.

being targeted as a burgeoning new industrial centre. There were some increases in commerce, transport and communication, restaurant and services. Yet the pace was still slow.

In the ensuing period of 1958–65, which includes the Second Five Year Plan Period and the Period of Restructuring of the Economy, there had been a major structural dislocation of employment in the city. The Great Leap Forward of 1958 brought a 50% increase in the city's total employment, i.e. an increase of 700 000 jobs in a single year. Those who filled the new jobs came mainly from the countryside of nearby provinces. They were being put into newly established heavy industrial plants. Yet the collapse of the Great Leap Forward ushered in a period of retrenchment that started in 1960, when a large number of the newly recruited labour force were sent back to their home villages. New demands for employment by graduating cohorts were met to a large extent through the 'Shang Shan Xia Xiang' movement, i.e. new graduates were sent to the countryside as 'educated peasants'. Thus there were much less spectacular increases in employment in 1957–65. Of all activities, industry netted a moderate increase, construction stagnated, while the sectors of commerce, restaurants and services (personal services) declined. Sectors that boosted the city as the nation's political, technology and education centre maintained sustained growth of more than 100% increase in jobs.

Further distortion to the employment structure in emphasizing 'production' and deemphasizing 'consumption' can be gleaned from changes in employment types during the Cultural Revolution of 1966–76. The effect of the baby-boom after World War II on the escalation of the labour force was keenly felt in this period. The annual increase of the labour force in the late 1960s reached about 10%, three times the figure for the previous decade. In all, 600 000 urban youths were sent to the countryside in the 'Shang Shan Xia Xiang' arrangement to solve the otherwise serious unemployment problem. In this period, total employment grew only by 35%, and about 90% of the growth was concentrated in industry. The other main impact of the political undertone of the Cultural Revolution was the slashing of employment in administration, R & D, culture and education, as educated cadres, technocrats and the intelligentsia in general were sent to the countryside and other parts of the nation for rustication (Table 6.2).

After 1977, those born in the 1960s' peak of births gradually entered the labour force, leading to a second round and yet higher job demand. Annually, an estimated 300 000 to 400 000 new jobs had to be created. In the 15 year period of 1975–90, 2.17 million new jobs had been generated. However, in this latter round of employment restructuring, the boom sectors turned to construction, commerce, restaurants, services, finance and insurance. R & D also benefited substantially. There was in general a return to tertiary activities as a result of policy change towards more emphasis on the rule of the market, and eradication of the former policy taboo of emphasizing the 'productive' sectors to the extent of harming basic services and activities to support the large urban population. A second characteristic of this period is the upsurge of the collective sector and the 'individual' or 'self-employed' sector, formerly discouraged or even forbidden. These new and flexible small and medium enterprises, dependent on local resources, capital and market, constituted a new force in revitalizing the urban economy and accounted for about 1 million jobs in 1990 (compared to 458 421 in 1975) (*Beijing Social and Economic Statistical Yearbook*, 1991). In addition, economic reform and liberalization provided much of the driving force not only for increasing employment but also for transforming Beijing's employment structure towards one which is more balanced in terms of 'productive' and 'consumptive' activities.

In spite of the increasing role of market forces, Beijing's employment composition in 1990 still bore much of the impact of its being the national capital. Of the administrative employees, 46.9% belonged to the central government. For R & D, higher education, culture and art, the respective percentages were: 81.7%, 80.0% and 77.5%. However, for industry, central government accounted for 231 007 of the total 1 608 233 jobs. The latter nevertheless only reflected the fact that the central government controlled mainly heavy industries and that, despite heavy financing, most of their ownership had been passed to the municipality in different periods of 'decentralization' of ownership and control within the industrial sector, as profits from them form the main source of municipal revenue. The preponderance of activities and employment belonging to central government remains clearly a distinct characteristic. It underlines the significance of administrative status and 'centralism' in the size and nature of Beijing's present-day urban economy, which nevertheless conforms both to the traditional Chinese concept as well as the socialist concept of the national capital.

Fast track and comprehensive industrial development

The urban economy of Beijing, as previously presented, has been predominated by the manufacturing sector. The driving force behind this has also been explained as the socialist objectives of bolstering the city as the socialist capital on a firm (or sizeable) foundation of a local industrial proletariat, and transforming the city from one of a capitalistic 'consumptive' to a 'productive' centre. The process of development since

1949, particularly after the First Five Year Plan of 1953–57, has demonstrated further characteristics which we may summarize briefly here but will be further elaborated later. These are:

1. Hectic pace of development.
2. Development of a full range of industries to facilitate their 'administration' and the R & D activities of respective industrial ministries.
3. Development of industries without regard for local limitations, such as fuel, water, market and other local resources as well as transport and environmental conditions.

In 1949, there was a total of 21 055 industrial enterprises, the bulk of which were administered by the municipality, and only 47 were centrally administered. 125 were owned by 'the whole people', 33 were collectives and 20 897 were privately owned. These establishments employed 159 317 persons, or 36.7% of the total employed labour force, and generated a total output value of Yn169 million (1952 price). By 1990, the number of industrial enterprises rose to 29 072, even excluding rural enterprises under the village-administration level and individually operated small firms (or self-employed handicrafts or small workshops). Centrally administered enterprises were small in number, i.e. 254, yet they generated 15.4% of total industrial output value and employed 10.3% of the entire manufacturing labour force. Establishments owned by 'the whole people' numbered 1877, yet produced 62.7% of total industrial output by value, and 53.8% of the total manufacturing labour force of 2.28 million persons. 'Collectives' numbered 27 030 enterprises, employed 960 000 persons and produced Yn218 billion value of output. In the year there were 99 joint ventures with foreign capital which employed 37 663 persons, and generated Yn45 billion (6% of total). Thus by 1990, the industrial sector of the city, the mainstay of the urban economy, remained very much 'socialist' in nature, i.e. owned by the public in the forms of 'whole people', or 'collective' enterprises, whereas privately owned and foreign joint ventures still remained insignificant. Within this overall frame, the control of the municipality on the industrial sector, as reflected by industrial output generated by enterprises under its administration, had been on the increase since 1970, reaching the 80% level or above. This is an important fact that must be borne in mind when deliberating environmental issues and the future transformation of the urban economy, as profits from industrial enterprises form the main source of revenue of the city, and there has been great reluctance on the part of decision makers to discourage further industrial growth or to relocate some of its lucrative enterprises outside the city limits for environmental and regional restructuring purposes.

The rapid growth of industries in Beijing may be succinctly illustrated by Figure 6.1a. Using 1952 as 100, the indicator shot to 6910 in 1988, or rose by 69 times within the period. We shall pursue in the later part of this section various aspects of Beijing's industrial economy. First we shall briefly review its history of speedy industrial growth.

History of industrial growth

The industrial base of Beijing was laid during the first two Five Year Plan periods. Immediately after 1949, three major industrial enterprises that had already existed before World War II were expanded. They were the Xin Hua Publishing, Qing He Woollen Factory and the Shijingshan Iron and Steel Works. However, major industrial expansion only took place after the start of the First Five Year Plan. The two driving forces were Soviet aid and the socialist transformation of existing capitalist industries and enterprises. During the period, electronics, textiles, machinery and construction materials were the main industrial branches fostered (Table 6.3). Total industrial output value rose by 13 times in 1949–57, and modern industrial branches accounted for 74.3%. During the Second Five Year Plan (1958–62), Beijing's industrial development was further emphasized, and the principles of advanced modern industries and wide-ranging industrial development through central planning were adopted.

The Great Leap Forward of 1958 provided additional impetus to a blunt and blind attempt at fast and much larger-scale industrial development. In particular, it generated a special stress on heavy industries, especially iron and steel industries. Beijing's resources were thus devoted to the 'foundation industries' of fuel and power, metallurgy, chemicals and construction materials (see Table 6.3). Coalfields in the western suburb were developed. Significant expansion of Shijingshan Iron and Steel Works into an integrated iron and steel plant took place. New plants for heavy electrical machinery and power generators were established in the western suburb, while auto-making and internal combustion engine manufacturing were set up in the eastern suburb, and over 10 new large-scale electronics manufacturers congregated in the north-eastern suburb. The new chemical industry, which produced fertilizers, medicines and farm medications, dyes and rubber products, etc., was located in the southern suburb. In addition to heavy industries, food industries received substantial investment and support. Textiles experienced moderate growth. The total industrial investment in the 10-year period was Yn3.5 billion, about one-third of all investment in the municipality. By 1962, total industrial output of the city reached 26.7

Table 6.3 Ten important industries in Beijing, 1949–90 (output in Yn million)

Industry	1949	1952	1957	1965	1970	1975	1980	1985	1990
Machinery	18	86	285	893	2 148	3 970	5 842	9 777	15 129
Chemical	2	17	57	306	856	1 419	4 166	5 737	7 704
Metallurgy	8	77	167	846	1 338	1 634	2 271	2 752	4 756
Textiles	18	77	138	171	298	379	823	1 210	2 909
Food	34	201	323	546	643	972	1 457	2 157	2 650
Cultural, sports and educational products	24	64	143	337	315	451	767	1 296	124 887
Garments	18	77	138	171	298	379	823	1 210	1 955
Construction materials	2	38	98	239	396	486	769	1 039	1 601
Electricity	8	14	42	254	418	626	743	781	975
Handicrafts	NA	NA	NA	NA	NA	162	333	674	777

NA = not available
Source: Beijing Social and Economic Statistical Yearbook, 1991.

times that of 1949. Growth had happened on average at 28.8% annually, while heavy industries had grown faster, at 32.2% annually. Industrial output then accounted for 92% of the combined gross output value of industry and agriculture, a tremendous change from its 55% share in 1949.

The Cultural Revolution (1966–76) saw few significant new developments except for the building of a new petrochemical complex (Beijing Yan Shan Petro Chemical). Further growth was propelled by expansion and improvement of existing facilities, particularly those within heavy industries. In 1970–79 there was a total of Yn6.6 billion invested, 89.5% in heavy industries, particularly the three branches of chemicals, machinery and metallurgy. Thus the bias towards these heavy, foundation industries since the Second Five Year Plan persisted until the restructuring of Beijing's industries after 1978. In terms of output value, heavy industries contributed 63.7% of the total for all industries in 1979, and the preponderance of the three heavy branches may be gleaned from Table 6.3 and the output figures for 1970–80 (Wu et al., 1988).

The Four Directives of the Central Communist Party of 1980 on Beijing's role and the State Council's 1983 Comment on Beijing's General Plan provided a new orientation for Beijing's industrial development. The city's industries have to be restructured both to suit local factors of supply and demand and to avoid contradicting the city's role as the nation's political, cultural, education, tourist and R & D centre. The main new directions are:

1. Movement towards light industries.
2. Movement towards non-polluting and environmentally friendly industries.
3. Movement away from water-intensive, energy-intensive heavy industries.
4. Movement towards technology-intensive and high value-added industries.

The most obvious evidence in the restructuring attempt is the increase in investment in light industries. For the entire period of 1949–79, on average only 12.4% of total industrial investment went to light industries, yet in 1979–88 it went up to 28.7%. In 1990, it stood at 26.1%. In the decade of 1980–90, gross industrial output of the city rose by 1.6 times to Yn56.2 billion, and light industries accounted for 43.4%. Indeed, contribution from light industries had stayed above the 40% level, except for 1985 when it was 36.7%, as compared to the long period of 1969–79 in which it stayed at the 30–40% level, while in 1971 was only 26.9%. Within the last decade of 1980–90, industrial output value grew at an average annual rate of 10%, yet those branches of industry which are sympathetic to Beijing's demand for a good environment as the national capital, and suited to its high concentration of technological strength and high-level urban consumption, had grown faster than the average rate. These industries include electronics, food, textiles, printing and car-making. Their rapid increases have been netted out in Table 6.3 (in which electronics and car-making have been subsumed under 'machinery').

Main characteristics

Rapid pace and broad range. In the 35 years of 1949–84, a total of Yn1750 billion had been cumulatively invested in Beijing's industries, guaranteeing their very speedy growth. In the period, total industrial gross output increased at an annual rate of 17.6%, making the city second to Shanghai as China's largest industrial base. Of the 164 industrial branches that existed in China, Beijing possessed 149, i.e. almost a complete range of industries. Machinery (including electronics and machine making), chemicals (including chemicals and petrochemicals) and textiles form the three pillars, accounting for about 60% of total industrial output in value. A number of industries figure significantly in the country's industrial economy. Measured by output value, petrochemicals ranked first among the 29 provincial-level regions in China, producing 22.7% of the country's total. Cultural, sports and educational products ranked second, accounting for 9.8% of the national total. Electronics and woollen textiles both ranked third, accounting for 8.5% and 8.3% respectively. Leather and garments accounted for 7.1% and 6.7% and both ranked fourth. Metallurgy, industrial equipment and daily electrical appliances ranked fifth with respective national shares in output of 4.7%, 4.9% and 6.1%. On product basis, Beijing equally ranked high in a broad range of industrial output. 1983 figures show that it was the largest producer in the country of rubber products, plastics, and refrigerators; second for pig iron, washing machines and personal computers; third for power generators, weight-lifting machines, coking coal, computers, colour TVs, woollen cloth and motor cars; fourth in cast iron, internal combustion engines, recorders and synthetic fibre; and fifth in steel, rolling stock, sewing machines, beer and furniture.

Unbalanced industrial structure. Beijing's industries, in spite of their wide range, are characterized by increasing imbalance towards intermediate industries, whereas light industries are less developed. The large share of intermediate industries has been an unreasonable and unhealthy structural fault. This is mainly reflected by a large amount of exports from the city of intermediate industrial outputs. On the other hand, most of the inputs into the intermediate industries come from outside. On average, Beijing needs to import 18 million tonnes of coal, 6 million tonnes of crude oil and 4 million tonnes of iron pellets and other raw materials annually. After they have been processed into intermediate products, a large proportion are exported out of the city, e.g. annually a large amount of pig iron and steel ingots (several hundred thousand tonnes each), over 1 million tonnes of coke and 2 million tonnes of petrochemical products are shipped out from the city. It was estimated that in 1982, 32% of the total of 21 major products under the Bureau of Chemical Industries, and 80% of the products of the Yan Shan Petrochemical Plant, were exported. In that year Beijing produced 300 000 tonnes of plastics of which only about a third was for consumption by local factories. Thus despite Beijing's broad range of industries, and its technical capability, there is insufficient vertical development to maximize the advantages of downstream and coordinated growth. It ends up with uneconomic exchanges with outside regions, which increase the burden on its inter-regional transport lines. Such two-way flow of raw materials and output for the intermediate industries represents tremendous waste, creates unnecessary transport problems and adds to the costs of the final products (Wu et al., 1988).

The imbalance between heavy and light industries has been touched on previously and in Table 6.1. In 1949–87, investment in heavy industries represented 87.6% of total investment in all industries and 63.7% of cumulative total industrial output (Chen, 1990). Within light industries, insufficient attention was paid to development of those branches that complement existing heavy industries by making use of their outputs as inputs, adding yet another structural imbalance. Beijing's light industries, until the 1980s (Table 6.4) still relied more heavily on farm inputs, whereas the intermediate outputs from heavy industries have been largely exported with little further processing to add to their value. In addition, some of the raw materials required by light industries have to be shipped in from long distances and some, e.g. wool, are even imported from foreign countries. Clearly, the supply of farm input as a factor for light industries to grow is much less favourable in Beijing than comparable cities such as Shanghai, Nanjing and Guangzhou which are supplied by large and productive hinterlands with cheaper means of and more convenient water transport.

Concentration in water- and energy-intensive and polluting industries. The heavy industries of Beijing are also characterized by a generally high intensity of water and energy consumption, as well as being generators

Table 6.4 Beijing's industrial structure (% by output value)

Year	Raw material/ intermediate industries	Fabricating/ processing industries	Light industries utilitising farming inputs	Light industries utilising industrial inputs
1957	34.5	65.5	82.0	18.0
1965	44.6	55.4	67.6	32.4
1975	45.2	54.8	60.9	39.1
1980	48.1	51.9	60.1	39.9
1985	45.9	54.1	61.4	38.6

Source: Wu, et al., 1988.

of pollutants. This is obviously unsuitable for Beijing which suffers from both water and energy shortages, and is at variance with its being the national capital with a population of 10 million. In 1989, industrial water consumption in the city amounted to 1.8 billion cu m, a large proportion of the 75% guaranteed supply of 3.74 billion cu m in 1990. Of the industrial consumption, 90% was consumed by heavy industries. On average, 50–60% of industrial branches within heavy industries registered an industrial output water consumption of 133 cu m per Yn10 000. The heavy consumers of cement making (759 cu m), paper (664 cu m), metallurgy (302 cu m), coking (277 cu m) and chemicals (245 cu m) consumed even more (Seventh Five-Year Plan Study, 1991).

Energy consumption in the industrial sector was 16 million TCE (Tonne Coal Equivalent) in 1989, and on average it amounted to 3.43 TCE per Yn10 000 industrial output value. Heavy industries consumed 84% of this total amount, with a per Yn10 000 consumption of 5.13 TCE, whereas that for an average light industry was only 1.22 TCE. The most energy-intensive industries are metallurgy, chemicals, coking and coal products and chemicals.

On the basis of five types of pollutants, i.e. water, sulphur dioxode, dust, smoke and solid waste, Beijing industries have been graded in terms of their pollution intensity. Again, the heavy industries of chemicals, metallurgy, construction materials, paper and coking and coal products ranked as highly polluting (Seventh Five-Year Plan Study, 1991, 44). The harmful effects of the predominance of undesirable industries on the urban environment will be further discussed in later chapters.

In spite of recent policy reorientation and efforts, industrial branches that are 'friendly' towards the urban environment and that suit Beijing's natural and human resources, such as electronics, auto-making and precision equipment, have not yet become significant within its industrial structure.

Economic viability and resources. Most factories face problems of economic viability and lack of incentives and resources for upgrading technology. A survey of 218 large–medium industrial enterprises in 1991 indicated an overall declining economic performance (Zhang, 1991). Both the ratios of profits and tax to capital and sales declined consistently and substantially in 1980–90. The annual growth rate for profit and tax for the period was 6.5%, yet the tax component grew only annually at 3.1%, whereas retained profits grew at 23%, indicating that there had been a redirection of resources from the government to individual enterprises, and hence raising the possibility of increased enterprise incentives for self-generated growth. However, the growth in profit and tax had not been evenly distributed among various industrial branches. The iron and steel industry and the chemical industries registered above average rates, whereas car-making, basic metallurgy, machine making, drugs, light engineering, printing, precision equipment, electronics, construction materials and textiles were all below average. The highest rate of the iron and steel industry of 59% was substantially higher than the lowest of 9% in electronics. The Capital Iron and Steel Company alone played the major role in the profit–loss situation of these 218 enterprises. Excluding it, the average annual growth rate of profits and tax for the period would become only 1.3%. In another survey of 383 large industrial enterprises (Beijing Technology Management Research Centre, 1991, 18), that single enterprise contributed 53% of the total profits and tax of all these enterprises, or 10% of the total of the entire manufacturing sector of Beijing. The pre-eminence of that company and the highly unsuitable iron and steel and chemical industries represent a market situation grossly distorted by a system of official price control and scarcity that upholds some industries and depresses others through differing profit–loss situations, with the result that industries suited to the national capital's urban and human resources environment have not been effectively encouraged.

Zhang's study (1991) also revealed a slow growth in labour productivity of 5.8% in the 218 Beijing factories in 1980–90, whereas costs for raw materials and energy inputs have grown at 16.8%, and labour cost at 18.1% per annum in 1986–90. In all, the profit margin or the ratio of capital to profits and tax had been on the decrease. It dropped from 45.1% in 1980 to 40.5% in 1985 and then to 26.2% in 1990. While the burden of centrally planned production targets remained unchanged for the period (30%), increasing the role of the market for inputs had been responsible for cutting into the profit margin and hence affecting the economic viability of those branches that have less market competitiveness in their outputs.

In the survey of 383 large and medium enterprises that formed the foundation of Beijing's industry, a similar picture of overall deficiency in economic viability has been confirmed. Among these enterprises, 20.6% reported a zero profit/capital ratio, 14.6% reported a rate of less than 1%, and those that exceeded 20% only amounted to 9.9% of the enterprises. Six reasons have been suggested for lack of economic viability:

1. Price increases in raw materials and fuel inputs.
2. Rising level of loan interest rate.
3. Gradual withdrawal of a number of state subsidies.
4. Increase in non-productive expenses, e.g. labour insurance and retirement benefit payments.
5. Rising wages.
6. Decreasing profits from exports as export price increases had been falling short of cost increases.

In addition, increases in inventory have been an important cause for a low and depressed profit/capital ratio, as they locked up a large amount of capital. In 1990, the stock of steel amounted to 307 days' normal demand. In a survey of 30 large and medium electrical goods establishments, 13.3% reported an inventory of less than 20%, 16.6% an inventory of 20–50%, and 63.3% with a rate of over 50%. Only two establishments had no increase of stock at year-end compared to the beginning of the year. In many cases, the inventory rate in 1989 was already very high, so the increase in 1990 is even more unreasonable. The root cause for this is the lack of flexibility in production planning according to market demand, so that many products without a real or sufficient demand were still produced. On top of that, many establishments kept up the tradition of maintaining quantitative expansion and disregarding economic viability, quality development, technical upgrading and increase in added value. Thus, though output value had been on the increase consistently, it was achieved at the expense of wasting valuable raw materials, energy and other inputs (Beijing Technology Management Research Centre, 1991, 56). Further evidence of insufficient attention towards technological upgrading, and expansion of industrial capacity through R & D, is the low level of input for technological improvement out of total annual capital investment for a number of important industrial branches in 1986–89. It amounted to 9.5% in machine-making, 7.9% in electronic equipment, 7.3% in car-making, 6.5 in textiles, and 6.3% in construction materials. Only in metallurgy was a higher figure of 32.3% reported, and in drugs and light engineering, 15.1% and 13% were reported. Of such small amounts of funds for technological improvement, taking machine-making as an example, 35.9% was used to increase quantity in production capacity, 12% in plant layout or relocation, 20.1%

for increasing the number of product types, while only 25.3% was spent on quality improvement (Beijing Technology Management Research Centre, 1991, 18).

Main industries

Beijing's industries currently fall into seven main branches. Here we shall present their general situation as at the end of 1990 as further substantiation on the structure, nature and problems of the city's present industrial economy.

1. *Basic metal industries.* Since 1983, all basic iron and steel industries have been put under the Capital Steel Corporation (CSC), whereas the non-ferrous basic metal industries have been grouped under another administrative heading, Head Office of Non-ferrous Basic Metals Industries (HONBMI). In 1978 CSC produced 2.45 million tonnes of pig iron. In 1990, it was raised to 4.06 million tonnes. Steel production stood at 1.17 million tonnes in 1978, but reached 3.81 million tonnes in 1990. CSC was an old enterprise that started in 1919. It produced only pig iron in 1949 and that amounted to only 26 000 tonnes. By 1990, it was the largest industrial enterprise in the city and employed 92 111 persons. It is a comprehensive and integrated iron and steel enterprise, with seven mines, 22 ore processing plants, four furnaces with a total capacity of 4139 cu m and a number of rolling mills. It ranked as one of the 10 largest integrated iron and steel plants in China. In 1988, it produced 7.8% of the nation's pig iron, 6.2% of raw steel, 6.7% of steel products and 1% of steel-alloys. The plant plans to increase its production two-fold in 1986–95. The main plant site is located 20 km from the urban districts in the western suburb of Shijingshan, occupying a total land area of 57 million sq m. From the point of view of market demand, Beijing requires such a large iron and steel plant. Yet the plant is located on the windward side of the city and forms a major urban pollution source. It is also an intensive consumer of energy and water. These characteristics make it 'unfriendly' to Beijing as a national political and cultural centre. The plant is nevertheless expanding rapidly in response to market demand. It is also capable of doing so as it has been a very profitable enterprise. It is not only able to generate its own investment capital for expansion, but also forms an important source of revenue for the municipal government. In 1990, CSC realized total profits and tax of Yn2625 million, out of which Yn1499 million was remitted to the municipality. The latter

represented 46% of all revenue derived from the industrial sector for the year for the entire city. HONBMI is composed of 22 plants. Its gross output was Yn357 million and it remitted Yn49 million in profits and tax to the municipality in 1990.

2. *Chemical and allied industries.* These industries cover chemicals, medicines and drugs, synthetic fibres, rubber products and plastics. In 1988, these industries had, respectively, 199, 42, 10, 43 and 163 individual enterprises and produced an annual output of Yn5.8 billion, 0.85 billion, 0.42 billion, 0.68 billion and 0.76 billion. Beijing's chemical industries are mostly medium to large-scale establishments. Yan Shan Petro-chemical is the largest and accounts for about a third of the output value of the capital's chemical industry. Most plants consisted of imported technology of later than the 1960s and are reckoned to be better than most competitors in the country in product quality and technological level. Although in general leading the nation in these two aspects, the industries suffer from the common ailments of bias towards production of intermediate products, commonplace and low-order products, with relatively low added value. Locational fault is clear for the largest plant, Yan Shan Petro-chemicals. The location within a small valley in Fangshan creates problems of pollution and limited space for development. The future direction for these industries is to rely on technological improvement to restructure themselves for vertical growth, more technology-intensive and downstream processing. At the same time they should shift their emphasis towards more economies in water and energy and less pollutive processes and products.

3. *Light engineering.* Light engineering includes a number of industries under the First and Second Bureaux for Light Industries, including watches, sewing machines, glasses, pens, lamps, metal tools, household electrical applicances, etc. In 1988, there were 239 enterprises with a product value of Yn39.2 billion, and total profits and tax amounted to Yn0.7 billion.

4. *Machinery.* Machine-making includes a range of high-technology industries such as printing machines, construction machines, general machines, power generators, pharmaceuticals, farm machines, and textile machines and equipment. In 1988, there were 726 enterprises in Beijing, employing 276 763 workers. They generated an output of Yn3.9 billion, or 2.9% of the national total, and profits and tax amounted to Yn0.76 billion. Beijing favours the development of these industries because the city has already developed a broad and firm industrial foundation with numerous medium–large enterprises, and leads the nation in high-level R & D and supply of technical personnel. Yet these industries suffer from structural

ailments resulting from past policies. The enterprises lack clear specialization guidelines, which leads to duplication of processes and products. Individual enterprises used to adopt a 'self-contained' and 'self-reliant' policy, such that most of them are all-rounders, with few linkages and division of labour between related enterprises. In general, there has been duplication of equipment and waste of resources. Products are of low quality and limited design and size range. Of the 740 products within the Bureau of Machinery, 600 are earmarked for upgrading and modernization of design. Old equipment plagues the enterprises as well. On average, they are products of the 1960s, having been in service for more than 30 years. Lack of standardization and specialization affected the growth of precision dies and casts and other machine tools, which adversely influences product quality and new product development.

5. *Car-making*. Sometimes grouped under machinery, Beijing's motor industry is one of the 'Big Four' in China's light vehicle sector. The city now leads the nation in the production of light vehicles, with an annual capacity of 100 000 cars, 200 000 engines, 1.5 million motorcycles and 200 000–250 000 sets of parts, whereas in 1979 it only produced 24 000 vehicles. Thus the industry has already grown into a self-contained system of light vehicle production. At present, there are 25 parts producers and 5 body-makers and assemblers. In 1990, these employed 57 259 persons, with 5110 being technical staff, and produced 82 089 light vehicles, 1.45 million motorcycles, and 151 763 engines. The total output value was Yn2.2 billion and profits and tax amounted to Yn0.5 billion. In the number of light vehicles, Beijing's production in that year was 16.1% of the national total. Beijing's present and future strength lies in light vehicles. It leads the 'Three Small' or light vehicle producers of Beijing, Tianjin and Guangzhou. As a high value-added, non-polluting industry generally not demanding of water and energy, the car industry has been singled out as one of the major 'friendly' industries for the capital, to be strongly promoted for future growth. Its future directions will lie with new models of enlarged capacity to reach economies of scale, improved parts production through inward standardization and specialization, and strengthening foreign technology transfer through joint ventures.

6. *Textiles*. Beijing and Tianjin together form North China's largest textiles centre. In 1988, there were 432 enterprises, employing 434 000 workers with an annual output of Yn8.1 billion, and total profits and tax of Yn1.24 billion. Cotton textiles predominate, generating 50.3% of the total output value, followed by woollen textiles and knitting, with 23.3% and 14.8% shares. The two cities

together produced 57.8% of the nation's cotton textiles, 14.2% of its woollen textiles and 10.6% of its knitwear. In Beijing alone, the textiles industry accounted for 7.6% of the city's total industrial output value, and employed 116 000 persons with the following production capacity: 462 600 cotton spindles, 87 000 wool spindles, 55 000 tonnes annually of chemical fibre, 24 420 cu m annually of dyeing and stencilling ability. The three main branches of cotton, woollens and knitting accounted for over 90% of the city's textile production. The former two have attained an edge in the national and export markets, with reasonably advanced technology, vertical and diagonal linkages, and high labour productivity. The latter exceeds that of Tianjin, North China and the national average. In 1988, textile exports formed 23% of total foreign exports of the city and amounted to US$16.8 million. The industry is located in three specialized textile industry areas, i.e. in the eastern suburb, in Qinghe, and in Shunyi. It still faces the problems of outdated equipment and technology and needs to attain further vertical deepening, stable production and quality production.

7. *Electronics*. Beijing ranks number four after Jiangsu, Guangdong and Shanghai as China's largest electronics production base. In 1989, it produced an output value of Yn4.1 billion, about 40% of the first rank base, or 6.6% of the national total. Yet Beijing's products are grossly different from the national pattern. In Beijing, 36.2% of the output is capital goods, 23.7% parts and components, and 40% consumer products, whereas the same set of figures for the nation is 15.8%, 30.9% and 53.3%. The three largest production bases are much less oriented to production goods, only 9.4, 19.8 and 7.8% of the electronics output of Jiangsu, Guangdong and Shanghai falling into this category. Further examination of the actual product mix of Beijing indicated such a pattern: products for communication, broadcasting and TV industry accounted for 44.7% of total output value of the industry; products of the computer segment 26.9%; components 20.8%; parts 7.6%. In the entire industry were 128 enterprises in 1989, employing 110 000 persons, among whom 15.5% are engineers or technical personnel. Among its products, some rank first in the nation, e.g. broadcasting and TV equipment and computers. In the Eighth Five Year Plan, the municipality plans to invest Yn3.5 billion in the industry, of which Yn1.5 would be foreign capital. By 1995, the industry is expected to generate an annual output of Yn7–10 billion.

The electronics industry was first set up in the north-east suburb in the 1950s with the establishment of 10 key enterprises. In the 1980s, in the Zhongguancun area of Haidian, a new high-tech electronics base began to take shape. It combined the R & D, production and sales functions of the industry and was designated in 1988 as the 'Laboratory for New Technology of Beijing'. As the area is located in China's highest density district for high-level manpower, its prospect for major future growth is great. Here are over 50 higher education institutions and over 140 research centres of the Academia Sinica and various central ministries, with a force of over 80 000 scientists and researchers and a university student body of over 100 000. In 1988, Zhongguancun produced Yn300 million of electronics products and was the nation's largest market for electronics components and parts.

Spatial characteristics

The location of industries within Beijing had been guided by a series of general plans for the city, although there had been several major disruptions leading to departures from original plans. Starting from 1949, newly established industries first concentrated in the eight patches of industrial areas in the outer rim of the inner city. Then in the First and Second Five Year Plan periods, 10 additional industrial districts gradually took shape (Fig. 6.2). The latter include the Shijingshan Iron and Steel and Electricity Industry Area, Fengtai Auto-making Industry Area, Chemical Industry Area of the South-east Suburb, Cotton Textiles Area of the Eastern Suburb, Jiuxianqiao Electronics Industry Area, Qinghe Woollen Textiles Area, Telecommunications Industry Area of the Northern Suburb, and the Construction Materials Industry of Fangshan. During the Cultural Revolution, a new petrochemical complex, the Yan Shan Petro-chemical Corporation, was added to Fangshan. With this exception, the spatial pattern of industries of Beijing remained little changed, adhering much to the planned constellations, as has been illustrated by Table 6.5 which shows the distribution of industrial land in 1987 and the planned situation for 2000. In 1987, about 95% of the industrial land of the planned urban area was within these planned industrial areas, and they accommodated 1879 enterprises and 920 000 industrial workers, respectively 34% and 52% of the municipal totals. However, the industrial density of the old city districts remained very high. In only 0.4% of the territory of the municipality, it accommodated 790 enterprises and 250 000 industrial workers.

A fair amount of factories within the old urban districts were the product of political excesses in the late 1960s, during which time over 1000 'May-Seventh Factories' were set up as a means to provide productive activities within residential and non-industrial districts in

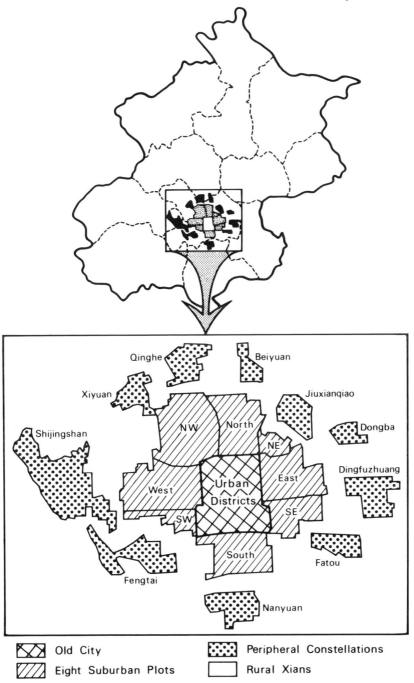

Figure 6.2 Industrial location of Beijing

Table 6.5 Distribution of industrial land in the planned urban area of Beijing, 1987–2000 (in hectares)

Location	1987	2000	Change 1987–2000
A. Old City Districts:	427	229	−198
East City	58	27	−32
West City	62	31	−31
Chongwen	113	92	−21
Xuanwu	194	80	−114
B. Eight Patches in Suburbs:	3955	3671	−284
North Suburb	400	421	+21
North-east Suburb	121	124	+3
East Suburb	764	679	−85
South-east Suburb	800	837	+37
South Suburb	750	790	+40
South-west Suburb	270	152	−118
West Suburb	430	329	−102
North-west Suburb	420	340	−80
C. Peripheral Constellations:	3628	5201	+1573
Beiyuan	83	181	+98
Jiuxianqiao	302	461	+159
Dongba	75	319	+244
Dingfuzhuang	313	654	+341
Fatou	266	687	+421
Nanyuan	46	126	+79
Fengtai	632	628	−5
Shijingshan	1343	1457	+114
Xiyuan	7	7	0
Qinghe	562	682	+120
Planned Urban Area Total	8010	9101	+1091

Source: Wu, 1990.

cities in China, to achieve Mao's target of mixing manual and non-manual labour and engaging all people in some productive activity. Later on some of these factories merged to form larger units and became the mainstay of industrial enterprises of the old city. Many of such factories are polluting and are inter-mixed with residential and other sensitive non-industrial uses, e.g. hospitals and schools, causing much damage to the urban environment as well as posing fire, health and other hazards. In 1980–90, 66 such enterprises had been relocated to outer districts of the municipality, releasing 72 hectares of land which was mostly reassigned for office use. Fifty-one of the factories had to be resettled because they were noise hazards, nine gave out polluted gas and water, two posed hazards of explosion and fire, two occupied designated cultural and historical preservation sites and two were sited outside the red demarcation line for buildings. Another 60 enterprises had yet to be relocated from the old urban districts for similar reasons as at the end of 1990.

Lack of planning control during the Cultural Revolution also led to coalescence of the suburban industrial districts between themselves and with the urban districts. The 'filling the gap' tactic advocated in the period had swollen most industrial districts, plundering former separating green belts (see Figure 6.2), leading to deterioration of the urban environment. In the outer suburbs (or rural *xians*), industrial plants had been deliberately located in a scattered and sporadic fashion, paying no heed to rational economic locational considerations of transport, raw material sources and markets, as the slogans at the time were 'be prepared for war', and seek 'hilly, dispersed and caved' locations. Such a pattern of industrial location resulted in high penalties in terms of production and sales inefficiency as well as sacrificing workers' welfare and convenience.

Future industrial expansion, as illustrated for the year 2000 in Table 6.5, will take place mostly in peripheral constellations. Between 1987–2000, they will expand 43.4% in area, adding 1573 hectares of new industrial land, while both the old city districts and the eight industrial patches in the suburbs will register a decline. The decline of the old city will be as much as 198 hectares, or 46% of its total of 427 hectares as of 1987, underlining the municipality's determination to clear the industrial sores left behind by the Cultural Revolution.

Conclusion: problems and plans for the urban economy

The rapid development of Beijing since 1949 into a major economic centre had been influenced by two predominant considerations, as reviewed in a lengthy speech by the mayor, Peng Zhen, in 1956. He first emphasized that the main role for the municipality after its liberation was 'to develop its productive enterprises, so that production of the city will not only be revived and expanded, but the city will turn from a consumptive one into one of a productive nature. Then, the people's government could be firmly established'. Peng then drafted the 1949 policy directive for Beijing entitled 'Revival and Expansion of Production is the Main Objective of Urban Works' (Ma, 1991). Secondly, Peng felt that from the point of view of urban finance, Beijing had to become a sizeable modern industrial area. The post-1949 construction works required by its being the new national capital put a huge demand on construction materials, equipment, and daily necessities such as clothing and food for those who supported the building of the national political and administrative centre. As the national capital, Beijing should not rely on transfer or import of materials from other places, or too much on subsidy from the central government. Besides its own contribution to the country, it should also be self-reliant.

Industries would provide the municipality with revenue as well as a means to modernize suburban agriculture to yield sufficient food supplies for the urban residents. Peng criticized those who cited Washington and Bonn as examples that the national capital does not need to be an economic centre and said they harboured ulterior motives. He countered the challenge that industries would 'disturb' city residents, commenting that industries provided employment and could raise income, thus would contribute to the welfare of the people and a stable and satisfied community. His views are shared by some even today. Ma (1991), for instance, argued that Beijing should naturally be an economic centre, though the Directives of the CCP in 1980 and the State Council in 1983 have clearly dropped 'economic centre' as one of the roles of the city. His reasons are simply that Beijing has been so since the 1950s, and is the nerve centre of the country in economic management and planning, as well as a financial centre with an already sizeable productive urban economy.

Nevertheless, it was widely admitted in the 1980s that the urban economy of Beijing had caused serious problems and required significant restructuring. Yang (1984), for example, noted that the decision makers had been misguided by the belief that the national capital should be 'a centre where a large proletariat congregates', and it should be 'a city with the most developed industries'. In 1958, it was even proclaimed as the city's target to develop into 'a modern socialist industrial base' in a matter of five years. Under such principles, over half the city's total capital investment in 1949–78 was spent on industries, of which 87.9% went into heavy industries leading to the predominance of machinery, metallurgy, electricity and chemicals and an imbalance of structure in favour of industries intensive in their use of capital, land, water and resources. These heavy industries are also highly polluting and of low added value. The latter is substantiated by an imbalance towards intermediate products. The industrial structure had in turn generated serious social and economic problems. The city had been over-expanded; its population growth was difficult to control; developable land was in short supply; and scarcity of water and electricity became endemic. On top of these are environmental deterioration, traffic congestion, and insufficient investment in housing and other urban infrastructure which were slighted as the authority regarded them as 'consumptive' in nature.

The CCP Directives in 1980 specified that 'Number one, the capital should be the nation's political centre, the nerve centre, centre for binding the Party and the People, *not necessarily an economic centre.* Number two, it is China's window to the outside world. The world also views China through Beijing'. More specifically, it requires that Beijing has to remain economically prosperous and should stress the development of tourism, service industries, food industry and light and electronics industries of a high-tech nature: 'We must be determined to develop such as the export of capital, equipment and technical personnel to other provinces, or through joint-ventures with the latter, to help to ease the population pressure of the capital'. The State Council's Directives of 1983 have further elaborated the capital's new industrial policy since the liberalization and reforms of 1978: 'Beijing must not henceforth develop heavy industries, especially those that are energy-intensive, water-intensive, demand much transport and land, and are proved to be a nuisance to nearby residents. Instead, it should develop industries of high value-added, state-of-the-art or advanced industries that are technology-intensive. At present, food processing, electronics and other light industries that suit the capital's situation have to be rapidly expanded'. In addition, it requested a substantial development in commerce and service industries within 'a short period of time', and that Beijing's economy should develop jointly and cooperatively with those of Tianjin and Tangshan and the surrounding areas.

The revised General Plan of 1992 has mapped out a broad scenario for the development of the urban economy of Beijing in 1991–2010 (Beijing Municipality, 1992). The economy as a whole is expected to grow at a moderate pace while undergoing major structural transformation. The GNP (1990 price) will increase from Yn50 billion in 1990 to Yn89–100 billion in 2000, at an annual average rate of 5.5–7%. In 2010, it may reach Yn145-165 billion, growing at an average annual rate of 5–6% at this later stage. The sectoral composition will change accordingly. In 1990, the primary sector contributed 8.8% to GNP, but it will decline to 6% in 2000, and 4% in 2010. The secondary sector's share will drop from 52.4% in 1990 to 49% in 2000, and 41% in 2010, whereas the tertiary's share will shift respectively from 38.8%, to 45% and thence to 55%.

While industry will remain for a long time the mainstay of the economy despite a relative decline compared to tertiary activities, it will be transformed structurally to the 'five small and two high' types, i.e. small consumption in energy, water, materials, land and transport, and high in added value and technology intensity. Industries ranked first in priority are electronics and car-making, the new pillars of the industrial sector. Other favoured industries are machinery, textiles and electricity. Existing heavy industries are to be subject to improvement, particularly chemicals, metallurgy and construction materials that consumed 70% of the city's industrial energy and half its industrial water consumption. Following the structural transformation, a spatial shift is expected. By 2000, the industrial output value of the urban and suburban districts will decline from 60–70% of the city's total to 55% and further to 50% in 2010. Polluting factories within the limit of the Third Ring Road would be relocated to the outer suburbs or completely transformed.

The tertiary sector will generate much of the growth. In 1990 it may reach Yn45 billion, based on an average 9% annual rate of growth. By 2010, it would become Yn82–88 billion, still expected to grow at a higher rate than GNP, i.e. 6–7% annually. The final aim of the plan is to set up the tertiary sector as the mainstay of the urban economy to serve the national capital and to orientate it towards the whole nation and the world. This includes a comprehensive development of finance, insurance, data information businesses and consultancy, property, commerce and tourism. In the period, a new CBD will be established outside Chaoyangmen in the eastern suburb. Below it, there will be a hierarchy of business centres with commercial and some office functions.

Details of the first phase of development for the industrial sector have been outlined by Lin et al. (1991). The guiding principle is to maximize both foreign and domestic market demands, with raised economic efficiency and technology as the key approaches. In the transformation, mainstream industries have to be identified to achieve a rational industrial composition that is economically efficient, technically advanced, non-polluting, not a heavy consumer of energy amd that fits the situation of Beijing. Besides the above-mentioned industrial policies, micro-electronics, aerospace and superconductors industries will also be fostered. In addition, there will be a new export orientation for the new industrial structure, and by 2000, it is expected to export as much as US$3 billion. To achieve these objectives in 1990–2000, of the planned Yn72 billion capital investment for industries, Yn54 billion will be earmarked for technology upgrading and only Yn18 billion for basic construction. In the actual disbursement of these funds, a policy bias towards electronics and car-making will be ensured. To facilitate movement of enterprises towards export markets, a number of export-oriented industrial zones will be set up in which enterprises will enjoy tax, price and foreign currency privileges. Enterprises that export 70% of their output or over US$30 million a year can enjoy the same privileges as foreign joint ventures. Sufficient and appropriate land would also be planned in advance to facilitate the achievement of the industrial goals. For example, electronics will be focused in Jiuxianqiao and Zhongguancun and the motor industry located in Shunyi, Daqing and Huairou.

Despite the awareness and the determination, the urban economy of Beijing by 1993 had not changed much, particularly so within the industrial sector. Prominent reasons include a shortage of capital which prevented the government from making any great progress. Particularly paradoxical is the fact that most of the polluting and energy- and water-intensive heavy industries remained the largest contributors to municipal revenue. Owing to high domestic demand and high product prices, these enterprises had been able to remain the most profitable, and thus able to generate their own funds for further growth and expansion. Perhaps it awaits at least the deepening of two types of reforms as a precondition for successful implementation of the plans for the transformation of Beijing's urban economy, viz:

1. Tax reforms to enable the municipal government to generate the necessary revenue from the growing economy to enable it to be financially capable.
2. Price reforms to enable sectoral policies to work through market mechanisms.

We shall discuss these points further in Chapter 12 on the new development strategy of Beijing.

7

Population growth and its spatial pattern

Socialist principles on size and composition of urban population

It has been noted in previous chapters that an important socialist urban planning target is to limit the size of the city. As the urban population provides labour supply for productive activities within a city, as well as demand for urban-based consumption of food, other daily consumables and services, it is a key factor within the system of central planning when applied to the spatial planning unit, the city, which includes both the supply and demand side variables in the equation involved in the allocation of resources. Thus in Soviet urban planning, population size has often been a major target in the general plans of cities, and administrative measures to control migration into cities, though with limited success, have been a consistent feature in urban administration (Zhang, 1984, 112–18). Although in Western urban planning population size targets are also commonplace, they are not as emphasized as in the socialist countries. The main reason is that migration of people in and out of cities in a market economy is difficult to monitor and predict, not to say control. Even in autocratic Third World cities such as Djakarta, the 'closed city' policy was difficult to enforce consistently over a long period of time. However, within socialist countries before 1989, i.e. before the downfall of the Soviet bloc, stringent migration control through population registration and job control methods, coupled with central planning on both economic activities and provision of social services, had put migration and hence urban population growth under reasonable control.

In China, more stringent rules had been applied on migration in the pre-1978 years. Urbanization, although it still existed, was under close official surveillance and manipulation. There had been minor departures, as will be reviewed in the case of Beijing, yet on a small scale compared to the tidal upsurge prevailing in most Third World countries in the years after World War II. The pattern of population growth within socialist cities, and for that matter Chinese cities, is also the outcome of the ideological principle that cities are mainly 'productive' centres, generating manufactured goods and services for the benefit of the masses, which include both the rural and urban population. The Stalinist interpretation of this function of the city emphasized its industrial role to the detriment of services. Stalin even believed that one day there would be the demise of the 'big city' as productive activities would have to be moved and dispersed into sites of rural setting (Sit, 1985). Although the Chinese had not taken this extreme interpretation, they put a lot of effort into dispersing new investment to smaller settlements in the interior of the country, away from the main and large urban centres along the coast. Mao's pragmatic view since 1956 had tempered such a national strategy by maintaining the role of such coastal centres under the rationale of utilizing their infrastructure and human resources for the benefit of overall faster growth of the nation.

Yet the above considerations alone cannot adequately explain Beijing's hectic post-1949 population growth. We must also go back to the traditional Chinese view that the national capital serves as the example for the nation to emulate. This, in the new socialist regime, included revised political and industrial roles for major cities in the PRC. As the top rank political centre of the nation, Beijing was given all the administrative functions that befit the national capital which it once was, but had gradually lost since the late Qing Dynasty and that had disappeared during the Kuomintang reign. Secondly, as the socialist national capital, it should set an example for all other Chinese cities as an industrial or productive centre, resting on a firm foundation of the modern industrial proletariat. Other major coastal cities with sizeable pre-1949 populations and modern urban functions, such as Shanghai, Guangzhou and Tianjin, were subject to population control and a crash course of functional transformation in rapidly scaling down their service roles, especially finance, commerce and personal services. Beijing in the post-1949 years had experienced the reverse: hectic growth of new 'basic' or productive activities accompanied by massive population increases. These events reflected the destiny of the new national capital, symbolic of the highly concentrated and centralized control of the new regime as well as the artificial creation of a new industrial centre for providing the new socialist headquarters with the physical and ideological comfort of being surrounded by a large modern industrial proletariat. In addition, industrial investment and its annual returns could be used to support the capital financially and materially, and to concentrate the material wealth which the new regime was able to amass from the rest of the nation.

All told, the size of Beijing has been determined by considerations of its need to be a large industrial centre, the socialist desire for centralized control through central planning, and the requirement for a socialist city to be self-sufficient. The combined effect was a large planned population from the start, as new governing headquarters were set up in the capital and a brand new administrative and political centre was established in and around the Zhong Nan Hai and the western suburb. With the help and advice of Soviet experts, the Chinese followed the example of Moscow and initially set a 20-year maximum target population of the city at 4 million. In 1953 when the formal general plan was drafted, the ceiling was raised to 5 million. Very soon, stimulated by Mao's new pragmatic view that capital cities should also develop to enhance the pace of the nation's economic growth, Beijing's territory and population limits were further raised. The entire city was extended to 8860 sq km, with a long-term (50-year) target maximum of 10 million people, whereas the urban population alone was to be 5–6 million. These new standards were laid down in the 1957 General Plan, which was set against the background that Beijing should quickly develop into a major centre of big industries. There have been twists and turns in the political scene of China and of Beijing since 1957, yet the 10 million maximum has stayed intact until very recently. In 1958 there was a once-for-all large increase in territory for the city, raising its area from 8700 sq km to 17 200 sq km (later modified to 16 800 sq km) in a single stroke. It was, however, largely a response to the principles that the city should be self-sufficient in daily food as much as possible, and that there should be closer integration between urban and rural activities (Beijing Construction History, 1987).

Post-1982 planning of Beijing scaled down much of the formal attention and effort on industrial growth of the city. Despite this, the tradition of putting a cap on the city's population growth has been maintained. Yet in this later period, the rationale is not based on central planning needs in respect of economic development, but on a realization of the harmful consequences of big city problems such as congestion, pollution and housing, as well as the limits of the ecological capacity of the Beijing area and environmental considerations for a healthy community, and awareness of Beijing's predominant role as the political and cultural centre of the nation. The 1982 plan put a limit of 4 million people for the urban areas while maintaining the 10 million maximum for the entire municipality, clearly demonstrating a strategy of decongestion and decentralization within the city's own boundaries. Real population figures for 1988 had exceeded these maxima (see Table 5.1). The latest revisions of the general plan in 1992 put these figures at 6.5 million and 12.5 million by the year 2010 respectively.

The critical importance attached to the size of the urban population, based on the estimated demand derived from the city's role, meant that population growth in a Chinese city under the PRC has been much more regulated, both in terms of its quantitative change and its employment structure, than is common in Third World cities after World War II. In the latter, rapid growth of over 7% annually had been frequent for the bigger cities. Such growth was fuelled both by a high natural increase of over 2% annually and a much higher rural–urban migration. Moreover, these are fairly consistent features that straddle decades from the 1950s to the present. They also do not seem to be led by industrialization or dynamic growth of the city's economy. Rather, it has been alleged to be influenced by the so-called 'Todaro effect', i.e. rural–urban migration being attracted into cities by unsustained, and often false, hopes of employment and better educational and social services against unemployment and under-employment as well as dull life in the rural areas (Kelley and Williamson, 1987). The temporal process of population growth in Beijing demonstrates the different setting of the Chinese cities. Much of the growth that had been recorded in China's cities occurred as an integral part of the nation's drive for rapid industrialization in the early history of the PRC. The rural–urban migration which fuelled such growth actually corresponded well with the expansion of the industrial sector. Despite this, looking at the long time span of 1949–92 the population growth of Beijing, or for that matter for most of the very large cities in the PRC, cannot be regarded as spectacular. The pace has been slow, and often corresponded to the natural growth rate. Yet against such a backdrop, there had been major in- and out-migrations, results of political events and the strong hand of government which are still seldom seen in other cities in the Third World.

Of course, as the national capital, Beijing receives a large daily flow of temporary population (as against permanent residents) who come into the city for business or as tourists. In 1991, the temporary population amounted to 713 000, or about 7% of the permanent population of 10 322 000. This number is expected to increase as China becomes more open and travel within the country is much less restricted.

In reviewing the population growth of Beijing, we should also note the significant turn of events in 1978 which marked the change from a much more rigid central-planning control system in 1949–78, to a much relaxed situation in the post-1978 years that emphasizes market forces, economics and more personal freedom of movement.

Periods of growth

Beijing's territory expanded in the 1949–61 period as a matter of policy in order to increase its jurisdiction for acquiring enough space for major industrial development, and for maintaining a degree of self-sufficiency in food and water supply. In the period, the actual administrative territory of the city increased 22.6 fold, i.e. from 707 sq km to 16 808 sq km. At the end of 1961, the population added onto Beijing through territorial expansion alone was reported to be 2.826 million (see Table 5.2 in Chapter 5), or the equivalent of 39.8% of the total population of the city of 7.21 million at the time (Li, 1987, 2–3). Even by 1984, of the population increase of 7.32 million since 1949, Li (1987) estimated that 35.9% was owing to boundary changes, whereas natural increase accounted for 46.8% and migration 17.3%.

Having noted the effect of boundary changes on Beijing's population growth, we have taken the precaution of excluding it as a factor in analysing the contribution of natural growth and migration, which are central to the socialist concept of controlling the size of the city. Indeed, the following tables in the chapter are based on population figures using the present administrative limits, thus excluding the impact of boundary changes. That is to say, the 1949 population of the city was 4.14 million, instead of 1.56 million (that was the population within the 707 sq km old city boundary). Indeed, all statistical yearbooks on Beijing reported historical population figures back to 1949 using such a procedure.

A marked contrast between Beijing and other Third World national capitals is its slow overall growth rate. In Table 7.1, between 1949 and 1990, the city added a total of 6.2 million persons. Although superficially an alarmingly large figure, expressed in average annual growth rate it is only 2.25%, or an annual addition of 151 000 persons on the 1949 figure of 4.14 million (Table 7.2). In contrast, Yeung (1988, 160) reported the following very high annual growth rates for selected national capitals in Asia: Bangkok grew at 7.8% in 1970–80; Kuala Lumpur at 7.6% in 1970–80; Seoul at 8.5% in 1960–70 and then 4.2% in 1970–80; Taipei at 6.0% in 1960–70 and then 4.7% in 1970–80; and Manila at 4.9% in 1960–70 and 4.1% in 1970–80. Rondinelli (1988, 299) reported much more alarming rates during 1960–70 and 1970–80 for the African nations. Out of a total of 36 national capitals (for some the largest city), 21 registered over 70% growth (for a 10-year period, i.e. about 6% annually) in either or both of the two periods. In general, Third World countries registered high natural increases of population after World War II of around 2%, and a much higher urbanization rate of about 4%. The national capitals have grown at an even faster pace of over 4%. The previous examples

Table 7.1 Population change in Beijing 1949–91, permanent population only (10 000s)

Period	Change in persons	Births	Deaths	Natural growth	Natural growth as % of change	Immigration	Emigration	Net migration gain	Migration as % change
1949–60	318.1	224.5	60.1	164.4	51.7	462.3	308.6	153.7	48.3
1960–70	39.1	198.0	57.0	141.0	360.6	87.6	189.5	–101.9	–260.6
1970–78	78.4	85.6	41.2	44.4	56.6	77.8	43.8	34.0	43.4
1978–83	83.7	73.3	26.3	47.0	56.2	66.5	29.8	36.7	43.8
1983–90	107.2	109.4	43.2	66.2	61.8	78.8	37.8	41.0	38.2
Cumulative total	626.5			463.0	74.0			164.5	26.3

Source: Li, 1987; *Forty Years of Beijing, 1949–1989* and *Social and Economic Statistics of Beijing, 1986–1990.*

Table 7.2 Population (in millions) and density of various parts of Beijing, 1935–90

	Pre-Liberation			1949			PRC Period 1964		1984		1990	
	Area (sq km)	1935 Population	Density	Area (sq km)	1949 Population	Density	Population	Density	Population	Density	Population	Density
City districts	62	1.11	17 967	87	1.41	16 172	2.31	26 494	2.38	27 310	2.42	27 862
Suburban	645	0.46	712	1 283	0.56	438	2.16	1 683	3.23	2 519	3.56	2 777
Outer suburbs				3 198	0.05	16	0.29	91	0.37	102	1.00	312
Rural Xians	16 101	2.14	133	12 240	2.11	172	2.89	236	3.47	283	3.34	272
Total	16 808	3.71	221	16 808	4.14	246	7.65	455	9.45	562	10.32	614

Source: Compiled from Li (1987) and *Beijing Social and Economic Statistical Yearbook* 1991.

demonstrate the frequent occurrence of 6% annual rates, particularly at the time of their most rapid growth. In any case, an overall long-term average annual rate of 4% and above seems to be the norm.

For China as a whole, the experiences after World War II have been distinctively different. Sit's analysis (1985, 11–12) shows that China in 1949–81 registered an average population growth rate of 1.92%, and an annual urbanization rate of 2.78%, both markedly below the average situation for the Third World. This reflects, in effect, the command economy and a development policy of balanced rural and urban growth. In addition, in most Third World countries urbanization has been the consequence of both natural increase and migration. McGee claimed that migration has contributed to about half the growth, a situation different from the nineteenth-century and early twentieth-century urbanization experiences of the industrialized economies. As for the nature of migration, it too is distinctly the outcome more of the rural 'push' than the more forceful urban 'pull' generated by industrialism, well expressed in the term 'Todaro Effect' (McGee, 1971). Sit's analysis (1985, 13) shows that China stands out in the Third World in such aspects as well, i.e. that natural increase contributed to 82% of urban population increase and that urban population increase correlates highly with programmes of industrialization. That is to say, China's migration streams have been urban pulled.

Beijing's contrast with other Third World national capitals is obvious. It registered a very low overall growth rate of 2.25% in 1949–90, and that growth is mainly owing to natural increase (74.1%). Yet, as the national capital, Beijing does draw some distance away from the rest of the country's big cities. For example, its growth rate is higher than the long-term average for other major cities such as Tianjin (1.97% in 1949–82) and Shanghai (1.29%) (Li, 1987, 61) and its migration component exceeded the national average of 18% by a substantial margin. The 'special treatment' received by Beijing as the national capital accounts for most of these differences. Yet its population growth dynamics, in broad terms, still reflect much of what is true of PRC cities. We shall attempt to illustrate how such dynamics have been shaped and hence correspond to the political and policy twists of the country since 1949 through analysing the different periods of population growth of the city.

1949–60

This is the period of fastest population growth (Table 7.1). The city's population increased by 3.18 million, or by 76.8% in a matter of 11 years. Such an increase accounted for 51.2% of the cumulative increase for the entire 1949–90 period. The bulk intake thus effectively raised the population base of the city and to a large extent set the momentum for later increases. On average the annual rate of increase for these 11 years was 5.25%, a rate that conforms with other Third World cities in the years immediately following World War II. Natural increase accounted for 51.7% and migration 48.3%, again fairly similar to the general Third World situation. The post-war baby boom of 1952–58 and the lack of birth control programmes were responsible for the high birth rate of 3.82% and high natural growth rate of 2.76%. When broken down further to conform with major economic and political periods, this reveals that the First Five Year Plan (1953–57) and Great Leap Forward (1958–60) did affect the population growth of Beijing in a significant way.

In the immediate post-civil war years of economic reconstruction, the natural increase was pulled down somewhat by a high death rate since food supply and medical and health services were not yet back to normal. Yet the city population was bolstered by a higher migration rate (2.52%) as Beijing started its development into the national capital and control headquarters of the country. Annual increase of population amounted to 209 000, with an annual rate of 4.74%.

During the First Five Year Plan Period (1953–57) large-scale construction projects to turn the city into a new industrial base and phased development of the central administrative machinery fuelled net migration in the order of 112 000 persons annually. It was, however, the baby boom, which happened in 1952–58, with an average annual birth rate of 3.96%, coupled with a fast declining death rate as a result of improved medical and health facilities and a stable politico-economic situation for the nation, that accounted for the high population growth rate of 5.17%. The natural growth rate also registered a high of 3.1%.

The Great Leap Forward years of 1958–60 had a drastic, yet negative, long-term effect on Beijing's population growth. These years coincide with the highest recorded natural increase rate of 3.6%. On top of that the overheated drive to develop Beijing rapidly into a major industrial base had drawn into the city a huge influx of construction and industrial labour, causing the migration rate to peak at 4.72%. The total population growth rate of these three years averaged 8.32% annually, the highest in Beijing since 1949, comparable to other Asian national capitals such as Seoul, Bangkok, Kuala Lumpur or Taipei at their post-war peak period of growth.

Overall, Beijing in the 1950s was more similar to Third World national capitals in having a high population growth rate with an equally high natural population growth rate, though migration into the city was more economically pulled than in other Third World cities.

1960–70

Population growth of Beijing was in the doldrums in the 1960s. Total population increased by only 391 000 persons in the decade, with an average annual growth rate of a mere 0.5%. The basic reason for this is negative migration. The city lost annually through migration 100 000 persons (Table 7.1). Detailed analysis of the period indicated that 1960–62 were years of bad harvests, natural calamities and collapse of the ill-planned Great Leap Forward. The nation adopted drastic retrenchment measures by cancelling many industrial and construction projects and returning a large number of workers to their home villages. Beijing lost 388 000 persons through migration, an annual rate of 2.68%. In these years, the city reduced its population absolutely by 42 000 persons, the only such record in its post-1949 history. In 1962–66, strict control over migration was enforced and the city went on losing population through migration at a rate of 0.6%. It nevertheless maintained its modest total population growth owing to the second post-1949 baby boom of 1962–64. In 1963, at the peak of the boom, the natural growth rate stood at 3.53% (Li, 1987, 73). Despite this, the total population growth rate was trimmed down to 1.33% annually because of loss through migration.

Lastly in 1966–70, with the onset and spread of the Cultural Revolution, the nation was once again in upheaval. The city's economy was greatly disrupted and that part of the urban population which comprised educated persons such as cadres, professionals and students was forced to rusticate in the countryside. Net loss through migration resulted in the migration rate reducing to –1.45%, i.e. the city shed 550 000 persons in these five years through migration. At the same time, the natural growth rate declined to 1.59%. The combined effects of these reasons produced a very low, or even stagnant population growth rate, i.e. an annual rate of 0.4%.

In the 1960s it was mainly the dysfunctioning of central planning and Maoist political fanaticism that twisted the population dynamics through forced repatriation of workers and rustication of the intelligentsia so that the population of Beijing seemingly remained stagnant in numerical terms. Urban growth was further frustrated by lack of food as well as a new ideology in favour of the countryside, whereas urban services and infrastructure were given a low priority and urbanity was at a low ebb. It was a situation which is not only quantitatively, but more so qualitatively, different from situations obtaining in other Third World cities.

1970–78

1970 began with a return to the normal situation after the heat of the Cultural Revolution. Increased political and social stability, as well as the return of normal economic production, had positive impacts on population growth, particularly through the return of formerly 'forced' out-migrants. Population in the period increased by 784 000, or about 100 000 annually, at a yearly rate of 1.22%. The migration rate returned to a positive 0.53% annually. This is also partly the outcome of major industrial projects, e.g. petrochemicals and iron and steel works, that necessitated recruitment of rural labourers, as well as a relaxed policy to allow some of the educated youth sent down to the countryside to return to the city. The overall population increase was modest, as more attention towards birth control slashed the birth rate substantially by 60% compared to the former period. The average natural population growth rate dipped to only 0.69%, with an annual addition of 55 000, a very small figure for a city of over 8 million.

A low birth rate and an effective control over migration distinguish Beijing from other Third World capitals with an annual increase of population at 1.22%.

1978–83

1978 was yet another political divide. The new era of Deng Xiao-ping meant much more relaxed control over migration, emphasis on economics and the rule of the market. Yet it also meant a reorientation of the role of the national capital. The industrial role of Beijing was de-emphasized and its administrative and cultural role as the national capital was stressed. The former factors led to heightened gains in migration, as the migration rate shot up to 0.85% annually, largely composed of cadres and college students returning from rustication programmes, a new influx of business from the rest of the country and joint ventures with foreign capital to cash in on the new economics and 'open door' strategy. The latter necessitated strict control on the city's population growth to maintain a conducive environment. On top of these, the Chinese government was shocked by the prospects of a population explosion after 2000. Many cities, Beijing included, were asked to adopt stringent measures to contain population and to put a cap on the potential of future population growth. In its 1982 General Plan, the 10 million maximum figure for the entire city was re-stressed, and a vigorous 'one-child policy' that restricted married couples to producing one child, or otherwise to be subject to economic, social and political penalties, was enforced. Despite this, the large amount of returning college students of marrying age and the lowering of the official marriage age boosted the birth rate and hence returned the natural growth rate to 1.04%, about 40% more than that of the former period.

The city as a whole registered 1.89% annual total population increase rate, the highest since 1960. Natural growth and migration had an almost equal share. In the five-year period the city added 837 000 persons, more than the former eight-year period.

1983–90

The upsurge of migrants after 1978 gradually petered out in the 1980s as returnees were exhausted and the municipality put stringent control on in-migration. The annual average migration increase rate dropped to 0.46%. This meant a yearly migration gain of 51 000 persons. It forms 38.2% of the total population growth of the city, making natural growth the obvious larger contributor. As Beijing enters into its third post-1949 baby boom of 1985–95, birth control becomes an obvious official priority. It is estimated that in this boom period, there will be annually 110 000 newly married couples. Even if they stick to the 'one-child policy', there will be 110 000 newborns a year. In fact, the average natural increase in 1983–90 was 94 000 persons. Considering the stable rate for deaths, this is a very low figure, indicating a successful implementation of the 'one-child policy'. Continued enforcement of the policy and encouragement of late marriage are indispensable for curbing a new tide of population increase. The municipality is committed to these as well as to strict control over migration, which we will discuss further in the next section.

For the entire 1983–90 period, despite relaxed control over people's movement and economic liberalization, Beijing had been growing very slowly, at 1.45% annually, and much of it through natural increase.

Migration and the reasons behind it

Although migration contributes about 30% of total population growth in Beijing in the long period of 1949–90, two elements of the migration stream have added significance regarding their long-term impact on the city. The first is the large scale in-migration in the 1950s which has a lasting impact on the scale and composition of the city's population. The second is that out-migrants since the 1960s have been largely of 'skill-intensive' people. Albeit small in number, 70% of them still maintain their families in Beijing. Thus there is a built-in returning potential for most of these out-migrants. In 1986 the municipality completed a two-year study on migration issues of the city which formed the basis of this section (Liu, 1986).

Impact of in-migrants

In 1985, there were 9.58 million permanent residents in the city, of which 5.86 million lived within the urban areas. Of the latter, 3.18 million or 54.3% migrated to Beijing after 1949. Only 0.72 million moved into the urban areas from the rural periphery. The bulk, 2.44 million, migrated into the city from other provinces. When the children of these migrants are included, permanent residents that were in-migrants since 1949 amounted to 74% of the total urban population.

In-migrants of the various periods had effectively raised the youthful age groups and satisfied the labour demands of these periods. Age analysis of the in-migrants showed that 24% of them were 20–24 year olds when they moved in; 20% were 15–19 year olds, 14.8% were 25–29 year olds, and 22.9% were 14 and below. Clearly the bulk were less than 30 years old, the majority of which in the most active age of 15–29. The sex ratio of the migrants shows a male dominance of 131.5:100. Bulk intake of these migrants has left an imprint on the sex ratio of the older people of the present population of 114.3:100, as compared to 93.9:100 for non-migrants at 65 years old and above. Of the female migrants, child-bearing age groups accounted for 72.4%. The most active child-bearing group of 20–34 alone accounted for 47.5%. Clearly, in-migrants represent a negative effect on the control of natural population increase.

The study revealed that in-migrants had a reasonably high level of education. College-level graduates accounted for 13.6% and middle school graduates 42%. Despite this, the large-scale influx of farmers into Beijing as labourers in the 1950s is also the explanation for 27.2% of the migrants with only primary school education, and 17.2% who are semi- or illiterate. Comparison of their jobs before and after in-migration sheds light on the fact that migrants had been mainly economically pulled. Figure 7.1 shows the close relationship between capital investment amounts and the twists and turns of in-migration before 1970. Stricter control over in-migration and increasing replacement of labour by machines and capital in the post-1970 years have been reasons why the

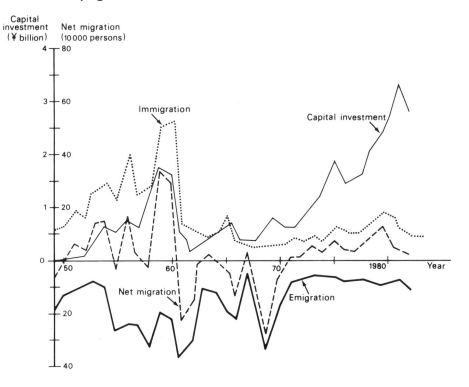

Figure 7.1 Net migration and capital investment for Beijing, 1949–1989. Source: compiled from Beijing Statistical Year Book various dates

two have not been as closely correlated as before. Before migration, 49.8% worked as labourers in the primary sector, 14.4% as technicians, 13.4% as administrative and office workers, 10.1% as transport workers, 4.6% as commerce and service workers, while 7.7% were unclassified. After migration, the distribution changed to: 31.1% as production and transport workers, 30.1% as administrative and office workers, 28% as technicians and 8.6% as commerce and service workers. The capital as the nation's political and administrative centre and the second largest industrial base seems to have drawn from the rest of the country people who finally meet its labour demand.

Impact of out-migrants

The other part of Liu's study is on out-migrants. There were two main waves of out-migration from Beijing. The first happened in 1949–70 and accounted for 85.1% of the total out-migrants in the 35 years of 1949–84. Within this period are three 'special occasions'. In 1949–50 a large proportion of Kuomintang officials, capitalists and old bureaucrats moved out 'to escape the new rule'. In 1961–62, forced decampment was carried out at the collapse of the Great Leap Forward which was followed by food scarcity. In 1968–70 out-migrants were mainly urban educated youth sent down to the countryside in the 'Shang Shan Xia Xiang' movement. These 'special occasions' accounted for only 14.9% of the out-migrants in the 35-year period, and the annual average flow is only half that of the previous period. Strict control over in-migration to some extent explained a psychological 'fear' that once a person had moved out, it would be difficult for him to move back. The characteristics of out-migrants in this second period throw into relief the relatively small amount of outward flow.

First, 87.8% of the out-migrants are within the economically active age groups, with an average age of 31.7 years. The sex ratio is very skewed, i.e. 380:100 and 95.8% of them moved out singly. Those moved with the family accounted for only 4.2%. Thus the larger proportion could move back to rejoin their relatives or families at any future date. They too are better educated. The average years of education for those above 6 years old is 10, compared to only 1.4 years for the whole city. 19.9% have college-level education as compared to 8.3% for the whole city.

The percentage of out-migrants who were currently employed was 56%, of which 43.5% were in the education, culture, science and research sectors, or were cadres of various ranks. Of the 44% currently not in employment, 65% moved out for study in a university or were allocated to new jobs after university graduation. They too were between 17 and 26 years old. These statistics underline the major dynamics for out-migration since 1971, i.e. 'brain-drain' as well as 'skill-uplifting', and that the out-migrants are largely skill intensive. Of the recent out-migrants, another notable feature is the outflow to foreign countries (15%) and to Taiwan, Hong Kong and Macao (3.9%).

Zhang and Liu (1991), in a long-range analysis of 1975–90, examined the various reasons behind both the in-and out-migration streams. 'Study' as a reason is responsible for a 191 000 net increase through migration. It is the most important migration factor. Before 1988, in-migration through study was also free of control, as long as the candidate was admitted to a college in Beijing. Of the college graduates that are residents of the city, less than 0.5% received job placements outside the city. Those who were recruited from outside had also been mainly employed within Beijing after graduation. The second important reason is 'to join relatives for livelihood'. This category added 134 000 net migrants in 1975–90. It is an increasing factor as the population goes on ageing. 'Military service or retirement from military service' are responsible for a 127 000 net gain in migration. Before the 1980s, out-migration was more than in-migration, yet it has been reversed in the 1980s. It is a category of migration that the authors claim can be easily controlled. 'Accompanying family' is the fourth significant factor which added 112 000 net migrants in the 15 years. It is the result of the tendency that the accompanying persons followed the migrant to come in, but often did not follow him to move out. On the contrary, their remaining in Beijing becomes a rationale for the out-migrant to move back to Beijing again at some future date. In the 15-year period, job migration has led to a net migration increase of 107 000 persons, or 12.5% of the total net migration gain. Although there had been a rule that all administrative units should observe the principle of balance in transferring personnel in and out of Beijing through job allocation, the reality is that in-migrants in such a category exceeded out-migrants by 40%. 'Marriage' as a reason accounted for 72 000 net migrants. Usually it is females from the surrounding rural areas that marry male Beijing residents. There is at present no control at all on such migration. Zhang and Liu's exposition of the latest situation revealed that migration had continued to be of significance in the growth of Beijing's population, particularly so as some of the in-flows are not subject to control whereas the control over others is quite lax.

Temporary population

In China all citizens are subject to household registration. Those who leave their permanent registered city or rural unit of domicile and move into other places are regarded as temporary population. The temporary population is the major part of Beijing's 'fluid' population, which includes also people in transit. In 1990, the daily 'fluid' population of Beijing was 1.27 million, of which 0.97 million were temporary residents and 300 000 in transit to other places. Of the temporary residents, 520 000 were contract and cyclical labourers recruited from surrounding rural areas by Beijing's businesses, as well as construction labourers brought in from the rest of the country. People for purposes such as business and services amounted to 160 000. There were 20 000 from outside serving as domestic helpers. The balance of 270 000 includes tourists, people on non-commercial business and other exchanges.

The size of the temporary population has grown significantly throughout the years, particularly after the open-door policy and the liberalization drive since 1978. Before 1970, except for the overheated Great Leap Forward years of 1958 and 1959, the temporary population remained well below a daily 200 000, and mostly around 100 000 persons. Since 1978 China has gradually expanded its relationship with foreign countries and started to woo foreign capital as well as to venture into a broad range of foreign trading and economic relationships. Economic reform and steady growth of the domestic economy have also created more need for the setting up of new businesses and for conferences in the national capital. As Beijing entered into a more 'open' economy as well as becoming an 'open' political centre with more intensive contacts and interaction with the rest of China and the rest of the world, both the volume as well as the purpose of the temporary population have changed drastically. In 1966–70, survey results indicated that two-thirds of the temporary residents were visiting relatives and friends, for medical treatment or for maternity reasons. In 1985, people coming for employment or business in industries, con- struction, commerce and services accounted for almost half the temporary residents, while those visiting relatives and friends dropped to 16% (Li, 1987, 176–7). With the further opening of China, and Beijing taking on more activities in the tertiary and quaternary sectors to fit its roles as the administrative and cultural centre of the nation, the amount of daily flow of temporary population will further rise. This is because most of these temporary residents fulfil a need which cannot be substituted. It is estimated that by 2000, the daily number will amount to 1.3 million persons, whilst those in transit could be 0.5 million. The burden of this large additional population on the city's infrastructure and on daily supplies must be carefully estimated and duly included in city plans.

Spatial distribution

The spatial distribution of population in Beijing is very uneven, and so is its growth over the years since 1949. Of the total permanent population of 10.32 million in 1990, 2.42 million or 23.4% were concentrated in the four city districts of a limited territory of 87 sq km. There, the density of population reached 27 862 per sq km (Table 7.2). In the four suburban districts with a total area of 1283 sq km were 34.5% or 3.56 million of the city's population. Yet its density was only about one-tenth that of the city districts. About a third of the population, largely rural, was scattered on the lowland parts of the outer suburbs or the rural *xians* which cover a wide space of 12 240 sq km. Within the outer suburbs there were two special districts singled out because of being the location of important heavy industries, i.e. Mentougu and Fangshan. In these two districts there were about one million people, some 70% of which congregated around the industrial complex in Fangshan. The overall density of Beijing was low, at 614 persons per sq km in 1990. Despite the low figure, it represents almost a three-fold increase since 1935 and a 2.5 fold increase since 1949 (Table 7.2).

The spatial dynamics of population growth in the Beijing area have demonstrated two distinct periods. In 1949–84, Beijing added 5.31 million population, 50.3% of the increase in the suburban districts. There the total population had increased from about half a million to 3.23 million. Two of them became million cities at 1984, i.e. Chaoyang and Haidian. The city districts added 1 million. This represents a 68.8% increase of its 1949 population leading to a very high density in its small territory. The increase in the outer suburbs looks colossal compared to its original small population, yet it is only actually 320 000 persons. Compaction of the city districts and expansion of the suburban industrial, educational and research institutions had been the main forces behind population build-up in the suburbs, particularly Chaoyang and Haidian.

In 1984–90, Beijing as a whole experienced a 10% increase of population, less than a million. This second period saw the outer suburbs as the main area for population build-up, especially for Fangshan which shot up from 70 000 in 1984 to over 700 000 in 1990 because of the petrochemical complex. In fact 72.4% of the population increase of this period of the whole city was accommodated in the two outer-suburban districts. It perhaps marks a new trend of decentralization to the outer suburbs. On the other hand, the rural *xians* experienced a 4.9% decline in population, largely owing to out-migration into the more urbanized districts. A survey on migrants from the rural *xians* of the city and suburban districts in Beijing in 1982 indicated that females accounted for 90.6% of the flow, of which 50.5% concentrated in the age group of 20–24 and 47.3% in the age group of 25–29. The survey found that of the total rural–urban migrants as many as 48.4% moved because of marriage (Ji et al., 1984). The loss in the rural *xians* through marriage was quite obvious. Its impact would be greater if it were not for replacement by higher rural birth rates than the city average.

The centripetal tendency of the post-1949 population dynamics of Beijing has been explained in Chapter 5 as the lack of economic opportunities and socio-economic infrastructure of the outer suburban districts and the rural *xians* before the 1980s. Despite explicit planning designs, genuine decentralization had not been able to go beyond the suburban districts. Thus not only has the population increased, but also its unbalanced spatial distribution has aggravated the city's population problems.

Population problems

Control over overall size

PRC scholars basically view the population problem of Beijing as one of 'over-size'. They also note other problems such as the mismatch between the structures of population and the economy and between the former and the social infrastructure, as well as overconcentration of people within the city districts.

The 'over-size' issue has been well presented by Cao (1991) based on Chinese planning principles and standards. Cao maintains that within the extended 1026 sq km of planned urban areas of the city, there should be a reservation for green fields, particularly for vegetable farms and production units of non-staple food. In addition, there are to be rivers and green open space, water conservation areas, airports, radio stations and space for high-wattage corridors, as well as green buffers between various constellations of urban development. Thus only about 600 sq km of the planned urban areas may be used for urban construction. Of these 500 sq km are taken up by the central mass and the 10 peripheral constellations, while 100 sq km are scattered between fields and green buffers. Within the 1026 sq km in 1989 lived a 5.59 million permanent population of which 5.12 million were urban, about 81.2% of Beijing's total urban population. In recent years, population within the planned urban areas grew at about 100 000 per year, accounting for about 80% of Beijing's total growth in urban population. In 2020–30, Beijing's urban population may reach 10–11 million and an estimated 8–9 million would be living within the planned urban areas. Cao's worry is how this 'over-sized' population could be accommodated within current planning standards.

According to standards promulgated on 1 March 1991, per capita planned urban built-up area is graded into four categories. The highest rank standard is 105.1–120 sq m; Beijing belongs to this category as it is the national capital. The standard for the other three categories applies to lesser cities and ranges between 60 and 105 sq m. In 1981, within the limits of the planned urban areas of Beijing, the total urban built-up area was 346 sq km, or an average of 83 sq m per person. In the 1982 General Plan, it was planned to raise the standard to 110 sq m in 20 years' time with further reserves for longer-term railways, roads and green areas to reach the ultimate standard of 120 sq m per capita. Yet the population projection of the 1982 General Plan was too conservative. It estimated the urban population within the planned urban areas in 2000 at 4 million and thus reserved a total of 480 sq km of urban built-up space. In 1991, the population within the planned urban areas had already reached 5.2 million and the actual urban built-up area close to 500 sq km. Then, the per capita urban built-up area was around 90 sq m. That is to say, in 10 years there had been an improvement of about 10 sq m, yet it is still below the designated standard. Cao suggested that in the 20 years of 1991–2010 the per capita standard has to be raised from 90 to 110 sq m. To achieve that the planned urban areas would only be able to accommodate 5.5 million people. He insists on the planning prerogative of making 110 sq m the target for per capita urban built-up area within the 1026 sq km of the planned urban areas. In the longer-term future, i.e. by 2050, the ultimate standard of 120 sq m should be reached and the population of the planned urban area should henceforth decline to about 5 million. Population growth within this core city of Beijing should be decentralized to the outer suburbs.

Growth rate

It is basically within the consideration of size that other issues of population have been framed. Rapid natural growth, in its third upturn since 1949, has been constantly feared. The baby boom of the 1950s had been the culprit. The birth rate reached two peaks in 1982 (2.04%) and 1987 (1.73%). In the 1980s the average natural growth rate stayed at 0.6%, or an average yearly net increase of 97 000. However in the 1990s and beyond 2000, natural population growth will further decline owing to the combined effects of low births in the 1970s, the ageing of the population and successful implementation of the 'one-child policy'. Since 1992, the 'one child policy' has been officially relaxed. The ratio of two-children families may increase. Despite this, the overall natural growth rate in the 20 years to come is expected to decline. In the 1980s it was 1.9%, in the 1990s it would be 0.3–0.5% and in the first decade of the twenty-first century, 0.2–0.4%. In the coming decade, the expected natural net growth will total 600 000–700 000, and for the next decade 400 000–500 000. Net natural growth alone will still add a further 1–1.2 million to the city in the coming 20 years.

Migration has seen a net addition of 504 000 in the 1980s. In the 1990s the expected total will also be in the region of half a million or around 45 000–50 000 a year. In 2001–2010, the rate of migration increase is expected to be 40 000–50 000 a year, equivalent to the forecasted natural growth. For migration additions to be contained within the projected figures, stringent in-migration measures have to be taken and out-migration has to be encouraged. At present, there are still plenty of loopholes in migration control which raise doubts about the possibility of strict control over migration. Zhang and Liu (1991) listed six such problems:

1. There are too many government offices with authority to approve in-migrants. The permanent ones numbered 94 and there are hundreds of *ad hoc* committees. Thus the authority on migration control is highly diffused.
2. Beijing does not have an annual migration plan to conform with its economic and physical plans.
3. There is no consistent and coordinated policy package. Most measures are *ad hoc*, unscientific and not devised within a comprehensive view.
4. Data and the information system of the control mechanisms have not been well developed. Statistics of the various approval and control offices are incomplete and not of consistent methodology or standards.
5. Control measures are all administrative in nature without resort to economic or other measures and incentives.
6. There is not yet a complete set of legislation to support existing measures. As a consequence, some measures lack the might of legal enforcement and others lack supervision by law.

Age structure

The age composition of Beijing's population shows marked shifts towards an increasing imbalance between the young and the old and an increasing working population as a result of past decades of migration and the last decade of birth control measures. The young age group (0–14) as a percentage of the total population dropped from 48.7 to 20.8% in 1964–90, while the old (over 65) had increased from 4.1–7.0%. The drastic decline of the young signified depressed demand for primary education which must change its goal to one of upgrading quality. The education system must also divert its resources to post-secondary and vocational activities. The ageing problem (according to international standard when the old age group reached beyond 7%) will increase as the twentieth century comes to a close. Facilities of medical and social welfare for the aged have to be planned ahead to meet the expected new demands. The enlarging bulk of the working population will continue to be an important stress on Beijing's employment situation until 2000. The problem has been partly caused by non-demographic reasons, including insufficient places at the secondary and post-secondary levels of education. Many young people had been forced to join the workforce while still at school age. In addition, because of economic and other reasons (housing and other fringe benefits) many employees keep on working beyond the official retirement age (60 for men and 55 for women), aggravating the unemployment situation.

The last main problem has been one of spatial imbalance in population distribution leading to overconcentration and congestion of the inner city, i.e. the city districts, and relative underdevelopment of the suburban districts and the satellite towns. These have been discussed in some detail in previous sections and Chapter 5.

Approaches to the population problems

The Chinese government's response to population issues is largely based on the point of view that the size and structure of a city's population have to be dictated by the nature, i.e. the role and function, of the city. The latter decides the size of the city and forms the principal problem in the planning of the city (Zhang and An 1984, 3; Sun and Zhang, 1991, 9).

The CCP and State Council's 'Reply on the General Plan of Beijing Municipality' in July 1983 stated clearly that the city's plan and its development plans for all economic and non-economic activities must conform with Beijing's role as the nation's political and cultural centre. According to such a role, population growth must be strictly controlled. Indeed, control of the total city population size as an approach to Beijing's population had a very early start when the Russian experts presented their report on issues of Beijing's urban planning in 1953:

> The socialist system aims to avoid over-concentration of population in big cities . . . Beijing has no major industries, but as a national capital, it should not only be a cultural, science and art centre, but also at the same time a city of big industries . . . At present Beijing's proletariat made up only 4% of the population, while in Moscow it is 25% . . . Based on these considerations it could be expected that Beijing's population will increase, not just by natural growth alone, but also through migration from the rest of the country. In 15–20 years' time, its population may double. (*Beijing Construction History*, 1987, 109–10)

The Soviet experts also laid down the standards for economic and physical planning based on the relationship between population and the function of the city. They divided the urban population into two according to their job nature: basic population and service population (those providing support to the former). The basic population includes those employed in government bureaucracies, industrial workers, professionals and those working and studying in high-level educational institutes and research units. The service population are the self-employed, employees of the municipality, internal security people, shopkeepers, traders and school teachers, etc. The ideal ratio of the two populations is 1:1. It is ruled that of the total population, ideally half will be working population. For the 1.3 million working population of Beijing at the time, accordingly the basic population should be composed of the following:

Industrial workers and cadres	400 000
Central government employees	150 000
Students	100 000
Total	650 000

To accommodate 400 000 to be employed in industries, and 100 000 service population that are to be attached to them, would require a total of 70 sq km of built-up land according to the standards that 1000 industrial workers are to occupy 7 hectares of factory land, 2 hectares per 1000 service workers and 100 sq m of residential land per person (*Beijing's Construction History*, 1987, 109–12). The Soviet experts' planning strategy thus has its source in the relationship between population and role of the city, and works down to details of land allocation on the basis of the size of varying categories of the working population and an assumed size of the dependent population.

The report of the National Planning Commission in 1954 faithfully adopted the Soviet advice in its report to the Beijing municipality regarding planning for the city, and worked out the projected size of the population for the various subcategories of basic and service populations and their accompanying land requirements (*Beijing Construction History*, 1987, 182–4). The General Plan of 1958 follows such a strand of thought and anticipates that its existing population of 6.3 million will increase to 10 million in future, as the plan envisages that 'we need also to turn it [Beijing] rapidly into a modern industrial base and a science and technology centre' (ibid., 206). This expansionist note was changed in the 1982 General Plan which follows the new consensus that the capital's main role should not be one of a major industrial centre but of the nation's political and cultural centre. For the first time in the series of general and draft general plans, it emphasized strict measures to limit the size of the city to a total of 10 million by the year 2000 (ibid., 221). This view was reiterated by the two 1983 documents which say: 'Hence Beijing's population should not exceed 10 million at any time,' and 'Strict control over migration to steadfastly control Beijing's population to within 10 million by 2000' (ibid., 314, 316).

Thus a general formula of: nature of the city → population → land requirement can be perceived in the planning logic for the Chinese city. Once the nature of the city has been fixed, then the key to planning is very much the control of the city's population.

In practice tripartite control measures have been applied, i.e. birth control, migration control and spatial regulation. Birth control has been subject to the cycle of births as well as a wavering policy. Stringent birth control measures have been applied only since the late 1970s which culminated in the 'one-child policy'. The birth rate for the whole city dropped to 1.36% in 1990 while for the city district it went down to 0.95%. 'One-child' families had reached 90% of the households for the city and suburban districts and 70% of the rural households in the outer suburbs in 1985. It is expected that by 2000, the respective percentages would be further raised to 95% and 80%, producing a negative natural growth of −0.19% or almost zero growth. Thus birth control has been the most successful of the control measures.

In controlling migration, some suggested two long-term targets, i.e. (1) an annual net migration addition of 27 000 until 2000; (2) a much lower annual rate of 10 000 persons (Beijing Municipality, 1981, 41). Yet these targets have been regarded as too low. In fact as previously explained, these targets have never been officially accepted, and the flow of migrants in the 1980s and those expected for the 1990s will very much exceed these low figures. Migration control has to address not only the quantitative aspects in maintaining an accepted population quantum at any given date, but to pay heed to three considerations. First, there should be due allowance to ensure inflow of young cadres to replace and fortify the central administrative machinery which Beijing alone is unable to satisfy. Secondly, the tradition of 'settlement' of professionals in Beijing as a consequence of net gains in migration, i.e. a large surplus of in-migrants over out-migrants, is a wasteful use of resources, particularly when they are skilled and education-intensive people. It turns Beijing into a 'closed system' in terms of flow of talents. New employment policies have to be devised to allow free flow of professionals and to turn it into an open system. Thirdly, most of the migrants end up in the city districts, and recently in the suburban districts, aggravating imbalances in population distribution.

The latest projections indicated that migration for the coming two decades will breach the low average figures for 1949–79 of less than 30 000 per annum. The revised figures allow for the needs of Beijing to perform its role as the political and cultural capital of an opening China with a fast pace of economic development. As the growth of population in 1979–88 had already breached the long-held maximum of 10 million, control over the total population spectrum, its structure for meeting the functional needs of the capital, and the planning goal of an improved urban living environment, demands much stronger and better co-ordinated measures. At present a number of measures have been under consideration by the authority.

Scientific migration control

This measure would fix the ideal size of population based on the nature of the city and projections from past experience, as has been reported previously for the years of 2000 and 2010. On this basis, annual in-migration targets will be set both for quantity and quality screening purposes. To implement this a joint Population Control Committee composed of representatives of the Central Committee of CCP, the State Council, the PLA and the Beijing Municipality has to be set up to take charge of the planning and coordinating roles. Annual quotas will then be discharged to lower-level authorities through these four major offices and a system of population registration cards is to be uniformly administered. Annual student intake from outside Beijing will be regarded as temporary population. If they are retained or employed in the Beijing area after graduation, they will be entered into the relevant quotas. In addition, an economic control measure will apply to all quota in-migrants, viz. the relevant units that use the quota have to pay an urban development tax on a per in-migrant basis.

Regional control over migrants

At present 60% of the population, and 60–70% of industrial output value, are concentrated in 6% of the whole city, i.e. in its planned urban areas. Green space, including the vegetable farms, water conservation areas and numerous rivers and lakes that serve as the ecological balance media of the city, has been under threat. In comparison, the vast area of 6000 sq km of flat land in the outer suburbs is still relatively sparsely populated. The municipal government has recently proclaimed 22 incentives for satellite town development in this area. Yet lack of infrastructure, communication and transport links with the urban areas are plagued by small-scale and uneconomic development, and most of the satellite towns remain unattractive for intra-urban migrants as well as being reception areas for in-migrants from outside Beijing. New measures suggested combine continued stringent restriction on development within the planned urban areas through plot ratio and building intensity controls, as well as strict vetting on development projects. There should be no further new factories, colleges or research units set up in the area. New residential developments may be approved only if they combine with inner city renewal schemes. The development of the 14 largest satellites would be bolstered with additional capital investment and new transport links with the urban areas, including rail and road links. Economic incentives have to be devised to attract relocation of enterprises into these centres as well as to attract migrants. *Xian* centres and market towns serve as important interception points for the flow of the outer suburban rural population into the planned urban areas. Their development will help to ease population pressure on the planned urban areas, while at the same time instilling growth in the rural *xians* by providing them with improved services and by acting as economic, political and cultural centres.

In the spatial approach to the population issue, another suggestion is to develop a 'secondary capital'. Three locations, i.e. Shunyi-Changping, Chunzhou and Langfang, have been suggested as possible candidates for developing into a 'secondary capital' of 800 000 to 1 million population. It could decentralize some of the functions of Beijing as the national capital and hence help reduce its population pressures.

Continual observance of the 'one-child policy' and control of the temporary population

Steadfast adherence to family planning and the 'one-child policy', measures to encourage out-migration at retirement and household moves in outward-bound job re-allocation, can help to hold down the total growth of population.

The burden on Beijing of a daily temporary population of over 1.3 million can be easily perceived. It places an extra demand on all sorts of urban facilities and food supplies as well as social and medical services. Until now there have been few suggestions as to how this transient population could be effectively contained. There has been talk about using economic measures such as tax, price and wages, yet there is a lack of concrete and viable proposals. As Beijing grows economically, further opens up for international business and relaxes its control over movement of people into it for business transactions and for tours, the problem is likely to aggravate.

Conclusion: population control in the Chinese city

Following the Soviet model, the PRC de-emphasized concentration of people and industries in major cities. Thus most of the big cities along the Chinese coast have grown very little in the post-1949 years in comparison with small and medium-sized cities. In fact, urbanization as a whole in the PRC has been straitjacketed by Maoist ideology on top of the socialist distaste for big cities. The overall pace of urbanization in China in the period is a meagre annual 2.75%, compared to the norm of 4% in the Third World. In spite of this national picture, Beijing as the new national capital has grown at a much faster rate within the ranks of big cities in the PRC. Even Soviet experts sent to advise China on the planning of the city in the early 1950s had to defer to other socialist principles which conflict with the rule on containment of city size: i.e. the national capital had to be a centre of big industries with a large proletariat besides being the political, administrative and cultural centre of the new socialist regime. To fulfil such roles, the population of Beijing underwent drastic quantitative increases and qualitative transformation, largely through massive influx. This gave rise to Beijing's high population growth rates in the 1950s, which in terms of proportionate increase may be compared to the general situation in Third World capitals after World War II. Yet Beijing's population growth, even in this period, demonstrates a clear link between the nature of the city and the size of its population. This is to say that population had been drawn into the city by positive economic demand, a reflection of the functions of the city destined by its administrative rank as well as the socialist goal of what a city should be. This is very different from the majority of cases in national capital growth in the Third World that are driven largely by rural push.

The first decade of population growth in Beijing obviously has significant ramifications for its population dynamics in later decades. It is especially the case that once Beijing had accommodated a large population influx in the 1950s, it very soon stepped into line with the overall trend of big city behaviour within the PRC. In general, its population growth trend had been stable and low in rate, though not uninteresting. It was marked by political events caused by Maoist ideology in the 1960s and early 1970s, rather than by economic factors or normal urban functional developments. As the national capital, Beijing did observe a traditional role in providing the rest of the nation with an example in implementing the leading ideology and its enshrined policies.

In a socialist state adopting central planning, population as a factor of labour supply as well as a consumer of goods and services obviously occupies a central location in economic and physical planning. Manipulation of migration and control of natural growth have been consistently applied in Beijing even after the gradual replacement of central planning by a new system of markets after 1978. The concern of the government and planners that a 'cap' should be put on population growth is a consistent feature in all the general plans from 1953 to 1992. The composition of that population and the methods to achieve it, as well as the underlying rationale, have however changed much since 1949. Before 1978, emphasis on the productive role of Beijing led to growth largely in the form of big industries, hence a bias in the employment structure of its population as revealed in Chapter 6. Lax control over natural growth for most of the pre-1978 years resulted in 1–3% annual natural growth rates, only to be balanced out by migration (in the 1960s and 1970s). The slow growth in the post-1978 period, which generally represents a time of fast economic development and liberalization of the bureaucracy, fortunately results from a successful birth control programme, in spite of the coming of a potential baby boom, and reasonable control over in-migration.

Post-liberalization (1978) Beijing still maintains, or puts more effort into controlling, its population compared to the period before. Very clearly, the underlying rationale has now moved to one of upgrading the population quality as well as a structural transformation of the economy and better living environment for the city's population. Some of these will be discussed in the following chapters on housing, transport and urban redevelopment.

Population growth in Beijing since 1949 thus departs markedly from experiences of other Third World national capitals. It can be distinguished from other Chinese cities as well, owing primarily to its status as the national capital.

8

Urban housing and housing reforms

Socialist approach to urban housing

Soviet experience

Socialist town planning intends to forge a new society. Bater (1980, 22) pinpointed this by the two overriding principles of (*a*) bridging the gap between proletariat and peasantry relationships; and (*b*) ensuring equality in the provision of items of collective consumption. To achieve these objectives in most Soviet and East European cities, a two-pronged policy has been followed: (1) the designing of urban expansion to provide jobs in proximity to, and services within, residential areas; and (2) the restructuring of inherited, pre-socialist areas by investing them with new socialist functions, new meaning and symbolism (Hamilton and Burnett, 1979, 265).

Thus providing each person with an equitable share of items of personal and collective consumption is a fundamental tenet of socialist town planning. This is most clearly demonstrated in the 10 principles embodied in the 1935 Moscow plan which makes a sharp distinction from capitalist town planning and sets a model for city plans in other socialist countries. In Chapter 4, we have listed these principles, four of which directly relate to urban housing. They set directions for urban housing development in the socialist city, and pinpoint its nature and the methods that could be utilized. These four principles are: (1) state control of housing, (2) planned development of residential areas, (3) spatial equality in the distribution of items of collective consumption, and (4) limited journey to work.

With the demise of private enterprise, the provision of all items of collective consumption would become the responsibility of planners. So too would the task of ensuring equality in their distribution within the city. The history of the USSR shows the gradual evolution of a system of urban housing management, provision and planning norms for the effective discharge of these planning objectives. Housing not only formed the basic collective and private consumption of urbanites, the integration into residential areas of other basic consumption and service items at designated planning standard makes it a key mechanism for achieving the socialist goals of both decent housing for the working class and equity in the allocation of consumptive items. Socialist neighbourhoods, favoured for organizing a more collective way of life, are also claimed to be the catalyst for real change in social behaviour (Hamilton and Burnett, 1979, 265). Urban real estates in Russia were municipalized in 1918. The basis for assigning urban housing was formally established in 1922 and the minimum sanitary allocation was 9 sq m of living space per person (i.e. living and dining rooms, bedrooms, excluding kitchen, bathroom and corridors). As the average living space per inhabitant at the time was about 4 sq m, the 9 sq m norm soon became the maximum assignable. From 1918 to 1950 about 350 million sq m of housing were built by the state or with state assistance throughout the country. However, due to rapid urbanization, urban housing standards dropped to less than 4 sq m per person in 1950. The need to economize on space produced apartment blocks with communal use of facilities. Frequently more than one family shared a 3- to 4-bedroom unit, and apartment designs often precluded single-family occupance.

Within this overall picture there was differentiation of standards at the micro level. Units for elites were above the 9 sq m limit and roughly two to two and a half times better than those for the average worker. The industrialization of housing construction in the 1950s and 1960s had resulted in obvious improvements in urban housing standards. In 1960–75 two-thirds of the population were rehoused and 1.55 billion sq m of new housing were built. In 1977, the per capita living space for the whole country improved to 8 sq m. For the 27 major cities, one exceeded the national average, three were on a par with it, while Moscow, the capital and largest city, attained the highest level of 10.3 sq m. In that year the state sector accounted for about 70% of the total housing stock of about 2 billion sq m, of which two-thirds were controlled by various ministries, departments and state enter-prises, as were three-fifths of state funds for housing construction. The continual 'departmentalist' approach to housing development is a consequence of central planning and the departments' reluctance to relinquish control over housing as a factor for attracting labour. The ill effects of such an approach are several: (1) shortfall of ancillary facilities as there were unlikely to be coordinated plans and funds to pair up with local housing projects; (2) spatial integration of housing projects was difficult to achieve; and (3) national goals of equity were less easy to achieve when funds were expended to meet ministerial objectives and needs (Bater, 1980, 99–107).

Cooperative and private housing accounted for a minor proportion of urban housing. The former was mostly for higher-level cadres with higher incomes, whereas the latter was mostly found in the inner parts of the big city or in smaller urban settlements.

As discussed before, urban housing is spatially organized with the provision of basic daily collective and personal consumption of goods and services. In the years after World War II, the *mikrorayon* emerged as the basic building block in Soviet town planning. At present about half the urban population in the former USSR live in *mikrorayons* which are comprised of 5–8 living complexes of 1000–1500 residents each. A *mikrorayon* has between 8000 and 12 000 residents with a set list of appropriate norms of shopping, educational, health and social service units to go with it. It provides a service radius of 50–100 m. Four to five *mikrorayons* make up a residential complex of 32 000– 60 000 people with a serving radius of 300–400 m. It has been noted that 'By so constructing the housing and consumer and cultural-services components of the urban system waste is minimised, efficiency maximised . . . If by social justice in housing we mean the equitable allocation of available living space it may be fairly said that the situation in the Soviet Union is far better than in most countries' (Bater, 1980, 109–11).

The space standard was greatly improved in the 1980s. The national housing survey of 1988 showed a total stock of 4.4 billion sq m, 15.5 sq m per capita, and a per capita living area of 10.5 sq m. The average in Moscow was a much higher 17 sq m. Despite such marked improve- ments, state control and state funding remained. In Moscow 70% of the residents lived in state housing and 20% in housing constructed by their work unit. The low rent policy was also maintained. The average rent was equivalent to 3% of average household income or 17 roubles (Feng and Zhou, 1990). Since 1991 the former USSR has moved away from the socialist system. In urban housing, major new trends are the expansion of cooperative housing and sales of state-owned flats.

PRC adaptation

The PRC government had inherited two very different situations in 1949: (1) a socialist ideology and commitment to socialist principles; and

(2) a semi-colonial China with backward development in economy and in urban infrastructure. Within urban housing, the Chinese launched an unprecedented large-scale government effort in housing construction and, within a matter of about a decade, put private housing under rigid official control so that it was in line with the low-rent policy of the public sector in spite of remaining private in ownership status. The Soviet strategy in integrating housing with provision of collective and personal consumption, down to the finer planning concepts of the *mikrorayon*, was adopted as well, with obvious modifications to suit China's conditions.

As early as the 1953 Draft General Plan, the overriding socialist principle for the planning of the national capital was stated in the form of six planning goals, one of which pledged to turn Beijing into a 'socialist city of collective living'. The municipality's all-out effort in housing construction and provision was certainly a way of achieving this goal. The plan stipulated one planning rule (out of eight) which explicitly introduced a modified Soviet residential area planning concept into Beijing: the residential areas were to be planned in the form of 'big neighbourhoods' of 9–15 hectares. To achieve savings in capital and space, the housing blocks were to have 4–5 storeys, while those along the edges of public squares may be 7–8 storeys or even higher. The neighbourhoods are to be centrally planned and designed. Their construction has to be comprehensive, with cultural and social welfare facilities, green areas and play areas, such that the neighbourhood will have sufficient sunshine and fresh air.

In the Draft Plan of 1957 there was more explicit adoption of Soviet principles in residential planning. It stressed the need to locate housing and workplaces in close proximity to cut down people's commuting time and the volume of intra-urban traffic. Public facilities were to be evenly spread and integrated with residential uses, based on the foundation of 'small districts' of 30–60 hectares, with a population of 10–20 000 people. These basic units replaced the former 'big neighbourhoods' and were closed to through traffic. Within a 'small district' were to be located middle and primary schools, infant institutes, shops and public services.

However, Chinese politics had influenced the theory and practice of urban housing in Beijing, especially in the long period of 1958–78. The Great Leap Forward that started in 1958 caused some revision of the city's plan. In the organization of residential areas, the principle of People's Commune was raised. In the planning of new residential areas facilities for collective living had to be provided. Starting from 1964, the planning profession of Beijing was criticized for being too capitalist, their planning standards were too high, and Beijing's urban development pace was too rushed. In the full swing of the Cultural Revolution, with the closing down of the planning office, residential planning came to a standstill. For five to six years, roughly until 1972, new urban housing construction was without planning and control. Individual enterprises were encouraged to fill whatever gap existed in the new rule of 'driving pins into any visible gaps', and low standards were equally encouraged as a virtue.

Another problem of theory and practice is not dissimilar to the situation in the USSR in the 1950s and 1960s. Development priority was given to productive activities, particularly in the development of industries which squeezed investment funds for housing to a minimum, leading to the imbalance of 'productive' and 'consumptive' investments, the so-called adverse 'bone' and 'flesh' relationship. In 1953–57, floor space constructed for productive uses and floor space for living and residence uses were more or less in balance, i.e. at a ratio of 1:1.12. In 1958–76, the ratio dropped to 1:0.9. In the Great Leap Forward years, it bottomed at 1:0.64. The imbalance started to be addressed only after the Cultural Revolution, particularly after 1978. In 1979–81, the ratio was at its post-1949 peak of 1:2.32, i.e. 70% of all construction was for living and residence use. Within the so-called living and residence use, the ratio of the two had also been raised in favour of socialization of household activities as women have been more and more employed since 1949 under the new socialist regime. The ratio at 1949 was 1:0.17 and it became 1:0.22 in 1981.

Planning of residential areas and the provision of urban housing are indeed part of the socialist control system for organizing the urban masses. It was felt by the 1982 General Plan that the 'small districts' failed to give the community a real community sense, except for providing residents the convenience of staple food and non-staple food stores. Other facilities such as middle and primary schools, post office, banks and housing management offices all have varying service radii. Very often these are not even provided for, as for quite some time housing construction had been decentralized to local government units or even state enterprises and municipal government had had insufficient funds to match up such housing construction with infrastructure and social facilities. The grassroots political and administrative organization, the residents committees, serve 400–800 households, and the upper-level street committees are also not in congruence with the 'small districts' in the territory. Thus the new plan requested a redefinition of the basic residential planning unit and decided to enlarge it to the 'residential districts' of 30–40 000 people with a total site of 60–100 hectares each. The planning of these new districts should take into consideration integration of basic community

Table 8.1 Examples of residential districts built after 1950

	Site (hectares)	Population	Average building height (floors)	Gross population (persons/ hectare)	Planning year
Small districts:					
Sanlitun	18.1	7 215	4.7	400	1957
Fujialou	25.3	11 730	4.4	464	1957
Hepingli	18.5	7 260	4.1	392	1959
Chui Yang Liu	20.9	7 320	4.2	351	1962
Longtan	10.3	6 800	5.0	661	1965
Xinyuenli	12.6	6 027	5.0	479	1966
Tongihu	39.8	33 800	6.7	849	1976
Wenweiyuen	11.0	7 653	5.2	697	1978
Zuo Zi Zhuang	43.9	31 988	8.2	729	1979
Ninhuahe	33.0	21 615	8.8	655	1981
Huangzhongnan	12.9	11 745	9.9	907	1981
Residential districts:					
Wuluju	85.8	66 000	46%*	769	1982
Fangzhuang	117.9	100 000	89%*	848	1984

* % of high-rise buildings (over 8 storeys) in all residential buildings.
Source: Compiled from: *Beijing City Construction Since Liberation*, 1985, 176–181.

and urban facilities as well as the boundaries of the grassroots administrative organs, i.e. to conform with the jurisdiction of the street committee. Within the residential district, 'small districts' still exist for detailed planning for a 'quiet and convenient' living environment. Though this is a belated emphasis, it does reflect the original planning goal of making use of urban housing and planning of residential areas as a means to organize the urban masses politically and for the disbursement of collective and personal consumption on socialist equity principles. Selected examples of 'small districts' and 'residential districts' planned and constructed in 1957–84 have been shown in Table 8.1.

As in the USSR, the PRC followed a low-rent policy to ensure that urban housing was affordable to all, and put a strict control over private housing so that their rental charges fell in line with the general low-rent situation. The latter was achieved in Beijing in 1958 when, as a national policy, the CCP decreed that renting of all private property should be the prerogative of the government. It hence effectively 'socialized' the private property rental market. The standards for rentals of both public and private properties changed a few times before 1958 and lacked a degree of uniformity. In 1958 the municipality, following the new national decree, promulgated the 'Standards for Public Housing Under Civil Use'. For residential housing, the average monthly rental was set at 27 cents per sq m, while the average for one-storey structures was 22 cents. Compared to the average monthly income of a worker household of Yn70, occupying an average flat of 30 sq m, the rental amounted to 9–11.5% of household income. In 1966, the rental was further revised downwards to 24 cents per sq m on average and 21 cents for one-storey structures. The State Council maintained even lower rentals for staff of the central government, as decreed in 1955. For them the average rental was 14 cents and for a one-storey structure 10 cents. Despite their higher average income and better housing standards in terms of size of the flat, facilities and environment, central government officials enjoyed a lower rent comparable to the 3% income level set up by the USSR. Since 1979, Beijing's rental policy was unified at 13.6 cents per sq m and 12.2 cents for one-storey structures. When the average household income of a city worker was around Yn100, the rental level was scaled down to 3.6–4% of average income. The standards for rentals of private property followed closely those for publicly owned housing. The property owner received a monthly payment of 20–40% of the monthly rental, charged according to his contract with the government (*Beijing City Construction Since Liberation*, 1985, 188–9).

Details of the spatial and locational aspects of Beijing's urban housing development after 1949 will be separately presented later. It is nevertheless clear that whilst the Soviet approach has largely been followed, the amount of urban housing provision in the PRC, its standards, as well as the level of rental charged and the integrated social, educational and cultural facilities fell behind standards set by the Soviet planners for the USSR. This underlines the much lower level of economic development of the PRC and the much worse urban housing situation faced by a less capable government in terms of the resources and productivity of its construction industry. Political ups and downs and their ideological implications also had obvious effects on all these aspects of urban housing in Beijing. Some form of privileged class in the provision of urban housing is also noted in Beijing, as is the generally accepted situation in the USSR.

The reality: development of urban housing in Beijing

In this section we turn to examine in more detail actual practice in urban housing provision in Beijing, through a historical description of major events since 1949.

The total housing stock in Beijing in 1949 was 20.5 million sq m of which 13.5 million sq m were domestic housing. Before 1949, most of the housing in Beijing was built in the Ming and Qing Dynasties, largely of the 'square courtyard' type of one-storey structures. Houses that rose above one-storey formed only 17% of all structures and were mainly 2–3 storeys high. A survey of the housing situation at 1949 revealed 280 000 publicly owned and 920 000 privately owned structures. Half of all properties were rented out. Of the 410 000 households in the city, 330 000 rented their accommodation, and only 25 000 households lived in their own properties. The dilapidated conditions of most old properties were revealed in a later survey in 1950. Dangerous housing (defined as 'less than 25% new') numbered 740 000 structures, with 10.7 million sq m floor area, or 61% of housing inside the city districts.

Housing development since 1949 may be described in the following four stages:

Adapting the old situation (1949–57)

Lack of experience, as well as the constraints of insufficient capital and building capability in meeting an urgent demand, combined to mean that most of the new residential houses constructed in the period were wood and brick one-storey structures. They provided urgently needed living space without accompanying living facilities and supporting services. The layout is barrack like. Minimum provision of non-staple food items and groceries is found on the side of the main street. The official line at the time was to depress the unit cost for non-productive construction. Even worse was that at some point in the period, the principle of 'combining short and long-term needs with emphasis on the long-term need' was followed, leading to a situation of 'rational design, irrational use', i.e. some housing was designed with large flats of 77 sq m and provided with self-contained facilities such as toilet and kitchen, but each of these was allocated to two or more households to share, a situation similar to that in Moscow in the 1950s.

Within the period, a total of 9.16 million sq m of domestic housing were built (Table 8.2), most of it in 1953–57, located at the fringe of the city districts and the suburban districts, between the Second and Third Ring roads (see Figure 8.1). In the earlier years of 1949–52 one-storey structures predominated. After 1953, economy on land dictated the building of 3–4-storey structures. The construction was mainly carried out, planned and managed by various departments, bureaus and ministries. Coordinated effort and a unified approach were not yet developed. Spatially, an obvious concentration of new housing in the

209

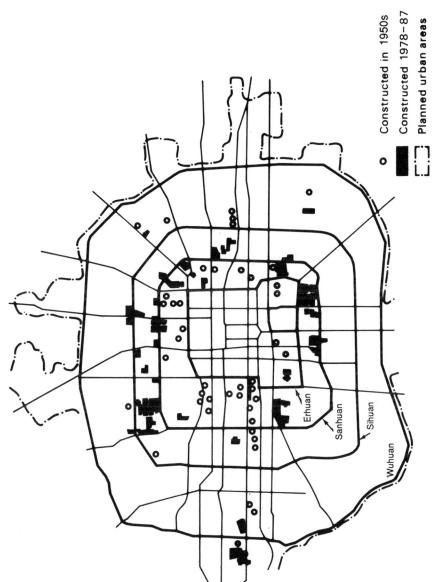

Figure 8.1 Distribution of public housing constructed after 1949. Source: Lu, 1989

o Constructed in 1950s

■ Constructed 1978–87

⌐⌐ Planned urban areas

western suburb underlined the demands of the rapidly growing central administrative machinery in that part of the city.

Socialist transformation (1958–65)

In 1957 the Soviet *mikrorayon* was adapted in the form of 'small districts' in which the central park and community facilities are placed in the middle of the area in a closed system. The first of those is the Sunset Lane small district which was planned in 1957. It has a site area of 15.3 hectares and was planned to accommodate 5087 persons. Building structures vary between three and four storeys, with a gross density of 332 persons/hectare. Other examples are shown in Table 8.1. The building height gradually increased to 4–5 storeys and larger sites and coordinated development fashioned after the Soviet model became the norm at the end of the 1950s. Coordinated approach involved the so-called 'Five-Unity', i.e. unified action in investment, land resumption, planning, construction and management. Residences built under the new approach exceeded 50% of the total construction area completed by the end of the decade. In addition, there were more variations in design and construction materials. Flats were also fully equipped with heating, toilet, bath and kitchen. Attention towards supporting facilities such as drainage, electricity and water supply, as well as detailed layout of the building to maximize sunlight, marked the new developments from the previous period.

The period also witnessed the set up of the system of 'lead-architect responsibility'. He was responsible for planning and implementing the construction of the small district based on the 'six maps', i.e. map of current situation, general layout plan, functional zone plan, comprehensive layout plan of over- and underground pipes, green plan and vertical design plan. The municipal government restructured the building materials industry of the city, cutting down the number of pre-fabricated parts and materials to attain economies of scale. The low-rent policy and rigid control over rentals of private properties started to be enforced within the period.

Despite the increased ability of the construction industry and a much more streamlined system of housing project planning and construction, the emphasis on productive construction and investment prevailing at the time gave residential housing construction a lower priority. In the eight years, only 8 million sq m were completed, an annual rate of about 1 million, lower than 1953–57. In the latter five years when China was hit by three years of natural calamities and two years of retrenchment, the annual construction rate was much lower (Table 8.2).

Table 8.2 Types of building completed in 1949–83 (10 000 sq m)

	Total		1949–52		1953–57		1958–60		1961–65		1966–76		1977–83		1979–83	
	34-year total	Annual average	Total	Annual average	Total	Annual average	Total	Annual average	Total	Annual average	Total	Annual average	Total	Annual average	Total	Annual average
Grand total	10 298.6	302.9	385.0	128.3	1 744.3	348.9	1 142.0	380.7	1 056.4	211.3	1 811.0	164.6	4 159.9	594.3	3 416.9	683.3
Industry	1 643.6	48.3	29.0	9.7	137.3	27.5	299.0	99.7	182.8	36.6	443.1	40.3	552.4	78.9	398.5	79.7
Warehouses	509.4	15.0	5.7	1.9	69.4	13.9	55.5	18.5	74.1	14.8	127.8	11.6	176.9	25.3	132.7	26.5
Offices	607.9	17.9	90.4	30.1	223.7	44.7	78.0	26.0	42.3	8.5	61.4	5.6	112.1	16.0	78.3	15.7
Residences	4 881.2	143.6	156.9	52.3	759.4	151.9	363.1	121.0	441.2	88.2	690.2	62.7	2 740.4	391.5	2 142.2	128.0
Education	709.4	20.9	54.1	18.0	208.2	41.6	91.9	30.6	102.4	20.5	122.9	11.2	129.9	18.6	108.6	21.7
Research	158.3	4.7					18.1	6.0	53.1	10.6	25.9	2.4	61.2	8.7	51.8	10.1
Medical	188.6	5.55	16.7	5.6	52.4	10.5	21.3	7.1	14.0	2.8	38.9	3.5	45.3	6.5	34.7	6.9
Commercial	185.4	5.4	10.6	3.5	43.8	8.8	4.5	1.5	4.7	0.9	32.4	2.9	89.4	12.8	62.5	12.5
Cultural and recreational	41.6	1.2	2.5	0.8	8.8	1.8	17.6	5.9	3.3	0.7	3.2	0.3	6.2	0.9	5.3	1.1
Theatres and cinemas	16.2	0.5	0.8	0.3	5.1	1.0	2.6	0.9	0.5	0.1	1.5	0.1	5.7	0.8	4.1	0.8
Nurseries	55.7	1.6	2.8	0.9	11.7	2.3	6.1	2.0	3.2	0.6	7.3	0.7	24.6	3.5	20.5	4.1
Hotels	119.6	3.5	3.5	1.2	34.7	6.9	21.4	7.1	6.7	1.3	21.1	1.9	32.2	4.6	26.0	5.2

Stagnation (1966–76)

The 10-year Cultural Revolution brought tremendous disruption to city planning in Beijing. Planners and other professionals and cadres were sent down to the countryside for rustication in great numbers. Beijing's town plan and its enforcement office were abandoned. At the same time large numbers of young college and middle-school graduates were sent down to the countryside and the rest of rural China in the 'Shang Shan Xia Xiang' movement. The urban population growth pressure relaxed significantly. In fact for one or two years (see Chapter 7) Beijing even lost population absolutely, to the extent that Dwyer, albeit wrongly, claimed that 'from the mid-1960s onwards, the solution of urban housing and other infrastructural problems was sought not so much through investment and construction but rather through the attempted expulsion of large numbers of urban dwellers, particularly young people, and their absorption into the countryside' (1986, 484). What was correctly interpreted by Western scholars was the highly publicized 'red versus expert' debate, which came down heavily on the side of being ideologically correct rather than technically expert. Planners and cadres in economic construction were penalized or intimidated into general inaction if not sent down for rustication. During the same time, because of the ideological bias towards the rural areas, little investment in urban housing took place (see Table 8.2). The average annual housing completed in Beijing hit the lowest record of 627 000 sq m in its post-1949 history, being only 41% of the highest level of 1953–57. In the 11 years only 6.9 million sq m were completed, virtually equivalent to the total amount of housing completed in a single year in 1991 (for residential use it was about 4.6 million sq m). General stagnation in urban housing construction may also be sustained by the fact that in the First Five Year Plan period, investment for housing took about 9% of all funds for capital construction, and it was halved in 1966–76 (Dwyer, 1986, 485).

The concept of 'small district' was effectively shelved and housing construction followed the advice of 'driving a pin into any visible gaps' without regard to urban plans, utility lines or their reservation space. In addition, the drive towards economy led to much worse quality housing than that constructed in the early 1950s. The average household construction area dropped to 31.5 sq m and the structure is described as 'narrow, small, low and thin'. More effort on housing construction was seen only after 1973 as the heat of the Cultural Revolution petered out and there was a rise in the urban population.

New development (post-1977)

Neglect of people's livelihood was realized and debated as a significant national political and planning issue since 1975. Starting from 1976, planning activity of the municipality gradually resumed and large-scale housing projects, e.g. Tongihu, were launched in 1976. Yet the real turning point was 1978. With a new leadership and a new governing philosophy, Beijing, like the whole country, was thrown into widespread construction work to redress the long neglect of the years since 1966. The annual construction activity, measured in total floor space completed, averaged 5.94 million sq m in 1977–83, and was further increased to 6.83 million sq m in 1979–83. For residential uses, comparable figures were 3.91 million sq m and 4.28 million sq m. These were 3–4 times higher than comparable figures of the previous peak in 1953–57 and about 7 times that of its lowest point in 1966–76 (Table 8.2).

In 1978–87, Beijing had built a total of 44 million sq m of new housing, 35 million sq m of which were completed in 1981–87. The proportion of residential floor space to total floor space completed had also been raised from 30–40% in the past decades to about 60% in the 1980s. With the new construction boom, the city's housing standard was raised from a per capita living area of 4.55 sq m in 1978 to 6.82 sq m in 1987, and 8.1 sq m in 1991.

Two major changes occurred in this period besides the much increased construction activities: (1) a gradual move away from the long-held low-rent policy towards charging an economic rent, and (2) commercialization of urban housing with new units constructed for sale, sale of some old units and the creation of an urban housing market.

In residential area planning, there was movement towards large and more comprehensive projects with more varied designs and attention to the living and built environment. The 1982 General Plan adopted the new concept of 'residential district', a larger area than 'small districts', and new provision standards for cultural, welfare, education, commercial, and service facilities within the 'residential districts' and 'small districts' were formally approved in 1985.

New housing projects designed and constructed in the period demonstrate the following qualities:

1. *More widely spread spatially.* In 1977–83, a total of over 60 projects were put on the drawing board. About half were located outside the Third Ring Road and are in general spread out in all directions in the suburban districts (Figure 8.1).
2. *Larger in scale.* The basic planning unit changed from 'small district' to 'residential district', hence the project size, which previously was

around 20 hectares with a few thousand to 10 000 population, became much larger in scale, ranging from 60–100 hectares with a population of 30 000–40 000. In a few projects, e.g. Fangzhuang, the site area covered 117.9 hectares with a designated population of about 100 000, thus effectively a sizeable urban settlement in its own right. Scale economies and comprehensive planning could be better achieved with the increased project size.

3. *Predominance of high-rise buildings.* The need to build quickly to meet long-held demand and to economize on land has resulted in a rush towards high-rise building design. High-rise blocks exceeding nine-storeys formed as much as 89% of all building space in the Fangzhuang project (Table 8.1). In the earlier years of the period (1978–83) the average was 30–50%. After 1987, there was a reversal of this trend as the municipality had then formed a policy on the control of building height as one of the means to control the city's urban design and urban environment.

4. *High density.* Density standard before the mid-1960s was low, varying around 400 persons per hectare gross. In 1982, the planning office instructed a new rule of 600–800 persons per hectare gross. For 'small districts' it is recommended to use the upper limit of 800, while 'residential districts' use the lower limit of 600. These standards were set against considerations of a guarantee of 1 sq m of public green space per capita, house separation at a ratio of no less than 1.6 and high-rises to form less than 40% of all buildings. However, in actual planning, some projects attained a higher density of over 900 persons per hectare gross (Table 8.1).

6. *New functional concept.* Commercial and service facilities have been planned along 'commercial and operational' lines instead of based on the old concept that they 'serve' the local community. Hence new plans place these facilities at the entrance to the housing district instead of at its geometric centre, turning a 'closed' approach into an 'open' approach. The new location remains convenient to local residents while it simultaneously makes the facilities equally attractive to passers-by and enhances their economic viability.

Current housing situation

At the end of 1991, Beijing had a total of 104.9 million sq m of residential floor area. It is about 7.7 times that of 1949. That is to say, Beijing had increased six times in terms of new housing construction since 1949. The standard of housing had also improved over the same period. Per capita living area (less than useable space as it excludes

toilet, bath, kitchen and corridors) improved from 4.75 sq m in 1949 to
8.1 sq m in 1991. By this latter standard which measures the improvement in citizens' average housing conditions, the improvement was
68.6%.

However, improvement in urban housing in Beijing took place almost
entirely within the 1980s. More than half the housing stock at 1991, i.e.
57.9 million sq m, was added only after 1980. In the three decades of
1949–80, addition of new housing was barely sufficient to meet
population increase, as per capita living space stayed the same in 1980
as in 1949. In fact it worsened in 1957 and 1965, i.e. 3.7 and 3.6 sq m per
person respectively, only to recover somewhat since 1978, i.e. around 4.7
sq m per person.

It is China's national goal to attain by 2000 a per capita living area of
8 sq m for urban residents and for each household to occupy a self-
contained urban housing unit. Beijing by 1991 had already attained the
first part of this national goal. Yet Beijing has set a higher standard for
itself for the year 2000, i.e. a per capita living space of 9 sq m, the
original USSR standard adopted in the first general plan of the city
(1953) (Fan, 1989b, 33). It looks highly possible that the 9 sq m goal
could be achieved, but accommodating each household in a self-
contained unit may not be feasible.

In the first national housing survey of the PRC done in 1985 (Fan,
1989b), Beijing was found to be not very impressive in housing
compared to other provinces in China. In terms of per capita useable
area, the national average was 10.01 sq m; Beijing registered 8.77 sq m,
ranking 22 among the country's 28 provincial-level administrative units,
and much below the national average. In living area, the national
average was 6.36 sq m, and Beijing's figure was 6.67 sq m. Of the 28
provincial administrative units, Beijing ranked 13. Beijing's lower
ranking in per capita living area generally reflects the prevailing
situation that, owing to differences in climate, the southern provinces
attach more auxiliary space to the housing unit than do northern
provinces.

The survey reported that 36.4% of housing in the nation was built in
the first five years of the 1980s, a situation similar to that of Beijing. In
the nation, 26.5% of households were described as 'overcrowded'. The
highest proportion is found in Shanghai, 49.98%. The figure for Beijing is
24.4%, ranking 9. In basic facilities, 96.7% of households had electricity.
Those with own kitchen, toilet and water tap were respectively 62.6%,
24.2% and 57.3% of all households. For Beijing, the relevant figures were
37.3% with own kitchen, 37.3% with own toilet and 49% with own water
tap. The proportion of households with bath, gas and heating facilities
for the nation as a whole was very low, varying from 6 to 8%. Beijing

ranked highest, yet the respective proportions are 6.8%, 17.8% and 41%. Thus in terms of reaching the national goal of self-contained units for all households by 2000, the prospect would be quite slim for Beijing and the nation as a whole. The 1985 survey revealed that of the total of 1.238 million households surveyed in Beijing, only 540 000 households or 43.9% occupied self-contained units. More than half were still below the national target. This formidable task aside, the 24.4% overcrowding means over 400 000 actual households were substandard. Half were 'inconvenient households', a third were 'overcrowded', and a sixth were 'houseless' households.

High-rise blocks: solution and problem

The debate on high-rise residential blocks started in the mid 1980s. High-rise blocks (nine storeys and above) were seen as an expedient means to economize on land and expensive infrastructure in a rapid rush to fill the pent-up need for residences in the late 1970s and early 1980s. People objecting to the proliferation of high-rise blocks pointed to their bad effects on the cityscape, particularly their intrusion into the profile and skyline of the low-rise traditional core of the Ming and Qing Dynasty preserve of the Forbidden City, as well as insufficient infrastructure to meet increased population load and the accompanying social and psychological problems of high-density and high-rise living.

The first high-rise residential block of nine storeys with lift was completed in 1960. In 1960–71 eight such blocks were constructed, less than one block a year. In 1972, two high-rises were put up as quarters for the foreign diplomatic corps in Beijing. It is only after 1976 that high-rises began to be frequently encountered in the skyline of Beijing. By 1985, the municipality had sanctioned applications for building 1310 high-rise residential blocks with a total floor space of 13.1 million sq m, or about the same area as all housing in old Beijing at 1949. In 1985 on average a new high-rise was approved every 1.3 days and the floor space of high-rises constituted about a third of all residential space completed in 1985 (Fan, 1988a). The 1985 housing survey shows that Beijing had the highest proportion of high-rises in its housing stock, i.e. 3.27% compared to 0.8% in Shanghai, 0.16% in Tianjin and the national average of 0.22% (Fan, 1989b).

Not only are high-rises more numerous, they become ever taller with the passage of time. Before 1971, they were invariably nine storeys high. Gradually they increased in height, especially after 1980 when the first 20-storey block appeared. In 1984, a 24-storey block was approved. By 1988, about 1000 high-rise residential blocks had been completed, with a total floor area of 11 million sq m. Another 270 blocks with 8 million sq m completed floor space were reported to be under construction in 1989. At 1988, high-rises accounted for one-eighth of total housing stock in Beijing and 20% of all housing constructed in 1972–88 (Lu, 1989). Thus high-rise blocks, though latecomers, have since 1980 become a prominent feature in urban housing in the city.

Spatially, 87% of the blocks lay on the two sides of the Third Ring Road, and 61% in the two city districts of Chaoyang and Haidian. Within the old city, 186 blocks were approved with a designated floor area of 1.84 million sq m. Such penetration of high buildings in the old city has certainly caused concern over their impact on the traditional city core. Despite these general statistics on their location, their actual distribution pattern within the Fourth Ring Road, as illustrated by a map by Fan (1989a), shows an alarming proliferation. They seem to be almost everywhere, except in the Forbidden City.

Three reasons have been advanced for the increasing proliferation of high-rise domestic blocks in Beijing.

1. Rapid increase of population and a shortage of housing. The average per capita living area in 1972 was 4.28 sq m. By 1990 it was raised to 7.72 sq m. The annual rate of improvement is about 0.25 sq m. The 1982 General Plan assumed a population for the planned urban areas of about 5 million and it had reserved 'residential land' on a per capita basis of 27 sq m, i.e. at a gross density of 370 persons per hectare. Since the urban population in the early 1980s had already exceeded the planned target, increasing the population density by building higher, with more living area per unit of building land, became an obvious solution for improving the average living situation and for accommodating more people.
2. To economize on land, particularly to cut down on conversion of good vegetable plots in the suburban districts into building land. In 1983, Beijing had a total of 390 000 mou (260 sq km) of vegetable fields, 58% of which were in the suburban districts. In that year alone 5000 mou (3.3 sq km) in the suburban districts were lost to urban encroachment. With recently increasing building activity in the order of 10 million sq m completed floor space a year (residential 6 million), building high has become a means for minimizing the amount of rural–urban land-use conversion for saving the city's 'vegetable basket'.
3. Official preference for building high and raising density standards. It was said that most high-ranking officials in Beijing are in favour of high-rise building. It is alleged to be a basic reason behind the large amount of approvals before 1987. It is only since 1989 that an official

policy of strictly controlling the amount of high-rise domestic blocks and bringing down the height of domestic housing was adopted (Fan, 1989a,b).

The economic argument on the side of the high-rise approach, besides saving on land and preserving suburban agriculture, includes minimum demolition for accommodating more people within the built-up areas. High density may also save on urban infrastructure, help to improve the built environment by varying designs and enhance the identity of a local district. The other side of the picture, however, includes higher building costs and higher maintenance costs, less sunlight and more unfavourable fire-protection conditions and congestion. It is estimated that on a per sq m building area basis, the high-rise approach costs Yn50 more than walk-up flats of a few storeys. Average household building maintenance cost is about Yn500 more on an annual basis (Lu, 1989). Of course, the debate on the high-rise approach has not been confined to the economic sphere. A survey of residents' opinions in 1985–86 indicates that provision of building infrastructure and its management in Beijing were still unsatisfactory and unfavourable to high-rise residents. Of 800 households surveyed, 42% reported that the lift was always out of order, 54% claimed that it sometimes went wrong. None of the lifts at the time was automatic, and they needed to stop operating when the operator was at meals twice a day. Electricity supply situation was much better, only 5% claimed frequent 'black-outs'. Problems of water pressure were cited by 43% of the households, while 17% claimed 'frequently without supply'. Piped gas was supplied to only 47% of the blocks, with 51% of the households enjoying this convenience; 42% of the households had to fetch portable pressurized gas for fuel. A telephone is a rare luxury possessed by a few households, most depended on public telephones. Of the 30 blocks, only two had a public telephone service on the ground floor, 19 blocks had to rely on that in other blocks within the small district. Thus 81% of the surveyed households complained of telephone inconvenience. Shortage of space for parking bicycles was a problem cited by 53% of the households. Monthly building management fees were expensive, amounting to Yn40–50 per household, yet the actual amount paid by the households was Yn1 or less. Thus living in a high-rise block means more inconvenience for households yet more subsidy from the state or enterprise.

On the psychological side, 34% of the households felt 'unsafe' living in high-rise blocks. They feared theft and burglary, fire, earthquakes and children falling from the balcony. Children 'almost had no chance to play with neighbouring children', claimed 62% of the households. Compared to former living in walk-up flats, 70% said their children had drastically reduced the frequency of play with neighbours. Some 84% of the households did not socialize with neighbours and 71% of the old people said they felt lonely in the day; 62% of households noted a reduction of social visits from relatives and friends after having moved into the high-rise block. In general more people 'don't like' high-rise living; 33% as against 28% who 'liked it', while 39% of the respondents had no opinion (Fan, 1987).

The spread of high-rise residential buildings in Chinese cities seems unavoidable, though it appears odd that Beijing was the launching ground for such an invasion. The issues of preservation of the skyline of the inner city and maintaining the aesthetic quality of historical parts of the city and its valuable traditional architecture have formed an important force behind the demand for stringent height zoning and building volume control, which we shall leave for further discussion in a later chapter. The flood-tide of high-rise blocks seems to have subsided since 1987 when the municipality finally placed a rigid and sensible control on the approval of high-rise structures.

Housing reform

Physical construction alone may not solve the quality, distribution and management problems of urban housing in Chinese cities. In Beijing, where over 50% of existing stock is cottage structure and without the basic utility provisions, the problem is thus not only one of new construction. More funds have to be generated and the older part of the stock has both to be better maintained and a large part of it redeveloped. In 1988, the State Council launched a national campaign on urban housing reform to address these issues. The core of the reform is to turn urban housing from a social good into a commodity which will be distributed according to market mechanisms instead of the sheer emphasis on building which was the case before 1988. The reform aims to take three to five years for gradual implementation in all towns and cities within the country (Ministry of Construction, 1990).

The reform attacks the root of socialist urban housing philosophy. 'In China, public housing is a form of brick-and-mortar wage as well as a redistributive tool', claimed a World Bank report (1992). Before 1988, the planner-driven approach to estimating housing demand without considering household income and preferences had been persistent. Housing quotas and housing approval had been given out to work units that had funds for housing construction, as well as to lower-level governments which usually had budgets for housing construction for civil servants. Access to housing for individuals was first influenced by whether their work unit had been allocated housing units or had the necessary funds for their construction or purchase. Then their political activism and political status were substantial qualifications. Age and working seniority formed other criteria. Couples were not eligible for new housing if their combined ages did not exceed fifty years (Dwyer, 1986). Statistics for Beijing for 1982 had borne out some of these facts: of the 660 000 households of housing shortage, 81 800 were 'waiting to get married', and 42 500 households were 'houseless after marriage'. Together they formed 19% of all households of housing shortage, or 8.7% of all households in the city (Beijing Urban Housing Research Committee, 1984).

The basic root to the urban housing problem has thus been 'state construction, administrative allocation and low rent'. With decentralization of power the bias has moved more in favour of work units with financial means and influence. In 1979, over 90% of all investments in housing construction were financed by the 'unified' state–local budget. By 1988, this had dropped to 22%. Most housing is now acquired or constructed by work units which currently finance 52% of all annual housing construction out of retained earnings, other 'extra-budgetary' funds or depreciation allowances. The residue is financed by collective enterprises (World Bank, 1992, 7). The World Bank claims that the situation of shortage has been aggravated by 'standard inflation', i.e. the Ministry of Construction recommended raising the 1972–77 average housing unit size of 34–38 sq m to 56 sq m. This encouraged work units with funds to demand larger flats and higher space standards; hence they transfer more of the nation's resources to housing through tax deduction, evasion or the use of funds for production and compensation in the form of subsidy in kind, whereas these may be better spent on meeting more urgent needs or for productive investment. The World Bank estimates that the weight of housing benefits has increased from 7% of total compensation to 16% in one decade (1978–88), with cash wages and bonuses declining to 62%. This massive and sustained shift of resources into urban housing suggests that shelter investment may be excessive. This is all the more likely as households bear almost none of the financial consequences involved (World Bank, 1992).

The situation in Beijing in the early 1980s revealed that when housing was considered not as a commodity, but as part of wage compensation in kind, untold inequality arose between work units of diversely different resources and between individuals within the same unit, not according to need but to other criteria based on political power. For example, in Beijing, the average per capita living area of workers in central government offices was 7.06 sq m in 1984, for municipal government workers it was 5.27 sq m, and for those working in city district offices it was even lower. Statistics that include all housing completed in 1976–83 showed that work units of different administrative rank had achieved housing constructed on different per capita levels. Those with per capita (worker) construction area completed of over 10 sq m are the Planning Bureau, Construction Bureau, Petrochemical Corporation, Metallurgical Bureau, Electricity Bureau and the National Agricultural and Forestry Service. Those with per capita of 5–6 sq m include the Urban Services Bureau, Utilities Bureau, Environmental Protection Bureau, Housing Corporation, Education Bureau and Higher Education Bureau. Work units belonging to the four city districts with over 400 000 workers registered an average per capita construction area of only 0.45 sq m. These statistics reflect a hierarchical arrangement of different work units in the ability to construct their own housing and hence different degrees of access to and standards of housing so obtained. According to existing rules work units can utilize the welfare fund, bonus fund and depreciation on non-productive capital construction for housing construction. In fact, most work units had utilized unapproved sources; i.e. after-tax profits and other funds, which respectively amounted to 41.2% and 61.4% of total funds for housing construction in 1982–83. In addition, when a work unit has the necessary capital it may still not be able to construct its own housing. It has to draw up a plan, find the land, organize construction material supply and hire the construction team. In such activities, small units with low administrative rank are definitely placed in an unfavourable position. Unified construction had been unable to solve the problem of the small units. By 1983, only 13% of the year's housing was constructed by such a means. Its unpopularity arises from the fact that the per sq m construction cost by the unified approach had been too high, i.e. varying between Yn450 around the Third Ring Road and Yn580 around the Second Ring Road. The high calculated selling price was the result of adding into the construction cost many other items of peripheral cost, i.e. demolition and resettlement, urban facilities, ancillary and supporting services. Actual construction cost itself amounted to roughly 40% of the listed cost only. As 60% of capital provided by those participating in the 'unified construction' schemes would be eaten up by these non-housing elements, the ability of small work units to solve their workers' housing problem had become more remote (World Bank, 1992).

The new housing reform of 1988 aims to attack the long-standing urban housing problems with four different approaches: (1) changing the present housing investment and maintenance and management funds from a mix of direct and indirect transfers and subsidies to a system of direct subsidy so that it is finally integrated into the worker's formal paypacket; (2) reorientating urban housing from a social good to become a real commodity in the market place; (3) reforming relevant taxes, wage, government budgetary and financial arrangements to ensure that there will be a practical housing finance market to ensure positive recycling of housing investment; and (4) setting up markets for housing, housing finance, construction, management and servicing.

To achieve these objectives, two short-term measures have been recommended for phased implementation in a five-year period. The first is the abandonment of the low-rent policy, replacing the uniform and minimal monthly per sq m rental of Yn0.13 by a new rental formula reflecting the various economic costs involved and the differences in location, floor level and facilities provided. The new rental policy will aim to cut down indirect subsidy in the initial stage by a rental coupon which provides a surrogate of subsidy in kind, finally to be integrated into the worker's wage packet. The new rental calculation also limits direct subsidy to an established space standard and facilities standard. Above-standard provisions would be additionally charged on a commercial basis. The five basic factors considered in the rental calculation are: depreciation over 60 years at 2%; maintenance fees at Yn2.1 per sq m per year; capital investment interest at 3% annually; management fee at 10% of the sum of the previous three items; and lastly housing tax at 12% of the rental. The basic rental for an average urban flat amounted to a monthly Yn1.28 per sq m, or an equivalent of 83.9% of the actual rental at cost of Yn1.53, or 53% of the commercial charge of Yn2.4. The basic rental will be added onto or subtracted from fixed amounts depending on location, floor, utilities and facilities provision or non-provision. The rental coupon is to be issued by the work unit to the worker as payment for subsidizing his housing, and can replace the same amount of cash rental payment. The monetary value of the coupon is set at 23.5% of monthly wage. The factor of 23.5% was derived from the average monthly wage, average floor area occupied, average current rental paid by the workers and average new housing unit rental per sq m. The rental coupon may also be used as bank deposit or as payment for housing mortgages (Ministry of Construction, 1990).

The second measure is the sale of public housing. Through the promotion of workers' purchasing their own housing units, the state aims to harness the community's savings and purchasing power for solving the current housing shortage. The sales price of new housing units would include the construction cost, land acquisition and sitting residents' resettlement costs. Cost of public utilities, tax for transport and energy funds, and public building within a residential project for commercial sales or leasing would not be included. With this new method of calculation, new units with full property rights can be sold at a preferential price of Yn258.43 per sq m in urban redevelopment sites and Yn256.51 in newly developed urban sites. Flats with full property rights are to be sold to individuals on a first come, first served basis. Such flats should amount to 10% of all units in any residential project. Work units with financial means may purchase new housing for sale to their staff at 70% of the preferential price. This category of housing has limited property rights. The owner may not resell, let, mortgage or give away his unit. In case he wants to sell it, the only way is to sell it back to his work unit at a price based on the original price depreciated according to the length of occupation. In buying a flat the worker has to pay a lum sum of 30%, and the balance is to be financed by long-term (10–20-year) low-interest bank loans.

The standard sales price for an old flat is to be determined by its replacement cost, depreciation and environmental and locational qualities. The minimum price should be Yn120 per sq m. Similarly, the purchaser has to pay a lump sum of 30%, the rest to be financed by low-interest bank loans of up to a repayment period of 10 years (Ministry of Construction, 1990).

The national urban housing reform was first started in the three centrally administered cities, i.e. Beijing, Tianjin and Shanghai. Beijing, being the national capital, obviously serves as the example for the whole nation to look up to. In the implementation of the reform measures, development of new areas as well as redevelopment of inner city districts have been combined with provision of new and improved housing. These will be illustrated by the three case studies of Beijing below.

Urban redevelopment

In 1991, Beijing had 202 plots of dilapidated housing waiting to be redeveloped. These had a total construction area of about 5 million sq m, about 5.3% of the city's total residential area, yet accounting for 20% of the city's households with serious housing problems. In phase one of the city's redevelopment, 37 of the largest plots will be developed, involving demolition of 1.6 million sq m and the construction of 5.3 million sq m of new building, of which 3.4 million sq m will be for residence. This effort alone will require a total capital of Yn6–8 billion. The municipal government will loan Yn0.2 billion as start-up capital. District governments of the various plots will supply a meagre addition through their budget. Individual contribution through housing reform helped to raise about 3% of the total. The balance, about 85%, would need to be financed through sales of commercial properties yielded by the redevelopment projects.

To increase the pace of redevelopment, encouragement to existing residents to seek their own arrangements for transit housing has become the rule. In some projects a Yn20 per day bonus and Yn20 per sq m removal subsidy were given to promote rapid vacation of old flats. 86–96% of the residents had chosen to arrange their own transit housing. For residents who choose to move back after redevelopment, the rule of 'one sq m compensation for one sq m demolition' is followed and all return residents have to participate in the housing reform. However, the municipality encourages permanent out-movers towards newly developed suburban housing. Measures like larger units (two-room as against one-room flats) and payment of an additional lump sum subsidy of Yn10 000–15 000 have been used to encourage their moving into outside new areas. Out-mover rates reached 45–99% in various redevelopment projects. Those who choose to move back are offered a house selling price of Yn240–380 per sq m, and a 15–20% discount will be offered for full cash payment. Yet only 5% of the residents affected had chosen to buy the redeveloped residences. As part of housing reform, new flats are charged new monthly rentals at Yn0.55–0.63 per sq m of living space. Some are at a much higher rate of Yn1.34. In addition, all renters have to pay a rental deposit of Yn40–80 per sq m construction area.

As sales of properties at commercial rates form the larger bulk of redevelopment finance, the redevelopment agents tried very hard to increase the 'commodity goods' rate of the project and to increase the gross population density. The market price that may be fetched by 'commodity' flats ranges from Yn2500 to 3000, about Yn1000–1500 per sq m in excess of the production cost. Commercial buildings like offices and shops can fetch even higher prices of about Yn3500 per sq m. In some redevelopments, these 'commodity goods' took 25–40% of the total newly constructed area. As much as 85% of the financing of urban redevelopment projects has to come from the sale of commodity goods, which is being constrained both by the number of old residents who like to move back and by planning controls regarding density and buildings used after redevelopment. More sympathetic planning policy re-adjustment will be required for the successful implementation of urban redevelopment and hence the elimination of dilapidated housing and improving the inner city (Research Office, Urban Construction Bureau, Beijing Municipality, 1991).

Cooperative of Juer Hutung

Juer Hutung (Chrysanthemum Lane), part of the inner city of Beijing, demonstrates a cooperative approach by residents to redevelop their dilapidated housing. The redevelopment site comprises 12 courtyard houses on a ground area of 4830 sq m. The residents within the site can freely join the 'redevelopment cooperative' which operates under the motto of 'Cooperative members contribute capital; work units provide subsidy; the state gives support; democratic management; self-help service'.

Members of the cooperative have preferential purchasing rights to the 5651 sq m of new housing to be developed. The selling price, if within the set space standard, is fixed at 600 Yn per sq m of construction area, of which the member pays Yn350 and his work unit Yn250. The standard price varies slightly according to aspect, floor level and facilities. If a member wants to purchase a flat larger than the set space standard (the leased space of his old flat) approval from the cooperative is required, and excess space will be charged at Yn2500 per sq m of construction area. The purchaser has full property rights which can be mortgaged, transferred and inherited, but the flat can only be sold after 5 years of occupation. If the selling price exceeded Yn350, the amount paid by the original purchaser, the excess would be proportionately distributed between the member, his work unit and the state according to the amount of investment each put in for constructing the flat and after considering the factor of inflation. In principle, the member pays the purchasing price in one go. If he is unable to do so he may arrange a loan from his work unit, or from the Beijing branch of the Construction Bank. In the latter case, his work unit must serve as the guarantor. In addition, the purchaser has to pay 3% of the selling price, together with 2% contribution from the cooperative from its receipt of the flat price payment, to serve as a 'public facilities maintenance fund'.

Residents who do not want to buy a new flat can arrange to exchange their rights for housing in other areas, or to be resettled by the Housing Bureau in public, cottage-type housing in no less than the former rented space. The owner–occupier of an old flat may purchase a new flat of no less than the space of his own residence. The assessed value of his old property is to be deducted from the selling price of the new flat. If owner-occupiers do not wish to be housed within the new development, the Housing Bureau may resettle them at no less than the space of their old flat in public cottage housing. If they want to retain their property rights, the cottage may be sold to them against the assessed value of their old property.

Besides serving as an example of the cooperative approach, Juer Hutung is also an experiment in using courtyard house and low-rise design to attain both the higher density and environmental preservation goals of urban redevelopment in the more historic and cultural parts of inner Beijing. The pilot site redevelopment started in 1987 in courtyard

41. It had 22 households and 79 residents. The average per capita construction area was 7.8 sq m. This was, however, attained through the addition of numerous small huts to the original brick houses, which raised the courtyard's built-up area from 56% to 83%. Public facilities were poorly supplied. There was only one water tap, one sewer, and the only toilet was 100 m away from the courtyard. The pilot scheme aims to attain a per capita construction area of 9 sq m, of low-rise high-density quasi-courtyard new housing in traditional Chinese cottage style. Finally, the pilot scheme was extended to a site of 2090 sq m, involving 7 courtyards, 40 households and 139 residents. The re-developed properties are 2–3 storeys high, comprising 46 self-contained units of an average space of 60 sq m. There is a total construction area of 2760 sq m at a plot ratio (the ratio between total floor area and the site area of a building) of 1.2. The scheme was completed in 1992 and fully occupied by the end of that year (Wu and Liu, 1989; Fang, 1989).

In 1989 there were only four housing cooperatives in the city with a membership of 558 households and a capital of Yn4.23 million. In the year, 130 households moved into newly built houses. In 1990, the number of cooperatives increased to 13, with 1404 household members. In the year Yn18.6 million capital was amassed and 350 households moved into new housing. In 1991, they gathered Yn60 million funds and rehoused 1000 households in new housing (*Beijing Social and Economic Statistical Yearbook*, various dates).

Sales of old flats of the Sixth Construction Company

Urban housing in China followed the welfare approach, i.e. 'construction by the government, allocation by the work unit, and low rent'. Such an approach is said to have created an incurable sickness for both the state and work units. Its two basic symptoms are the increasing housing construction burden on the state and unfair housing allocation. In addition, work units are burdened by an increasing need to subsidize workers through maintaining their housing. The Sixth Construction Company is one of 10 pilots testing the housing reform at the enterprise level. Its rental revenue from public housing was around Yn140 000 per year recently, yet it had to foot annual maintenance expenses of Yn900 000. Thus maintenance subsidy alone amounted to Yn760 000 a year. Since 1988, the company has implemented the new housing reform by raising rent and selling old flats to the occupiers. As a first step, it sold some old public housing at a discount price and recouped Yn3.77 million, enough capital for constructing 15 000 sq m of new housing for sale to houseless staff or staff with cramped living conditions.

Concurrently, the company has abandoned the allocation system for distributing new housing. All newly completed or acquired public housing will be sold to its staff, with the aim of phasing out housing as a welfare element in the company's compensation system.

The company's sales of old flats are based on the 'semi-commodity' principle. The standard price is set at Yn357 per sq m of construction area. Sitting tenants of old flats are offered three types of discount for purchases made before a certain date: (1) 30% discount of expenses involved in land resumption, demolition and removal compensation; (2) 20% of the standard price; and (3) a yearly 0.5% discount according to length of service within the company. With these discounts, the average per sq m price becomes Yn150 and varies between Yn122 and Yn186. In addition, further discounts of 20%, 18% and 15% are given to buyers who pay off the whole price within 1 to 3 years. Payment by instalments over 10–15 years can be arranged, with a downpayment of 30%, the rest to be deducted monthly from the pay packet at the normal interest rate charged by state banks. The standard prices for three types of old flats are: Yn6000 for a one-room flat; Yn9000 for a two-room flat and Yn11 000 for a three-room flat. Since the first instalment varies between Yn2000 and Yn3000, and the average annual wage of a worker is around Yn2000, most of the staff can afford to buy a flat. The company also takes on a five-year responsibility for maintaining the communal parts of housing blocks, whereas internal parts of the flat are to be maintained by the new owner. Within two months, 504 staff households applied to buy their flats, about 34.7% of the 1450 flats scheduled for the purpose (Gu and Zhu, 1989).

For Beijing as a whole in 1989, there were sales of 158 000 sq m of residential property, 77 000 sq m of which was new housing. In terms of number of flats, 1405 old flats and 1189 new flats were sold. In 1990, 99 000 sq m or 1830 flats were sold and Yn21.5 million recouped. In addition 183 flats were sold at a commercial price, a total of Yn16.8 million. New rents were charged on 7.62 million sq m of housing, which represented Yn3.1 million above the total revenue from standard rent, in addition to a total rental deposit of Yn5.8 million. In 1991, 90% of Beijing's housing under the administration of the municipality had implemented the housing reform. This is equivalent to 43 million sq m. It had recouped a total of Yn280 million from individuals. Of this capital Yn150 million was raised by selling 12 000 flats (total 700 000 sq m) to workers or residents, Yn50 million from individuals in urban redevelopment projects in which 6000 households had been re-accommodated in new housing, and Yn20 million from newly increased rentals and the newly created rental deposits (*Beijing Statistical Yearbook*, various dates).

Conclusion: new phase in urban housing

> For housing reform, the cities look up to the provincial capital; the
> provincial capitals look up to the national capital. (Gu and Zhu, 1989, 13)

It is true that in urban housing, Beijing, like the traditional Chinese
national capitals in history, serves as the pace and standard setter for the
whole nation. The post-1949 twists and turns in housing investment and
housing provision, and the system of allocation in Beijing, reflect the
national tenet in these aspects. Perhaps there is a need to note that in
most cases what Beijing represents is a 'little better' than the national
average. The post-1978 housing construction boom in Beijing, as is the
situation for the rest of the country, has underlined a massive transfer of
resources from productive to consumptive use. This certainly begs
sympathy from outsiders, as the nation as a whole had suffered almost
two decades of underprovision of basic urban facilities and items of
collective consumption including housing, the so-called 'flesh' and 'bone'
imbalance.

Yet it is equally easy to appreciate the World Bank's comment on the
'excessive' flow of scarce resources to urban housing, without due
regard to market demand and consumer choice. What is more at fault is
that such investment, under the low-rent policy, only creates more
problems of unfair distribution, uneconomic use, lack of management,
insufficient maintenance, i.e. a negative drain of resources whereby
input feeds on more input without output in the form of a recycling
fund. At present it is widely accepted that the principle of welfare
approach, implemented by the rule of 'state construction, work unit
allocation and low rent', is at odds with efficient use of resources,
fairness and equity. A return to the rule of the market through raising
old rentals and sales of old and new flats is, in essence, the real
substance of the current housing reform. As the World Bank has noted,
the real solution to urban housing in China lies beyond the confines of
housing itself. It calls for the government to restrict its role to providing
(*a*) a local regulatory environment conducive to the emergence of
diversified sources of production; (*b*) a legal framework that redefines
property rights; (*c*) a local planning framework that helps extend
affordable serviced land development in core areas of a city; and (*d*) a
mortgage finance framework that is consistent with macro-economic
priorities and allows for the emergence of financing mechanisms that are
self-sustaining and require no subsidization. It recommends reforms to
restore consumer choice and redirect construction to respond to
household preferences and income levels. The link between work units
and household housing choice must be broken, by transferring control

over existing units' allocation and maintenance to rental companies; and the state and state-owned enterprises have to withdraw gradually from the market. There is need to introduce fixed-term renewable leases for rental units, and restrictions on the generation of income from private property should be lifted completely. New construction of rental units is to be financed by rental income being used to pay off mortgages provided by financial intermediaries, and both the nature and number of construction and management companies are to shift in the direction of real market competition (World Bank, 1992).

The preponderance of central ministries, departments and bureaus in Beijing and their control of resources over their small empires, as well as their ability to transfer resources from enterprises they control and their power and influence within Beijing, to some extent accounted for the hectic building boom of residential housing construction in 1979–87. It certainly contributed to some degree of amelioration of the city's housing problem in terms of more living quarters for allocation. The improvement of the city's overall per capita living area from 6 sq m in the early 1980s to 8.01 sq m in 1991 is evidence for this fact. Better design and improved community, social and cultural provisions, as set by the 1985 new residential district planning standards, equally bolstered the overall positive change of urban housing in the city. However, the non-economic force behind these changes and improvements, deriving largely from Beijing being the national capital, fits in very well with the traditional Chinese concept of the dictate of the sovereign and his wish that his capital should be the best. To this extent, Beijing's example had been copied by cities lower down the administrative hierarchy. The fact of the national capital being better does impress on the visitor to Chinese cities in recent years that urban housing in Beijing is certainly more remarkable in its better design, higher construction quality, much more numerous new blocks, and many more high-rises, as compared even to Shanghai, Tianjin and Guangzhou. Despite the superficial glamour and achievements, urban housing development in Beijing in the 10 years of 1978–87 has not broken out of the confines of the unbelievable yet realistic combined influence of socialism and feudalism.

The 1988 housing reform may be seen as a significant departure from these two forces in the making of the city. Yet the rule of the market is in its infancy. By the end of 1991, 43 million sq m of housing was covered by various stages and measures of the housing reform, equivalent to about 40% of the total domestic living area in the city, or 90% of that under the control of the municipality. In the period of 1989–91, 16 424 new and old flats with a total of 956 000 sq m had been sold to workers at a preferential price. In terms of construction space, this only amounts to 10% of the newly completed residential housing or 0.9% of the city's whole stock in 1991. Cooperative housing generated from household members a meagre capital of Yn82.8 million and was only able to rehouse 2962 households in the three years. Thus quantitatively, privatization of urban housing still has a long way to go. The extent and progress of rental coupon issue and raising of old rentals are still not publicly known. The world is watching with great interest this new round of change in Beijing, putting urban housing on a new economic and commercial footing. If successfully implemented, the reform would drastically change not only the quality of living for its citizens, but given time would produce a new cityscape as well as a revised urban human ecology in the form of a fresh pattern of social areas. As a pace setter, Beijing's changes will trickle down to lesser members of the administrative–urban hierarchy.

9

Urban environment and preserving the old city

Environment of the national capital

The urban environment may mean different things to different people. Even for a defined 'urban environment', it may be further examined at different scale levels. Here, we adopt a view that Beijing's environment combines its historical value, i.e. that part of its physical environment that preserves the traditional Chinese city culture, and the broad natural and built environment that contains the functioning totality of the present-day metropolis.

Present-day Beijing, to both Chinese and foreigners, effectively evokes the symbolism of traditional Chinese culture through its well-preserved city core that dates back to the Ming Dynasty of about five centuries ago, as well as a modern socialist big city predominated by a huge bureaucracy and major modern industries. Indeed, these two images or roles of Beijing have since the founding of the PRC in 1949 been in constant conflict with each other. The debate in 1949–50 between Liang and the Soviet experts on whether the old city within its wall was to be completely preserved, and whether the new political and administrative centre was to be set up on green turf or within the old core for economy and expedience, started the row between these two seemingly divergent roles of Beijing. Rapid industrialization since the First Five Year Plan, especially the development of polluting heavy industries, has led to deterioration of the urban environment, including defacing of valuable marble statues and carvings of historic value by acid rain and infringement by non-conforming industrial uses into groups of historical buildings, causing damage to the aesthetics of the traditional built form. Pollution aside, energy- and water-intensive heavy industries aggravated the city's water shortage and transport problems. The huge labour demand generated by the crash course of industrialization is itself a heavy burden on the natural environment, to the extent that some claim that Beijing's environmental capacity is already overloaded.

Since the new Directives of 1980 and 1983, Beijing has re-emphasized its role as the political and cultural centre of the nation and wants to restrict further growth of industries while striving to shift existing ones to a more environmentally friendly structure. The 1980 Directives further stipulated that one of the four objectives of the city's development is to 'develop into the nation's cleanest, most hygienic, and most beautiful city, and one of the better cities of the world in these scores'. It argues that Beijing would be able to achieve this 'because it has hills and rivers, good climate and plenty of cultural and archeological relics' (Beijing Construction History, Vol. 1, 1987, 313).

The 1983 Directives also elaborated on the significance of Beijing's being a cultural city in history and that the municipality should preserve it as such:

> Beijing is our country's capital. It is at the same time a historical cultural city. Urban planning and construction in Beijing should reflect the historic culture of the Chinese people as well as the revolutionary tradition and socialist characteristics of the capital. Valuable revolutionary artifacts, historical relics, old architecture, and old archeological sites of value have to be preserved. The built form and volume surrounding such sites must be appropriately controlled. The old city has to be gradually redeveloped in a wholesale manner . . . not only to improve existing basic infrastructure and attain a level of modernization, but also for inheriting and enhancing the tradition of it being a historical cultural city. (*Beijing Construction History*, 1987, Vol. 1, 317).

Environmental construction work, which includes preservation of the environment, curing of pollution, greening of the city and raising the hygienic conditions of the city, improving its rivers and water courses and reinforcing the development of tourist areas and natural preserves, is viewed as a necessary corollary of achieving the political and cultural roles of the city. Such work is indeed indispensable for turning Beijing into 'a clean, pretty and ecologically healthy city'.

In short, there are two direct aims of environmental preservation for Beijing: (1) preserving the cultural and historic core of the city; and (2) improving its natural environment to make the city beautiful, healthy and clean. To achieve these aims, indirect methods of controlling the size of the population, constraining growth of heavy, polluting and water- and energy-intensive industries, promotion of tertiary activities and 'clean' industries have been suggested.

Li and Li (1990) said that Beijing is a social system with a very complicated structure formed under a specific historical setting. As the nation's political centre, it administered the function of a socialist capital. Yet as a big city grown under special historical circumstances, it demonstrates many of the functions of a big metropolis.

The nature of a city determines its roles. With adequate 'functional support', the roles may be fulfilled. Functional support in essence is a safeguard of a city's nature, and is there to ensure its functioning by means of material and spiritual support which includes 10 variables: population, resources, information system, environment and ecology, social values, culture, housing, public services and utilities, transport, and social security and protection. Of the 10 variables, environment and ecology and culture are to be dealt with in this chapter. However, the nature of Beijing, for a very long period in 1953–78, had been distorted in favour of building up 'big industries'. Present-day Beijing has inherited much of the excesses of overemphasis on industries in past decades. As a consequence, some of the supporting elements had either been neglected or over-exploited, to the extent that their supportive role to Beijing's future growth as the nation's political and cultural centre is endangered. The focus of this chapter is on such a theme. It will first outline the main environmental issues of the capital. Then it will trace the debate and the consequential means for preserving old Beijing. The municipality's methods for tackling pollution will then be presented. It will conclude with some environmental targets and a discussion on the city's present environmental policy.

Main environmental issues

Beijing, as the capital of China, occupies a special position in environmental problems and environmental protection for the rest of the country. Such a fact conforms with the traditional Chinese view that the national capital serves as the example for other cities to follow. The city's environmental issues are the consequences of interaction of its natural environment, social environment and economic activities. To tackle and solve Beijing's environmental problems, one should take a long-term perspective and combine environmental protection with urban redevelopment, urban construction and development of the economy. Water shortages and environmental pollution have been two important constraints to Beijing's future development in economic terms as well as in terms of building a beautiful, healthy and clean capital to serve as the nation's political and cultural centre. We shall first describe these main environmental issues before discussing their implications and possible solutions.

Water shortage

Of the 300-odd cities in China, about 180 are classified as having a 'shortage in water resource'. Beijing is one of the worst 40 cities. Its problem is largely a consequence of its geography. It is located in the north-west part of the North China Plain, an area known for inadequate water resources. The average annual precipitation of the city is 626 mm, with a total rainfall of 10.5 billion cu m. Water catchment and storage facilities, both man-made and natural (including underground aquifers), are capable of utilizing 4.2–4.5 billion cu m of these resources annually. In dry years, that amount shrinks further to 3.3–3.5 billion cu m. On a per capita basis, Beijing's useable water resources are only 19.2% of the national average, and 3.4% of the world average. Because of rapid urbanization and industrialization, the city's annual water consumption has already reached 4.4 billion cu m, the limit of its useable annual supply in a 'good' year (Zheng, 1990).

The water shortage problem is the product both of the characteristics of its supply and hectic growth of demand. Annual and seasonal fluctuations have been a significant factor in Beijing's water problem. The trend of annual precipitation also tends to shrink. In the 1950s it was 781.9 mm, 1960s 628 mm, and 1970s 567.8 mm. Of the total annual precipitation, over 80% falls between June and September. Against a shrinking supply, Beijing's consumption has been on the increase. Industrial use had increased from 0.01 billion cu m in the early 1950s to 1.35 billion cu m in 1983. Even given strict adherence to the principle of not developing any water-intensive industries, the estimated consumption by 2000 is still 2 billion cu m. Increase in municipal use has been concurrent to the build-up of the population. But after 1983, improving standards of living have been mainly responsible for raising consumption to 1 billion cu m by 2000. In addition, a 22-fold extension in the irrigated area in 1949–83 and an increasing emphasis on self-sufficiency in grain and vegetables have been important reasons behind the huge increase in consumption by the farm sector. In future, rural consumption has to be held constant to relieve the water shortage problem (Huo, 1989).

Given the estimates for the year 2000, shortages of water will become more and more serious, as the estimated 5.5–6 billion cu m annual consumption will exceed average supply by a large margin. In the past, particularly in the 1980s, short supply was made good by exploiting underground storage. This averaged 0.7 billion cu m annually. However, in most years, the amount extracted from this source exceeded 3 billion cu m, well over the estimated annual 'bearable' maximum of 2.5 billion cu m. As the extraction takes place mainly in the main urban mass where the urban population, industries and vegetable fields concentrate, a huge water-table funnel of about 1000 sq km has been created by lowering the water-table and decreasing the quality of water (Huo, 1989)

Of the annual total consumption, industrial use takes 28%, farm use 64% and municipal use 8%. Thus industrial use constitutes 70–80% of total consumption within the urban (non-farm) uses. Statistics in 1983 show that metallurgy, chemicals and paper-making accounted for 51.3% of total industrial water consumption. In these industries, the rate of recycling of water had then reached 80.2%. Thus there is little scope to reduce further their consumption through recycling. A water-saving office was only set up in 1980 by the municipality to advise enterprises on how to save water. In 1980–84, it had brought down industrial water consumption by 14.5%. Yet there is doubt as to the effectiveness of the approach without restructuring of industries towards less water-intensive varieties.

Rural use consumes 2.5–3 billion cu m of water annually. The productivity of water in farming is low. The consumption per Yn10 000 farm output is 200 000 tonnes of water, and 1 tonne of water can only yield 0.5 kg of grain. The latter compares very unfavourably with 1.7 kg of grain in areas of even drier conditions in other parts of the country. Types of crop, particularly winter wheat and wet paddy, are heavy consumers of water. Restriction on their acreage and replacing some of them by other crops, or adopting new breeds such as dry-farming paddy, may both safeguard production as well as achieve savings in water consumption. Irrigation by channels and ditches, which are the prevailing methods at present, leads to 50% loss of irrigation water. Even the well and bucket method registers a loss of 20%. Sprinkling and dripping methods, which are highly water efficient, have to be gradually adopted to cut down on wasteful use of water.

A long-term solution to Beijing's water shortage problem may thus not be found within its territory. The environmental capacity of Beijing in this respect has been over-loaded. Remedial measures via outside sources are now being considered.

Damage to the natural ecology

Owing to its structural characteristics as well as erosion by rivers, there are a number of geomorphological gaps that effectively turn into wind tunnels facilitating the rush of north-east winds into the plain areas to the south-east. The weather in spring is usually dry, and the soil on the hills and slopes is thin and does not favour the growth of grass and scrub. In addition, the ratio of natural vegetation coverage is low. These

considerations combine to yield a tenuous natural ecology, easily sus-
ceptible to the onslaught of the north-east winds and human
disturbances such as deforestation and over-grazing. For a long time
in the 1950s and 1960s, agricultural policy which emphasized mono-
culture of grain led to encroachment of cultivation onto grazing land
and the clearing of forests. This further reduced the already slight
vegetation coverage. Application of large amounts of organic
agrochemicals and chemical fertilizers also damaged the farm ecology.
At the moment, forest coverage in Beijing area is only about 15%.
Another 23.3% is under grass and scrub. Per capita forest area is 0.27
mou (one sq km = 1500 mou), or one-fifteenth of the national average.

Soil erosion has been serious, both owing to wind-blown effects as
well as torrential rains in the summer. Soil erosion has led to silting of
the major reservoirs as well as generation of badlands. For example, an
annual intake of 31 million cu m of sand is registered in the Kunting
Reservoir. It cumulatively decreased the reservoir's capacity by a quarter
and there are 410 000 mou (273 sq km) of badlands. Damage to the
natural environment also decreased the flow in the middle and lower
reaches of rivers. For example, the Yungding River has turned dry for
over 20 years in the section below the Marco Polo Bridge. The beds of
long sections of the Chaobai and Yungding rivers have become heaps of
sand and they reinforce the hazards of sandstorms when the north-east
wind blows. Large areas of ponds and lakes in the plains have turned
into patches of derelict land. This damage to the environment further
weakens its ability to withstand and combat natural hazards like
sandstorms, floods and drought, and reduces plant, insect and animal
life in the area, besides undermining its capacity for farming and
supplying water for the city.

Water pollution

Beijing's waste water has been increasing very rapidly. Data for the
urban and suburban areas for 1954–80 show that the waste water
discharge had increased from 0.77 cu m/min to 23 cu m/min. The daily
discharge in 1980 was 1.8 million tonnes, 60% of which was industrial
waste. Of this, 244 000 tonnes were poisonous. Only 8% of the waste
water was then treated, and the rest was directly discharged into rivers
and streams. In 1991, the situation was not greatly improved. While the
daily discharge increased to 3.45 million tonnes, the treatment capacity
remained low. The three treatment plants of the city could handle a
daily amount of 304 000 tonnes, or 6.6% of the total discharge. The
urban and suburban areas contributed 74.8% of the discharge, a

reflection of the direct link between urbanization and industrialization on water pollution. The actual discharge in 1991 had exceeded the estimated figure for the year 2000 made in the early 1980s and indicates the rapid deterioration of the situation.

A survey in 1980 revealed that within the discharge, there were five major toxic substances: 0.078 tonnes of mercury, 5.2 tonnes of chromium, 16.3 tonnes of zinc, 22.7 tonnes of cyanide compound, and 299 tonnes of phenolic compounds. Some of these are heavy metals that are difficult to dissolve and they accumulate in the mud on the river-bed, causing long-term health hazards. The 1980 survey also revealed a daily discharge of 46 000 cu m of water polluted by bacteria from Beijing's 330 hospitals and clinics, 90% of which had not been treated. Spot checks at 59 hospitals indicated that the discharge exceeded the safety standard of 500 bacteria/litre, and its *E. coli* count exceeded the national standard by 80%. Polluted surface water contaminated the ground water as well. The 1980 study showed that 17% of the 482 wells tested contained water with higher than specified safety maxima of phenolic compounds, cyanide compounds, zinc, mercury and chromium. As a result of pollution, the hardness of the ground water has increased. In 1949, with the exception of a few areas, it was mostly 270 mg/litre (measured by calcium carbonate – $CaCO_3$). With increasing urbanization and industrial activities, areas that exceeded the standard of 450 mg/litre gradually increased, and in 1980 covered 216.9 sq km. By 1985, they had extended to 254.5 sq km (Beijing National Land Agency, 1990).

Air pollution

Air pollution in Beijing is typical of the coal-smoke type, dictated by its heavy dependence on coal as the energy source for both industrial and domestic uses. Such a pattern is especially obvious in winter when domestic heating in the form of inefficient direct burning of coal in small heating stoves raises the level of air pollutants substantially. It also underlines the unique combination of Beijing's modern heavy industries and its low standard of living and backward urban infrastructural development. The latter may be comparable to most Third World cities. A second contribution to air pollution is direct ground discharge of particles, caused by both industry and sandstorms. The latter is the outcome of its geography and mismanagement of the environment through overgrazing and deforestation as previously mentioned. The last main source is exhaust fumes from motor vehicles, a fact of life of a metropolis with an ever-increasing fleet of cars.

The pollution sources are mainly the city districts and the suburbs, including some county capitals and new towns. In 1981–85, sulphur dioxide in the air showed an increasing trend during the heating season (winter), while the change in intensity of carbon monoxide and nitrogen oxides was not obvious. In 1985, the city consumed 205 million tonnes of coal, which accounted for 60.6% of the total energy consumed. Crude oil consumed was about 8.81 million tonnes coal equivalent, or 33.7% of the total energy consumed. This pattern of primary energy source had not changed much in 1991. In that year, 20.7 million tonnes of coal were consumed, and 9.5 million tonnes coal equivalent of crude oil were consumed, respectively 60.3% and 38.9% of the total consumption (*Beijing Statistical Yearbook*, 1992). Industrial consumption took about 70% of the total consumption and domestic use took 20%. In the 1980s, coal consumption grew at an average annual rate of 2.2%. In the heating season, daily consumption was 30% above average. Central heating devices and small stoves that burn coal directly accounted almost equally for the heating use of coal. The two were responsible for 48.2% of sulphur dioxide content of the lower atmosphere in the heating season (Beijing National Land Agency, 1990).

Sulphur dioxide (SO$_2$). A study in 1979 showed that for the four city districts, the average daily sulphur dioxide content of the air was 0.23 mg/cu m during the heating season, and 0.05 mg/cu m in the rest of the year. The figure for the heating season was as high as the 1958 figure for London before it abandoned direct firing of coal as a means of heating. In comparison, Beijing's content was 20% higher than Shanghai, 30% higher than Tianjin and 30–70% higher than Los Angeles, Tokyo, Osaka and New York in the mid-70s.

Figure 9.1 measures the content of SO$_2$ in the air in 1986 through the formation of SO$_3$ under chemical reaction. The intensity of SO$_x$ was on the increase in Beijing as a whole and the main sources are the city districts and the heavy industrial complex at Shijingshan. Seasonal variation according to the heating or non-heating period may vary the measured content 3–6-fold. Heavy concentration in the city districts, much more than the heavy industrial district in the heating season, underlines the Third World city phenomenon of inadequate urban infrastructure in a cold environment. The suburbs and outer suburbs, with their much lower population densities, did not figure in the SO$_3$ content in either map.

Nitrogen oxides (NO$_x$). The main source of nitrogen monoxide is exhaust fumes of motor vehicles and that of nitrogen dioxide is the burning of coal. Statistics for 1984–87 show an increasing trend for NO$_x$,

A. Non-heating Season

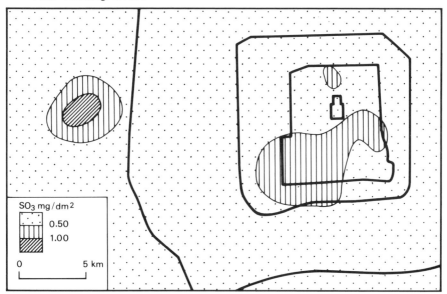

B. Heating Season

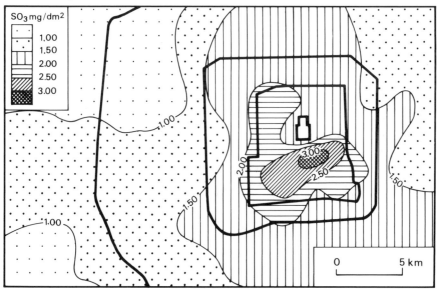

Figure 9.1 Sulphur oxides in the air, Beijing 1986

particularly in areas with heavy vehicular traffic. The NO_x content at seven monitoring stations during the heating season registered an average intensity of 94 ml/cu m in 1984 and 115 ml/cu m in 1987, respectively 31.7% and 46.1% above the accepted environmental standards. Vehicular exhaust fumes show a net pattern with higher values at road junctions and along major arteries. There are two high concentration areas: south-east and north-east of the city districts. The two areas combined have 6 sq km above the safety limit.

Carbon monoxide (CO). This is sourced from incomplete burning of fuel, both in small coal stoves and by motor vehicles in slow motion. The burning of coal in the heating season and heavy and congested traffic are the two main causes. Data of 1984–87 confirmed a rising trend. In 1984 the average daily figure was 1.9 ml/cu m and it rose to 2.3 ml/cu m in 1987, respectively 8.1% and 12.1% higher than accepted environmental standards. Time and spatial distribution underline that in the heating season there is a higher pollutant content in the air than the rest of the year, and the city districts also have higher figures than the suburbs.

Dust. This refers to particles that hang in and fall from the lower atmosphere. Since 1981, the city districts and suburbs have registered a decline in dust fall. In 1981, the monthly figure was 30 tonnes/sq km. By 1987, it dropped to 26 tonnes/sq km. In the outer suburbs, in industrial areas like Fangshan and Shijingshan, it was higher, i.e. 27–34 tonnes/sq km, while in other parts of the territory it was below 20 tonnes/sq km.

The total of air pollutants emitted into the atmosphere from the city as a whole was estimated to be 1.1 million tonnes in 1987. Of this, 81.9% came from burning of fuel, 14.5% came from industrial processing. The five major pollutants are, by order of their contribution to total air pollution: carbon monoxide (31.5%), sulphur dioxide (23.3%), soot (20.8%), dust (14%) and nitrogen oxides (9.8%). The spatial distribution of these pollutants shows a heavy bias in the suburbs; it centres around the Capital Iron and Steel Corporation and thins out in all directions.

We can generalize that Beijing has a serious air pollution problem, especially during its heating season. In the 611 sq km of monitoring centred around the city districts, the composite air pollution index as a whole reached over 1, showing that the average pollution situation has exceeded the national average. During the non-heating period of the year, the area with a composite index of over 1 extends for 60 sq km. Thus Beijing's air quality is definitely poor. This may be felt even by the average tourist who would find plenty of soot and dust in his or her hair after a half-day tour in any part of the city. Worse still is the fact that in Beijing's air there is a high content of the cancer-inducing chemical BaP (Benzo[a]pyrene). The presence of the chemical correlates highly with deaths from lung cancer. In 1958 Beijing registered a death rate from that disease of 7.9 persons in every 100 000; in 1979, this rose to 15.5 persons in every 100 000. BaP forms three high concentration areas within the planned urban area and thins out towards the periphery. The first area is within the old city, with Da Shan Lan as the centre. The second is centred at the Capital Iron and Steel Corporation and the third at the coking plant in the eastern suburb. The correlation between industrial production and BaP concentration is obvious, yet its high content within the old city is much more worrying as the population density, and hence its harmful effect, is much higher there. In the heating season, the area above the accepted level of concentration covers 500 sq km in the planned urban areas. Improving the energy and fuel consumption pattern of the residents hence becomes an urgent need so as to bring down the risk of this deadly chemical. In the non-heating season, the intensity and the area of high intensity both decrease. In the old city, only limited areas exceed the standard (1 mg/100 cu m), whilst in areas of the iron and steel plant and the coking plant the intensity remains above 4 mg/100 cu m. It illustrates the harmful effect of these heavy industries to the average Beijing resident (Beijing Urban Ecological System Research Group, 1991, 63).

Solid waste

There are about 8000 enterprises that release solid industrial waste, some of which are poisonous. The 1985 total industrial solid waste production was 8.14 million tonnes, 138 000 tonnes of which were poisonous. Of the amount produced, 4.36 million tonnes were dumped. Although 99.5% was general waste, 24 500 tonnes were poisonous, 1.47 million tonnes of the dumped waste were tailings from mines and the construction materials industry; 1.11 million tonnes were coal treatment waste mainly generated in Fangshan and Mentougu, centres of the coal industry. Waste from furnaces amounted to 910 000 tonnes. The last major item was pulverized fuel ash from the iron and steel plant and from electricity power plants. These four types constituted 87.7% of all solid waste. The recycling rate of industrial solid waste was only 42.2% and 36% was treated. For poisonous waste, the respective rates were 70.7% and 11.6%. These ratios were all lower than the national average.

In 1985, domestic solid waste amounted to 2.48 million tonnes, and night-soil 947 000 tonnes. In 1980–85, the per capita daily domestic solid waste generation increased at an average rate of 11.2%. Figures in 1991 show a total of domestic solid waste of 3.97 million tonnes, an increase of 60% in a matter of six years. The rate of increase remains great. Night-soil amounted to 2.1 million tonnes, and its rate of increase was even larger (*Beijing Statistical Yearbook*, 1992; and Beijing National Land Agency, 1990).

Disposal of solid waste consumes much valuable urban land, besides presenting health hazards and eyesores. Aerial photograph studies reveal that within the 750 sq km of planned urban areas, solid waste heaps 64 sq m in area numbered around 5000. They occupied a total of 5.76 sq km. Solid waste disposal landfills are scattered on the four sides of the city districts and are more concentrated in the suburb around the Third Ring Road. Recently, the municipal government marked out an additional 5700 mou (3.8 sq km) of land for constructing eight transhipment centres, four disposal grounds and eight fill areas.

Noise pollution

With the development of large-scale, high-speed and more forceful machines in manufacturing and transport industries, noise pollution has become an increasing urban problem. Noise pollution accounts for a significant number of complaint letters received by the municipality, i.e. 4% in 1977 and 41% in 1978 (*Beijing Metropolis*, 1985). A long period of exposure above 90 acoustic decibels (dBA) would damage one's hearing capability; 60–90 dBa would affect productivity and conversation, 40–60 dBA would affect sleep, and 30–40 dBA would cause unpleasant feelings. In industrialized countries, stringent noise standards are enforced in cities (Table 9.1).

A study in 1978 in the city districts of Beijing showed that the average noise level at 65 monitoring stations was 73.5 dBA. In the residential area of Qienmen, a survey of 67 households indicated that 90% of the residents felt the noise level was too high and people living in rooms facing the street could not sleep before 11 pm. The standards of Beijing, as shown in Table 9.2, are lower than those in Japan.

The 1979 noise census for the city districts indicated an average noise level of 60 dBA. This was highest in Xuanwu District, i.e. 64 dBA, followed by Chongwen (63 dBA), East City (59 dBA) and West City (53 dBA). The same survey also found that the noise impact index for the city districts was 0.235, about 100% more than the standard index of 0.1. The noise pollution problem of the city was thus serious. The municipality has since adopted a number of measures to cut down the

Table 9.1   Noise standards in Japan (dBA)

Land use	Day	Morning, evening	Night
Resort and places of quietness	45	40	35
Residential	50	45	40
Commercial, industrial	60	55	50

Source: *Beijing Metropolis*, 1985.

Table 9.2   Noise standards in Beijing (dBA)

Land use	Day	Night
Special use	45	35
Residential, educational, cultural	50	40
Mixed uses I (residential + commercial)	55	45
Mixed uses II (residential + commercial + industrial)	60	50
Industrial	65	55
Main road arteries	70	55

Source: *Beijing Metropolis*, 1985.

urban noise level. For example, from 1983 onwards, motor vehicles were forbidden to use their horns in 15 major streets. That measure alone decreased the average dBA of the city districts by 3.6.

Urban heat island

The urban heat island effect is illustrated by the difference in average temperature between the inner city and the suburbs (Figure 9.2). When the difference exceeds 0.5°C, the urban heat island effect is said to exist. Statistics for 20 major cities of the world show the prevalence of such a phenomenon, with average temperature difference of 0.7°C. The effect leads to convectional currents between the inner city and its suburbs. It tends to spread pollutants from the inner city over a much wider territory. In some extreme cases, areas without pollution sources may have more serious pollution as a consequence of the urban heat island effect.

Beijing's urban heat island effect is very strong; the difference in average temperature between the city districts and the suburbs is 1.7°C and in the worst part of the year it reaches 2.5°C. The effect is most marked in winter, the heating season. Figure 9.2 shows a very strong effect of 5.1°C in 1987 in a day of brightness and little wind.

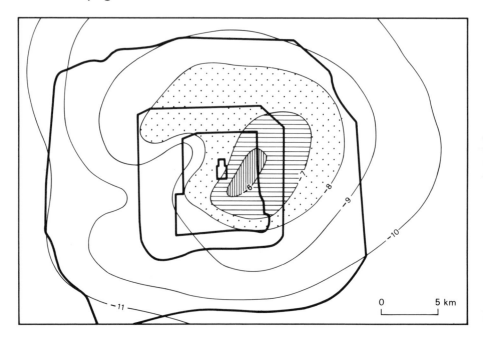

Figure 9.2   Heating island isotherms (in C°, 2 Jan. 1987, 8 pm)

Preserving Old Beijing

Preserving the traditional core of the city started as soon as Beijing was made the capital of the PRC in 1949. The debate centred around the issue of where to put the new administrative headquarters of the central government. Local planners led by Professor Liang put forward the proposal that the PRC central government headquarters should be established in the western suburb (see Figure. 9.3), whereas the opposite point of view, that space could be found within the old city for accommodating this new function, was represented by the Soviet experts. In fact, the essence of the debate was the manner in which the old city should be preserved. Liang and Chen, in their formal proposal to the central government in 1950, stated that the old city of Beijing (within its wall) had preserved the best of Chinese urban planning and should be completely preserved. They proposed that the Chinese government should take up the responsibility conscientiously and steadfastly to protect the old city, a cultural artifact of historic and art value, for the people (Beijing Construction History, 1987).

The arguments of the Soviet experts were based on the experience in

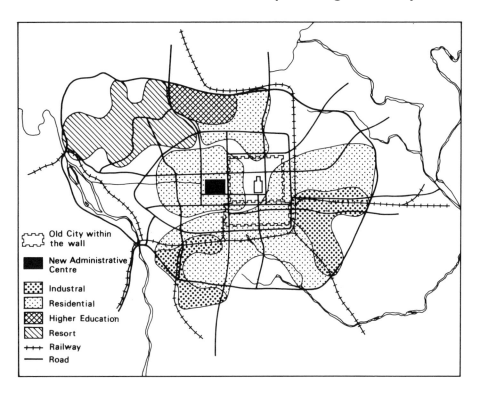

Figure 9.3 Liang's General Plan for Beijing, 1950

the USSR that setting up the new administrative centre within the old city could minimize cost, as some housing and infrastructure that already existed there could be immediately exploited. It would also save time compared to setting it up on a greenfield site. In addition, they did not seem to be too serious about the preservation of the old city:

> We have such type of suggestion too, i.e. to turn the old city of Moscow into a museum, and build a new city by its side. We had turned it down and reconstructed Moscow. The result is not bad at all. Demolition of old buildings in Beijing is a task that must be done somewhere in time. Rickshaw drivers are now employed as factory hands. What means of transport through the Hutung [small lanes] you [Liang and Chen] can now rely on? (Beijing Construction History, 1987)

With economic expedience and modernization arguments, the Soviet experts won the day. The new administrative quarter was soon set up in the south and south-western part of the old city, immediately outside the Forbidden City. In the course of redevelopment and construction for accommodating the new function and housing its large number of employees and their dependants, there had been some disturbance and demolition of historic buildings and loss of character of some areas within the old city. The wall and its gates were soon gone as obvious casualties of the approach. However, there are long-term consequences that still remain, such as overcrowding and severe traffic jams, as the administrative and cultural functions overlap each other as well as overlap with the city's main shopping and retailing centres.

The second main event in the preservation of old Beijing was the restructuring of Tian An Men Square in 1954–60. In an exhibition in 1954, 10 proposals had been revealed. Later in 1956, under the leadership of Soviet experts, another 11 proposals were formulated and shown to the public together with the general plan of the city.

Obviously, the restructuring of Tian An Men Square led to another debate that involved the preservation of the old city and the tradition of Chinese city planning that it represents. The debate centred around four issues:

1. *Nature of the Square.* Some viewed it as the pivot of politics in the country, a symbol of the nation which should be surrounded by offices of central ministries, the seat of central government, and museums of the revolution and of its military history. Others viewed it as the pivot of culture which should thus be dominated by libraries and museums.
2. *Built form.* Some felt that the square represented the great achievement of socialist construction. New buildings should line its sides and even occupy its centre, to form the highest point and centre for all buildings within the city. The opposing view is that new buildings should not be taller than Tian An Men or the Memorial of the People's Heroes.
3. *Treatment for old buildings.* Some slighted old buildings in and around the square and regarded them as insignificant in the new era of socialism. They proposed that these old buildings should be gradually replaced by new tall ones that show the spirit of socialism and communism. The opposite view is that old buildings there are valuable historical assets of the nation and should be preserved.
4. *Size of the Square.* Some felt that the Square is the central space for political movements and public rallies of the people. It should be large and some proposed 30–40 hectares as appropriate. Others held the view that the Square should not be too large, to maintain a reasonable scale in relation to surrounding buildings.

The final decision was that the Square is to be a political centre. On its two sides are to be the Hall of the People, and the Museum of Revolution and Museum of History. Zhong Hua Men (gate) was demolished but Chao Yang Men (gate) and Jinlou (archery tower) remained. The red walls on the two sides were taken down to make way for the new buildings and for extending the size of the Square from the original 11 hectares to 40 hectares (see Figure 9.4). Tram-rails on East and West Changan Avenue were dismantled, creating a 390 m long and 80 m wide passage in front of Tian An Men for public rallies. The old north–south central axis of the traditional plan of the old city is preserved. It is now marked by the Memorial of the People's Heroes located at the centre of the new Square, and this is taller than the highest point of Tian An Men and Tai He Dian (throne hall) (Beijing Construction History, 1987).

The main purpose of the new arrangement is to transform the former forbidden square of the imperial rule into a new centre of socialism based on the rule of the people. It wants to reverse people's attention and reverence from one of northward orientation towards the Forbidden City and hence Tai He Dian and its symbolic mandate of Heaven, to a southward orientation marked by the national flag and the Memorial of the People's Heroes, and the Hall of the People that represents the highest seat of government of the new regime. In fact, the new arrangement has bolstered the attractiveness of Tian An Men and the Forbidden City which lies beyond (Zhao, 1989). This is especially so at night as Tian An Men is beautifully lit while the rest of the Square remains dim. Although Chairman Mao's portrait has since been hung above the main entrance to Tian An Men, thus effectively reminding people of the existence of the new regime, it underlines the feudalistic inclination of the new leadership based on personal cult and tales of the mandate of Heaven. In spirit, Mao's portrait at that location reinforces the feudalistic tradition and the symbolism of traditional Chinese city planning centred around the myth of the Son of Heaven. There are, however, clear elements of Western concepts introduced by the Soviet experts in the course of the planning and reconstruction of the Square. The concept of a huge open square for public rallies is itself non-Chinese. Old Beijing only had courtyards, a *yang* type of design. The new Square is a Western and a *yin* design (Rui, 1989; Pu, 1989). The Memorial of the People's Heroes in the form of an epitaph is also Western, though the shape and design of the structure are Chinese in style. The new buildings of the Hall of the People, Museum of History and Museum of Revolution are mixtures of Western styles, particularly of Soviet style modified here and there by Chinese ways. In the final analysis, the Square may be seen as representative of post-1949 Beijing, combining the traditional Chinese

248

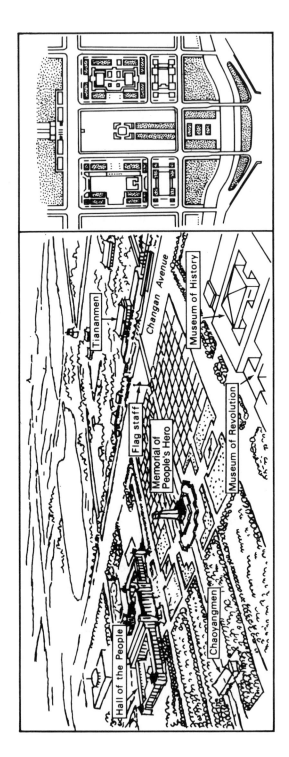

Figure 9.4 The final design of Tian An Men Square

city with imported alien elements through the Soviet experts. In 1980, following Mao's death in 1976, a new Chairman Mao Mausoleum was constructed in the southern portion of the Square. It too has reinforced the non-Chinese element of the Square, as no Chinese, particularly Chinese leaders, were not to be buried underground. The grey, grim and non-Chinese design of the structure seems to be out of place in the Square. It has not only reduced the size of the Square, but further diluted its original planning concept of being 'a political square' of the people. From the traditional Chinese city planning point of view, the Mausoleum is an unacceptable farce.

The restructured Tian An Men Square and its officially proclaimed nature emanating from the Soviet city model have formed the basis of the socialist transformation of nearly all urban centres in China, most notably in Shanghai, Nanjing, Hangzhou and Guangzhou, where the city centre is marked by a new people's square. A non-Chinese element in city planning has thus been successfully grafted onto the core of the Chinese city since 1960. The leading role of the national capital once again demonstrates its effectiveness.

Despite significant disturbances and alteration to the landscape of the old city, it still remains to this day the most comprehensively preserved example of traditional Chinese city planning. The Forbidden City, in particular, has not been touched by the two major events previously described. Large sums of money had been voted for its upkeep. It remains as glamorous as before, and forms a source of substantial pride for the Chinese in their history and culture. It attracts annually millions of Chinese as well as non-Chinese tourists and is one of the world's most valued and spectacular art pieces and archaeological remains. Preserving the Forbidden City, enhancing its present value as the cultural and historic inheritance of China and maximizing its positive impact on tourism and on the city's role as the cultural centre of the country have spurred on a new demand for more effective preservation through modern town-planning approaches.

In this revival of attention to preserve old Beijing, a comprehensive approach has emerged. It combined preservation with urban renewal and the importance of urban infrastructure. It also calls for due attention to the four relationships, i.e. (1) preservation of the old capital and modern urban living; (2) preservation of the old city and improvement of the living conditions of its residents; (3) relationship between the historical cultural centre and the modern political and cultural centre; and (4) relationship between old and new buildings.

Before 1960, within the old city, a total of 540 000 sq m of old buildings had been demolished. Yet only 530 000 sq m of new buildings were erected. The new and bulky buildings around Tian An Men Square and along Changan Avenue are the main reasons for the demolition as well as for the major alterations made to the old city. In the 20 years that followed, the annual demolition rate was less than 100 000 sq m. Yet since 1978, many work units began construction of tall buildings within their courtyards. In 1978–92, the annual demolition amounted to 100 000 sq m, but the annual addition of new floor space was in the order of 700 000–800 000 sq m. In 1983–85, the demolition rate had further increased to 160 000–220 000 annually, while new construction completed exceeded an annual figure of 1 million sq m. These statistics showed that post-1949 construction, especially that since 1978, was mainly set on empty space within the old city, whereas of the 10 million sq m or so old cottage houses inherited in 1949, only about a third had been redeveloped (Tong, 1987). The threat to the old city has arisen mainly since the open policy of 1978 and it takes two main forms: the invasion of over 100 tall buildings which threaten the traditional skyline of the Imperial City, some even threatening the central axis of the Forbidden City; new developments taking up courtyards and empty spaces, doing a great deal of damage to the traditional built form of courtyard houses, royal gardens, old temples and traditional mandarin houses. Traditional or old Beijing is a horizontal city with key landmarks at commanding heights to provide identity and direction to the spatial ordering of the city. Rui (1989) identified six major characteristics of the old city which need to be considered worthy of preserving. The predominant characteristic is the north–south axis. It not only links the Forbidden City and Tiantan, two major groups of historic and cultural artifacts of old Beijing, to form the backbone of the city, but also forms a central or base-line for the whole of urban Beijing. The height of buildings along the axis that would impinge on it has to be strictly controlled through planning regulations. The second element is formed by the six huge ponds (*hai*) and their accompanying systems of gardens and open spaces. They complement and provide a green setting for the central axis. The third element is the small neighbourhoods between the main roads. They provide the city with a uniform and complete set of buildings arranged in the *yang* style, with smooth correlations in building height, colour and spatial structure. Fourthly, the chessboard pattern of streets dates back to the Song style of the Yuan city. Fifthly, the markets, shopping streets and religious buildings reflect the evolution as well as the multi-faceted cultural, religious and racial elements of old Beijing. Sixthly, though the old city wall was demolished in the 1950s and lost as an artifact, its site, particularly within the Second Ring Road, still remains. The wall provides the old city with a frame to make it complete. Thus the old site needs to be utilized in such a way that a 'new wall' fitting such a perceived image of the old city may re-emerge.

Arising from increasing concern and more importantly as a direct consequence of the new directives of the CCP and central government (1980) on the nature of Beijing, official preservation legislation started in 1982. In that year the State Council proclaimed the first list of 'historical cultural cities' and Beijing heads the list. The document states that 'Our country is an old civilized nation. Protecting a group of historical cultural cities has positive implications on inheriting our long cultural assets, promoting our proud revolutionary tradition, facilitating education on patriotism, constructing spiritual civilization of socialism and extending our international influence' (Li, 1990). The Forbidden City was also listed by UNESCO as 'the World's Cultural Asset'. In the same year, legislation on cultural asset protection was promulgated. Within Beijing 35 examples of historic architecture were proclaimed as 'national'-level protection subjects. In addition, there were 174 at municipal level and 854 at *xian* (county) level proclaimed as cultural assets to be protected by law. Around the protected architecture of municipal level and above, 187 development control zones have been promulgated according to the Cultural Asset Protection Law. Further larger-scale protection aimed at the three-dimensional aesthetic approach to preserve the style and spirit of the old city took the form of the *Regulation on Building Height of the Planned Urban Areas* in 1985, and *Land Use and Height Control Planning Measures of the Old City of Beijing* in 1987. The latter also restricts land use and plot ratio in areas with protected cultural assets. In brief, there have been three main types of protective measures: protection of the artifact itself; height control of surrounding areas; and land-use and building control in surrounding areas.

In implementing building control, building height was classified into six categories in 1982, i.e. single-storey or cottage type of building (3.3 m), below 9 m, below 18 m, below 30 m, below 45 m, and below 60 m. '18 m' forms an important threshold as lifts and indoor fire hydrants would be required above this height (Wang, 1989). A city's skyline may exhibit three patterns (Figure 9.5): the pyramidal model, common in North America as cities there are dominated by the central business district and capitalism in the form of tall offices, financial and commercial buildings; the basin model, of which the most commonly found are cultural cities of long history with a well-protected core; the saddle model, combining protection of the core and concentrated development at the rim of the old city, from which the building height declines outwards. The 1985 height control regulation in general incorporated the basin model. However, according to Wang (1989), the saddle pattern would be more apt for Beijing. The two 'peaks' are to be set along the Second Ring Road. Higher building there can maximize more convenient transport and proximity to the city centre. Thus it would

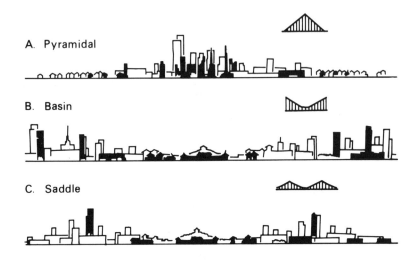

Figure 9.5 Three possible models for the skyline of central Beijing. Source: Fan, 1989

effectively draw away from the centre tall buildings that are bound by locational considerations to be tied to more central locations. Accordingly Wang proposed an overall height zone plan for Beijing (Figure 9.6).

Besides height control, the whole of Beijing may be classified into five types of area in the spirit of the Cultural Asset Protection Law (Li, 1987; Tong 1987):

1. *Cultural Protection Area.* This is an area zoned according to the Cultural Asset Protection Law and administered by relevant government agents. Within the area, all buildings are under strict protection. Maintenance and rebuilding have to follow the exact original style and form. No new buildings or additions are allowed.
2. *Style Protection Area.* Within the area, it is the identity of the locale that is under protection. Buildings may be demolished or newly constructed if they do not impair the style of the area. The height, volume, style, density and colour of new buildings will be screened to ensure that they agree with or promote the identity of the area.
3. *Cultural Control Area.* These are areas under height control of type II (cottage), III (9 m) and IV (18 m) for maintaining a complementary setting of individually scattered cultural assets. New buildings are controlled in height, volume, style and colour variously according to their distance from the cultural asset.

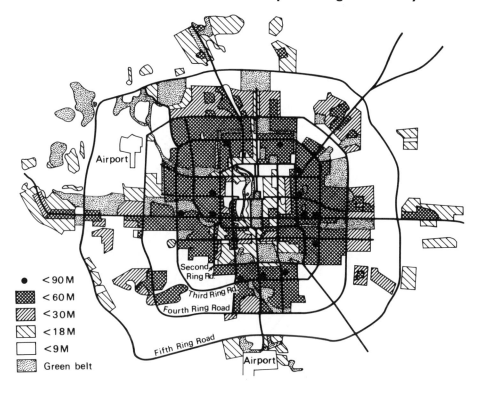

Figure 9.6 Suggested height control for Beijing. Source: Wang, 1989

4. *Transitional Area.* Areas outside the previous three control zones. Control measures are more relaxed. Despite this, an awareness of the need to protect the style and image of the old city will always be necessary.
5. *New Development Areas.* They are large tracts of land within the planned urban areas outside the old city, excluding the northwestern suburb. Building density and height are subject to general planning control only.

Li (1990) presented a similar category of protection areas. His Grade One Protection Area is the equivalent of the Cultural Protection Area, and covers 20 sq km of land which includes the whole of the Forbidden City and the San Hai. His Grade Two Protection Area is the equivalent of the Style Protection Area and the Cultural Control Area combined, while the Grade Three Protection Area is the same as the Transitional Area. Li's protection area has been shown graphically as well (Figure 9.7). Within

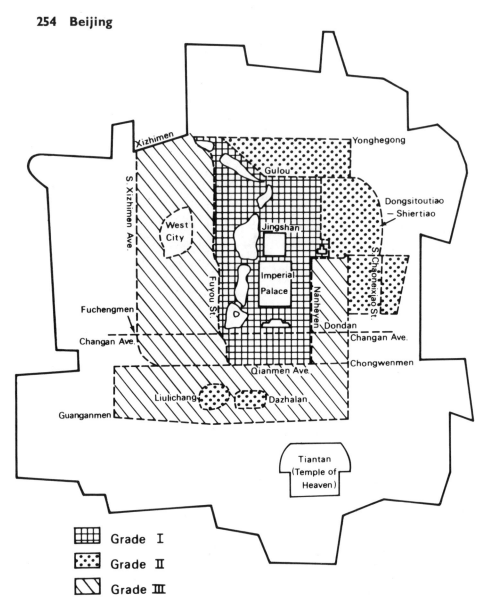

Figure 9.7 Cultural asset protection areas. Source: Li, 1990

the 62 sq km old city, areas under different intensity of building height control and cultural asset protection take up about a quarter of the total area. It underlines the rich cultural asset as well as the municipality's dedication to preserving such a valuable inheritance. Indeed, by both measures, Beijing stands out as a unique case in the world.

Tackling pollution

Energy

To a large degree, air pollution in Beijing is contributed to by its heavy dependence on direct burning of coal as a fuel. By 2000, its coal consumption may reach 30 million tonnes, about 1.79 times its 1980 consumption. In the heating season, there are over 6000 heating furnaces and over 1 million small coal pellet stoves releasing a large amount of pollutants into the lower atmosphere. The short-term policy is to improve the quality of coal and of the small heating stoves to raise their efficiency. In the long term, direct burning of coal by over 600 000 households has to be replaced by electricity or use of cleaner energy such as gas and portable liquefied gas. Use of portable liquefied gas for cooking has been on the increase. In 1980, only 62.2% of households were using it; by 1991, this became 85.1% of households. Burning of coal for heating by means of individual small stoves is still predominant, as central heating only accounted for 13.1% of domestic heating in the mid-1980s. Increasing electricity supply while improving the quality of coal products and small heating stoves, and providing Beijing with more natural gas and liquefied petroleum products, are ways to restructure its energy consumption pattern for a cleaner city.

Industrial restructuring

A strong concentration on energy-intensive, water-intensive and hence pollution-prone heavy industries has been a significant source of Beijing's pollution problems and a cause of its deteriorating environment. It is now the standing policy of the government to discourage further growth of these industries, while existing industries are forced to combat pollution through turning to more efficient processes or changing to new products and those located within sensitive areas are asked to relocate or close down.

Within the city districts enclosed by the Third Ring Road there are 1531 industrial enterprises, about half of which are serious pollution sources. The location of these factories in close proximity to dense residential areas is naturally a cause for concern. The municipal Environmental Protection Bureau and Economic Committee have joined forces to tackle the industrial pollution of the so-called 'one patch', i.e. the area within the Third Ring Road; the 'big three', i.e. the Capital Iron and Steel Corporation, Yan Shan Chemical Corporation and the Electricity Corporation; and the 'two small', i.e. rural collective industrial enterprises and 'street factories'. Since 1980, 800 of the more serious pollution sources within the Third Ring Road had been subjected to combination, conversion, closure and relocation. Of these, 226 were relocated, 25 heavy energy- and water-consuming and heavy polluting enterprises were closed, 135 changed their product line and 53 factories solved their pollution problems by restructuring their product mix.

In addition to the above, industrial specialization and division of labour between enterprises have been promoted as means to cut down the number of pollution sources and reduce pollution. This is especially vigorous in metal casting and welding, heat treatment and electroplating. For the city as a whole, there were 1486 such processing locations; by 1982 351 had been eliminated and 31 inside the city districts had been completely closed or relocated. Electroplating units inside the Third Ring Road had been reduced by 36% in the same period, and heat treatment locations within the city districts dropped from 176 to 105. Encouragement to recycle pollutants and waste has been provided through tax exemptions, retainment of profits and low-interest loans. The industrial bureaus also set up purification devices for their large plants and areas of concentration of polluting plants.

Water pollution in the seven rivers is also closely related to industries. In 1983 alone, 450 pollution sources along the rivers had been treated. Industrial waste water was largely untreated in 1973 (3%). By 1983, the rate had increased to 39% and the waste water recycling rate had also been raised to 69%. The reduction in pollutants in stream water in 1973–83 had been obvious, e.g. mercury had decreased by 97%. In that 10-year period, the length of underground sewers increased by 33%, diverting much of the flow of industrial and domestic waste water from streams, reducing the pollution of their upper and middle reaches.

Action on protecting the water sources of the city's main reservoirs forms part of combating industrial pollution. Poisonous chemicals from factories on the upstream side of Kunting Reservoir once posed serious problems to its water quality. A special committee was set up in 1972. Within three years, the committee managed to take action on the pollution sources and maintained the water quality standard for the reservoir.

Ecological agriculture

Since 1982, re-emphasis on the rule of law in protecting the rural environment had basically halted the uncontrolled felling of trees, grazing of animals and opening of new fields on hill slopes. Since then efforts on replanting have been organized annually. In 1991 the forest coverage rate of the municipality had regained 16%. In the plain areas, about 2 million mou (1333 sq km) of farm land have been protected by a green net of trees. An attack on pollution by insecticides and agro-chemicals had also been launched. The two popular yet highly poisonous drugs, 666 and DDT, though banned in other countries long ago, were still widely applied in Beijing in the 1970s. In 1976, the municipal government set up a Working Group on Prevention of Farm Pollution. The group formulated a policy on low-pollution farm chemicals and requested the Chemical Bureau to arrange production of advanced farm chemicals of low pollution effects. The use of organochlorine has since dropped from an annual 9000 tonnes in 1975 to 1700 tonnes in 1981. By 1984, 666 and DDT had been completely phased out. Residuals in the soil from 666 declined markedly and samples of grain, vegetables and milk which previously showed organochlorine above the safety limit returned to the national hygienic standards.

The use of the biotic approach to cure plant diseases and fight pests was successful as well. In 1981–83, a type of bee was used to combat pests on corn. It successfully protected the crop without application of any farm drug. Control of larvae by biotic means in pine trees in the main water catchment areas of the two largest reservoirs saved a substantial amount of chemicals, i.e. 150 000 tonnes, and reduced their pollution of the rural ecology.

Development of new breeds of crops to save water and to maximize the productivity of the soil are other means to attain a better ecological balance which have been previously mentioned.

Controlling the size of the city and infrastructural development

Heavy concentration of population and human activities within the 350 sq km core of the planned urban areas is a main contributing factor to the poor environment in Beijing. Within this area, about 2% of the total territory of the municipality, are 45% of its population, 82% of its building floor area and 80% of its energy consumption. On top of that, urban infrastructure has been lagging behind population and industrial development. A vast amount of industrial and domestic waste is hence emitted or discharged into the air and water courses without treatment. Decentralization of population and industries into the suburbs and beyond, particularly to new towns in the outer suburbs, and controlling the overall population size of the city are seen as necessary measures to reduce the burden on the ecology and protecting the environment. At the request of the municipal government, protection of the environment has become an important issue for the Planning Committee in its plan on economic development, the Economic Committee in its plan on industrial restructuring and technological improvement, and the Town Planning Commission in its national land planning. In Beijing's recent Five Year Plans, i.e. the sixth, seventh and eighth Plan, environmental protection targets have been set and relevant measures have been included. Various legislation at municipal level has been enacted to set standards for environmental protection and for punishing those who disregard the law. It covers areas ranging from the emission of smoke and dust from furnaces, urban tree planting, urban noise pollution, emission of waste gases, to waste water, etc. It is also a must for all new construction, expansion and redevelopment of urban infrastructure to ensure that environmental protection devices are simultaneously planned, constructed and put to use. As a new source of environmental protection revenue and a deterrent to pollution, pollution charges have been established for emission of pollutants above the set standards. The money has been used to subsidize pollution abatement at source.

Conclusion

Beijing in 1949 had inherited a macro environment which was not ideal for a capital city. It is too dry and exposed to the onslaught of sand-storms and other natural hazards. The hills had for very long periods in history been subject to deforestation and overgrazing. Despite this, Beijing also inherited a priceless fortune in the form of the ancient cultural complex of the old city, the national capital of Chinese dynasties for over 600 years. This latter asset is sufficient reason to qualify it as the capital of the PRC and hence as its political and cultural headquarters.

Post-1949 policies have since been much at variance with Beijing's environment. Forced industrialization with undue emphasis on heavy industries has not only created significant pollution sources and depleted water resources, it has also led to rapid increases in population. Government policy emphasis on 'production' and de-emphasis on 'consumption' aggravated environmental issues as the imbalance between urban infrastructure and increased industrial and urban waste worsened. The policy of local self-reliance and subsistence in food supply had promoted a rural economic policy of mono-culture of grain, disregarding the environmental capability of the area. This also led to further extension of cultivation to grazing land and further destruction of forests.

By almost all measurements, Beijing's water, air and solid waste pollution problems are serious, and so is its noise pollution. The re-orientation of Beijing's role as the nation's political and cultural centre since 1980, the overall change in philosophy of the Chinese government in respect to economic development based on the market system, and the emphasis on the need to improve people's quality and standard of living, have all dramatically changed the situation. Environmental protection legislation and measures have hence become important in the realms of economic planning and urban construction approvals. Substantial improvements have been made in the city's air and water quality as well as in noise levels. Yet until the early 1990s, Beijing could still be seen as one of the more polluted cities, and was far away from its set goal of being a clean, hygienic and beautiful city. Continual efforts by the government are necessary on a number of fronts to achieve such a goal. More precisely, the city has set environmental standards for the year 2000 as shown in Table 9.3.

The decades since 1949 underline very well the imbalance between economic development and attention towards the environment. Slighting the latter means equally slighting the long-term benefits to the community. In such a respect, Beijing is similar to major Third World cities where public good in the form of a hygienic and clean environment has not been an important item in the government's policy list. As a low latitude city, insufficient urban infrastructure in the form of central heating makes it unique in heavy air pollution in the heating season, as there are over 1 million small heating stoves burning coal directly to generate heat. In a way, its pollution may partly be related to a low level of economic development, in addition to the policy imbalance between 'productive' and 'consumptive' investments.

As the most completely preserved ancient capital of the world, Beijing's urban environment and environmental protection should include the unique element of the preservation of the old capital. In this chapter, we have discussed issues concerning the siting of the new administrative centre, the redevelopment of Tian An Men Square, and recent discussions and measures on control of building height and preservation of cultural assets within the old city. Economic expedience was the main reason for rejecting sensible local planners' proposals to preserve the Imperial City comprehensively and completely and to develop the new administrative centre of the nation in the western suburb. Concern about economics had been the main reason behind the lack of preservation of the old city for 20 years after 1960. Ideological biases may partly explain this. This concern had also been responsible for some of the invasion of non-Chinese designs into the new Tian An Men Square, at present an artifact in itself, to reflect the fusion of traditional Chinese feudalism and socialist idealism. Although in some ways somewhat damaged and altered, in most parts the Imperial City, particularly the Forbidden City, remains China's best preserved example

Table 9.3 Environmental standards of Beijing for the year 2000

Pollutant		mg/cu m (Air*)	Water*	ml/l (except where indicated)	Land use	Noise (dBA) Day	Night
Particulates	daily average	0.30	pH (value)	6.5–8.5	Special	45	35
	any time	1.00	Colour (grade)	< 15	Residential	50	40
Dust	daily average	0.15	Smell (grade)	1	cultural mixed I.	55	45
	any time	0.50	Dissolved oxygen (%)	> 6	Mixed II, Commercial	60	50
NO_x	daily average	0.10	Biochemical oxygen demand (days)	< 3	Industrial	65	55
	any time	0.15	Chemical oxygen demand (grade)	< 4	Main arteries	70	55
SO_2	daily average	0.15	Phenolic compounds	< 0.005			
	any time	0.50	Oxidized material	< 0.05			
CO	daily average	4.00	Zinc	< 0.04			
	any time	10.00	Total mercury	< 0.0005			
O_3	hourly average	0.16	Cadmium	< 0.005			
			Chromium (+6)	< 0.02			
			Lead	< 0.05			
			Copper	< 0.01			
			Oil	< 0.3			
			E. Coli (no. per litre)	< 10 000/litre			
			Total phosphorus	< 0.1			
			Total nitrogen	< 0.1			

* Grade Two standard
Source: Beijing Metropolis, 1985.

of the planning of the national capital and the important ideology behind the ordering of urban structures and urban living in traditional Chinese civilization. This important element of the urban environment of Beijing will remain the most notable reminder of what Beijing is, historically, culturally, ideologically and even environmentally.

10

Transport: walking on two legs?

The efficiency of an urban transport system is greatly influenced by its management, its capacity, the conditions under which it operates, and the demands made upon it as a result of the settlement's geographical location, its population size, urban form and urban function. Whereas the variables of location, population size, urban form and urban function may be unique to a city, the ruling philosophy and the predominant public goal of the state greatly affect former variables of management, capacity and operating conditions of the urban transport system. We shall briefly review the general situations obtaining in other parts of the world as background to the treatment of Beijing.

Soviet bloc countries

Studies of former Soviet bloc countries show that there is an established 'socialist' urban transport-planning philosophy (Bater, 1980). It combines three basic principles. First, the journey to work should be minimized. Secondly, spatial mobility should in general be based on public transport. Thirdly, public transport fares are to be heavily subsidized. The first is to be achieved through rational planning of employment and residential areas. Journey-to-work time for large cities of over half a million population is based on a norm of 40 minutes, while for smaller centres it is about 25 minutes. Economic expedience and low wage levels in general dictated the predominance of public transport. Although the trend of rising ownership of cars began to emerge in the 1970s, reliance on public transport was still obvious in the USSR. Lack of choice in residential location was another important reason why urban residents had to be dependent on public transport (French, 1979). Besides frequency of service, low flat-rate fare structure was a characteristic. The situation was said to be the envy of the

Western world, which reminds the Western commuter of 'an age long since past' (Compton, 1979, 483).

Despite the three main characteristics, there had been a big margin between theory and practice. In reality, irrational location of employment nodes in relation to residential areas had often lengthened journeys to work to much above the norm. The fact that low wage levels usually forced a family to have more than one wage earner also upset the planning target of relating workplace to residence. Large-scale redevelopment and rehousing in city centres in the 1950s and 1960s equally led to lengthening of journeys to work. Lastly, the lag between construction of housing and provision of services, and a large 'unplanned' and 'fluid' population within the city, were other major reasons worsening the situation in public transport. In the mid-1960s Muscovites on average spent 37 minutes on their journey to work; in the late 1970s one hour became the realistic average. Thus it was observed that a prolonged journey to work became a new trend in the USSR, in addition to a rising trend of private cars (Bater, 1980, 112–13).

Industrialized Western countries

While the former Soviet bloc countries still depended greatly on public transport, in cities of Western industrialized countries private cars have dominated urban transport since World War II. The trend persisted in the 1970s and 1980s as passenger car numbers continued to increase and car ownership reached well over 15 vehicles per 100 persons in most of these countries (Button and Ruthengatter, 1993, 28). A high standard of living, coupled with the freedom of movement offered by private cars and continued government efforts in construction of roads, substantiated the continuing preference for the private car as the main means of transport in these cities. In the bigger cities, congestion in the city centre led to development of mass transit systems, e.g. the underground train, yet for a number of such countries, such as the Netherlands, Germany and France, the intended infrastructure investments in the 1990s are still biased towards popular use of the car, since highway construction will take up from 50% to over 80% of all transport infrastructural investments in the period. Even within the Netherlands, popular demand on environmental grounds has opted for a policy of restricted use of the car in favour of public transport, yet the car remains the travel mode with the highest growth rate in projections made for the year 2010. It will have 46% growth compared to 1986, while trips by trains will grow by 39%, by other public transport 11%, and those by bicycle and walking will decline to 97% of their 1986 level (Rietveld, 1993).

Third World countries

Urban transportation in Third World cities may generally be described as sharing a number of characteristics. First, there is a mix of transportation technologies, highlighted by the sharing of road space by fast-moving motorized vehicles with slow human-powered bicycles, rickshaws and animal-drawn carts. In addition to traffic conflict, this has led to road congestion and road safety problems. Second is the misuse of transport technology. The most common example is the misuse of the tractor as a light goods vehicle or a light goods vehicle as a passenger car; or misuse of means of transport for inappropriate distances, such as trains for cargo shipment over less than 100 km. Third are the deficiencies of urban public transport. In most Third World cities, low income levels forbid a high car ownership ratio and thus most of the residents have to depend on public transport. The example of São Paulo indicates that public transport shared over 60% of daily trips in both 1960 and 1990, and buses accounted for over 80% of public transport trips. Cars, though increasing in number, contributed to less than a third of all daily trips. São Paulo is already a more advanced developed city in the Third World than Calcutta or Accra.

In many more Third World cities, rapid urbanization has outstripped public sector investment in public transport, leading to inadequacy of services. This may be measured by the base line suggested by the World Bank, i.e. less than one bus per 1000 population. Insufficient funds also lead to poor maintenance, low efficiency of operation and operating deficits. A low availability rate of less than 80% was registered in a number of cities whose operating km per day per bus was also low, as was the ratio of operating revenue to total costs. The fourth characteristic is evidenced by available data indicating that, whereas in cities of developed countries roads typically occupy 15% to 25% of total urban areas, in the Third World the ratio often falls below 10% (World Bank, 1975). An inadequate road network is a function of lack of government investment. The situation is getting increasingly worse; their fleets of motor vehicles, particularly private cars, are increasing at high annual rates of 10% or more.

Besides the above characteristics, the provision of urban transport also involves issues of social justice. Access to transport facilities is very important to the urban poor. They earn less than US$200 per annum and form 20–30% of the population in Latin American cities, or as much as 50% in big Indian cities such as Calcutta or Madras. Essential to the understanding of the urban transport problem of the Third World is therefore that part of the urban population simply cannot afford to use any form of motorized transport on a regular basis. US¢10 a working day – typical fares for two bus rides – represents about 10% of an income of US$300 a year. Not surprisingly, walking and cycling are even more important than public transport in terms of number of trips (World Bank, 1975). Household expenditure surveys indicate that the urban poor tend to devote 1–10% of their income to transport. Transport-related problems among this low income urban group are exacerbated by rising transport costs and the subsequent need for the poor to travel longer distances in search of employment, often owing to residential displacement to the urban periphery (Dimitriou, 1990c).

Beijing: a Third World situation?

Beijing before 1949 remained very much a traditionally planned Chinese national capital of the Ming and Qing Dynasties. As has been described in Chapter 3 the city was dominated by the Forbidden City and laid out according to the traditional philosophy of Confucianism with the mandate of Heaven, the symbolism of the unity of man and Heaven, and benevolence of the imperial reign being guiding principles. There was little heed to the requirements of economics, far less so to the movements of traffic. The Forbidden City, the seat of imperial govern-ance and abode of the Son of Heaven, occupies about one-ninth of the city, right at the centre, rigidly following the dictate of *Zhou Li*, a book written about 3000 years ago. Within the wall of the old city, a 62 sq km area, there had been no east–west through roads, except one in the 'outer city' from Guanganmen to Guangjimen.

Thus Beijing inherited a city form and a road network very unfit for a modern capital and a modern economy. In 1949, the city had only 215 km of surfaced roads with a total area of 1.4 million sq m. The widest road ran from Dongdan to Xidan for a length of 3.8 km, and its widest part did not exceed 11 m. In addition, the east and west portions of the latter, Changan Avenue, were not joined, as the two were separated by a T-shaped imperial square in front of Tian An Men. Elsewhere were over 3000 small lanes, locally called *hutongs*. Most of them were unsurfaced and ran in straight lines in the east–west direction, and were 4–6 m wide. They were rigidly laid out according to a separation of about 80 m within the 'inner city' or *nei cheng*.

The overall hindrance presented by the Forbidden City, since 1912 preserved as a museum and cultural asset, most of the San Hai (Three Seas) of the Imperial city, as well as the dense chessboard of *hutongs* put a straitjacket on the urban transport development of Beijing, particularly of its city districts. The pre-industrial character of the large city core and its richness in cultural relics, hence the need for preservation, make

Beijing a special case among Third World cities in its urban transport problems. Of course, Beijing also shares with them common features, including the imbalance between development of the road network and urban transport demand, poor public transport development and heavy dependence on informal modes of transport. But Beijing does have its 'socialist' features which distinguish it from other Third World cities, i.e. the large volume of daily trips by bicycle, an efficient, low-fare and predominant public transport of buses, and a cargo transport beset by problems of lack of incentives under the socialist 'big rice-bowl' protection leading to inefficient use of vehicles and roads. We shall review these in the light of post-1949 development, with emphasis on the most recent changes.

The road network

Post-1949 road development obviously saw the opening of east–west and north–south arteries as the most urgent work. It is vital to the development of the new suburbs for industries, high-level education, R & D and administration as well as for residential use. The road mileage of the urban areas within the city and suburban districts increased from 164 km in 1949 to 3276 km in 1991, about a 19-fold increase. Yet the motorized vehicle number increased from 2328 to 384 451 in 1950–90, or 164-fold, and the total urban public transport volume increased from 29 million persons in 1949 to 3523 million in 1991, or 120-fold (*Beijing Statistical Yearbook*, various dates). The ratio of road mileage to car population increase has been 1:8, and road mileage to public transport volume 1:6 (Quan, 1988a). These too are common features of most Third World cities, as previously mentioned. In Beijing, available data showed that (excluding the underground train) Beijing's capital investment in urban public transport for many years had been less than 1% of the city's total infrastructural investment. In the first three years after 1949, it registered a high point of 2.2%. For comparison, Shanghai's current rate is 1.3%. In addition, much of the construction and improvement has been carried out in recent years since the Open Door policy. Quan (1988a) showed that in 1978–88, the city invested a total of Yn4.3 billion in transport construction. In annual average terms, this was six times that of the years before. In these 10 years, 6.23 million sq m of urban roads had been added, or 38.7% of the total at 1978.

The major achievements in improving the urban road network include: (1) opening up and/or widening of five east–west trunk roads and one north–south trunk road; (2) construction of 10 arteries of 6–10 km in newly developed residential areas including six north–south and three east–west district roads; (3) in the suburbs, over ten major radiating roads have been built to link up the old city with new developments; (4) a number of ring roads have been constructed to reduce traffic in the old city. They are the Inner Ring Road, the main artery of the central area; the Second Ring Road, partially completed in 1980 on the former wall of the old city (completed in 1993); the Third Ring Road of 48 km, completed in 1981 and serving mainly as the link between the suburban districts; and the Fourth Ring Road of 65 km, partly completed at present. The Fourth Ring Road is to serve mainly intra-urban and inter-urban cargo transport. Over the Second and Third Ring Roads, by 1989, 40 flyovers had been completed at busy road junctions (Figure 10.1).

Thus post-1949 road building has greatly altered the old chessboard pattern of the road network, overlaying it with a mixture of ring roads and radial roads. The Third Ring Road marks the divide between the old city's chessboard pattern and the predominance of radial roads in the outer urban areas in the suburbs.

Another important feature of the road network is the recent emergence of a circulatory system for bicycles. In 1949–65, most new main roads contained 14–21 m wide lanes for cars, in the so-called 'one-slab' style, without separation for motorized and non-motorized traffic. With the growing use of bicycles in the city, the first 'three-slabs' style main road was constructed in 1965, providing separations for the two different modes. It contains two motorized vehicular lanes of 14 m each, and two bicycle lanes of 4 m each. In between them are green vegetated separation belts 2.5–5.5 m wide. By the end of 1983, there were 103 km of 'three-slabs' main roads, which increased to 242 km (173 within the city and suburban districts) in 1991.

In spite of the fast pace of road construction, on average about 74 km per year, the urban transport situation has continued to deteriorate. More hectic growth of motor cars and of transport demand arising from economic and population growth have been given as some of the main reasons above. Yet imbalance in spatial growth of the network makes a contribution as well. Within the central area, i.e. the old city of 62 sq km, the road density (roads of 7 m width and above) appears to be the highest of all the urban zones, i.e. 2.84 km/sq km, compared to 2.11 km/sq km between the Second and Third Ring Roads, and 0.75 km/sq km between the planning boundary and the Third Ring Road. Yet the quality of roads in the old city is low. Roads with a surfaced width of 7 m and above accounted for 9% of all roads within it, and there are limited through-roads. Despite this, in 1988 the old city accommodated 28.7% of the urban traffic and was the origin of 53% of the city's commuting trips, and its road network had already reached a capacity

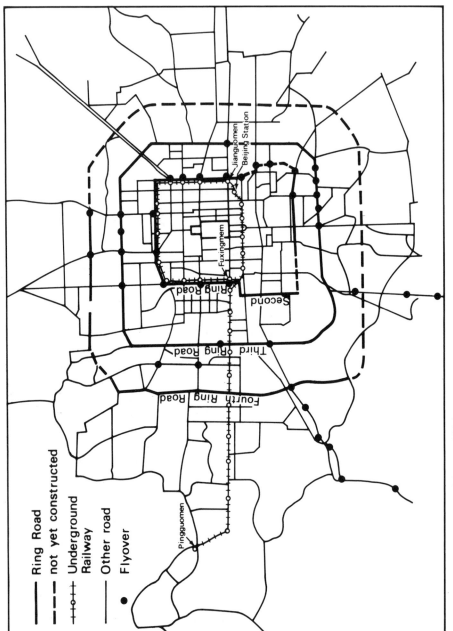

Figure 10.1 Road pattern of Beijing, 1984

Table 10.1 Road network and car and bicycle populations of Beijing compared to other cities (1980–82)

City	Road area (%)	Per capita road area (sq m)	Road density (km/ sq km)	Road length (km)	Cars No. ('000s)	Cars Ownership (%)	Bicycles No. ('000s)	Bicycles Ownership (%)
Beijing	16.4	6.2	7.5	2 234	116	1.3	3 283	36.4
Shanghai	6.4	1.6	6.8	964	30	0.7	2 022	17.4
Tianjin	3.8	2.2	4.1	800	53	0.7	2 877	37.8
Guangzhou	6.4	2.0	7.2	1 394	44	0.8	1 140	19.5
New York	24.1	28.0	12.1	10 000	4 631	43.2	–	–
Tokyo	13.8	9.7	18.5	10 900	3 054	26.2	–	–
London	16.6	26.3	8.0	12 800	2 259	32.7	–	–
Paris	25.0	9.3	NA	2 100	4 040	35.0	–	–

Source: Zhang (1987).

of 90% and the traffic volume was growing at a rate of 4.6% per year, exceeding the city average of 3% (Quan, 1990a).

Traffic surveys of 1986 and 1987 show that within the old city, the speed of motorized vehicles on main roads dropped 40% in one year alone, with an average of 20 km/hour, while on 23 main roads it was only 10 km/hour.

The inadequacy of main through-roads, arising both from the need to preserve the Forbidden City and San Hai and the high costs and problems of resettlement of the dense population involved in road-widening schemes, have been effective constraints on urban transport improvement of old Beijing. In addition, the insufficient number of ring roads poses another constraint. The Inner Ring Road is still incomplete and of low standard as the costs and trouble for demolition of existing housing are too high. As a consequence, most inter-district traffic has to be channelled through the Second Ring Road, which is also still incomplete in its southern half, leading to many congestion problems in its northern section which is currently in use and contains over 30% of the traffic in the whole of the old city.

Traffic surveys indicated that 93% of the flow is in an east–west direction and 25% of the inter-city flow passes through the inner city. This pattern of traffic flow is in conflict with the traditional street pattern of the old city. A higher-standard Second Ring Road and a completed Fourth Ring Road are certainly necessary in order to improve the situation. At the moment most of the traffic of the old city is concentrated on the northern section of the Second Ring Road, Changan Avenue and Qien Sanmen Avenue, which together account for 66.4% of all east–west flow. In addition, 53.5% of the north–south flow is concentrated in the eastern and western portion of the Second Ring Road. The incomplete Fourth Ring Road also forced most cargo traffic onto the Third Ring Road, leading to major congestion problems.

The standards of the radiating roads are also very low. For the most part, they contain only two lanes for motorized vehicles, and sections on the inside of the Third Ring Road are largely still incomplete. The overall low quality of the network may be further reflected by statistics on road widths. Of the 2069 km of roads within the 650 sq km of the planned urban area, only 824 km, or 39.8%, are over 7 m in width and able to be used by motorized vehicles. High-standard roads with four lanes and a total surfaced width of over 21 m amounted to only 104 km, or 5% of the total road network. Road width of 12–21 m, which allows for some separation of motorized and non-motorized traffic, accounted for 235 km or 11.4% of the roads; 60.2% of the road network is below 7 m in width and cannot normally be used for motorized traffic. Only about 497 km may be used by ambulances, fire-engines and refuse-collecting vehicles. The balance, or 748 km, are only used for bicycles and pedestrian traffic (Civil Engineering Bureau, 1987).

Level-crossings at road junctions reduce the efficiency of the road network. Improvements in the form of flyovers are difficult and costly to construct, especially so within the old city. Design and construction of flyovers are also constrained by the maxim that provision must be made for bicycle traffic. This factor and the lack of space at junctions make it even more difficult to attempt the channellization approach for flow improvement at major road junctions. It is estimated that of the 164 junctions presently under traffic light control, half cannot be improved by this method. Moreover, the network has 136 crossings with railways, of which 99 are level-crossings.

Thus constraints on the road network are caused by the urban form with inherited land use and chessboard pattern of *hutongs* of the old city unsuitable for modern urban traffic, as well as inadequate investment for improving urban roads. However, Beijing has also demonstrated another unique feature in its post-1949 road network planning: the debate on road widths. Despite lack of capital, and the general unwillingness to invest in 'unproductive' items such as roads, for many years the nation's and the municipality's leaders insisted on a policy of 'wide boulevards' in Beijing, especially for the arteries and main roads in newly developed urban areas. Such wide, straight and green-bordered roads have invoked some sense of symbolism that Beijing is the national capital, and hence is beautiful, imposing and better than the national norm. In the General Plan of 1953, it was suggested that the 'construction red lines' of main arteries should be 60–100 m wide, and other arteries about 40 m wide. This was objected to by the National Planning Commission which felt that the standard was impracticable and too extravagant. In the 1957 General Plan, this criticism of 'wide boulevards' went unheeded, and the respective widths set are 60–90 m and 40–50 m, while branch roads are to be 30–40 m and Changan Avenue is to be 120 m wide. In 1964, the general road widths were amended downwards. During the Cultural Revolution, 'wide-boulevard-ism' was attacked as an expression of capitalist-revisionism. The new attitude affected the construction of some roads at the time. In 1982, the new General Plan affirmed the lenient width provision and specified that main arteries are to be 60–80 m, secondary arteries 40–50 m, branch roads 30 m, and Changan Avenue 110–120 m. The rationale behind 'wide-boulevardism' is that the width of 'construction red lines' has to be considered on the basis of not only traffic demand, but also sunlight penetration, building height on the two sides, green open space separation, earthquake refuge and, perhaps more importantly, the reservation of space for road widening to meet future traffic demand

(Beijing Construction History, 1987). Obviously, this is in contradiction to the usual economic expedience argument used for speeding up industrialization and de-emphasizing 'consumptive' investment, and belies perhaps the deep-seated 'feudalistic' principle in the minds of the leadership, who were possibly subconsciously following the *Zhou Li* in that roads in the national capital must be wider than those in lesser cities and the width should be set to reflect the status of the Son of Heaven's place of abode. Transport technology and spatial pattern of demand will change quickly over time. There is little sense for a planner in a Third World city to argue for constructing at a lavish standard to meet yet unqualifiable and unquantifiable distant future demand.

Despite this exception, Beijing's road provision is very low compared to capitals of the developed nations. In Table 10.1, both the low ratio of car ownership and high ratio of bicycle ownership reflect the city's common character with Third World cities, which we shall turn to discuss in the coming paragraphs.

Public passenger transport

General principles and development history

Zhu and Zhang (1987) considered the following to be China's main features in urban passenger transport:

1. Owing to the 'low consumption' level arising from a low and generally flat wage level, urban residents have little choice but to opt for cheap means of transport. Thus the bicycle becomes a dominant urban transport mode in Chinese cities.
2. As China is a socialist country, public transport must serve the public at large and be made accessible to all of them.
3. As time unit economic cost in China is still very low, so the services provided by urban transport are not too costly. This leads to an unavoidable situation of mixed modes (motorized and non-motorized) in urban areas.
4. As China is a developing country with a low level of economic development, the urban road network and the structure of both passenger and cargo transport are simple and mostly of surface modes.

They believe that in the planning and development of urban transport, China has been following three basic principles: (1) to maintain parity with national economic development; (2) to follow the socialist principle

Table 10.2 Commuting modes (% of trips) of Chinese cities

City	Public transport	Bicycles	Walking	Others	Survey year
Beijing	29.5	37.0	29.9	3.6	1983
Shanghai	28.6	13.3	57.0	1.2	1982
Tianjin	10.3	44.5	42.6	2.5	1981
Xuzhou	4.6	41.8	52.2	1.4	1982

Source: Zhu and Zhang (1987).

of equity; and (3) to maximize returns on investment. They are indeed correct on the second principle, but there is doubt as to the first and third principles. Much criticism has been levelled about playing down 'consumptive' investment so that the growth of the road network and investment in public transport have been trailing behind demand and the growth of the economy. Disregard for economics and efficiency has also been found in the management of both public passenger and cargo transport within Beijing. Nevertheless, the prevalence of the bicycle in daily trips is definitely a Chinese characteristic, while public transport is the main motorized means for moving about in Chinese cities.

Table 10.2 shows the situation of urban passenger transport in the major Chinese cities of Beijing, Shanghai, Tianjin and a medium-sized city, Xuzhou. The bicycle is clearly the main means for daily commuting trips in the big cities with the exception of Shanghai. The latter's much more compact urban form and its policy bias toward bolstering public transport are well known. As a consequence, Shanghai stands out among Chinese cities as one where the bicycle plays a lesser role in daily commuting trips. In smaller cities, e.g. Xuzhou, the bicycle and walking have accounted for the bulk of daily trips while public transport plays a much lesser role. Beijing may represent the general situation of the big cities. If walking is not to be counted, then the ratio of the bicycle to public transport is roughly 56 to 44. Tianjin is widely known for its heavy dependence on the bicycle and represents the other category of big cities in terms of daily commuting modes, with Shanghai on the other extreme.

In Beijing, as in most Chinese cities, public transport means transport by publicly owned buses, although the situation has changed somewhat since the late 1980s with the growing fleet of taxis and a number of collective and even private enterprises running a number of routes of minibuses. Table 10.3 provides an overview of the composition and development of urban public transport in Beijing in 1949–91.

The history of urban public transport of Beijing is short. It started in 1921 with the setting up of a tram company. By 1947, the city had 82

Table 10.3 Urban public transport in Beijing

Mode	1949	1957	1965	1978	1987		1991
Service routes							
Buses	4	36	64	106	179	(173)*	223
Electric trams	7	11	16	12	13	(13)	13
Underground	–	–	–	1	2	(2)	2
Service mileage (km)							
Buses	34	449	956	1 274	2 197	(2 139)	2 568
Electric trams	43	98	174	132	145	(145)	147
Underground	–	–	–	24	40	(40)	40
Service							
Buses	61	545	1 124	2 223	3 990	(3 861)	4 366
Electric trams	103	333	447	404	534	(534)	511
Underground	–	–	–	116	252	(25)	305
Passenger volume (millions)							
Bus and Trams	29	452	824	1 695	3 112	(3 086)	3 074
Underground	–	–	–	31	192	(192)	371
Total	29	452	824	1 726	3 304	(3 272)	3 445
Rented cars	–	577	803	1 452	11 893		14 354
Passengers (millions)	–	106	5	10	63		78

* Bracketed figures for city and suburban districts.
Source: *Beijing Statistical Yearbook* (various dates).

trams and carried a daily passenger volume of 60–70 000. The first bus company was formed in 1935 and in 1947 there were a total of 132 buses, but serving buses numbered only 30–40, on six routes, and with a total serving mileage of 34.3 km (*Beijing City Construction Since Liberation*, 1985). At the end of 1991, the total mileage of bus routes was 2568 km with a serving fleet of 4366 buses. They handled a passenger volume of 3.1 billion (with trams), accounting for 87% of total public transport volume. Electric trams had not been emphasized in 1957–80, though their number picked up again in the 1980s. Though much cleaner than buses, they are less flexible and are less adapted to the intricate road network of the old city, and have not been treated as an efficient form of public transport. Their passenger volume has not even been separately released.

Underground

As the first Chinese city with an underground train, Beijing stands above many Third World cities in its early acquisition of this approach to solving the urban transport problem. Yet the construction of the underground in Beijing proved to be another symbol of the national

275

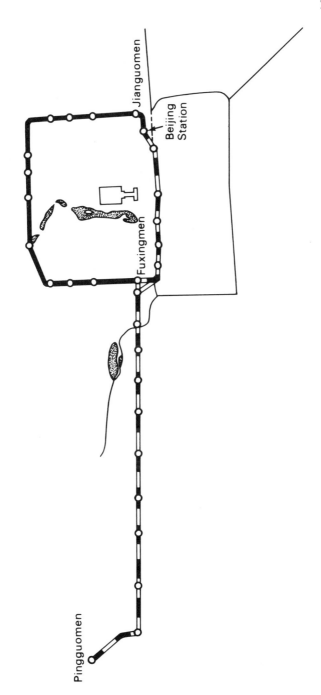

Figure 10.2 Route plan of the completed Underground in Beijing

capital rather than a genuine and serious attempt at tackling the transport issue, at least until 1978, the year of the Open Door and a turn in the governing philosophy in the PRC.

Phase One of construction of the east–west line from Pingguoyuan to Beijing Railway Station started in 1965. It is 23.6 km in length with 17 stations, and connects the western suburb with the old city (see Figure 10.1). It only took about four years to complete. However the line took a much longer period for trial run, i.e. 12 years, and was only officially open for commercial operation in 1981. In 1981, it took only 8.3 million passengers, whereas in 1983 it carried almost ten times that number, i.e. 82 million. The second line, or Phase Two, started construction in 1971 and took 13.5 years to complete. This new line is 16 km long, with 12 stations. It forms a complete circle with a section of Line One, following the old city wall. With the completion of Phase Two, the first line shortened its routing making it run from Pingguoyuan to Fuxingmen only, whereas the rest of Phase One and Phase Two form the new Circle Line. The rearranged Line One is 17 km in length, and Line Two (Circle Line) 23 km. The new arrangement has bolstered the efficiency of both lines. In 1991, they together carried 371 million passengers, or more than 1 million daily. This raised the underground's share in public transport passenger volume from 5.7% in 1987 to 11.8% in 1991 (Table 10.3).

The lesson from Beijing's underground is a reflection of the high costs involved in a closed-door approach to doing everything. The Chinese then adopted a self-reliant policy regarding its construction. The civil engineering works and rolling stock design and manufacture were 100% localized. It not only took many years to stock up and equip Phase One but a long trial period to ensure that the system worked smoothly. In the meantime, a large amount of capital had been immobilized while the urban transport situation deteriorated. Above all, the rolling stock, which was produced by many different factories and with parts sometimes incompatible with each other, has now become obsolete and needs to be phased out. Despite this, the city and the nation have for many years taken pride in the fact that it is the only Third World city with an underground train, built and equipped without reliance on technology from the developed countries. Again, in this case, urban infrastructural construction has not been treated with regard to technical and economic sense or useability, but rather a symbolism that is at variance with efficiency and practical general welfare.

Buses and trams

Table 10.3 also shows the emergence of taxis and other forms of hired cars as a means of public transport since 1978. The vehicle numbers increased almost 10 times in 1978–91 and their passenger volume almost eight-fold. Such a trend underlines the increasing cosmopolitanization and internationalization of Beijing as a tourist, political and business centre and its rapidly rising standard of living.

Nevertheless, for Beijing citizens, public buses and trams are still the means to go around the city, if not the bicycle. They are facing a worsening supply situation as increasing urban congestion and deteriorating quality of service have been undermining the services of buses and trams. Careful study of Table 10.3 reveals that, whereas the volume carried by buses and trams increased 91.4% in 1978–87, it stagnated in 1987–91; in fact there was a 1.2% decline. For a city of over 10 million, the provision of public buses and trams in Beijing can only be described as 'poor', especially considering the lack of other motorized means and the short mileage of the fast track mode, i.e. the 40 km of underground, and comparing it with a similar sized socialist capital, Moscow, in 1989. Even considering its population within the 2000-odd sq km of city and suburban districts, the provision of buses and trams was roughly 1.4 to every 2000 population, only marginally above the World Bank definition of 'poor provision' of 1 to every 2000 persons, and was much worse than Abidjan, Cairo, São Paulo, and Kuala Lumpur (Dimitriou, 1990b). If we include the 'floating population' which amounted to about 1 million, and the entire permanent urban population of the city, then the population served is increased to 8.78 million, and the number of buses and trams to population decreases to 1.1 for every 2000 population. Although superficially this represents a substantial improvement from the 1965 ratio of 0.7 per 2000 population, much of the improvement has been written off in practice by congestion and the slow turn-around time for the vehicles. In such a context, Beijing may not be just regarded as a Third World city, but possibly a 'poorer' and more 'impoverished' Third World city in public transport provision.

Poor quantitative supply of buses and trams and an inefficient road network contributed to much of the urban transport problem of what the locals in Beijing called 'difficulty in getting a bus'. On top of that are also the inefficient management of public transport service and the rigidity of the 'socialist way' in the running of public transport services.

It was reported that during the peak hours riding bicycles for journeys to work is 18% faster than riding buses and trams. It is more comfortable too, as 20% of these public modes reported an excessive load ratio of over 110% (Quan, 1988a). Although public bus and tram companies have since 1983 been annually provided with about 300 more new vehicles, the volume of passengers they carried has since stagnated. Part of the reason is the annual drop in motor vehicle speed of

Table 10.4 Passenger trip distribution in Beijing's city and suburban districts

Mode	By trip no. (10 millions)	(%)	By no. of modes (10 millions)	(%)
Buses and trams	171.4	33.4	302.7	45.9
Underground	18.7	3.6	30.7	4.7
Taxis	5.9	1.1	5.9	0.9
Other cars	24.7	4.8	24.7	3.8
Bicycles and other non-motorized vehicles	294.9	57.1	294.9	44.9
Total	515.6	100.0	658.9	100.0

Source: Quan, 1990b.

1–2 km/hour within the city and increasing congestion at road junctions. Detailed studies by Zhang and Zhang (1987) showed that if 250 m is taken as the maximum walking distance a person is willing to take to catch a bus or tram, then 70% of the city districts are not covered by these services. If 500 m is to be considered as the maximum limit, then only 17% of the city and suburban districts, or 52.2% of their population are covered. In addition, the survey found that within the 500 m radius catchment area, only 26.3% of people commuted by buses and trams, and they reported that walking to and from bus stops from origin and to destination plus waiting time constituted 37% of their total trip time. It may indicate that in the arrangement of routes, note has not been taken of customer convenience. In addition, stations of different routes for interchange are often separated by over 250 m distance, some even by over 400 m. The routings are such that it is difficult to avoid changing bus routes in order to complete a trip. As much as a quarter of the trips by public transport were reported to involve changing a bus or tram route (Quan, 1990b). The 1988 Beijing commuting trips survey shows a much more frequent need to take two public transport routings to complete a trip (Table 10.4). Scarcity of public transport routes is another reason behind these complaints of long walking distances to reach them and the need to change a route. The situation of Beijing, with a route density of 1.69 km/sq km within the area bounded by the Third Ring Road, and 2.16 km/sq km within the Second Ring Road, is certainly poor compared to cities in advanced countries, i.e. in Toyko and Paris where the respective densities are 4.42 km/sq km and 2.95 km/sq km in addition to a dense network of metros, and in comparison to other Chinese cities like Shanghai and Tianjin, where the overall densities in the urban districts are respectively 2.66 and 1.96 km/sq km (1986 data, Zhang and Zhang, 1987). The situation within the old city is no better. The high route density there hides the fact that many routes overlap with each other along the three north–south and the six east–west through-roads, particularly Changan Avenue which has 10 routes. Within the area enclosed by the Third Ring Road, 80 km of roads of a width of 6.5 m or above which can be used by buses are without any bus route. In the 1950s and 1960s many bus routes served narrow streets of 6–7 m width. With widening of some roads, these routes had moved to them and the abandoned old routes have not been replaced.

The capacity and quality of service of buses and trams have not been improved in the years since the Open Door Policy of 1978, and have also not been matching with increasing demand. In 1978–88, the seat number of public buses and trams increased by 92%, yet their turnover rate dropped by 17%. The real increase in seat capacity is thus only 60%, whereas the passenger volume increased by about 80% in the period. This had aggravated the poor service of the public transport system and forced 58% of the increased passenger volume to bicycles and collectively owned and privately run cars (Quan, 1990b). The bicycle as a means of commuting in 1983 and 1988 (Tables 10.2 and 10.4) increased from 52.7% to 57.1% of total trips, excluding walking, while the share by buses and trams dipped from 42% to 33.4%. In the decade of 1978–88, the average trip time by buses and trams increased 10.3%; 16% of the trips made between the Third Ring Road and the city centre took more than 45 minutes; and 64% of the trips took longer than riding a bicycle (Quan, 1990b).

The institutional reasons behind declining services and productivity of public buses and trams reveal the rigidity of public transport management under the Chinese socialist system as well as the difficulty involved in maintaining such services as a social and welfare good. In Beijing, public buses and trams are run by three public companies, all of them subsidized by the municipal government and operated under its instruction. In 1988, they had a total of 4300 vehicles (including 600 trams) and employed about 50 000 people. The total operating lines numbered 182 with an aggregate route mileage of 2200 km and a yearly passenger volume of 3.2 billion. More up-to-date figures can be found in Table 10.3. The companies operate on a low-fare policy as instructed by the municipal government, which is a national policy. As a consequence of this, the companies receive government subsidy to the extent of any deficit. Such rule by the government is said to be based on two reasons: (1) the low-fare policy is a feature of the welfare nature of socialism and is the explicit implementation of equity in access to public transport; (2) public transport provides a necessary social service to the whole community and hence helps to raise the efficiency and productivity of all economic and non-economic activities of the urban community. All urban enterprises pay tax and submit part of their profits to the government. In a way they have paid their costs for convenient urban public transport to the state. Public subsidy to the public transport system merely reflects such a circuitous payment. Maintaining a low fare, in addition, contributes to stabilizing the prices of goods and hence aids the social stability of the community. It also provides the government with a lever in regulating urban transport (Beijing Public Transport Corporation, 1987). Yet this external factor in determining the fares of Beijing's public transport has also been criticized as constraining the latter's growth and contribution. For instance, the municipality, out of a genuine fear of increased subsidies, has hesitated in adopting the principle that public transport should be the main form of urban transport development; fast and fixed-rail transit has not been emphasized; and it fails to promote public transport through relevant measures on capital investment, fare structure and fare level, and tax incentives. The companies' internal management structure and quality are also said to be disappointing.

In the past 40-odd years, because of lower fares in line with government policy, the public transport system experienced decreasing profits. As a supportive measure to safeguard development of public transport in the period of Open Door and Enterprise Reform, the municipal government adopted a new policy of complete and open subsidy, i.e. 'monthly ticket subsidy and financial underwriting', since 1988. A fixed subsidy was set at Yn1300 million in 1988 and the companies guarantee social and economic economies. They may raise fare charges, in which case half the extra revenue raised has to be submitted to the government. If the fares are not raised in a particular year, the fixed subsidy may be increased by Yn10 million. The underground also received an annual subsidy in a slightly different way from the government since 1980. In 1988–90, the total subsidy to the underground was Yn2100 million. The actual subsidy for selected years is Yn4.7 million for 1980, Yn86 million for 1985 and Yn225.7 million for 1988 (*Forty Years of Beijing*, 1990). Increasing subsidy has maintained a constantly low fare in the public transport system. Transportation expenses have therefore formed a very minor item of the total expenditure of urban households in Beijing: 2% in 1984 and 1.54% in 1991 (*Beijing Statistical Yearbook*, various dates).

Yet the heavy subsidy has not helped the development and improvement of services of the public transport system. The surface system suffered from a number of problems arising from the unconcerned attitude of the municipality, whose attention has been too much attracted towards the heavy burden of subsidy rather than on how the system should be revamped to become viable and efficient. More precisely these problems are (Wang, 1988):

1. Insufficient capital investment. For 1949–83, investment in the surface system was only 0.9% of the municipality's total investment in infrastructural projects. In 1983–88, it was raised to 1.18%, an annual average of Yn34 million, still a very small amount compared to increasing demand.
2. The heavy bias of the subsidy to monthly tickets had for a long time worked against improving the service. For example, deficit arising from sales of monthly tickets in 1986 alone amounted to Yn55 million, or Yn3.71 per ticket. This worked against any incentive of the companies or the municipal government to develop and improve the system, as that meant a heavier burden on the public coffers and no economic gain by the companies.
3. Heavy burden of taxes and supplementary fees. For the entire period 1949–83, taxes and supplementary fees took away only 9.6% of total revenue. In 1985 it reached 17% of total revenue.
4. The low depreciation rate and the requirement that 20% of the depreciation should be submitted to the municipality. According to such practice, a vehicle has to serve 30 years before it can be completely written off.

Thus Beijing's main public transport, buses and trams, demonstrated the common socialist characteristics of cheap fares and heavy public subsidy. However owing to the Third World city character of Beijing, it had not been economically capable of launching a massive underground train construction programme like that in Moscow since 1931. Thus for Beijing, public transport has remained more or less solely dependent on traditional surface modes of buses and trams. These modes have been increasingly constrained by the pattern and quality of the road network, particularly that part of it within the Third Ring Road or the inner city. Increasing input to the bus and tram system has since experienced diminishing return, which is evident in increasing deficits, stagnation in passenger volume, and declining productivity. Mass transit in the form of underground trains had not been seriously considered until very recently. In the long period of 1965–84, only 40 km of underground had been built, i.e. about an average of 2 km a year. Increasing demand for public transport, especially since 1980, has thus not been met by increased supply. Many trips have thus turned to non-motorized means, i.e. the bicycle.

Bicycles

Table 10.5 shows the change in vehicle population of Beijing in 1950–90. The number of bicycles doubled about every decade in 1960–80, yet in

Table 10.5 Vehicle population in Beijing, 1950–90

	1950	1960	1970	1980	1985	1990
1. Motorized	1 836	21 609	22 768	99 301	217 354	384 451
Vehicles	1 691	17 519	18 812	80 866	161 480	270 655
Goods	531	8 600	11 532	47 745	95 952	157 776
Large	475	8 264	8 839	43 233	60 921	54 676
Passenger	1 160	8 346	6 252	28 856	57 924	104 422
Small	982	6 610	3 838	13 719	37 491	89 373
Special	NA	573	1 028	4 265	7 604	8 457
Motorcycles	66	3 721	4 998	19 514	56 541	112 984
Trams	79	369	336	482	699	812
2. Non-motorized	23	83	151	385	561	872
Bicycles (0000)	19	76	145	288	551	838
Trishaws	NA	NA	NA	NA	NA	322 058
Animal carts	NA	NA	NA	NA	NA	25 422

Source: Forty Years of Beijing, 1990; Beijing Statistical Yearbook, 1991.

1980–90 it increased by about two-fold, though it had a very large base already in 1980. In 1949–67 the annual increase of bicycles was about 50 000. In 1967–81, it was about 150 000. Since 1982, the annual addition exceeds half a million. In 1990, on average a household owned more than two bicycles, as the population of bicycles numbered 8.32 million. Beijing is certainly the largest 'bicycle city' of the world, even surpassing Shanghai which has a larger population.

The ratio of public transport means to the bicycle for commuting trips in Beijing in 1983 was 29.5:37. In 1988, the ratio changed to 37:57.1 in favour of the bicycle (Tables 10.2 and 10.4). As the previous paragraphs have explained, diminishing returns in the public modes have left the demand of increased public transport unfulfilled. In a more compact city like Shanghai, most of this may be resolved by walking. Yet in Beijing, since increased activities lie in the newly developed industrial and residential areas, the bicycle provides a better means as the distance involved is longer. Within the old city, the network of narrow *hutongs* which has not been served by motorized modes of transport also provides effective conduits for the flow of bicycles. Studies in other Third World cities indicate that the average speed for transport modes of walking, buses, bicycles and cars are respectively 3.5, 7.8, 6.0 and 8.3 km/hr, and the average trip lengths are 1.1, 4.4, 2.8 and 4.9 km. For large cities in China the average trip length of the bicycle has clearly extended to that of the bus in a situation of deteriorating bus services. Surveys in Beijing reveal that the average trip length is below 6 km, those within 1 km accounting for 7%, and those that were 2–4 km and ideal for the bicycle accounting for 42%. Experts estimate that even for 6 km the bicycle remains an attractive mode (Quan, 1990b). Comparable data for 1983 also show that the average speed of public buses was 15 km/hr, and for the bicycle 12 km/hr. This has been sustained by commuting surveys which indicate that the bicycle has become the predominant mode of urban transport, even if walking is also taken into account.

The predominance of the bicycle is related not only to consideration of the substitution factor when means of public transport are deteriorating, it is also related to China's increasing capability in producing the bicycle leading to its falling prices, as well as the prevalence of an encourage- ment policy for the use of the bicycle. In the early 1980s, the average price of a bicycle, Yn400, was about two months' average income of a worker. In 1991, the average price of Yn300 was only about his monthly income. The falling price of the bicycle is also a consequence of rapid expansion in production. In 1988, it was reported that there were 10 million bicycles in stock. In most work units, journey to work by the bicycle is encouraged through a monthly subsidy as it guarantees punctual attendance by the worker.

The increasing use of the bicycle has contributed to the deteriorating congestion of the urban road network, particularly at road junctions. A 1986 survey that covers 178 main road junctions within the 750 sq km of the planned urban area illustrated the increased bicycle flow during the morning peak hour of 7–8 am. Road junctions registering bicycle flow in excess of 20 000 during the peak hour numbered 14 in 1986, a tremendous increase over 3 for 1978. Those with a flow of over 10 000 vehicles numbered 106, compared to 53 in 1978. The massive flow of bicycles has led to declining average speed for motorized traffic and serious congestion problems. It is especially marked within the old city, as only about 10% of the road network provides separation for motorized and non-motorized traffic. Even for those areas with separation, the chaos at road junctions is still problematic (Ma, 1988). Rough estimates in 1987 worked out that problems of mixed traffic on roads and at road junctions had contributed a 30–40% reduction in flow capacity of the roads (Quan, 1990b). Ma (1988) also reported that 74 of the 97 arteries of the urban areas registered 'saturated' or 'over-saturated' bicycle flow during the two peak hours of the day.

Bicycle parking has created another problem for the city districts. Within the Third Ring Road there were over 900 bicycle parking lots in 1988, with actual parking for 370 000 bicycles/hour and occupying 92 220 sq m of land, 74.2% of which were on pedestrian paths and roads (Quan, 1990b).

Compared to public transport modes of the bus and tram, the bicycle shows a number of disadvantages. Its carrying capacity is low on a per seat basis. It occupies more road space, has a slow speed and is unsuitable for long-distance trips. For stationary transport the road space occupied per passenger as a ratio between the bicycle and the bus is 2:1; when in motion, the ratio changes to 10:1. Thus the trend in Beijing since 1980 of moving increasingly towards the bicycle for commuting reflects an unhealthy situation, both considering the existing pattern of concentration of people and activities, commuting trips and the structure of the road network within the city and suburban districts.

Intra-urban cargo transport

Modern cargo transport by goods vehicles started in Beijing only in 1913 and the first government-owned transport company opened in 1918. By 1950, there were 960 goods vehicles and 480 were engaged in commercial goods transport, mostly owned by private companies. The Transport Bureau then inherited about 150 goods vehicles from the Kuomintang government, of which about 50 were still roadworthy. In addition, cargo was also moved by about 1700 privately operated horse-carriages and about 500 trishaws. Private operation of cargo transport was largely transferred to public ownership in 1956 and rigidly regulated by central planning. In 1979, under the new Open Policy and Enterprise Reform, unitary operation under the Transport Bureau was broken with the formation of four publicly owned transport companies. A new wave of 'commercialization' of cargo transport emerged. The four companies also worked hard under the official policy of 'road–rail split', redirecting short-distance cargo movement of 50–100 km from its former rail traffic to road traffic, relieving congestion of the railways and increasing 'door-to-door' services in goods movement. In 1983, Beijing possessed 73 300 goods vehicles, about a 75-fold increase of its 1950 fleet. Short-distance cargo movement within the city districts accounted for 70% of the total traffic. Of the flow in the city districts, construction materials and fuel (coal) accounted for 66.1% and 13.8% of the traffic. The balance was made up of industrial raw materials and products, food and daily consumables (*Beijing City Construction Since Liberation*, 1985).

More recent development of intra-urban cargo transport has been revealed by the 1988 survey. In the decade of 1978–88, total cargo volume increased 1.4-fold, at an average annual rate of 6%. Road transport took 84% of all traffic at the end of 1987, and railways only accounted for 12%. The road traffic was mainly made up of exchanges between the city and suburban districts with a predominant centripetal flow, i.e. the centre-ward and centre-out flow ratio was 2:1. Within the decade, specialized cargo transport firms, i.e. the four public companies, registered a 22% drop in their share of the total flow. In 1988, public cargo transport companies owned 3.5% of the goods vehicles and contributed 20.8% of total cargo transport volume. Of the entire flow of the metropolis 61% happened within the urban areas, predominantly within the four suburban districts which alone constituted 55% of the entire cargo traffic of the city. Peak hours of the flow coincided with peak hours of the passenger flow, with 91% of the total flow concentrated in daytime (7 am–5 pm) (Quan, 1990a). These general characteristics revealed a number of issues concerning Beijing's intra-urban cargo transport:

1. *Falling level of specialization and social division of labour.* The Open Policy and Enterprise Reforms since 1978 have provided many work units with the opportunity to purchase their own goods vehicles. Many of these have done so and chosen to purchase small vehicles which often double up as or are even solely used as passenger carriers (Table 10.5). For these work units, the new move towards 'self-catering' in cargo transport has also been encouraged by the

Table 10.6 Comparing economic indices of transport efficiency between specialized firms and self-catering cargo transport

Index	Specialized firms	Self-catering transport
Mileage rate (%)	52.2	41.1
Tonnage rate (%)	106.1	97.6
Daily productivity (tonnes/car tonne/km)	89.5	28.4
Daily car mileage (km)	155.1	88.4
Usable car rate (%)	89.4	92.1
Working car rate (%)	72.1	63.1
Gas consumption/000 tonnes/km (litre)	6.4	15.4

Source: Quan, 1991.

system of accounting, as the capital and expenses so incurred can be treated as production cost. Of the total goods vehicle fleet, the share of the public sector firms dropped from 50.6% in 1957 to 9% in 1978, then to 6.7% in 1983, and recently to 3.5% in 1991. The cargo volume carried by the public sector firms declined more sharply, i.e. from 100% in 1950, to 45.4% in 1978, 35.8% in 1983 and then 20.8% in 1991. The overall efficiency of the urban cargo transport sector has similarly declined, as may be substantiated by comparison of a number of indices between the specialized companies and the other half of the sector, i.e. 'self-catering' cargo transport, as shown in Table 10.6. Besides much lower transport efficiency, there is a large waste of scarce resources such as capital and fuel, in addition to aggravated problems of cargo transport control and planning, as 'self-catering' operation is being carried out by over 50 000 work units and private individuals (or individual enterprises employing a few persons each).

2. *Imbalance of vehicle size.* Road cargo transport in Beijing has always been dominated by weighty and bulky cargo that requires large vehicles. Construction materials, coal and industrial raw materials have consistently accounted for 60–70% of total cargo volume and been more efficiently moved by large and medium-sized vehicles (Wang, 1987). However, these goods vehicles accounted for only 30% of the fleet while small vehicles of less than 2 tonnes' capacity accounted for 70%.

3. *Imbalance in distribution between transport capacity and transport demand.* A detailed survey in 1983 showed that the four city districts accounted for 7.5% of the total cargo carried, yet they possessed 30.9% of the transport capacity. Most of the vehicles of the city districts go out of the districts for transport orders and return to it in

the night with an empty vehicle rate of 50%. There is also an imbalance between the eastern and western part of the city (Beijing Public Transport Corporation, 1987).

The main sources of cargo lie within the suburban districts, a fact dictated by the location of industries and warehouses as well as the distribution of resources. The spread of cargo sources in the three broad spatial areas of city districts, suburban districts and outer suburbs are 8.1%, 64.3% and 29.7%. The two largest source points are Shijingshan and the south-west suburb. They accounted for over 20% of the cargo dispatches. The distribution of destinations of cargo by the three broad areas of city districts, suburban districts and outer suburbs are 8.7%, 70.1% and 21.2%. The two largest destination points are the north-west and south-west suburbs, which accounted for 23% of the total cargo (Wang, 1987).

4. *Low vehicle usage rate and productivity.* The 1983 survey revealed an overall vehicle usage rate of 57.9% for the 18 474 vehicles surveyed, i.e. as many as 7771 vehicles or 40% were lying idle. The survey reported three main reasons for this: no transport orders; in maintenance; and the work unit was on its rest day. Of these, the majority reported lack of orders.

The average car productivity is 11 tonnes per day, i.e. an annual production of 4000 tonnes per vehicle. The average annual production was 9000 tonnes for the 4911 vehicles of the specialized transportation firms surveyed, and only 600 tonnes for the 50 243 'self-catering' vehicles (Wang, 1987).

Considering the generally higher efficiency of the specialized transport companies, the trend of fast decline of their contribution to urban cargo transport is thus alarming. Lax control over purchase of self-catering goods vehicles and disregard of transport economics by most work units since 1978 have been the main reasons. Yet rigid control over the state-owned sector, to the extent that it is not even allowed the financial means to renew its fleet and upgrade its vehicles in the face of changing demand, has been an important reason behind their falling share in total cargo transport as well (Beijing Public Transport Corporation, 1987).

The rapid increase of small goods vehicles in recent years in Beijing demonstrates a special characteristic of the socialist system in flux. In some measure it is another expression of the increase in private cars in Third World capitals, as many small goods vehicles are used solely or double up as a passenger vehicle. It serves to underlie the relatively more relaxed control over approval for purchase of goods vehicles compared to passenger vehicles by the work units. As the wage level of work unit managers and heads is still low, private ownership of passenger cars is much lower than in other Third World cities. The use of public (work unit) funds to acquire either the passenger vehicle or a small dual-purpose vehicle for more or less personal use has become a frequent phenomenon in Beijing.

Solving transport problems

The policy division of the municipality CCP in its detailed review of the urban transport situation of the city summarized the following as main issues:

1. Rapid increase of number of motor vehicles.
2. Congestion and inconvenience of public transport leading to rapid increase in bicycles.
3. Serious inadequacy in urban roads and their uneven distribution.
4. Low level of road traffic management and its low level of technical provision.

It thus sets as the long-term goal for Beijing (for the year 2000):

> to basically complete a road network with relevant facilities which will meet the needs of the city, with fair distribution, and with the separations of pedestrians and vehicles, motorized and non-motorized vehicles, and slow and fast moving vehicles; to set up passenger and cargo transport systems based on the leading role of public transport and public cargo firms which are of high efficiency and economies; to employ modern and advanced technical means to manage the transport system to ensure swift, convenient, safe, economical and low level of pollution in urban transport. (CCP of Beijing, 1987)

These general objectives have been incorporated in a number of quantified targets to be achieved in the year 2000 against the relative situation in the early 1980s:

1. To reduce journey-to-work time by 10%, and monthly ticket holders will have a single trip time of an average of 44 minutes.
2. Increase motor vehicle speed in the urban areas by 10%; public buses and trams within the city districts will have their average speed raised from 16 km to 18 km/hr.
3. To increase road density of the urban areas from 1.1 km to 1.5 km/ sq km; the area within the Third Ring Road will have its road area raised from 9% to 10.6%.
4. To raise the ratio of public transport vehicles (buses and trams) to

total population from one per 1470 to one per 1000 persons; to maintain a 85–90% loading rate per vehicle at peak hours and 65–70% loading rate at off-peak times.

5. To popularize the signal system on road management to ensure all arteries will be 'line-controlled' and some districts 'area-controlled'.
6. The ratio of public transport to the bicycle in commuting trips will be changed from 57:43 to 63:37.
7. The cargo volume handled by specialized transport firms will be raised from 35.6% to 42%.
8. To reduce accident numbers and pollution level.

To achieve these objectives, short-term direct measurements aimed at road management and traffic volume control have been launched since the early 1980s. Longer-term policies such as economic incentives and new forms of subsidy have been tried to boost the performance of public passenger and cargo companies and to provide them with more freedom in their business operation. In the realm of public passenger transport, emphasis on underground train development has been argued for, and an overall increase in public investment on urban transport has been proposed. We shall briefly summarize those measures for the public transport sector.

Public passenger transport

Since 1988, new measures on subsidies to the bus and tram companies enable them to take the initiative about increasing fares, and the old system of subsidy based on monthly tickets sold has been replaced by a lump sum. These provide the companies with more freedom in managing their economics. Despite this improvement, more needs to be done such as exemption from taxes, supply of cheap fuel, and increased investment from the government to modernize and increase the fleet as well as further 'separation' between the Transport Bureau and the companies in their operation, in addition to prioritization of road space for buses and trams on major roads to boost their predominance in the share of commuting trips. Control of the bicycle has been proposed as a means for raising the efficiency of the road network and increasing the productivity of public transport. Measures proposed include a restriction on the use of main arteries by bicycles as in Shanghai, imposing a bicycle licence fee, and the abandonment of the bicycle subsidy by work units to their employees (Ren, 1990). However, the most effective long-term solution in improving public transport in Beijing lies with a dedicated underground construction programme.

At present the public passenger transport system is mainly composed of buses; the existing two lines of underground only account for about 11% of all public passenger volume. According to the 1974 long-term underground train development plan, the city should have eight routes with a total mileage of about 200 km. Underground train construction in future would take two stages in the medium term. In stage one, two lines would be constructed. One would lead from Jianguomen to Fuxingmen, about 6 km long. The other runs from Hepingli to Songjiazhuang, a distance of 16 km. With the completion of these two new lines, the underground system would be able to carry 2.8–3 million passengers daily, or 30% of the daily flow. Stage two would add one east–west and one north–south line with a total length of 35 km. They may be completed by the year 2000. By then, the whole system would comprise about 100 km of track and a daily capacity of 3.5–4 million passengers, or 45% of the daily public transport volume. In addition, construction of light rails with a single direction capacity of about 40 000 persons/hr along the radial roads joining the old city to densely settled suburban residential areas can release the road network as well as provide convenient and fast means of public transport for the city (Zheng, Zu, 1988).

Public goods transport

The public sector in goods transport, if efficiently developed, would contribute to a drastic reduction of road congestion, savings for the entire economy in scarce capital, as well as lowering of actual transport costs. To achieve this, the basic approach is to provide an operational environment for these firms so that profits can be generated to modernize and raise the efficiency of their fleet. The CCP of Beijing (1987) suggested implementation of six measures: (1) exemption from turnover tax; (2) raising their depreciation rate from 4.9% to 8%; (3) depreciation funds will not be submitted to the Transport Bureau; (4) exemption from tax on transport fuel; (5) granting of low-interest loans for the construction of cargo handling centres; and (6) freedom to adjust charges for small orders.

To put into effect the new government measures requires a major change of attitude on the part of the government towards urban transport. First, the government should realize that improvement of urban transport is not a 'consumptive' pursuit. It will enhance the overall efficiency of the urban economy and improve the urban environment. Thus more government input would be required. Quan (1990b) reported an official proposal that urban transport should share

10% of the municipality's total annual infrastructural investment. Among the various elements of urban transport, their share in the annual investment fund should be as follows: road development, 30%; fixed rail development, 35%; public passenger transport, 15%; public cargo transport, 14%; and transport management, 6%. According to the municipality's budget for 1991, such a percentage distribution represents the following capital investment sums for the respective elements: Yn270 million, Yn316 million, Yn135 million, Yn126 million, and Yn56 million. The emphasis on road development and fixed-rail transport is obvious, reflecting their high priority in the minds of the bureaucrats.

The second change involves a shift from low fares and equal access to public passenger transport to the new principle of an increased element of 'consumers pay' policy. Official encouragement to public transport is still required, yet it should be given simultaneously with the granting to public passenger companies of the right to raise fares and increase their profitability under the supply and demand rules of the market. Lastly, there is the need to solve the urban transport problem in cooperation with other agencies of the municipal government. For example, such cooperation is necessary for a coordinated transport policy package combining legislation using economic sanctions, such as tax, registration fees, depreciation rate, and administrative sanctions, such as car purchase approvals and licensing to restrict the use of the bicycle and the 'self-catering' type of goods vehicles. In areas of urban planning and population control for the whole city, coordination is also necessary. The old city is already a headache for urban transport planners, yet it is still experiencing the addition of large hotels, shopping centres and other tertiary developments that would attract more commuters and traffic into it, such as the new hotels in Huangfujing. Effective town planning can reduce traffic demand. For example, in the 1970s, 200 000 bicycles were reported going out of the old city in the morning peak for journeys to work. By 1986, as a consequence of large-scale residential development in the suburbs, this flow was reduced by half (Quan, 1988). Controlling the population, especially the 'fluid' or floating population, would also contribute to reducing public passenger demand, as they contributed 35.5% of the total public transport passenger volume of the city in 1988 (Quan, 1990b).

Conclusion

In summarizing urban transport in Beijing three characteristics must be noted:

1. *Socialist character.* By this we mean in particular the long-held policy of cheap fares in public passenger transport and its use to effect the government's industrial and residential dispersal policies. Besides this, the general low wage level and central allocation in job placement and residential location had combined to work in favour of public transport, as ownership of the private car was and is still impossible for the large majority of the population. Public ownership of passenger transport and the large amount of subsidy for ensuring the low-fare policy, as well as the almost universal monthly bicycle subsidy by work units to workers using the bicycle, has maintained a very low cost of commuting trips for the average household. It persistently remains less than 2% of total household expenditure and is clearly a positive feature of socialism, compared to the situation of the Third World in which 10% of household expenditure devoted to transport is quite common.

2. *Third World characteristics.* Being a developing country, the PRC, including its capital, is in general lacking in resources to develop an efficient three-dimensional system of public transport within its cities. The road network has not been expanding at the pace demanded by the growth of the population and the urban economy. Inadequate financial resources have not only prohibited the municipality from embarking on a vigorous underground train programme, they have also for a long time restrained it from providing sufficient resources for developing and improving public bus and tram services on which the populace so much depends. The road space is characteristically shared by different modes of transport, including motorized and non-motorized modes. These are also inadequately managed by modern signals. There is thus a mixture of transport technologies, both in the modes of transport and in road management.

3. *Chinese feudalism.* The development of urban transport in Beijing has also been affected by the persistent feudal ideas of traditional Confucianism. The construction of the first underground line and its long period of testing before it finally opened for public use reveal that the decisions involved stem from the more philosophical perspective that the national capital must set an example for the rest of the country for key state policies. The first underground of the PRC symbolizes in itself the developed industrial might of the nation, the policy of self-reliance, the drive to 'be prepared for war', as well as China's attempt to develop a modern means of transport. The 'wide-boulevard' policy, which is still officially claimed as correct, underlines a great waste of resources in a Third World situation and in some measure is responsible for the 37% walking

and waiting time for a bus trip, and as an important factor for the popularity of the bicycle over the bus and tram, is still the norm in road building at the present. Economic expedience, which was sometimes the key in important decisions, e.g. the crash course of industrialization, has been forgotten with the unsound excuses of the 'beauty' and 'leadership' role of the capital.

These three elements are interlocking to produce the present-day urban transport situation of Beijing. Some of the phenomena which we have examined, such as the increasing number of small goods vehicles owned by a large number of work units and the continual growth in the number of motor cars (mainly owned by work units as well), reflect the possible combination of the socialist and Third World characteristics. The low-wage system has deprived the majority of people of the ability to purchase a private car, yet controlling a work unit with its sizeable financial means could enable one to acquire a motorized means with public funds. This is particularly so with lax control over work unit financing in the new age of Open Door and Enterprise Reform. It has led to much misuse of transport technology and hence a waste of resources.

In presenting their situation to the outside world, the Chinese often claim that theirs is a unique case and thus should require unique treatment. The role of the bicycle in urban transport is one of these examples (Li, 1987). There still is very strong support for the bicycle in Beijing and within the PRC in general as a long-term mode in urban transport. The present position may be reflected by Quan (1990b), who considers that the bicycle is an efficient mode for distances of less than 6 km and it would not be withdrawn from the urban transport scene for a long time to come. In fact Chen and Huang (1990) estimate that the distribution of passenger trips for Beijing for the year 2000 would be: walking 15%; bicycle (including private cars) 34%; public transport, 51%. At an estimated car ownership rate of 80/1000, the 34% may be effectively interpreted as largely made up of bicycles, though the breakdown is not available. Superficially, these projections of the continued role of the bicycle rest on the physical properties of the various modes, i.e. the bicycle can be an effective means for distances under 6 km, the bus for distances over 12 km. etc. They have masked the real reason: that the planners turn a blind eye to the problem of the bicycle, as for densely built-up and high-density Chinese cities, no operating space of 6 km can be safely claimed not to interfere with the operating space of other modes, particularly when the bicycle has to share the same conduit with public transport – roads, even for distances shorter than 6 km. Such physical properties of the different modes are indeed true for all cities of the world, yet the predominance of the bicycle is seldom found in others. Thus the 'Chineseness' of the bicycle problem is self-created by the Chinese. It hampers the search for a sensible solution for solving urban transport problems in the Chinese city. Could such a claim of uniqueness or 'Chineseness' be yet another example of traditional Confucianism?

11

Social areas in Beijing

Residential segregation within cities

Cities are a form of high-density, non-agricultural and large-size human settlement. They are massive congregations of people and of secondary and tertiary activities. Within a city, how activities are ordered in space and how people of different socio-economic and other characteristics segregate form enquiries in urban studies, which are important not only as a reflection of the nature of the respective city and the processes of urbanization involved, but also are the basis for planning the economic and physical development of the city.

The existing pattern of land uses is often studied and described in the form of the internal structure of a city. It is the product of historical development, planning and the combination of locational requirements of various urban functions and attributes of different locations of a city. In Western cities where market forces operate, land value or economic rent has been put forward as the predominant factor behind the urban land-use structure. In socialist cities where central planning is the norm both for economic activities and for the provision of consumptive services, the internal structure of the city is more the product of planning, particularly in new cities or in new parts of an old city that have been developed under the socialist system. Of course, even within the socialist city, historical development and deviations of practice from theory have produced divergent patterns between actual examples and the ideal model and between socialist cities themselves.

Contemporary cities in the Western world have been subject to increasing segregation by new forces that essentially reflect the new rules of the market economy. People with 'might', defined more in terms of money, have priority access to better residential locations. This allows a larger measure of personal preference to influence residential location, and has ushered in the secondary factors of family or life-cycle effects as well as individual perception and choice regarding what is an acceptable neighbourhood and acceptable distance for commuting. Historical developments in the form of established neighbourhood character, existing physical infrastructure and housing stock do play some role in affecting and attracting different people to different residential locations. Planning and official and institutional influences on mortgages and access to different to types of housing also play a role in affecting the spatial differentiation of residents in Western cities.

Within socialist cities of China, to what extent does residential segregation exist? What are the factors responsible? Answers to these questions are important in understanding the nature of Beijing under the influence of its long history and Confucian culture, as well as the vigorous post-1949 'socialist bending' and industrial and urban developments. In particular, it can reveal in detail the housing conditions and the social processes that shape the spatial structure of present-day Beijing.

Distribution of people and housing in Beijing

It is a popular belief that within socialist countries, socio-spatial disparities had diminished compared to their historical past and compared to cities in market economies (French and Hamilton, 1979, 18). The basic reason behind this is the socialist ruling philosophy of equity in a classless society. The state implemented it through its ownership of land and control over allocation of housing. In Hamilton and Burnett's (1979) study of social processes and residential structure of socialist cities, they acknowledge that planners of socialist societies had been attempting to create uniform residential areas according to Marxist-Leninist principles to eliminate social segregation, but also note that despite superficial uniformity, urban neighbourhoods in some cities are neither physically nor socially uniform. Notable differences existed between housing estates arising from their respective locations, age and other features, such as open space, architectural styles and elevations. Rent and land values were irrelevant in explaining social segregation in the socialist city, as they were neither differentiated by location nor by housing quality. Yet it is reasonably clear that in some East European cities and the former USSR, the legacy of the pre-socialist past and the fault of post-war socialist planning had created situations of considerable differentiation of housing quality, a private sector housing market as well as a shortage in supply. Such circumstances had allowed the operation of processes of social segregation in space within the socialist city. In addition, allocation policy had always favoured, in conditions of housing shortage, younger families with many children. With enterprise reforms, in the mid-1960s the state diminished its housing construction and cooperative housing developed. Larger enterprises and institutions usually purchased dwellings from cooperatives in order to pass them on to workers whom they intended to keep or to recruit. This again favoured the higher educational groups.

Chinese cities are a mixture of the socialist city of the former USSR and East European model, with their long-established and unique urbanism under Confucianism, and the hard reality of being poor in development like many other Third World cities. They thus form an interesting category in the overall research into urban social spatial segregation. There has been no doubt that the Chinese had been following general socialist principles in the planning and development of their cities since 1949. It has been particularly the case in the transformation of the city economy and in the provision of urban housing, as has been discussed in previous chapters. Other than these, China faced a serious shortage in urban housing. The situation was only to some extent relieved in the late 1980s with massive construction programmes and noticeable improvement of the per capita living space, from a low of 4 sq m to about 6–7 sq m for most cities. Social strata had not been sorted out through the market, with economics the predominant factor and personal choice and preference the secondary factors. They are the consequence of state policy working through the allocation system of the municipality and respective working units.

The earliest works on social areas in PRC cities were on Shanghai (Xu, 1985; and Yu, 1986) and on Guangzhou (Xu et al., 1989). They also provide evidence that some of the factors in the Shevky-Bell construct in Western literature of socio-economic attributes, family status and ethnicity (Shevky and Williams, 1949; Shevky and Bell, 1955) do operate in the PRC. These are education, occupation, and age. The underlying reasons have largely been suggested as being the outcome of urban land-use planning and the system of housing allocation. Housing characteristics, which have a partial historical element, also seem to have some significance, yet they appear to work through the variables of education and occupation.

Thus before we consider the social areas in Beijing, let us turn to a general survey of where people do live and their general housing situation in Beijing. By the latter we mean the physical properties of housing, such as age, height, construction, space standards and facilities provided. These considerations reflect the low standards within Beijing both as a Third World city and a socialist one. Our examination will be based on the municipality of Beijing, i.e. the inner city and the suburban areas which cover the central mass and the 'dispersed constellations', or,

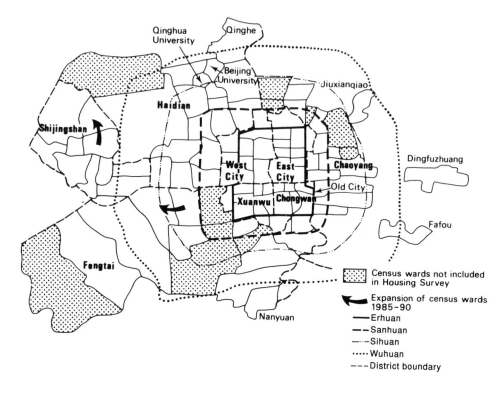

Figure 11.1   Census wards used in Beijing factorial analysis

in general, the largely built-up area within the Fifth Ring Road (Wuhuan Lu). The data come from the 1990 Population Census and the 1985 Housing Survey.

Density and the spread of people with different attributes

To facilitate our examination, we have plotted in Figure 11.1 the four urban districts of the inner city, i.e. West City, East City, Xuanwu and Chongwen, and the four suburb districts, i.e. Shijingshan, Fengtai, Haidian and Chaoyang, as well as the four ring roads and major local areas.

The old city, comprising most of the four urban districts, is where the population density is highest. With the exception of the Forbidden City, the San Hai Gardens and the locale of the Altars of Heaven and Agriculture, in the old city the census wards register a population

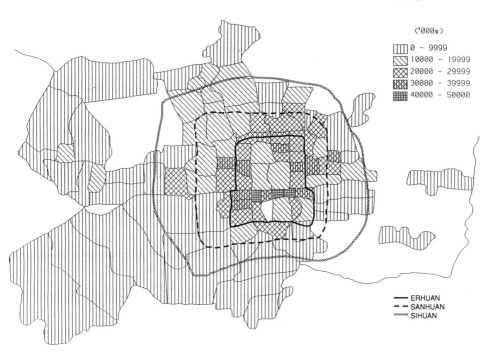

Figure 11.2   The distribution of population density

density in excess of 20 000 persons per sq km. The wards south of Qianmen register the highest density of 40 000–50 000 persons per sq km. In the suburban districts outside the Sanhuan Road (Third Ring Road), the population density is in general less than 10 000 persons per sq km (Figure 11.2). However, lower density does not necessarily mean better housing standards in terms of per capita floor space, as will be discussed in a later part of this section. High density of population is more a function of high density of houses or accommodation units.

The spread of population is also uneven in terms of age and employment. For age, we take those who are young (5 or less) and those who are old (60 and above) for illustration. The infant population aged 5 or less are proportionately higher in the suburban districts in Shijingshan, Fengtai and Nanyuan, i.e. 5.97–7.41% of the population. They are less than the mean (5.51%) which is generally registered in the periphery of the urban districts in the newly developing housing estates that lie on the two sides of the Third Ring Road. In general, the old city is close to the mean as well, except its southern part where there is a much denser population. Older people of over 60 are also proportionately more prevalent in the suburbs and less than the mean in the periphery of the urban districts. In the old city, the mean generally prevails, except for some slightly higher concentrations in a few northern wards. The higher infant population in the suburbs may be due partly to the existence of farm households in some wards and young families in new housing in others.

The distribution of government cadres reflects the spatial concentration of major government functions in parts of the city. The most concentrated wards with 15–24.9% employed as cadres are immediately outside Chaoyangmen, one ward immediately outside the East City district north of Xibianmen, the wards of the Forbidden City and the San Hai Gardens, and a ward north of Nanyuan in the south of the city. The professionals are much more represented (20–30.9%) in the 'dispersed constellations' housing the industrial districts and science parks (in the north-east). As a reflection of Beijing's rich supply of higher-level manpower, professionals account for 10–19.9% of the employed in almost all the wards in the area enclosed by the Fourth Ring Road.

Housing conditions and facilities

Age of housing testifies to the spatial growth of Beijing after 1949. Houses built before the 1940s were concentrated mainly in the old city and Nanyuan. In the 1950s the periphery and a few outlying suburban industrial districts were added. There had not been much development in the 1960s and 1970s. Major and widespread additions of new housing were seen only in the 1980s, mostly in areas that lie between the Third and Fourth Ring Roads.

Most of the pre-1949 old houses are of brick and wooden structure, as is quite a large proportion of housing in the suburban wards (Figure 11.3). In most wards of the old city these account for over 60% of all housing, a reflection of the old urban fabric of the inner city. In some suburban wards, they indicate the relatively high proportion of rural housing.

Of course, self-contained flats, locally known as 'suite apartments', are only a feature of post-1949 development, hence most of the old city wards are of accommodation units of shared facilities (Figure 11.4). 'Suite apartments' predominate (60–100%) in the periphery of the urban districts and the 'dispersed constellations'. They are supplied with their own toilets, water taps and in many cases heating. In the old city, all wards register less than 20% of flats being 'suite apartments', except a few on the eastern and western edge of the outer city built after the 1950s. The supply of gas is a luxury for the municipality as a whole.

(percentage)

▥	0.00 - 9.99
▧	10.00 - 19.99
▨	20.00 - 39.99
▦	40.00 - 59.99
▤	60.00 - 79.99
▩	80.00 - 100.00

——— ERHUAN
– – SANHUAN
∞∞∞ SIHUAN

Figure 11.3 The distribution of brick and wood structure houses

Most wards reported less than 20% of households with a gas supply. Only a few wards outside East City district, in Chaoyang district, and in a few suburban wards in Shijingshan reported 40% and more flats with a gas supply (Figure 11.5). A bathroom is yet another luxury, over 80% of the wards reporting less than 10% of the households with their own bathrooms, 100% for the old city. Only in four wards in the western suburb did the percentage with own bathroom reach over 60% (Figure 11.6). Shared facilities add a further headache to the already congested area of poor structure in the old city, and hence more urgency for urban renewal and redevelopment there.

However, in spite of marked differences in the provision of housing facilities, the old city and the newly built housing areas do not differ so greatly in terms of per capita living space. The categories of space of 0–2, 2–4, 4–6 and 6–8 sq m per capita when plotted on maps show no noticeable spatial variation nor differences between houses built at varying times or with varying facility provision. The very crowded situation of 0–2 sq m per capita represents less than 3% of the households for almost all wards. The crowded situation of 2–4 sq m per

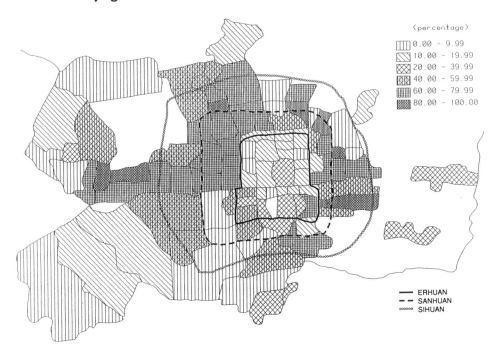

(percentage)

▦ 0.00 - 9.99
▧ 10.00 - 19.99
▨ 20.00 - 39.99
▥ 40.00 - 59.99
▤ 60.00 - 79.99
▦ 80.00 - 100.00

——— ERHUAN
– – SANHUAN
ooooo SIHUAN

Figure 11.4   The distribution of suite apartments

capita is slightly more prevalent in the old city, whose wards reported 10–20% such households, whereas five wards even reported 20–40%. Elsewhere in the city, wards largely register less than 10%. The higher space standard of 6–8 sq m per capita, in contrast, is more frequently found in the 'dispersed constellations' which reported 20–40% of their households in this category. However, within the old city, there are still as a general rule 10–20% of households with a similar space standard. In terms of space allocation one would tend to conclude that a uniform standard seems to have been observed. The poorer standards within the old city may be due to 'older-established' households, or people who like to cling onto a central location in spite of the possibility of improving their space standard by moving to newer areas.

Lastly, Beijing is still largely a low-rise city. With the exception of eight wards, all the 89 wards under examination reported over 90% of their housing being structures of walk-up flats of up to eight storeys. The exceptions are found mainly on the sides of the eastern section of the Third Ring Road in areas of hectic post-1975 housing construction (Figure 11.7). In these eight wards houses in excess of eight storeys

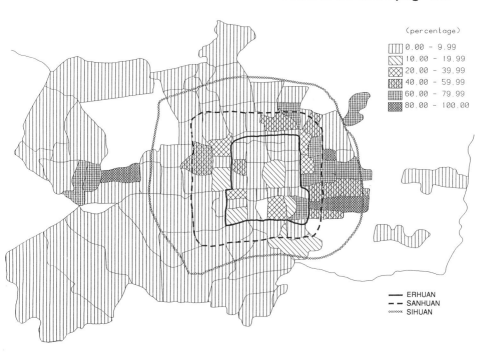

(percentage)

0.00 – 9.99
10.00 – 19.99
20.00 – 39.99
40.00 – 59.99
60.00 – 79.99
80.00 – 100.00

—— ERHUAN
– – SANHUAN
∞∞∞ SIHUAN

Figure 11.5   The distribution of households with gas supply

accounted for 20–40% of the total of the residential units. In the old city, the wards are predominated by single-storey structures. In the 'inner city' (i.e. the northern part of the old city), except the Forbidden City, all wards register 60–100% of households in single-storey structures. Only in parts of the outer city do some wards register 20–40% of such structures owing to their being affected by post-1950 developments. Thus Beijing is still very much a flat city, particularly so in the old city. Preservation and height control, because of the city's role as the traditional national capital, has added further weight to maintaining a strict limit on building height within the old city. Post-1950 development up to the early 1970s still mainly consists of walk-up flats of 4–6 storeys. It thus generates, within the old city, a basin-like building height profile that increases in height once we pass beyond the limit of the old city. Yet the rim of the basin is not a narrow ridge. It takes quite a uniform plateau shape of basically 4–6-storey worker housing.

With the above general background, we tend to think that social areas do exist in Beijing. People of similar socio-economic traits tend to be pulled together by the situation of housing, history of development of

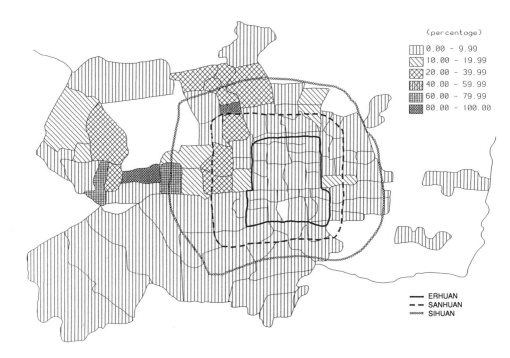

Figure 11.6 The distribution of households with a bathroom

the area and the spatial disposition of different land uses. It is with such a notion that we have performed a factorial ecological analysis of Beijing, using the 1990 Population Census and the 1985 Housing Survey data. The census wards used in the analysis have been mapped out in Figure 11.1.

Social areas in Beijing

Social areas are basic components of the urban human ecology. They are, put simply, discrete areas within a city with distinctive socio-economic, family status, and ethnicity attributes. Of the three sets of factors, the socio-economic factor plays a predominant role. As social area studies were pioneered by Shevky and Williams (1949) and Shevky and Bell (1955) based on cities in the USA, this is easy to understand. In such a market economy, the allocation, or rather the take-up, of residential units by individuals or households is largely based on economic might. For this reason, the variables used to measure this

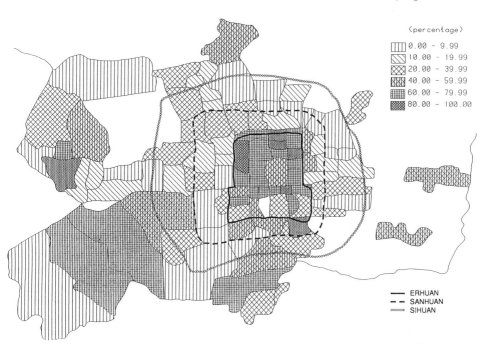

(percentage)

▥	0.00 - 9.99
▨	10.00 - 19.99
▩	20.00 - 39.99
▦	40.00 - 59.99
▦	60.00 - 79.99
▦	80.00 - 100.00

—— ERHUAN
– – SANHUAN
∞∞∞ SIHUAN

Figure 11.7   The distribution of single-storey houses

factor are often income, education and occupation. As a person's
housing need, his perception of a conducive residential environment,
and the ideal commuting time and distance vary at different stages of
his life or family cycle, they form a general yet secondary factor in
spatial ordering of people within the US city. Ethnicity, a factor that
continues to have a role in the USA's persistent policy of letting in
migrants from outside, as well as its long-standing racial situation of
negroes versus 'whites', has added a reality in American social area
studies that may or may not be similarly found in other countries. The
variables used for these two sets of factors are: for family cycle, family
size, portions of the age pyramid and fertility; and for ethnicity,
minority group concentration, dialects or languages and length of
residence (Abu-Lughod, 1969; Berry and Rees, 1969).

The methodology of social area derivation is simply first the division
of the city into census wards and then obtaining data on the variables
that reflect the three sets of factors. Factorial analytical techniques are
then used to identify the predominant dimensions that differentiate the
census wards. Clustering analysis follows for grouping similar census

wards into social areas, each of which is dominated by one dimension. Thus the urban residential space will be broken up into different parts with different types of people predominating, a fact generally accepted in the Western capitalist world.

A total of 89 variables have been used. Respectively, they may be classified as pertaining to the key processes of the Shevky-Bell construct, as follows:

1. Modernization (socio-economic status): education, demographic, employment, occupation, house-ownership.
2. Urbanization (family status): age, sex, resident status, household characteristics, ethnicity, density.

In addition to the above, there is a long list of housing variables. In Beijing's setting, these variables not only reflect the reality of data available from the Housing Survey, but also the situation in contemporary Chinese cities in which the age, facilities and space standards of housing correlate highly with the socio-economic status of the household head and his migratory history into the city, as supported by studies on Shanghai and Guangzhou, and to some extent also sustained by studies in some formerly socialist East European cities.

The census wards of Beijing have been grouped into eight social areas. The spatial pattern of the eight social areas has been mapped in Figure 11.8.

Inner city slum

This area covers the entire old city except one ward on its south-west margin which was largely developed after 1949 and five wards that extend out from it in the four margins. Thus it is an area already built up before 1949 which has since been subject to very little redevelopment. The area is mainly of old structures of wood and bricks, generally of one-storey courtyard houses of the Ming and Qing Dynasties. Per capita living space is very small and housing units are equipped with few modern facilities. Water tap, toilet, kitchen and heating are usually shared or not provided. It is an area also with a larger proportion of older people, which is reflected in its higher death rate. Besides the poor quality of housing, most of the population without housing provision are also found there. Employment-wise, commercial, restaurants and storage figure prominently, as is the usual case for the established part of a city.

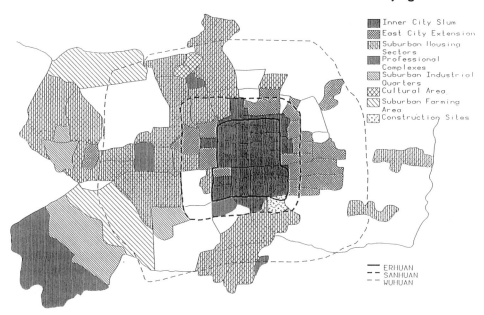

Figure 11.8   Social areas of Beijing, 1990

East city extension

This area covers mainly the eastern suburb immediately outside the old
eastern wall of Beijing. Ten wards are included in the social area,
extending from the Second Ring Road to beyond the Fourth Ring Road
to reach Jiuxianqiao and Dingfuzhuang, two of the major peripheral
constellations devoted to light industries. They, together with the east
and south-east patches of the 'eight suburban plots', form a large
industrial zone in the eastern suburb mainly concentrating on electronics,
chemicals and textiles, with machinery, construction materials and food
industries of secondary importance. They represent the large-scale
development of the suburban areas in the periphery of the city districts
for residential and industrial use in the 1960s and 1970s. The housing
estates comprise better equipped and taller structures. There are three
such wards on the northern and western margins outside the old wall.

Suburban housing sectors

This social area occupies the largest space within urban Beijing. It covers
the north-west, west, south-west and south of the 'eight suburban plots'

developed in the 1960s and the industrial 'dispersed constellations' of Nanyuan, Xiyuan and Qinghe. It is marked by mature families of industrial and commercial employment, low to medium level of education, a high birth rate in 1982–90 and a high population density. Houses are better equipped and more modern than those in the old city, with higher living space standards.

Professional complexes

This area exists in the form of four widely dispersed small patches in the suburban areas of Beijing. All of them are located conveniently in terms of transport, i.e. the south patch is next to Nanyuan airport, the southeast patch is between the Second and Third Ring Roads, while the west patch is dissected by the Fourth Ring Road. In addition, most of them are close to or within areas of concentration of research and technology land uses (see 'Urban and Suburban Land-uses' in Beijing National Land Agency, 1990). These four wards show predominance of the mature age groups and R & D, professional and technical employment.

Suburban industrial quarters

The cluster analysis has put the three wards so labelled into the same cluster as 'Inner City Slum'. Indeed, they share some of the characteristics of census wards there. They are the three large and earlier developed industrial suburbs of Shijingshan (mainly on iron and steel and other metallurgy industries), Fengtai (mainly on automobiles, textiles and construction materials) and Changxiandian (mainly on machinery). Shijingshan Iron and Steel Plant existed before 1949, the other two started construction in the First Five Year Plan (1953–57). Thus their common denominator is poor-quality and low-rise structures built in the early years of the PRC, besides the obvious location factor.

Cultural area

This comprises two small wards in the north-west suburb. It is the area of the two top and largest universities of the nation: Qinghua and Beijing University. They form therefore a distinct social area of university students and staff, and the families of the latter.

Suburban farming area

This includes two large, distant wards in the north-west and south-west suburb beyond the Fifth Ring Road. They score extremely high negatively in employment in the primary industries. This pattern reflects the concentration of the suburban farming community.

Construction sites

This social area may only be regarded as a temporary feature in the social space of Beijing. The large army of construction workers concentrated in a single ward at the time of the 1990 census led to its being identified.

Factors behind Beijing's social areas

Figure 11.8 shows various concentric layers of the social areas of the city. In general, we can observe, in addition to the concentric layers, sectoral and clustered types of development of the social areas. The process of compaction and peripheral accretion arising from a low level of economic development and a shortage of funds for housing and transport development, as described by Pannell (1980) and Shen and Yao (1985), are responsible for the concentric layers around the dense core of poor living conditions. Nationalization of most housing, central direction in its distribution and a low-rent policy combined to create a more mixed situation in socio-economic characteristics than the inner city of the Western world which is populated by the lowest income and education group of residents. In spite of this, Beijing also shares some of the features of the Western inner city. In its Inner City Slum, there is a higher proportion of old people, a higher death rate, a higher proportion of employment in the commercial, restaurant and storage sector, and generally people of a lower level of education. Initial post-1949 development followed the manner of peripheral accretion, though there had also been clustered developments around major old and new industrial projects. Within the extended periphery, there is better housing than the old core, and such development, similar to those that sprang up around industrial projects such as Shijingshan and Fengtai, is also industry led.

   The adoption of Soviet planning in Beijing also led to sectoral growth of new suburban housing after 1949, particularly in the west, south and north-western sectors of the planned urban areas following the 'dispersed constellations' pattern. Inevitably these areas are based on newly planned industrial growth as well. These housing areas are set between green buffers, largely vegetable fields, some of which have since been engulfed by built-up areas and a few have been integrated into the urban wards, though retaining their predominant farming character. The appearance of the Cultural Area and Professional Complexes owes much to Soviet planning as well. These areas of specialized activities have turned into distinct social areas of strong socio-economic and family cycle attributes. These activities occupy a location of good environment in the suburban areas and their work units are usually gifted with decision power, particularly in respect of providing housing to their students and staff. These social areas therefore distinctly bear out the basic Shevky-Bell construct, as they contain the most distinct social groups by age, education level, employment and housing quality.

Post-1978 liberalization and modernization led to a rush in housing construction of higher standards than previously. More significantly, larger residential areas are being constructed with a larger proportion of high-rise blocks. In spatial form and appearance, they become a new element within Beijing's cityscape. The residents in such areas tend to be cadres and financial sector employees, who presumably have more decision-making power than the average citizen. As a dimension for social area formation, this has been successfully netted out as one component in the factorial analysis, though in the cluster analysis it has been subsumed under East City Extension and Suburban Housing Sectors.

In short, 'nationalization' of old housing, central planning in location of major land uses and the general rule of placing residence close to employment are responsible for generating the social areas described above. Such a pattern falls in line with case studies for Shanghai and Guangzhou.

Conclusion

It is suggested that the superficially uniform residential spatial pattern of socialist cities has masked real differences in physical conditions of the urban housing stock, as well as differentiation in the socio-economic characteristics of the residents. In the East European countries, formerly residential differentiation by means of the key dimension of professional– manual workers has been supported by a number of studies. The existence of private housing and owner-occupier cooperative housing provided the necessary milieu for the sorting process to proceed according to such a dimension. The factors of age, education and housing types are found to be key variables which underline the social areas for these socialist cities. Studies in the PRC on Shanghai and Guangzhou pointed to the existence of social areas, and the operation of the variables of age, education and occupation. Of particular interest is that the occupation factor points to 'political status' in the form of a 'cadre' and 'non-cadre' division of individuals, suggestive of a new class structure and its influence on the residential spatial pattern in the Chinese socialist city. The notions of a classless society and a uniform pattern of neighbourhood have thus been put in doubt.

In Beijing, it does appear that residential segregation exists. Age, education, employment and type of household are found to be responsible for the social area of high concentration of university students, academics and R & D and research professionals. This reconfirms similar areas found in Warsaw, Guangzhou and Shanghai, a situation seemingly commonplace in socialist land-use and urban-planning arrangements. The shortage of housing, the general non-existence of private housing and the private rental market, the uniform allocation system through the work units, low rental policy and uniform and low public transport fares have combined to create two forces contributing to Beijing's pattern of social areas. The first is the spatial process of development of the housing stock; the second is the correlation between employment, occupation and residential location. In the 1950s, the predominant process at work was compaction within the old city and then the building up of the peripheral wards of the city districts for accommodating the political and administrative staff and their dependants, as Beijing took on the role of the national capital. The worsening of the inner city into a slum and the creation of old suburban areas are the consequences, though the latter happened some years later. Simultaneously, the north-west suburb was developed into a Soviet-style new area for higher education and research, in addition to its historical and environmental attributes for being a resort area. Such development stems from the capital's role as the nation's cultural centre, and its growth had not only been propelled by new development, there had also been a relocation of many research and educational units from the former national capital, Nanjing.

In the 1960s, large-scale industrialization of the city took place spatially in the form of 'dispersed constellations'. Allocation of housing units through the work units and a close correlation between housing provision and industrial estate development led to the formation of planned clusters of industrial workers' quarters in the suburban areas on the downwind sides of the inner city. Post-1978 liberalization and the emphasis on modernization and consumerism have led to a new change in the supply of and demand for residences in Beijing. The spatial response, though still much guided by planning, has been the emergence of high-rise complexes of larger scale than before. They have improved living space and equipment standards and are to be purchased by the work units or individuals. The socio-economic characteristics of residents appear to be either persons of political influence in the allocation process, or professionals which the work unit wants to retain or recruit, or individuals who can afford the higher rental or sale price of such housing. At present, the analysis has not yet netted out these complexes as a distinct social area. Nevertheless, it is evident that they represent a new process in residential segregation in Beijing.

The force of the historical and cultural factor in the creation of social areas of Beijing does not need to be emphasized. Preservation within the old city has been an important reason for the low amount of redevelopment of the predominant single-storey structures there so far. The nature of Beijing as the political and cultural centre of the nation has both enhanced the attraction of the inner city as a residential location and the development of the 'cultural area' in the north-western suburb and the Professional Complexes. Of course, the attraction is effected through the collective view of general land-use planning, as evidenced by the 1949–50 debate on where to locate the administrative centre, rather than by personal choice of individuals. Unlike some East European cities, i.e. Warsaw, these social areas do not lie within the inner city, but on newly developed and planned sites of good environment in the suburbs. The allocation of housing through work units, and the allocation of jobs through central planning on graduation, had made the ethnic factor insignificant against the background of hectic increase of population since 1949. The factor of income has not been included in our analysis owing to the lack of data. Nevertheless, as income has been generally low and uniform for different types of occupation within the city, it is believed to be an insignificant variable in reflecting the socio-economic status of the households.

Of course, what are left to be commented on are two main points that have been raised earlier, i.e. the social processes responsible for the creation of the social areas; and whether the replacement of the market by administrative means has led to more equality.

In general, we can only observe that the social processes at work are the struggle of the individual to get into the universities or polytechnics which may land him temporarily in the Cultural Area and part of the Professional Complexes, i.e. Haidian where many higher-level education institutions also congregate. At graduation he is allocated to a work unit. Then his place and type of residence are dependent on the resources and location of the work unit. Those who fail to get into the higher-level education institutes are to be allocated to manual or clerical jobs in the commercial or industrial sectors. Their housing condition and/or possibility are dependent both on the resources of their work units, their work age, and their position within the work unit. At least this had been the situation up to 1991 when self-effort to seek employment and private housing and a private rental market had only just started to emerge on a very small scale.

The claim by some authors (Konrad and Szelenyi, 1969) that replacement of the market in the allocation of urban housing by an administrative mechanism within socialist cities had not done away with inequality, but added to disparity of income and increased discrepancy of real rewards between professionals and manual workers, may not necessarily be true in the case of Beijing. Allocation of housing by the work unit created differences in housing benefits depending on the resources of the work unit rather than the professional–manual labour dimension. It is indeed true that distinct groups of work units do have more means to provide housing for their employees, as revealed in Chapter 8, yet a large 'profitable' factory like the Capital Iron and Steel Corporation provides much more decent housing to its manual workers than a municipal level bureau with limited financial means does to its professionals. Despite this note, in our analysis we have found distinct social areas of professional complexes, largely of R & D and professional and technical employees, as well as a new 'cadre'-dominated area in the making. Finally, the variables of age, education, employment, and occupation of the original Shevky-Bell construct do seem to be effective in the derivation of social areas for PRC cities. Lack of an obvious discrepancy in income between different occupations, as well as a situation of administrative allocation with low rentals, would conceptually make the variable of income ineffective. Segregation does exist, though to a much lower extent than in both the Western cities and other Third World cities. Even up to 1990, owing to the general lack of a private sector rental market and an owner-occupier housing sector different in its allocation, space and rental standards from the central and work unit allocation system, Beijing's residential segregation is much less than in the East European cities in the late 1970s. The characteristic of socialist equity seems to be largely prevailing in Beijing, though evidently new market forces have since started to operate and are casting doubt on the long-term validity of the present pattern.

12

Open and economic-minded Beijing: a new departure?

Introduction

The pros and cons of the post-1949 development of Beijing have indeed been a hot topic for both public and informed academic debates within the PRC, particularly so within Beijing itself in the past decade. This concern is made urgent and material because the PRC as a whole turned a new page in 1978 after Deng Xiao-ping took over in Chinese politics. Under him a new approach in managing and in development for the country has begun under the rubric of Open Door and Enterprise Reform. The long-held central planning system is being gradually replaced by a 'socialist market economy', emphasizing the rule of the market. Economic enterprises have been given more and more freedom in managing their own affairs as the official bureaus which formerly directed them in production and allocated to them the relevant inputs have now relinquished direct control, retaining only macro policy matters. Production or service enterprises are now mainly (though not entirely) responsible for their own profits and losses, and are given complete control over price setting, purchases of inputs, production planning and the raising of funds. For labour hiring and wage setting, they also enjoy much more autonomy than before. Most of these reforms started in 1982 and gradually deepened in 1990–92 (Huang and Bong, 1992).

At the beginning of 1993, the new system of 'socialist market economy' in replacement of 'planned commodity production' was formally announced. Thus chapters 4–11, which cover various facets of the urban geography of Beijing, straddle the pre-reform period of 1949–77 as well as the reform period of 1978–92. In each of these chapters we have attempted to comment on the experiences of the two different periods and have made our own observations as to the possible future prospects of the respective urban facet that is being dealt with. In this chapter, we have gathered from relevant sources Beijing's own evaluation of its post-1949 experience, as well as the municipality's strategy for guiding the city's development up to the year 2050. We hope to provide, from the Chinese point of view, a summary of about 40 years' experience of development under the PRC rule, and what the municipality sees as the main directions for the city's future growth in the coming half century or so.

Diagnosing the sources of post-1949 problems

Beijing Municipal Government, in its 1987 long-term strategic study of the city's development, expressed the source of the city's problems as follows:

> Due to natural constraints, present economic structure, and restrictions of the present administrative and enterprise management systems, within its limited space, Beijing's limited resources cannot be completely utilized for economic development. Thus what can be supplied from the city's own economic growth for the city's needs is highly inadequate. Yet demands from the political centre, urban needs and economic needs have been expanding, leading to a demand explosion in excess of what the city's natural and social resources can sustain. (Chen et al., 1989a)

The imbalance of supply and demand stems directly from the rapid growth of the city's population, pushing up total demand. The average annual growth rate of the city's population between 1949 and 1987 was 4.4%, much in excess of PRC's rate of urbanization, even of the growth of its cities with over 1 million population. In 1949, Beijing had only 2.03 million people. By 1986, there were 9.17 permanent residents. When an average daily floating population of 1.1 million are counted, the actual population of the city that demands food, services and various infrastructural and utilities support amounts to 11 million.

The second reason behind the imbalance is excessive urban construction programmes. The city's fixed capital investments have been overexpanded and overextended, making its urban demand explosion well above the PRC's urban average. Starting from the Fourth Five Year Plan, the fixed capital investment amount of Beijing increased by 100% every five years. For instance, in 1986, there were 27.6 million sq m of housing under construction. In 1987, the amount increased to 57.5 million sq m. Such hectic growth in construction had not only exceeded the city's construction ability and what its resources could afford, it also lengthened the construction cycle and forced a decrease in investment returns, causing problems for material supply, financing and for allocation of natural and social resources.

In terms of pressures on natural resources, the supply of water and developable land are good examples. Beijing has a serious water shortage problem. The useable water resource in a normal year is around 4–4.2 billion cu m. Rapid urban and industrial growth have pushed demand well beyond this limit in recent years, forcing the city to tap its underground water supply at an annual rate of 0.2–0.3 billion cu m. Demand increase will further mean an annual total of 5.5–6 billion cu m by the year 2000. Further demand growth will only be met by long-distance and highly costly water transfer from south China, i.e. from the Yangtze River. Supply of developable land to meet unrestrained growth of population, economic enterprises and administrative units of the central and local governments is particularly serious in central Beijing, as these all tend to be pulled to the city centre. Within the 440 sq km of the planned urban area in the mid-1980s, all developable space has either been built up or allocated. In the latest plan, the planned urban area has been extended to 1000 sq km. This means massive further urban encroachment onto the vegetable farms and green open space that serve as urban lungs and environmental hedges for the congested city.

For a long period, Beijing's urban infrastructure has been overloaded as its growth had always lagged behind urban population and economic growth. Under normal circumstances, investments for basic infrastructure should form 35% of total fixed capital investments. In 1949–86, Beijing's aggregated sums for urban infrastructural investment were only 21.9% of its total fixed capital investments. The short supply of urban infrastructure may be reflected in the balance sheet of supply and demand for basic urban facilities at the end of 1986. For example, water supply facilities were capable of yielding a daily total of 1.4 million tonnes, 150 000–200 000 tonnes below the daily peak demand; underground sewers were extended to only 27% of the built-up area, and sewage treatment facilities could handle just 10% of the waste water. Serious shortages were similarly reported in the utilities: central heating reached only 13% of households; electricity supply fell short of demand by 250 000 kwh; the urban telephone installation rate was only 6.7% and the connection rate 30%.

While the demand for construction funds is high, the supply of investment capital has fallen much behind. Under the present administrative and fiscal arrangements, the most profitable enterprises that benefit from the capital status of the city, e.g. financial institutions and centrally administered enterprises, submit their entire amount of profits and tax to the coffers of the central government. On the other hand, municipal-administered enterprises are currently under the 'split-profit' system and have to submit the larger proportion of their revenue to the central government as well, leaving limited funds as municipal revenue. In the 15-year period of 1985–2000, it is estimated that Beijing would require Yn38.4 billion from local sources for basic infrastructural projects. Under the present fiscal and enterprise management arrangements, only an estimated Yn12 billion may be raised in this way.

Structural imbalances existed in the age and education structure of the population, in the size and pace of growth of the economic sectors, as well as in productive and consumptive investments. Beijing has been facing an ageing problem in its population since the mid-1980s. In 1985, old people made up 9.2% of the population; by 2000, it will be increased to 14.7%. The situation projected for 2032 is 28.7% or an absolute older population of 3.14 million, i.e. one old person in every 3.1 persons. The rapid increase of old people has led to a structural shortage of labour, and will have an impact on the capital's future consumption pattern, economic structure, and demands for various social welfare facilities. Compared to most PRC cities, Beijing's population enjoys a higher educational attainment. Yet as the 1990 census revealed, 63% of the population had lower than junior high school level of education. Thus its quality of human resources still falls short of its role as the nation's political and cultural centre.

Beijing's overemphasis on industrial development has produced an obvious imbalance in its urban economy. In 1991, the share of the three economic sectors by value of output and by employment are: primary, 8.1% and 14.3%; secondary 52.2% and 44.1%; and tertiary, 39.7% and 41.6%. Though the government had made a great effort to redress the situation, and some improvements have been achieved, the situation was still only slightly better than what it was some years ago. The energy-intensive, water-intensive and raw material-intensive nature of the industrial sector has only been marginally changed. Historical factors and the central planning system have created internal imbalances in the form of excessive capacity among different enterprises and different products, ranging from below 30% in steel and microprocessors, to 31–40% in electric fans, farm drugs, and 41–50% in watches, bearings, and 51–60% in diesel engines and synthetic board (Capital Social and Economic Development Research Institute, 1989, 91).

These structural faults in the economy exerted pressure on the urban space, and restricted the scale and smooth running of other administrative and productive activities, as well as interfering with people's daily lives. Since the 1980s, the municipality has invested heavily in a number of new industries producing consumer durables. As these new industries depend on foreign capital to some extent, they have created a new constraint on industrial growth in the city, on top of the traditional constraints of water, land and energy. To foster structural trans-formation of the economy requires not only spatial readjustment by shifting some industries out of the inner city into suburban and new town locations as previously discussed, but also new taxation and fiscal arrangements so that old enterprises will bear heavier taxation and will surrender some of their resources for the development of new industries (Chen et al. 1989a, 8–11).

Inadequate investment in basic infrastructure compared to other investment has been a long-standing problem in the city, the so-called 'bone' and 'flesh' divergence. Until the mid-1980s productive investment projects as well as housing construction projects were still formulated and implemented by various ministries and their subordinate work units in a vertical style. Whether the municipal government had the resources to provide all the necessary supporting basic infrastructure was not their concern. In a situation of inadequate funds, the municipal government had not been able to match these development projects with basic infrastructural construction. In the years since 1949, of the total fixed capital investments made in the city, 53% were those by the various ministries, while the municipal government was responsible for 47% (Table 12.1). These figures underline the lack of control as well as the inadequacy of the resources of the municipal government to deal with the imbalance between urban growth and infrastructural construction. In the Fourth Five Year Plan (1971–75), basic infrastructural investment formed 26.3% of the total fixed capital investments of the city. In the Sixth Five Year Plan (1981–85), it fell further to 17.2%. For the entire post-1949 history, the cumulative total represents an overall 22.3% of total municipal investments, much lower than the norm of 35% (Capital Social and Economic Development Research Institute, 1989).

The causes of the above problems, besides the limitation of the city's natural resources, historical constraints and policy faults, include the following as the key factor:

> The primary reason being the society is still in the early development phase of socialism. Its level of productivity and social division of labour are still at a low level. It is also immature in its system and operating mechanisms. These deterministic features become much more obvious in the socio-economic development of big cities like Beijing. (Chen et al. 1989a, 13).

Using the yardstick created by an American expert on modernization, Beijing in 1985 was still a long way from the early phase of a modern-ized community (Ma and Fan, 1989, 42–8; Table 12.2). Its productivity

Table 12.1   Fixed capital investment of Beijing by sources of funds (in %)

Period	Total Central	Local*	Municipal infrastructure Central	Local	Commerce and services Central	Local
1949–50	55	45	–	100	–	–
1951–56	80	20	–	100	95	5
1957–60	65	35	30	70	28	72
1961–64	70	30	55	45	55	45
1965–70	74	26	15	85	40	60
1971–75	50	50	1	99	18	82
1976–80	44	56	31	69	18	82
1981–84	44	56	16	84	21	79
Cumulative total	53	47	35	65	26	74

* Municipal government
Source: Capital Social and Economic Development Research Institute (1989).

Table 12.2   Key indicators of community development

Indicator	Phase One of modernized community	Beijing in 1985
(1) GDP per capita	> US$3000	US$920
(2) Primary sector (% of GDP)	< 15%	6.9%
(3) Tertiary sector (% of GDP)	> 45%	33.3%
(4) % in non-farm occupation	> 70%	82.3%
(5) Literacy ratio of population	> 80%	90.5%
(6) Right age cohort with higher level education	30–50%	11.5%
(7) % of urban population	> 50%	59.8%
(8) Persons per doctor	800	255
(9) Life expectancy (yrs.)	60	73.2
(10) Newspaper circulation/person	0.3	1.5

Source: Capital Social and Economic Development Research Institute (1989).

and level of economic development were about 30% of the relevant criteria. The quality of its population, measured by the young age group with a higher level of education, was only about a third of the standard. Commodity production and social services were lagging behind as the tertiary sector was not much developed. However, of the various social indicators that reflect the quality of life of the masses, Beijing had attained higher standards, underlining that socialism does have its edge in certain aspects that affect people's basic welfare.

Put simply, the combination of socialism, Third World level of development, and the lack of relevant and effective administrative and enterprise management systems is believed to be the main source of the city's problems. The pursuit of equity in access to urban facilities and services has been an important goal for both the individual and work units. Yet the municipal government had, in the past, not provided constraint mechanisms such as pricing, taxation and other regulating measures. Thus what resulted was an obvious imbalance of supply and demand. The municipality lost its control over demand while being at the same time incapable of providing adequate supply. As the national capital, the host of numerous central government ministries and the military and CCP headquarters, Beijing has been confronted with a more difficult problem. These work units, with their rank and influence well above the municipal government, often compete among themselves for limited resources within the city's territory. What they do may also not even require the approval of the municipal government. Thus the latter with its limited authority had little means to coordinate, not to say to regulate, the activities of these 'super' work units to effect the necessary control over utilization of local resources and hence balanced and planned development in the various facets of the city.

Overloading of the city of Beijing may seem unavoidable even without a major disaster in the future. The most conservative estimate of the city's population at 2000 is 14 million, composed of 12 million permanent and 2 million floating population, with 8.5 million within the planned urban area. To meet the demand of such a community will require total fixed capital investments in the region of Yn150–170 billion in the 15-year period of 1985–2000, of which the municipality has to provide about Yn40 billion (Capital Social and Economic Research Institute, 1989). Beijing must make the best of the recent Open Door and Enterprise Reform to derive a new strategy to control inflationary demand and regulate development for meeting the planning targets for a beautiful, environmentally sound and efficient national capital.

Redefining the role of Beijing

The strategic position of the present-day as well as the future role of Beijing has been stated clearly in the following terms by the 1987 Strategic Long-term Study of the city:

> Beijing is the national capital of Socialist China. It is the world's famous civilized old city as well as a modern cultural city. At the same time it is a composite productive city in Asia and the Asian Pacific Region. (Chen et al. 1989a).

National capital of the PRC

As the national capital of the PRC, Beijing serves as the political centre and administrative nerve centre of the Chinese socialist system. 'It is the nerve centre that links the hearts of the people and the Party together' . . . 'It is also the "model district" for guiding the nation in modernization' (Chen, 1989a, 2). To foreign nations, Beijing is the display window of contemporary Chinese material and cultural achievements, as well as the bridge for international political, economic, cultural and scientific exchanges. As the headquarters of the CCP, it also claims the role as the base for enriching the theories of Marxism and socialism in general.

Civilized old capital and modern cultural city

Among the world's 76 famous historical cities, Beijing ranks fourth in length of history in urban development and thirteenth in length of history as a national capital. The city possesses 24 items as the nation's 'National Protected Cultural Relics', i.e. 9.6% of the nation's total, ranking number one with Shenxi Province. Its 'Protected Cultural Relics' at municipal grade accounted for 5% of the nation's total, ranking sixth among the provincial units. Post-1949 development in economy, science and culture has bolstered the city as the 'best district' in the country in science, culture, art and people's morality.

From 1949, the city has been planned as a new base for higher education and R & D in China. The large patch of special land use devoted to these functions in the north-western suburb illustrates this very well. Statistics in 1984 show that Beijing had 562 research and development units of various disciplines, representing 5.7% of the total number in the country. Higher-level education institutes numbered 77, about a quarter of the national total. Its R & D staff numbered 108 957 persons, or 18.4% of the nation's total. These two assets of the city form the special basis for its cultural character. Thus it possesses the best of the cultural heritage of the Chinese races, as well as the best of contemporary China in cultural and spiritual achievements (Chen et al., 1989a, 3).

Composite productive city in the Asian Pacific region

After more than four decades of industrial construction, Beijing now ranks number two as China's largest industrial base, second only to Shanghai. In the recent drive in structural transformation, high-tech industries, such as space, micro-electronics and biotechnology, are developing very fast. In the tertiary sector, Beijing aims to develop comprehensive and high-quality tertiary activities, not only to serve its own population but also the whole of North China, with a significant impact on the whole country. With the Open Door Policy, the city's international trade as well as foreign investments and joint ventures have grown rapidly. It is already the largest multi-functional regional city and the largest open city in North China.

The municipal government believes that Beijing has been fulfilling its historical tasks of transforming from a pre-1949 consumptive city into a productive city in accordance with socialist principles. Yet as China is still at the 'early phase of socialism', Beijing by all measurements remains a city of the Third World. Its economic development still lags behind most large cities of the industrialized countries. The capability of Beijing falls short of what is demanded of the national capital of a major nation.

Symbol of socialist China

As the national capital and the headquarters of the CCP, the symbol of Beijing carries with it a mandate which the rest of the country, particularly its cities, would look up to and replicate within their own spatial territory.

Within the social and cultural realms, the municipality feels that the 'communist morality', as well as concepts of socialist democracy and the rule of law of the masses, are still inadequate. Municipal management that befits its national capital role is yet to be established and improved. As such, the municipality sees four long-term targets for guiding Beijing's growth and development: (1) maintaining stable growth and prosperity; (2) development of a modern socialist culture; (3) strengthening the guiding and demonstration role of Beijing in the nation; and (4) development of an international exchange centre (Chen et al. 1989a, 6–7).

The new strategy

The municipality pledges to construct a socialist national capital with Chinese characteristics, and to abandon the traditional closed system of development and narrow-mindedness in managing Beijing by replacing it with a new scientific and pioneering spirit in maximizing opportunities offered by the recent Open Door Policy and Enterprise Reform (Chen, 1989a, 15–18). The components of the new strategy are:

1. Gradual transformation of the urban economy and the urban social development model to provide a more relaxed and liberal operating environment for the city. New growth is to be based on internal dynamics and careful balancing of various sectors of supply and demand. The city's total growth volume has to be strictly controlled. Short-term resource capability would be used as the criterion to gauge the suitable scale and nature of economic and social construction and development, and with this as a basis, the municipality would then plan its revenue, finance, material supply and the balance in foreign currency. A package of economic, administrative and legislative measures would need to be devised to achieve the balance of total social supply and demand and the healthy and stable growth of various economic sectors.

2. Achieving a new spatial order. Scale economies and economies of agglomeration have to be considered in balancing concentration of development within the inner city and a new style of dispersal of excessive and unsuitable activities from central locations. The city centre should concentrate Beijing's functions for fulfilling its role as the nation's political centre. Excessive concentrations there of educational and cultural institutions, R & D and unsuitable economic activities have to be dispersed to new urban districts and secondary centres within the suburban areas. The new spatial concept should involve a wider territory, and break away from the traditional administrative straitjacket of searching for a solution within the municipality's own jurisdiction. Inter-urban and inter-region cooperation and locational choice should be fostered whenever they are of higher returns and benefits for the parties concerned.

3. Emphasis on the cultural and brain-power of Beijing and its cosmopolitanization impact. In the long term, the city should develop its multi-functions to serve the central government and the whole country. The present economic and social structures should be transformed so that Beijing's vast potential in high-level manpower can be released and utilized as the predominant force in promoting the development of a high-tech, environmentally friendly, and high added-value urban economy and the growth of a high-level socialist civilization.

4. Deepening reforms in the management of the urban economy and municipal administration. A new administrative system for Beijing must be evolved. This may be achieved on the one hand by reforms in China's political system and economic systems, leading to the setting up of a system of macro regulation for the development of the capital. This is to use economic measures, administrative directives as well as legislation to constrain the growth impulse of

various work units in the city in order to restrain the growth of total demand. On the other hand, the city should move onto the path of the socialist market economy. Enterprise reforms to provide enterprises with autonomy in their own business and to inject into them the profit motive, together with reform in the price system, the creation of various markets and improving the system of urban taxes and fees, would be required to facilitate a reasonable disposition and flow of resources, so that the city can develop its own momentum for accumulation, development and self-adjustment.

In quantifiable terms, the municipality plans to achieve its strategic targets through three phased developments:

Phase One (1986–2000). There will be major efforts to effect a new urban development model for Beijing, emphasizing its macro regulatory capability to relieve the present serious imbalances between total supply and demand and serious structural imbalances in the economy. The present bottlenecks in development and the weak and yet desirable sectors will be bolstered. Reforms will be followed through to effect policy changes and inter-relationships for a new municipal administrative system to promote long-term and stable growth and development.

Phase Two (2000–20). This is the strategic adjustment and development stage. Within it, Beijing will strive to complete the structural transformation of its urban-rural economy. It will have to set up its new urban municipal operating system, form the capital region production circle, achieve comprehensive redistribution of its population and the setting up of a new urban system. The city's development will then enter a positive cycle of growth.

Phase Three (2020–50). This is the take-off period for comprehensive economic and social improvements so that the city can serve as the modern national capital and an international world-class central city for leading the PRC's urbanization.

Short- and medium-term policies

To achieve Beijing's long-term strategic objectives will be a long process. In the short and medium term, a number of key policy areas have been identified. They focus on concrete measures for the control of the city's population, spatial rearrangement to relieve pressure on the inner city and setting up of a capital city region, building up a new urban economy, emphasizing the construction of the basic infrastructure to modernize and boost the city's services, exploiting the brain-power of the city for economic and social development, reforming the municipal administration, and the promotion of spiritual development for cultivating a new 'Beijing Spirit'. Successes in these policy areas would make achievement of the strategy attainable and would enable the city to take initiatives in its future development.

Population control

As the nation's political and cultural centre with a prosperous economy, Beijing offers many attractions as a place of employment and residence. Measures have to be taken to ensure that population growth does not exceed the city's bearable limit, yet meets demands for its economic growth. By 2000, the total population should be within 12 million and those within the planned urban areas 6.5 million (Ma and Fan, 1989, 67). The basic policy includes elements of positive rearrangement of the city's population and economic activities into a rational pattern of concentric rings, persistent efforts to disperse the population into a larger territory, and the use of administrative and economic sanctions to restrict in-migration into the capital. Annual and five year plans for migration should be incorporated into the city's economic and social development plan. Quotas with enforceable directives should be issued to control population growth rigidly. The decision not to approve in-migration of whole work units into the city must be strictly implemented. The household registration scheme has to be improved to enforce effective hierarchical control of the permanent population. A per capita urban development tax should be collected from in-migrants approved under the urban population control plans. A 10% 'bed tax' has already been put into effect to tax tourists and to constrain the growth of the floating population, in addition to a 10% *ad valorem* tax on sales of goods and services related to tourists (Ma and Liu, 1989, 157). New town development should be fostered by special privileges to form secondary centres for effecting population dispersal. In addition, the Municipal Planning Commission should be made the authority to take charge on population control matters.

New spatial planning and formation of the capital city region

To redress the overconcentration of people and activities within the inner city, Beijing seeks to redistribute people and activities within and outside its municipal limits. This redistribution effort, to be completed by 2020 through a series of general plans with the force of law, would produce four concentric spatial rings of development, and achieve a new spatial organization for more rational use and disposition of resources and activities, and for improving the spatial and environmental balance.

The inner city. This is the core of the metropolis within the Second Ring Road. Its main function is to be the political centre and to retain the cityscape and atmosphere of the historic and cultural city of old Beijing. Work units within the core have to be those directly related to the CCP and the central government. Other work units have to be gradually resettled into new urban districts or the suburbs. New investments in the core will have to be confined to basic infrastructure, protection and preservation of historic structures and maintenance and improvement of existing office buildings and residential housing. In general, new office and residential development would not be allowed. The core will gradually become a purely political centre for the headquarters of the CCP, central government and the military. Its population density will decrease from the present figure of 27 000 per sq km to below 20 000 per sq km.

New urban districts. Extending outwards from the Third Ring Road to cover about 1026 sq km of territory will be the new urban districts. This will be the main area for investments in urban construction. The entire area will be planned in the form of 'dispersed constellations', each separated by green belts and gardens. Population will be clustered into residential districts and activities into 'work districts', each supported by adequate and comprehensive urban basic infrastructure and services. The present density of these areas of 2700 persons per sq km will be increased in future to 10 000–15 000 persons per sq km. Existing factories in the territory will either have to be transformed so that they are not polluting or relocated. The territory will also be unsuitable for large-scale development and expansion of R & D or cultural institutions.

Suburban districts. This ring has served the municipality as its base for production of subsidiary food and other farm products, the urban ecology protection belt and an important tourist and resort area. In future, it will add the functions of the city's industrial, trade, R & D and educational bases. Within it, several medium-sized cities of 300 000–500 000 population will be set up. Among them, the larger and longer-established ones such as Fangshan and Huangcun will be administered as 'urban districts', and utilized as reception grounds for industrial, educational, R & D concerns and subsidiary work units of the central government to be moved out of the inner city. On top of these, there will be about 10 expanded county capitals of 100 000–150 000 population for absorbing the dispersed population from the inner city and for acting as interception points for rural–urban migrants. A lower-end category of market towns of 30–50 000 persons for fostering the growth of rural collective enterprises would provide non-farm employment enabling rural people pushed out of the farm sector to remain within their native county.

The capital city. To consider Beijing's future growth in a wider spatial perspective and to suit new urbanization trends, an integrated urban system with Beijing as its core and spreading eastwards towards the coast should be fostered. Under the coordination and leadership of the central government, a long-term regional plan of the area should be developed to effect intra-regional cooperation and to achieve multi-centre, multi-enterprise and multi-sectoral diagonal and horizontal linkages. Policies to foster this as well as to encourage exchanges in the R & D, cultural and community spheres would also be hammered out (Liang and Li, 1989).

Adjustment of the economy to establish a new structure

Structural adjustment of the economy is essential to solve many of Beijing's urban problems. The adjustment should aim both to attain a reasonable balance of the primary, secondary and tertiary sectors, as well as to improve their quality and productivity. While promoting the flow of factors of production from the primary towards the secondary and tertiary sectors, the main direction is towards technical deepening and intensification, i.e. rapid growth of high-tech activities that suit the characteristics of the capital, upgrading and transforming traditional industries, and promoting the development of high-level manpower resources and substitution of urgent demands. It is intended that by the beginning of the twenty-first century, Beijing's economy would be based on high-tech sectors with an export and high added-value focus. Output from the electronics and machinery industries would make up 42% of total industrial output, while annual production of motor cars would reach 300 000 vehicles. In addition, the tertiary sector will form the mainstay of the urban economy, with high-level, high-value services as the new characteristics. By 2000, in terms of total employment, the share of the primary, secondary and tertiary sectors would be 9%, 42% and

49%, and their relative share of GDP would become 3.7%, 51.4% and 44.3% (Chen et al., 1989b, 151).

To achieve this goal, strong sectoral policies would be required to direct the urban economy towards the planned structure and composition. As the tertiary sector will be the preferred sector, a positive environment has to be created for it to move rapidly towards privatization and social division of labour, such as the device of a reasonable pricing policy and investment policy. Special attention would be made towards new sectors using high-level human resources so that a new enterprise system that reflects and reinforces the role and comparative advantage of the capital could be rapidly established.

In manufacturing industries, the old model of a closed system based on internal dynamics, quantitative growth and local market would be abandoned and replaced by an externally oriented model that would maximize Beijing's R & D and developed economic base to confront successfully challenges of competition in the market and in new technologies both within and outside China. Export-oriented and import-substitution types of industries would be the preferred branches with gradual movement away from low-level and superficial processing and intermediate goods industries towards high-technology input and high added-value production. Concurrently, traditional industries, basic industries and light vehicle manufacture, as well as high-tech machinery, textiles and garments and food industries, should be upgraded in technology and added value.

Spatially, the principle of 'redevelop industrial areas of the city districts, develop suburban industrial areas and form a linkage web with industries in the region' would be followed. In the year 2000, in terms of output value, the spatial spread of industries in the urban districts, suburban districts and the outer suburbs would be 17.8%, 52.8% and 29.4% (Capital Social and Economic Development Research Institute, 1989, 274). In future, the inner city would only serve as the nerve centre for new product development, business services, information and consultancy, while urbanization economies for industries are to be achieved through externally oriented horizontal linkages and the formation of consortia.

The rural economy of the suburban and rural *xians* would be based on self-sufficiency in staple food and for supplying the vast urban market. Increased input of technology and deepening of processing through setting up processing bases for non-staple food items are the main directions of development. The territory should also receive overspilled and relocated people and economic activities from the inner city. It should also serve as the ecological protective belt for the capital.

Speedy construction of basic infrastructure

In future, investment in basic infrastructure as a percentage of total fixed capital investments for the entire city will be fixed and implemented accordingly. For any five-year period, it should be no less than 25%; for individual years, effort should be made to attain 30% or higher. Concomitant with Open Door and Enterprise Reform, concrete measurements have to be implemented to collect land rent, user charges on municipal utilities and services, and charges for connecting with basic infrastructure, and to effect a general development levy. Bonds for raising funds for basic infrastructure construction would also be tried. Within infrastructural planning, four main areas of attention have been identified:

1. *Water.* Before the year 2000, the main effort lies in saving water. Reforms in the management of water resources will help to enforce comprehensive regulation on the use of water and put a control over the total volume demanded. The long-term solution beyond 2000 has to be long-distance diversion of water from outside. Feasibility studies by the relevant central ministries on the diversion of water from the Yellow River and Yangtze River into Beijing have to be urgently pursued, so that by about 2000 there may be some new water resources available for the city.
2. *Transport and communication.* Bottlenecks at present are the product of chaotic land-use patterns and bad management. The basic solution to the city's traffic jams lies with its passenger transport structure. Construction of rapid mass transit, especially the under-ground passenger train, would be one solution. In communication, expansion of the number of telephones within the city and an increased long-distance call capability are the principal methods.
3. *Energy.* There is an acute shortage of secondary energy, leading to a low level of economies in both social and environmental terms. This has already formed one significant constraint for building a modern capital. As a Third World city, Beijing may only take gradual steps to speed up the construction of power plants and the electricity grid, while at the same time encouraging saving in energy use. Development of central heating and increasing imports of natural gas are other measures for diversifying the pattern of energy consumption.
4. *Environment.* To prevent further deterioration and to improve the environment, all development in the city must pay heed to environ-mental protection. In the planning of all new projects, economic study, urban planning and environmental impact assessment must go hand in hand. For the short and medium term, district-wise

comprehensive environmental improvement would be launched. Industrial and some of the domestic pollution sources would be put under discharge volume control. The pace of green open space construction would also be increased. The main target is to achieve environmental improvement in strategic target areas and some urban districts.

Unleash the leading role of R & D

R & D activities of the city would be oriented towards economic applications, to serve modernization of the city infrastructure and municipal management, and for improving the livelihood of the people. Cooperation between central and local R & D units would be promoted for upgrading the traditional economic sectors and selectively developing a number of high-tech industries. To achieve this, the administrative separatism of the former central command economy has to be broken to allow horizontal linkages and combination of efforts to speed up R & D effects. R & D units are encouraged to join forces with enterprises and to form new types of joint venture for effectively tackling R & D problems in the economy and in urban construction, especially for enhancing the technology and innovativeness of large and medium-sized state enterprises.

To promote Beijing's R & D strength effectively, the development of 'science and technology development areas' such as the one in Zhongguancun would play an important role. Within such areas will concentrate specialists in space, super-conductivity, micro-electronics, biotechnology and laser fields. They will be organized into target teams for applied research with the aim of generating commercialized final products. Within the areas, special open policy measures on personnel, technology, capital, foreign currency and foreign trade are to be granted to both local and foreign enterprises.

Municipal reform and municipal finance

Two measures have been suggested. In the short term, under the present system, the supply and demand relationship and the distribution of resources of the city must be forcefully directed by a bureaucracy with central government-level status. It is therefore necessary to set up a new administrative organ for the planning and construction of the capital which has central government rank and is directly led by the CCP and the State Council. The new unit is to be responsible for coordinating all policies related to the urban and social construction and development of Beijing and to the use and distribution of its resources. In the long term, there should be a move towards localization by strengthening the roles of the People's Congress of Beijing Municipality and the municipal government. Simultaneously, developments along the lines of democracy and the rule of law should be followed. There would be gradual development of various types of markets for micro-level regulation of the flow of resources and of supply and demand. These include the establishment of a property market for the promotion of renewal within the old city and dispersal of population and activities into the outer areas. Establishment of the capital's financial market is essential to raise funds for urban construction, economic development, and to allow the rational flow of resources to the preferred sectors to effect structural transformation.

The price system of the city must also be changed to enable various markets to function. Before 1984, the price level of the city was at the bottom compared to the rest of the country, a consequence of a deliberate subsidy to maintain a special image for the national capital. Such a subsidy has also been necessary because as the national capital, the CCP and the central government have requested high urban standards there. In addition, it provides services for the central government and the whole country. Subsidy from municipal revenue for various items of daily life in Beijing amounted to Yn1.2 billion in 1985, or about a third of total municipal expenditure for the year, and is increasing at a very rapid rate. Its burden is thus much heavier than other provincial units. With the advent of the 'socialist market economy', such a subsidy would be absurd (Ma and Liu, 1989). As the national capital with busy intercourse with the outside world, and being the concentration of high-level manpower and high added-value activities, Beijing exerts a large demand on high-quality commodities. Under the prevailing situation of lack of local resources and a high population pressure, the price level of the city should normally be higher than the rest of the country. Indeed, price mechanism has to be utilized as an effective means to regulate the flow of resources and people between the city and other areas and to arbitrate the relationship of supply and demand.

To solve the problem of a serious shortage of investment capital, a positive overhaul of the present municipal finance, taxation, credit and foreign currency management systems is necessary. The following are methods to be implemented towards such an end (Ma and Liu, 1989, 154–62):

1. Setting up 'Capital City Finance'. According to the present arrangement, the local finance of the municipality has great difficulty in

bearing the responsibility of construction and development of the national capital. A special arrangement has to be considered within the finance of the central government, i.e. the setting up of a 'Special Fund for Assisting the Construction of the National Capital'. In 1986, Beijing could only retain 49.55% of its revenue for meeting municipal expenses. The central government in return provided an annually variable amount of subsidy for specific construction projects. In 1981–86, this averaged about Yn0.7 billion. The proposed Special Fund is to replace this variable central government subsidy and was initially set at Yn0.8 billion a year, and may be revised upwards. The second proposed source of funds is a further retention of 15–20% of the municipal revenue for Beijing's own use.

2. A gradual increase in local taxes and official fee items, which will be at a level higher than the rest of the country as a reflection of the national capital status and for recouping the cost of outlays for providing the services and facilities.

3. Expanding the range of activities and power of the municipal banks and to allow them to issue 'Capital Construction Bonds', at about Yn0.2 billion per year, and other utility bonds, so that the financial sector will be boosted and more funds can be generated to support construction and development of the capital.

4. Increasing the city's retention of its foreign currency receipts from the present 25% to 40% and expanding its powers to approve foreign capital utilization and the import of foreign technology to the limit of US$50 million, on a par with those enjoyed by the Coastal Open Cities of Shanghai and Tianjin. In addition, the annual allocation of foreign currency from the central government should be raised from US$0.2 to 0.3 billion.

Enhancing development of the spirit of socialism

The basic purpose of developing Beijing's spirit of socialism is said to be to create a new 'socialist man' who could take up the challenges of further opening and reform under the general guidance of communist principles and the tradition of the Chinese communists, the so-called 'Yenan Spirit'. This new 'Beijing man' will be fostered through the education system, art, culture and the media, and his image will be projected to the whole country to form a new ideology and model for the general public to follow.

Following the 'Four Directives' of 1980 and the 'Comments' of 1983, Beijing aims to develop into a 'culture-oriented city' of socialist material civilization and spiritual civilization with the following characteristics:

1. A population with a high level of education.
2. A city that can provide services for the whole country and with a modernized urban infrastructure that communicates with the world. In addition, it will be clean and environmentally healthy.
3. The economy will be composed of sectors of high added-value, with high input in technology, saving in water, energy and land, and not demanding in transport as well as non-polluting.
4. It will have a comprehensive R & D system.
5. It will have an education system that produces trained manpower to meet the challenges of modernization, and is able to measure up to world standards and meet demands of the future.
6. It will be able to inherit and enhance traditional Chinese culture and be a centre for developing advanced contemporary civilization, and be the bridgehead and bastion for war against invasion of the capitalist ideology.
7. It will be the base for the development and nurturing of the new socialist man, and the renaissance of the Chinese socialist spiritual achievement (Chen et al., 1989b, 163).

In phase one, i.e. up to 2000, Beijing will aim to develop into a culturally advanced city by emphasizing the leading role of education, science and technology and promoting the growth of some sectors and products to advanced world standards, while it will become the best city in the PRC in social stability, security and social morality. In the next phase, to be completed in another 20 years, it will complete its historical goal of the CCP's 'Four Directives', to be a city of 'seven best' and 'three firsts', and will then cross the threshold of becoming an information-led city.

The capital city region

Of the various targets of the new strategy and the proposed policy measures, most are indeed matters of national significance and are related to the development of the recent Open Door policy and Enterprise Reform in general. How the nation proceeds would influence whether similar measures would be taken or could succeed within Beijing. However, among the policy measures, some are specific to Beijing, especially the proposal to form the 'capital city region'. In the past decades, policy emphasis on self-reliance and self-sufficiency in the PRC has produced closed systems at all levels, creating hindrance to social division of labour, specialization and horizontal linkages. This is not only true for business or industrial enterprises, but equally true for bigger and multi-functional units like a city.

Beijing's big expansion in industries in the 1950s and 1960s was closely related to the need to be self-sufficient in industrial products, and the tax and profits from industrial enterprises used to form the main source of municipal revenue. In 1985, it was claimed that industries provided 50% of the commodities available in the city's shops, 92% of the municipal revenue and 80% of the city's total export in terms of value, in addition to 1.7 million jobs. So industrial development has been crucial to the survival and self-sufficiency of the Chinese socialist city (Economic Committee of Beijing Municipality, 1989, 268). Yet, as the national capital where the central government is located, self-sufficiency has espoused another element which no other province and city can share, i.e. most central ministries set up their own work units and ancillaries in the city to be 'self-reliant'. This latter 'self-reliant' spirit is to be copied by the respective ministries' subordinates in other cities and provinces. It is in such a light that the comment that Beijing is a closed system should be interpreted, because from a certain angle the national capital is not 'closed'. Beijing does not only have national pre-eminence, it plays the role as the model, vanguard and lead for the rest of the country, like the national capital in the old dynasties of China. Nevertheless, it is fair to say that Beijing's attention, besides combining the need to be self-sufficient and fulfilling its traditional model role for the whole country, has indeed been largely inward looking and not much related to its immediate neighbourhood, as would be the case for most cities in the non-socialist world.

To some extent, problems created by the lack of an adequate relationship with its natural hinterland had at times grown so serious that the solution of extending the spatial limit of the closed system had been resorted to. The advantage of such a method is to avoid upsetting the existing system and the way of doing things. Recently a similar method has been suggested by the authority of Changping Xian (Wan, 1987), i.e. incorporating 6000 sq km of territory of Hebei Province to the east and south of present-day Beijing into the city. The major role of Beijing as the national capital and its function as the political and cultural centre may have little relevance to its relationship with its immediate hinterland, but as a multi-functional city it has been for a long time constricted and made inefficient by the closed system approach. Indeed, the political and cultural centre functions had also been for a long time badly squeezed as limited resources had been channelled to support industrial growth and the swollen population which had thus been generated. Recasting Beijing's role as a multi-functional city in its natural hinterland and fostering rational economic linkages with its close neighbours mean an important turn in Beijing's path of development from what was already established after 1949 under socialism.

The concept of a 'capital city region' is not new in China's long history of urbanization. In all feudal dynasties of China, a large tract of land surrounding the national capital was usually zoned out as the 'capital territory' to be directly administered by the minister responsible for the national capital. In the Qing Dynasty, the region embraced a large urban system lying 300–400 km from the centre of the capital, and included important cities such as Baoding, Tianjin, Tangshan, Qinhuang-dao, Chengde and Zhangjiakou (see Figure 12.1). Each of these cities within the 'capital city region' had its special function in an integrated division of labour for supporting the national capital. For example, Tianjin was a transport and trading city serving the conduit of grain from South China through the Grand Canal and through coastal shipping into the capital (Huang, 1991). Thus it was the long-established rule that Beijing was economically linked with the surrounding hinterland and with the Yangtze Basin. The post-1949 socialist trans-formation, whereby 'consumptive' Beijing was turned into a 'productive' Beijing relying heavily on industries, as well as the breaking up administratively of the former 'capital city region' into several closed systems of cities and districts, had been most untraditional in Beijing's history of development. As a national capital, Beijing's main functions should be the political, military and cultural centre of the country. Whereas in pre-modern China the economic needs of the national capital could be achieved through an organized city system with a clear-cut division of labour, it is indeed a mockery that in the post-1949 period of modern transport and communication, Beijing had to develop along lines of self-sufficiency and comprehensive development, putting an unnecessary strain on its natural and human resources (Huang, 1991).

The first official revival of the 'capital city region' idea can be found in the 1982 General Plan. In the literature so engendered, the 'capital city region' may be seen as comprising two rings. The inner ring comprises the jurisdiction of five municipalities, i.e. Beijing, Tianjin, Tangshan, Langfang and Qinhuangdao (see Figure 12.1). It covers a total territory of 52,000 sq km, about 0.55% of the national total, and had an urban population of 13.45 million and a total population of 27.5 million in 1982, respectively 6.5% and 2.7% of the national total. The second ring includes the neighbouring districts of Chengde, Zhangjiakou, Baoding and Cangzhou. The entire region had a territory of 168 000 sq km, a population of 50.3 million and an urban population of 36.5 million in 1989 (Huang, 1987; Zhang and Zhang, 1991) (see Figure 12.1).

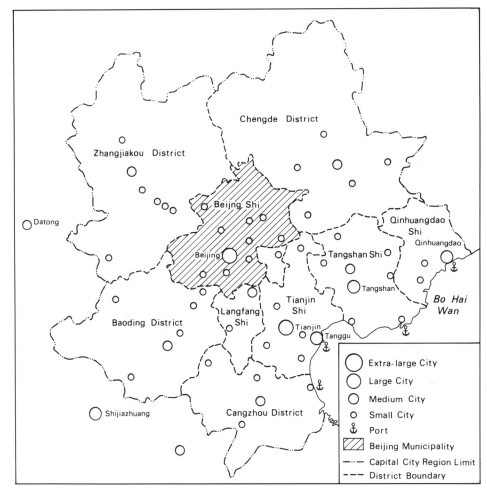

Figure 12.1   The administrative composition of the capital city region. Source: Regional Development Strategy Research Institute, 1991

At present most industrial developments are concentrated in the city districts of Beijing and Tianjin. In the western and northern parts, and the eastern coastal belt of the region, there is still plenty of undeveloped wasteland which may be opened up for urban and industrial development. The low-lying and salty coastal strip is ideal for heavy industries. Lack of fresh water prevents it from being used for agricultural activities, yet its coastal location offers convenience for factories. Overall, the region has been well served by major railways, roads, airports and seaports. It also possesses the highest concentration in the country of science and research personnel and technical personnel. In 1989, Beijing, Tianjin and Hebei Province together had about 1.11 million engineering, technical, R & D and teaching personnel, about 12% of the national total and more than the combined figure for Shanghai and Jiangsu Province.

However, the region has been suffering from a number of defects. Shortage of water is a major constraint. Overconcentration and overpopulation in the built-up areas of Beijing and Tianjin have created 'big city problems' of inadequate housing, traffic jams and deteriorating quality of the environment. In addition, the old Soviet-style system of central planning and administration had for a long time prohibited complementary development and coordinated growth in the region, constraining industrial division of labour and horizontal linkages. The motor car and iron and steel industries may illustrate this point (Regional Development Strategy Research Institute, 1991):

1. *Motor car industry.* The region has over 40 years' experience in the industry with Beijing, Tianjin and Tangshan as the three production centres. As the region possesses iron and steel, rubber, plastics, paint, glass, textiles and leather industries, it can supply most of the materials and intermediate goods required by the car industry. The strong machinery, electronics and precision equipment industries also provided the necessary support. The large market in North China forms another favourable factor. However, unco-ordinated development has led to the proliferation of over 260 small factories and an undesirably small scale of production. Lack of common parts and components as well as too many car models further undermined quality and price-competitiveness. Coordinated effort by the main producers in Beijing and Tianjin for a unified parts and components production system, and division of labour to allow specialization of key parts such as bodies and engines by the largest manufacturers, are key to the further growth of the industry.

2. *Iron and steel industry.* This industry made up 8.9% of total industrial output by value and forms one of the nation's main production bases. The capacity of the industry is spread between Beijing, Tangshan and Tianjin, with small plants in Xuanhua and Chengde. Location of the industry in the latter two cities is obviously unreasonable. The local resource of iron ore at Xuanhua has already been exhausted, and the location in Chengde has caused pollution in the historic cultural city and is in conflict with its role as a tourist centre. Beijing is the region's largest producer, yet it has neither iron ore nor coking coal; both have to be brought

in from outside. Lack of water resources also posed a definite constraint on its growth there. For a long time Beijing had much more capacity in iron-making, leading to wasteful transport of bulky input and output. For example, in the early 1980s, pig iron production in Beijing accounted for 82% of the region's total, steel and steel products were respectively 46% and 44% of the region's total (Li, 1985). In Tianjin, the second largest producer, for a very long time there was steel-making capacity but no iron-making industry so that it relied heavily on inputs from Beijing and Shanghai. In addition, Tianjin's industry is spread out in numerous disparate locations within the city, causing grave pollution and transport problems. Tangshan had also for a very long time much more capacity in steel-making than iron-making, necessitating the transport of pig iron and steel ingots from Beijing and other places. The region's iron and steel industry needs to be restructured by focusing it on the eastern coastal belt where both coal and iron ore are found in plenty. Detailed investigations for a large-scale integrated iron and steel plant site in the area have been made in 1989 and 1990. Wangtan (Figure 12.2) has been identified as an ideal location. Setting up a huge new production base there, financed and joint ventured by existing plants in the three cities, would be a significant step towards solving the pollution problems of these cities as well as easing their urban land scarcity and water shortage problems, and lifting the industry onto a higher-quality and more efficient platform.

Thus Zhang and Zhang (1991) consider that the enlarged space of the region could offer a number of opportunities for solving the post-1949 problems of the city development of Beijing, as well as a new strategy of economic restructuring and growth for it and other cities in the region. First, the region may help to disperse some of Beijing's overcongested urban functions. Beijing's overdeveloped heavy industries have been a constant problem. Quite a number of these industries could be relocated to the coastal belt of the region and to Tangshan, where there are local resources and much more space for development.

Besides dispersal of economic and administration activities, Beijing's residents are to be encouraged to resettle in the nearby cities, which should also include the small towns of Yenxiao and Zhuzhou. Beijing's enterprises are to be encouraged to expand by means of setting up branch units in these cities. With the new branches, some of the staff and dependants have to be simultaneously resettled. The enterprises and the municipality could also adopt positive measures such as higher wage scales, and flexible household registration which allows out-moved

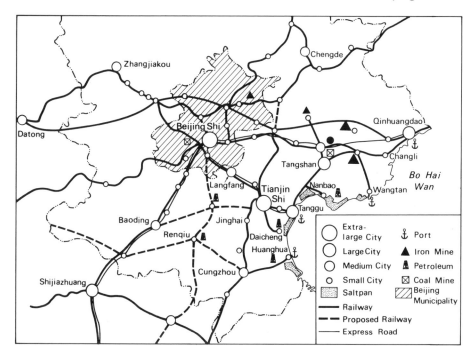

Figure 12.2   Major resources, transport lines and cities in the capital city region.
Source: Regional Development Strategy Research Institute, 1991

households to retain their Beijing registration, as a means to encourage resettlement by out-migration of whole households.

Secondly, Beijing can utilize the region to attain economic restructuring so that energy-intensive, land-intensive and polluting industries may be relocated to more suitable locations within the region, while the city will channel its land and other resources to its key functions as the political and cultural centre of the nation. In such restructuring the entire region may benefit from further growth, as resources in the rest of the region take advantage of Beijing's outflow to attain more rational and higher-level development.

Thirdly, transport development in the region can be so coordinated that Beijing's pressure may be released. What has been under way already and is to be completed by 1996 is a new north–south railway trunk line in China, the Beijing–Kowloon Line. It is 2360 km long and will provide Beijing with another major link with southern China. It will start from Huangcun in the southern suburb of Beijing (Figure 12.2). Another new line to be constructed is the Tianjin–Baoding Line which will take away part of the cargo flow from the northern part of North

China and the passenger traffic from east and west of Beijing. A proposal on building Beijing's second airport outside the municipality, in Langfang, has recently received much attention. The new move may decentralize air traffic from Beijing, leading to concurrent decentralization of some of the city's activities to Langfang. The last proposal on the transport front is to construct an expressway paralleling the Qinhuangdao–Datong Line and linking a stretch of 400 km of highly urbanized belt to facilitate dispersal of activities from the core of the region to its coastal periphery. Of course, construction of modernized port facilities at Huangtan, Tanggu and Huanghua in graduated steps are necessary for providing additional coastal outlets for Beijing and the region as a whole.

Fourthly, development of the tourist potential of Chengde, Baoding and Qinhuangdao would not only enhance the region's attractiveness for tourism, it would also take away the existing concentration of the industry in the national capital. Development of road and other transport facilities, basic infrastructure and hotel and service facilities in these cities will benefit not only tourism, but also their attractiveness as overspill towns for Beijing.

Lastly, regional cooperation through interpenetration of investment and exchanges of technology and personnel will help to foster higher-level efficiency in the production of daily consumables from both industrial and primary sector origins. Many activities have been going on; for example, Beijing has signed numerous production contracts with surrounding counties and cities for large-scale purchases of beef, seafood, vegetables, poultry, fruits, cotton and tobacco. It has become a trend for Beijing to search for its daily supplies from the region rather than this being confined to its own municipal limit as before (Research Reports on Planning for the Seventh Five Year Plan, Beijing, 1991).

Beijing is unsuited for significant growth of heavy industries. Forced industrialization has been the predominant factor, leading to its 'big city problems' and undermining Beijing's role as the political and cultural centre of the country. On the other hand, the well-established pre-1949 industrial base and relatively much better located city, Tianjin, had not been utilized for much further industrial growth. In 1949, Beijing's industrial output value was only about a quarter of that of Tianjin. In 1990, it rose to Yn78 billion, Yn6 billion more than that of Tianjin. In the entire post-1949 period (1949–89), Tianjin submitted Yn62.5 billion to the central government in profits and taxes, while it only received Yn21.2 billion of investment from it. In the same period, Beijing received Yn44.9 billion, about double that of Tianjin. Administrative independence and vertical hierarchical central direction had also prohibited rational complementary growth of the two cities. Their industrial structure shows a close resemblance, i.e. the five major industries of machinery, chemicals, textiles, food and metallurgy accounted for 61.4% and 62.6% of the total industrial output for Beijing and Tianjin respectively. Thus both cities have failed to attain scale economies in most industrial activities and their per capita labour productivity falls far behind Shanghai. The post-1980 re-emphasis on Beijing's role as the political and cultural centre of the country, and the call for restructuring its economy to suit the main role of the city, provided a new impetus for Tianjin to revive its role as the economic centre in the region. It is proposed that a planning committee, headed by the National Planning Committee with participation of the leaders of the two cities, be formed to foster closer cooperation between the two cities as a lead to coordinated development in the lesser urban centres within the region. On that basis, the lesser cities would become useful receptive locations for dispersal of industries from the two core cities (Research Reports on Planning for the Seventh Five Year Plan, 1991).

The development of a coastal economic belt encompassing industries, ports and tourism would also provide impetus for further growth of the region. In Tanggu and New Port of Tianjin, export-oriented science development parks have started to pioneer new high-tech and export-oriented industries. At Huangtan, a new integrated iron and steel complex of a scale similar to Baoshan Steel of Shanghai will be established. A good natural harbour, Huangtan will develop into a major port with diverse industries related to its basic iron and steel industries. Nanbao will have potential for important marine chemical industries and Changli and Huanghua will be developed into medium-sized industrial towns. In short, the coastal belt will provide the necessary space for new industrial development, which will itself support continued industrial expansion of a high-tech and high-added-value nature in the two core cities by supplying them with intermediate inputs and machinery, as well as providing them with coastal port outlets.

In addition, the setting up of a 'secondary capital' to relieve pressure on Beijing has also been discussed for some time and incorporated in the strategic proposal for the city. Three locations have been suggested, i.e. Sanhe Xian east of the capital, somewhere between Changping and Shunyi; Langfang; and Zhuzhou to the south of Beijing (Research Reports on Planning for the Seventh Five Year Plan, 1991).

The region should be treated similarly to the Pearl River Delta and the Yangtze Delta Economic Region, to be directed in its macro-economic matters and planning by a unified authority. In the long term, the administrative arrangements for the capital city region should also be reconsidered.

Conclusion

Sit (1985) observed that urbanization in post-1949 PRC has produced a unique type of city with multiple characteristics emphasizing the productive role, equity in the distribution of consumptive items including housing, self-sufficiency based on an extended urban jurisdiction to encompass a large rural territory in the form of a 'city region', and the central role of very large cities in its natural hinterland. Detailed study of Beijing in the present book has revealed that PRC cities are in general closed systems. Of course, this is not to say that the city is completely cut off from other places that lie beyond its administrative boundary, as was impossible even at the height of extreme leftist ideology during the Cultural Revolution. The city has been all along promoted as a productive agent to provide goods and services for the countryside. In addition to industries, educational, cultural, medical and health services and political influence have all been urban based in the PRC. Cities, particularly the very large cities, do develop regional linkages as providers of such services. They have been sourcing supplies from distant places of food, energy and materials for feeding their population and factories. The claim that they are 'closed systems' has therefore to be interpreted with this kind of allowance. Compared to what they were before 1949 and what is current in the Western world, they are to a large extent 'closed', particularly in the sense that they have little economic cooperation and linkages with neighbouring administrative units based on exchanges under the rule of economic principles.

There are many more administrative hurdles for cross-territory flow of goods and people in the PRC. Of course, even where there are inter-city and inter-regional flows of people and resources, they have been mainly administratively directed. It is in this sense that the Chinese cities since 1949 have not been given the economic incentive to grow and develop according to their natural and social resource endowment, but to thrive on internal dynamics and what has been allowed and arranged through central planning. Such a lack of initiative in development may be the essence of the claim of the 'closedness' of PRC cities. It is from this 'closedness' that the present government wants to break away in the new spirit of Open Door and Enterprise Reform. The new strategy for the future development of Beijing emphasizes the political and cultural centre role and the natural and social environment of the city as a basis for planning its restructuring in economic activities and in its spatial rearrangement. The approach as well as the detailed policies mapped out in this chapter illustrate a departure from the former 'closedness' character in the city's development to one which takes into consideration a wider range of factors, involving market forces to a greater extent, as well as extending beyond the city limits. In short, it is a much more 'open' approach.

In its 1987 strategic study, the municipal government saw the main sources of Beijing's present-day problem as being: the imbalance of supply and demand arising from the rapid post-1949 development of industries which generated large population increases; overloading of the urban infrastructure as the municipality has insufficient funds and insufficient capital to match development by infrastructure construction; and structural faults in the economy arising from the emphasis on 'productive' over 'consumptive' activities and the imbalance between natural resources and the structure of the industries developed. Clearly, these arise mainly from the dysfunctioning of central planning and the misconception of the role of the national capital, i.e. one which is of necessity a large industrial base and self-sufficient as much as possible. The municipality's claim that these problems originated from the low level of productivity and social division of labour characteristic of the early stage of socialism is indeed not pointing to the basic facts. Nor is its list of problems all true. Shortage of funds is only a superficial problem, as a large amount of fixed investment has been directed towards construction of large industries that are neither efficient, nor conducive to the natural and human environment of the national capital. The total outcome would be different if the same amount of funds had been used differently. Inadequate technical and professional capacity is yet another false claim. In the context of the PRC, Beijing has been the best 'endowed' city in such aspects, and is indeed comparable to some cities in the advanced industrialized countries. Of course, it is better than almost all other cities in the Third World in such aspects. Thus the real problem lies with the system rather than the superficial technical issues of overpopulation, shortage of water resources, etc.

We can further grasp the essence of the matter by analysing the municipality's three redefined roles for Beijing. The role of 'a large industrial base' has been dropped in the 1987 strategy. Replaced in pre-eminence is its political role as a national capital for 'linking the hearts of the people and Party together', serving as a 'model district' for guiding the nation in modernization, and being a base of advancement for the theories of Marxism. In a sense, the role of the traditional Chinese capital as the seat of government of the Son of Heaven, in which symbolically man and universe interact and from which the blessing of Heaven for a harmonious and potent reign would be sourced, has been revived in the redefined basic role of Beijing, though couched in different jargon and with an obviously new ideological inclination. Despite these superficial differences, the present-day and future national capital has to serve a classic role that has been true for thousands of years, as the centre for invoking unity of the 'people' and the 'Party', a model for the nation's modernization drive, a place to represent the Chinese cultural heritage and new spiritual achievements, and even developments in the theories of socialism. It is being treated clearly as the fountain-head of the legitimacy to rule as well as the embodiment of both the style and ways of the present regime, and a reflection of its acceptance or popularity within the nation. This vital element has been echoed in the policy objective of creating a 'socialist man' for projection to the whole of the country to form a new ideology and model for the public to follow, and that Beijing should become a bastion against capitalism and the place for the renaissance of Chinese socialism. Although the redefined role has retained an element of 'being an economic base', i.e. Beijing has to be a composite productive city in the Asian Pacific region, it is only a secondary role for maintaining the city and its population. It is thus on the basic question of what the role of Beijing is that we feel there exists an interesting agreement between the long tradition of the Chinese culture, the Confucian definition of the role of the national capital, and socialism. Of course, the meaning of 'socialism' in this latest round of Chinese political developments means merely upholding the Party and its new interpretation of economics in the form of the 'socialist market economy', and the basic role of the state at such an early phase of socialism is to be one of economic development. Thus, there has been a subtle yet significant transformation from the former dominance of Soviet-style socialism to a new round of Confucianism plus a 'socialist market economy'. In less ideological terms, the new stage differs from the former in that it allows a much more 'open' and 'economic' (rule of the market) approach to the development of the city. The basic strategic elements of transformation of the urban economy, new spatial order, and reforms of enterprise management, municipal administration and financing not only aim to readjust the city in a way that suits its predominant role, but also to provide the municipality with the authority, the financial capability, and the right urban and economic environment for achieving its strategic goals.

How Beijing will fare under the new approach and new strategy will have a great deal to do with the success or failure of the Chinese government in engineering and implementing new reforms for a 'socialist market economy'. Superficially, the Chinese want to combine the best of two worlds, i.e. equity and public ownership in general under socialism and efficiency in production and disposition of goods and services under the rule of the market in the fashion of the capitalist system. Up to the time of writing, the Chinese have made substantial headway in the building of the new system. It is nevertheless yet unknown what will happen next, particularly since the summer of 1993 when hyper-inflation, a rush of capital into stock market and property market speculation and the outflow of capital into Hong Kong caused the central government to adopt restraining measures on loans and new project approvals. Stricter control over enterprise behaviour may not follow widespread alarm about enterprise fraud and corruption, but the new system has definitely not yet been clearly spelled out in sets of enforceable rules and regulations that are efficient and cost-effective to implement. The reforms are still in a stage of transition in which some new elements have been tried out and installed, while a good deal of the old system still remains and keeps on functioning. Thus Beijing, after almost half a century under socialism, is still at the crossroads. In this new round of change, the guiding principles seem to be a mixture of traditional Confucianism, 'socialism' and capitalism based on the rule of the market. We feel it is difficult to predict how the city may be in 2050, though in this chapter we have presented what has been attempted by the municipal government. The difficulty in doing this is even greater than when the sage kings tried to forsee the coming harvest by gazing into the sky through the central opening of the Ming T'ang.

13

Conclusion: is there a Chinese socialist city model?

Cultural roots of Beijing

In this book on Beijing, we have taken an approach which combines the historical and cultural exposition of what is the traditional Chinese perspective of a city, particularly the role and configuration of the Chinese national capital, and the post-1949 situation and development of Beijing under the new political and economic realities of a socialist government in a Third World setting.

Thus the book spans a wide latitude both in time and in aspects of the urban geography of the city. At the start, three chapters were devoted to unravel the historical facts and interpretations which show that the traditional Chinese concept of the city is quite different from what has been accepted in the Western world. Nine chapters were then used to portray and explain developments in key facets of Beijing, including planning concepts, urban growth patterns, economy, population change, housing, urban transport, urban environment, the preservation of the old city core and social segregation. We shall briefly recapitulate the main points in these chapters before discussing the keynote of the book: what is Beijing and is it unique?

Culture has a strong influence on a city's role, physical form, and the social processes that lead to its growth in population and formation of social areas. As an old-established national capital of China, Beijing is deeply rooted in traditional Chinese cultural traits regarding what a city is. Put simply, in traditional China cities did not arise owing to demands for trade, nor did they rely on the development of other urban economic functions such as handicrafts. Economics had little role in the formation of Chinese cities until very late, i.e. about the Song Dynasty. Within the Chinese city in history, and more markedly in the national capital, residential neighbourhoods were enclosed by walls whose gates were shut at night under curfews, while trade and commerce were strictly regulated and restricted by officials within the markets which occupied discrete and very limited space within the city. Thus the traditional Chinese city served primarily as the seat of government and the place for the location of law-enforcement institutes. This concept is believed to originate from the ancient institution called Ming T'ang. Though all civilizations seem to share the same origin for the earliest permanent settlement, the locale of a wise man or sage from which he could read the stars and foretell conditions of rain or shine and the coming harvest, the Chinese have developed and institutionalized this into their traditional world view in the form of Confucianism and incorporated it into the layout of the Ming T'ang. Indeed the Ming T'ang concept has defined and perpetuated the traditional Chinese perspective of what the city was to be, viz.:

1. An institution to enable man to keep in harmony with nature.
2. A seat of governance aimed at orderliness through a system of rituals and code of behaviour, symbolized by both the layout of the city and ritual performances by the resident officials.
3. A service centre, more in the political, law and order, education and cultural senses for the surrounding countryside that unites with it into a harmonious unity.

Thus *Zhou Li* (Tian Gong chapter) says that the national capital is 'to form a centre and moral yardstick to which his people may look'. A similar role was to be performed by cities of lesser administrative status for their respective rural hinterlands. It is following such a vein that we may better appreciate Mote's (1977) claim that the traditional Chinese cities are 'knots of a net', basically of the same substance as the countryside, though possibly stronger and more intense in their concentration. In traditional China, for 5000 years, an urban culture distinct from what was prevailing in the countryside did not evolve. The town–country unity was both culturally and physically (in architect, use and built materials) true.

Originally the Ming T'ang was a simple thatched hut where the sage king watched the sky to communicate with Heaven and receive omens that might affect the harvest and other well-being of his people. Later, the 'observation' or communication with Heaven was developed into a system of rituals involving offering of sacrifices to Heaven in different parts of the year, offerings to spirits and dead ancestors, and other forms of rituals. The structure and organization of the Ming T'ang had similarly and gradually evolved into a more complicated form. First it was turned into a multi-room structure, then into groups of buildings, and then into the palace city of the feudal hereditary and dynastic

kingships who succeeded the early sage kings. The expansion of empire
and secularization of some of the functions performed by former sage
kings led to the expansion and separation in space of some of the
functions of the Ming T'ang, while some functions formerly performed
by the sage king were deputized to officials of the sovereign. It is clear
that the national capital layout of later dynasties in traditional China
was fashioned after the Ming T'ang, with the palace of the sovereign, the
Son of Heaven at its core, as he had the mandate of Heaven, and
through him the blessing of Heaven or universe to man will flow. Thus
the sovereign became the source of potency and orderliness. Details of
the layout of the palace, particularly the residential chamber of the Son
of Heaven, are therefore central to the concept of the traditional Chinese
city, as this where the harmony of man and Heaven is symbolized by
the intercourse of the vital ethers, *yin* (represented by the sovereign) and
yang (represented by the empress). The location of the sovereign's Court
Hall and the Temple and Altar on which he performed major sacrifices
had all been highly symbolic and rigidly laid out according to *Kao Gong
Ji* of *Zhou Li*. The wall of the national capital as well as its moat took
their form from the Pi Yong of the Ming T'ang. The wall symbolizes the
earth, the moat the flow of the sovereign's benevolent rule on Earth.
They are categorically different from the defensive notion of such urban
features to which we are so accustomed.

Lesser cities look up to the national capital, and are laid out on a
smaller scale with less magnificence, yet in similar principle, according to
their respective administrative ranks. Indeed, the same layout is in
principle replicated in the average person's residence. In short, the
national capital and the entire city notion have been a form of life in the
traditional Chinese world, centred around the man and Heaven
relationship and a system of rituals and social behaviour that had evolved
for the maintenance of order in society and the potency of the land.

As the abode of the Son of Heaven, the ideal location of the national
capital obviously is to be the centre of his reign. As the territory of
various dynasties changed in response to the expansion of Han
dominance to South China through migration and the opening up of the
Huai and then the Yangtze river basins, the notion of centrality changed
when it applied to the location of the national capital. Moreover, two
subsidiary principles had been considered as well, i.e. defence and
harmonious man and Heaven relationship. In practice, centrality means
to be the centre of an economic region, rather than of itself an economic
centre. The east and southward shift of the economic focus of China
following the opening up of the Yangtze and Huai river basins
necessitated separation of the political centre from the 'economic centre'
(central location of the most prosperous economic region) of China. In

the long history of China, various methods had been resorted to in order to overcome the difficulty of maintaining the national capital despite it not being at the centre of the most prosperous region, including digging long canals to facilitate transport and the adoption of the 'dual capitals' system. As a supplementary method the national capital was also provided with a large 'capital city region' for its upkeep. Historical facts show that the Chinese national capital was usually linked closely with its immediate hinterland and the rest of the country, yet it had never been an economic centre. It functioned as an open system for providing the nation with a unique service (political, cultural and military centre) while drawing economic support from the entire nation in return.

We may summarize by saying that the traditional Chinese capital city concept has within it the following distinctive features:

1. It is the centre for linking the nation with Heaven (which may be interpreted as the destiny of the nation).
2. It is not an economic centre. It serves as the political, cultural and military headquarters of the nation.
3. It is an open system, closely linked with the rest of the country through material and non-material flows.
4. It is the model of the nation for all matters of significance, and is the top-ranking place for all these matters.
5. It is the summary of the ruling philosophy as well as the embodiment of the social and cultural norms of the entire nation.
6. It is a well-planned settlement, laid out according to the ruling philosophy and rituals that bind the entire nation by set values and social behaviour.
7. Its size and functions are strictly restrained so that it can perform its role efficiently, i.e. without excessive population burden and land uses that do not conform with the standards of the traditional layout for observing its roles.

As the traditional national capital of the Ming and Qing Dynasties some of these features of Beijing have persisted beyond 1949, while others have been transformed owing to the advancement of modernization, or grossly altered by the new socialist ideology and its application in the post-1949 development of the city.

Post-1949 Beijing

Physical and human setting

Beijing municipality has a total area of 16 800 sq km, about half the size of Taiwan. Its lowland areas extend to about a third of its size.

Historically it served as the major transport node between North-east China, Mongolia and North China. The area is plagued by limited and variable precipitation. It is also subject to a number of other serious natural hazards. The most recent destroyed nearby Tangshan in 1976. The physical qualities of the territory are thus unfavourable to the city's growth into a major industrial and multi-functional super-city with a population in excess of 10 million.

Beijing was not the centre of the country in the economic sense in the Ming and Qing Dynasties. Yet its 'centrality' has improved in modern times with railway building and industrialization. North-east China has become the largest industrial base of China since the 1920s, and Shanghai the second largest, while the Beijing–Tianjin–Tangshan region is the third, so within the part of China east of longitude 110°E which is most developed, industrialized, intensively farmed, populated and where most of the lowlands are located, Beijing does appear to be the centre. Modern means of railway and air transport, which has only gradually developed in China since the 1920s, similarly place Beijing as the hub for the country. In the human–economic sense, Beijing's strategic position in the whole nation has thus been much improved. On this score it is definitely a good choice as a national capital. The choice of Beijing in 1949 as the national capital by the PRC instead of retaining Nanjing may also be owing to the traditional consideration of the bad 'omen' of a fallen dynasty.

Socialist planning principles

Traditional Chinese locational considerations for the national capital of a newly founded dynasty thus do seem to play a role in Beijing's revival in 1949 as the national capital of China. Indeed, such traditional considerations still have an influence, for economic centrality, psychological, historical and cultural factors are much subscribed to and have real impact even up to the present. The ideology of the new socialist government, in contrast, did not seem to have much impact on the siting of the national capital, although socialist ideas and concepts strongly influenced the role and physical planning of the new capital. The most significant socialist city planning principles that were adopted by the PRC were:

1. The rule of equity in the distribution of consumptive goods and services.
2. Economics in the role of the city, i.e. it has to be 'productive' in nature. More specifically, cities need to become centres of industries for fulfilling the production targets of central plans.

3. Resources for building construction, investment in productive activities and disbursement of land are to be based on central allocation and not the market. The system of allocation works through the vertical hierarchies of various ministries so that municipal authorities have relatively little control, and sometimes even knowledge, of the city's many facets of development.

In addition, Beijing also adopted the physical planning concepts of industrial and residential land-use segregation, locating land uses to achieve minimum volume of transport and minimum commuting trips, and the use of 'micro-districts' for constructing residential areas. Soviet influence was particularly obvious in the early years of the PRC. Soviet expert teams were invited in 1949, 1953 and 1955 to assist Beijing in drawing up its general plans. They were successful in grafting Soviet principles onto the various early general plans of the city which set the foundation for its later development. The emphasis on Beijing as a large industrial base for the PRC underlines the principle of economics and the ideological bias of 'productive' over the 'consumptive' role of the socialist city. Putting a limit on the size of the city and providing it with a new pattern of ring and radial roads, the development of new towns and the adoption of a 'dispersed constellations' style of growth of the urban areas are other notable Soviet elements in the city's physical development.

Chinese planning elements

Yet in the course of formulating the general plan, Chinese elements are seen to play an equally significant role in affecting the urban planning and construction of the city. Disputes in 1949–57 over the location of the administrative centre, whether Beijing should be developed into a centre of big industries, and on 'wide-boulevardism' reveal that some of the traditional Chinese views on city planning were alive and strong. The concept that Beijing should be a centre of big industries is not quite socialist, although socialist cities are to be productive in nature. The underlying argument was much more related to the traditional notion that the national capital should be the top-ranking place for everything. Thus it should be a big industrial centre in modern times when the national ideology was based on the industrial poletariat and the PRC's prevailing policy was rapid industrialization. In addition, the various industrial ministries needed to set up their 'showpiece' factories for demonstrating to other provinces. Beijing's generous standards regarding road widths can also be traced back to *Kao Gong Ji* which specifies that roads in the capital should be much wider than in lesser cities. The view of local planners against the location of the administrative centre within the old city reflects the significance attached by them to preservation of the old city as a valued cultural relic for the Chinese race, whereas the Soviet experts were only concerned about economic expedience. In the Great Leap Forward of 1958 and its aftermath, the urge for rural–urban convergence and an early leapfrog into communism had effected an extension of the city boundary and lowered its planning standards. During the Cultural Revolution in 1966–76 many of the ultra-leftist ideas of the Great Leap Forward were carried even further. The general plan of the city was suspended and the Planning Bureau was dismantled. Planning and urban construction in general came almost to a standstill. Mixed land uses within the city and the outer suburbs were generally promoted according to Mao's idea that different employment sectors should be intermixed and learn from each other. Thus until 1978, for almost 30 years under the new regime, urban planning had been in effect either seriously disrupted or suspended for more than half the time. In such times, professionals in town planning and urban construction, who were basically USSR trained or inclined, were much suppressed under the political movements of the day inspired by local Maoist ideas that differed substantially from the socialist planning concepts of the USSR.

Pattern of urban growth

The urban growth rate in Beijing, measured in built-up area, amounted to an annual 6.26 sq km in 1949–83, mainly pulled by industrial land uses, with administration, education and research land uses of secondary significance. Before 1980, growth was largely concentrated in the 'central mass'. After 1980 growth happened in the fashion of 'filling up the gap' between the central mass and the dispersed constellations. There is a lack of genuine dispersal so far, and growth has taken place by compaction and peripheral accretion. In 1949–79, statistics show that the central mass accounted for 62% of the physical growth of built-up areas and 76% of the increase in urban population. Lack of funds and cutbacks of project investment in the new towns after the failure of the Great Leap Forward are the main underlying reasons. Decentralization in the forms of 'dispersed constellations' and the 'mother–children' pattern of settlement hierarchy is emphatic in word but not in deed. The growth of the built-up area and urban growth at large reflect the imbalance between the 'consumptive' and 'productive' roles of the city, as can be substantiated by a declining ratio of building space to two categories of use, i.e. 'living space' and 'working space', of 1.55:1 in 1949 to 0.61:1 in 1979. Of the entire addition of building land in 1949–79, 16.2% was taken up by industrial uses.

Viewed from an ideological platform, the rapid growth of the built-up area may be attributed to the factors of centralism, symbolism, and top-ranking status that used to affect the national capital. Centralization of power and control in both feudalistic and socialist settings requires the development of multiple functions and hence a large share of both population and related activities. These bolstered the city's urban growth. Being the national capital of a socialist country, the Chinese leaders' interpretation was that the city should have a large proletariat of industrial workers. It should also set a model for the rest of the country. These entailed large-scale industrial development and a grand-scale establishment of a large education and resort area, industrial estates and generous standards for road widths and per capita urban land in general. The notion that the capital should be the top in rank for all matters of significance equally contributed to an escalation in land demand.

Complementary to centralism is the development of the city-region. Local self-sufficiency is believed to offer the security on which centralism can be based. Such a concept is inward looking and treats the city as a closed system. It is distinctive of the position of the capital in feudal times when it was supplied by almost the entire country.

Urban economy

Measured by a number of economic indicators, Beijing's economy had performed very well over 1953–88 with consistent and high rates of growth. In comparison, the direct share of labour in the benefits of economic growth was not high, as wages only increased at an annual rate of 5% against a background of 2.3% annual rate of inflation and 2.2% annual rise in cost of living. Government subsidy for a wide variety of consumptive items, including food, transport, housing and some consumer light manufacturing, had thus been important for maintaining a slightly improved standard of living. While the economy had expanded substantially physically, the per capita wage at 1991 was still Yn2877, effectively putting Beijing into the category of Third World or developing countries' status by level of economic development.

Beijing's economy also exhibits another characteristic, i.e. the pre-dominance of the secondary sector. This usually accounted for 60–70% of GNP, and recently remains at over 50%. The overwhelming significance of industries is clearly the result of the basic policy laid down in the early 1950s to develop Beijing into the nation's major industrial base. The demand for 'top rank' and 'demonstration effect' of the various industrial ministries espoused a wide range of industries, particularly heavy and intermediate products industries which Soviet-style industrialization often stresses. This industrial structure had been purposely fostered without regard to Beijing's natural environment, natural resources and whether they are suitable for a national capital whose main role should be as the nation's political and cultural centre. The industrial structure therefore shows important faults such as a bias towards heavy, intermediate goods, and water- and energy-intensive and polluting industries. In 1991, the industrial sector still employed 1.58 million out of the total labour force of 4.66 million.

A closed-system approach had been followed in the development of the urban economy, with little diagonal and other linkage between related enterprises, and even less industrial division of labour with neighbouring cities and regions. In addition some large plants were located in Beijing, largely because of Beijing's national capital status. The development of the suburban and rural economy based on the staple food and non-staple food demand of the urban population is yet another aspect of the closed system approach wrapped up in a label of local self-sufficiency in developing the urban economy.

Population

Central to Chinese city planning and urban economic planning is control over the size of the population. Beijing's development into a large industrial base necessitated a massive influx of population in the 1950s and a large planned population target. Despite this, the city's population has been under the same rigid household registration control as in all socialist cities. As a rule, various general plans do put a 'cap' on the maximum population, though large-scale industrial growth planned in the 1950s expanded the maximum figure twice in 1953–57 from the original 4 million to 6 million.

Most of the growth stems from the migration and boundary extension which happened in the 1950s. The average annual population growth rate in that decade exceeded 6%, though in later periods of 1960–70 and 1970–88 growth was respectively only 0.5% and 1.22% annually. Even in 1978–83, when major policy changes allowed for lax migration control and the return of people sent down to other places during the Cultural Revolution, the growth rate only stayed at 1.89% annually. Over the long period of 1949–84, the average annual rate of increase was thus only 2.25%, much lower than the comparable rate of 4% for the Third

World in general, and over 6% for its prime cities. In addition, growth was largely concentrated in the 1950s and was economically led. These situations confirmed that the post-1949 urbanization of Beijing was distinct from other Third World capitals.

In sum, the population growth of Beijing has been under strict control. The bulk of the increase was deliberate and economically led, and later population changes largely corresponded with major political events of the PRC which usually de-emphasized urban population growth and urban concentration. Like the traditional national capital which maintained rigid control over its population size through forced repatriation of retiring officials to their home village or town, and banishment of all people who were without approved business to be inside the city, post-1949 Beijing maintains a rigid control over its population for reasons of facilitating central planning and ensuring a large degree of self-sufficiency within the capital.

Housing and social segregation

Lack of investment capital, arising from a low level of economic development and a policy bias towards investments in 'productive' projects over 'consumptive' construction, led to very low standards of housing measured in terms of both per capita living space and housing provision, particularly before 1978. The policy objective of equity has, however, put Beijing in a different category compared to other Third World national capitals. A low-rent policy and lack of a private sector market resulted in a generally monotonous distribution of housing as a consumptive good. The combination of these factors produced a situation in which the city was merely capable of generating minimum housing for meeting expanding demands. Thus per capita living space remained at about 4.5 sq m for the entire 1949–79 period.

Massive new construction since 1980 has led to a visible improvement in the housing situation. It drastically increased the per capita living space to 8.1 sq m by 1991. The factors behind the new development are the 1980 Directives of the CCP and State Council, which corrected the previous bias on 'productive' investment, and called for meeting the consumptive needs of the people. Enterprise Reform also enabled work units with resources to channel some of their retained profits and funds into financing and acquiring housing units for their workers. However, the new change has been in substance a redirection of limited capital by resourceful work units to consumption that is not necessarily rational and fair, while state and local governments have been deprived of some of their revenue in tax and remitted profits from such work units. The principle of equity in housing has thus been gradually eroded. Housing disparity increased further after the 1988 housing reform when the private sale and rental markets were deliberately encouraged.

In spite of the recent changes, the social areas study of Beijing mapped out the social segregation of the city based on education, employment, cadre–non-cadre occupation and the history of the housing constructed. The extent of social differentiation is however found to be much less than in both the Western and Third World city under the market economy. The old city, being the earliest developed, the cultural and historical core of Beijing and the best area in terms of public transport, municipal services and shopping facilities, remains attractive as a place of residence, though it is very cramped. The cultural area and professional complexes in Haidian and other areas and numerous industrial workers' quarters between the Third and Fifth Ring Roads reflect the effect of socialist planning on the formation of social areas.

Urban transport

Beijing in 1949 had not only inherited a Third World level of economy, it also inherited an urban road network laid out according to rules laid down in *Kao Gong Ji*, i.e. a chessboard pattern with a completely closed central block, the Forbidden City. The archaic pattern is unfit for modern intra-urban transport. Yet the need to preserve old Beijing with its feudal system of urban *hutongs* (lanes) seriously restricted the possibilities for developing and improving urban transport, except by constructing an underground system. Construction of the latter did happen very early; in fact it was the first underground ever built in any Third World city. However, the reason for its being built relates more to the political and defence functions that the leadership considered at the time, and the use of the underground as a symbol of the technological might of the nation. The high standards adopted for the city's new roads demonstrate yet another feudalistic view that the national capital should be 'best' in standard which was made a political issue during the Cultural Revolution. Besides the new demonstration of traditional feudalism just mentioned, the city was also building ring roads and radial roads fashioned according Soviet planning concepts.

The bias of Soviet-style central planning against 'consumptive' investments had its casualty in limited funds for the construction and improvement of the road network, operation of public buses and trams and the construction of the underground train. Although Beijing is by no means a poor city within the Third World, according to the World Bank's standard, its urban public transport provision is definitely poor.

Even goods transport had been regarded as 'consumptive', and was similarly constricted in its growth and improvement by lack of funds.

The above considerations, in addition to a general encouragement policy on the use of the bicycle, have made Beijing the 'bicycle kingdom'. Indeed, riding the bicycle is 18% faster than taking the bus or tram during rush hours and it becomes the predominant mode of commuting within the city. Yet the bicycle has also added problems to the transport scene by causing congestion on existing roads, particularly at road junctions, and has frustrated more liberal programmes for a system of flyovers within the old city to solve the congestion problem, as flyovers are unfriendly to the bicycle and city officials dare not offend a large number of bicycle users. A strange situation of mixed manual and motorized modes therefore characterizes Beijing's urban passenger transport and is expected to last beyond the year 2000.

In the recent Open Door and Enterprise Reform period, increased enterprise and work unit freedom has led to a rapid increase in both the passenger motor car and the light goods vehicle. The latter often doubles up or is solely used as a passenger car. Rising vehicle numbers from such sources represent an inefficient diversion of scarce capital and have contributed to increasing congestion on the roads and opened Beijing to a new set of urban transport problems.

Environment

The 1980 CCP Directive that calls on Beijing 'to develop into the nation's cleanest, most hygienic and most beautiful city, and be one of the better cities of the world in these scores' pales against the city's badly polluted environment. Four decades of overconcentration on heavy industries, as well as the severe imbalance in investments for the 'flesh' and 'bones' of the city, left Beijing in a very poor state of affairs. Most of the nation's standards for water, air, noise and solid waste discharges have been breached. The majority of its industries are polluting types. Added to this is the still underdeveloped electricity supply and central heating, so that direct burning of coal for cooking and heating in the winter is responsible for a large amount of air pollution. Long disregard for 'consumptive' investments and lack of municipal authority to coordinate and control developments result in the city being grossly inadequate in the provision of basic urban infrastructure. Toxic chemicals emitted from industries, such as BaP, have been a proven threat to the health of the residents. Rapid industrialization and modernization after 1949 have therefore seriously damaged the city's environment and threatened its ecological balance. This is perhaps one of the important costs, in both the short and long term, of the overemphasis on economics in the national capital since 1949.

The preservation of old Beijing has also been a hard struggle from the beginning when the city was made the national capital of the PRC. The Soviet experts, with their contempt for traditional Chinese culture and historic inheritance, and superficial interpretation of economic expedience, did not see the need to preserve the old city as a museum of Chinese culture. With the support of Mao they won their day in arguing for the setting up of the administrative machinery of the new central government within the old city, greatly damaging parts of its historic relics. The walls of the old city were taken down in the 1950s. The design and construction of Tian An Men Square represent another major Soviet invasion into the traditional layout in the core of the Chinese national capital. All aspects of the finally implemented plan, i.e. the nature, size and built form of the Square, are non-Chinese. Despite this, similar squares have since been constructed in other Chinese cities, though of lesser scale and grandeur, and have become a new element of the Chinese socialist city. Will Tian An Men Square be restructured? In spite of its non-Chinese elements, it is a historical artifact in itself, i.e. it testifies to the fusion of Confucian tradition with the Soviet style of socialist principles. It seems that the imprints of post-1949 developments under socialism in Beijing have been so deeply engraved into its Confucian background that the present image of the city appears to be a mixture of both.

The municipality's new strategy

The municipality in 1987 saw the following as Beijing's five main problems:

1. Over-population.
2. Water shortage.
3. Shortage of investment funds.
4. Inadequate technological and professional capacities.
5. Deteriorating environment.

These problems are believed to have arisen through the imbalance between total supply and demand which was a consequence of the structural faults of the urban economy, leading to overloading of the basic infrastructure and the environmental capacity of the city. To redress these problems, the municipality recommended a combination of socialist principles and the market-oriented Western approach. In the former, a re-emphasis on population control and the exhortation of the spirit of socialism are called for. The latter includes restructuring the urban economy based on new enterprise autonomy and market forces, and municipal reform to allow the city authority much wider planning and development control power as well as the right to charge users according to the market rule. A new spatial reorganization with regard to the city's larger natural hinterland and an emphasis on the social division of labour and the comparative advantages of different locations have been proposed. This new approach, while it incorporates more openness and economic sense, still possesses the clear tint of centralism and central planning, remnants of Confucianism and socialism. The new strategy has been implemented in the late 1980s. Up to the time of writing some marked changes have already been in evidence, as has been described in the relevant chapters, such as those on urban development, urban economy, transport and housing.

Conclusion: Chinese socialist city model?

Post-1949 Beijing, as it seems to us, has been primarily busying itself in a struggle along three fronts. First, it wants to lead the nation, by actual example, in moving from an underdeveloped Third World situation to a higher level of economic development through a crash course in industrialization. Secondly, for the newly founded regime, the national capital has to play a major part in the unification of the country and in strengthening the new regime. Beijing is the power-house of the new regime. It has to give the new nation an identity as well as the inspiration to be on its feet and to move forward. Thirdly, as a socialist country, the PRC has adopted 'equity' as a basic policy. Beijing has been striving for equity in its urban services and daily provisions to its residents.

The achievement in the four decades under socialism has been obvious. The city's population grew from 2.5 million in 1949 to 12 million in 1992. This growth has been largely regulated according to the needs of industrial development and the development of other functions of the national capital. There has never been a notable unemployment problem nor a widespread informal sector that both symbolize urbanization without comparable growth of the economy, a situation of subsistence urbanization as is the case in major Third World cities. There has been a steady rise in average income, though at a pace slower than growth of the economy. Housing and basic urban infrastructural provisions, including public transport, have been provided at low standards and are in some senses inadequate. Nevertheless, equity seems to have generally prevailed through low-level charges, official subsidies and a system of generally impartial allocation. Thus the shortage has never led to political or social instability.

Of course, the question is whether Beijing and its residents deserve better. Has the old system of central planning slowed down development both in quantitative and qualitative terms, rather than enhancing it? These are questions that may have no clear-cut answers. Overemphasis on the 'production' role of the city to the extent of slighting 'consumption', as well as a lack of economic sense moulded by the market and social division of labour coordinated by enterprises with profit motives, have been pointed out as the underlying dimensions for Beijing's present 'big city problems'. The situation would certainly be worse if 'socialist' control over population movements and enterprise development had not been enforced.

In commenting on Beijing's post-1949 development it is necessary to divide the time span into pre-1978 and post-1978 periods. In the former, 'socialism' prevailed in general. It is, however, Soviet 'socialism', at times modified by the Chinese local interpretation and development, particularly during the Great Leap Forward and the Cultural Revolution when it may be more aptly described as 'Maoism'. Under 'Maoism', the economics of the Soviet-style socialism were at their lowest ebb when the ruling philosophy was dominated by an urge for a quick leap into communism and when political and spiritual qualities were exhorted. Post-1978 developments have been marked by a return to the emphasis on pragmatism and economics, tending towards the rule of the market rather than central planning. It is a period of much more open-mindedness and economic sense. The control of the ministries on urban developments has been either trimmed or relaxed, while the municipality has been bolstered in its managing and regulating role. In this period, two versions of the general plan have been produced and the city's role and development strategy redefined.

The latest development, as reported by *Asiaweek* (30/6/93), showed increased efforts on improving the infrastructure and rapid progress in attracting foreign investment. Beijing spent $3.2 billion on its infrastructure in the 1980s. For the 1991–95 period the authority intends to invest another $4 billion on 30 projects to improve the telephone system, airport, and supplies of power, gas and water. In 1992, the upgrading of the Second Ring Road was completed at a cost of $435 million. Similar work on the Third Ring Road was 30% finished. The problem of increasing car numbers deepened; in 1992, 100 000 new motor vehicle licences were issued. As an answer to the long-term intra-urban transport problem, the first phase of the underground train extension programme was under construction in 1992. It is a 12 km east–west line under Changan Avenue. The first station at Xidan opened at the end of 1992. Talks are under way to solicit foreign partners for the north–south line, and the authority is considering sales of rights to develop above-station sites. A long-distance rail station is under construction in the south-western part of the city, to be opened in 1995. The plan to completely redevelop the old city's residential uses, targeted at 10 million sq m of floor space occupied by 2 million people, has started in 1992. In that year 1 million sq m was completed.

The new strategy also sparked a dramatic increase in foreign investment. In 1992 the city approved 2208 ventures involving outside capital, compared to 724 in 1991. Another 1200 were sanctioned in the first four months of 1993. Cumulatively there were 4970 joint ventures involving foreign capital with a total of $6.43 billion foreign investment. Taxes from foreign-funded ventures already accounted for 10% of the municipality's revenue and are its fastest growing source. In domestic economic reform, the market has been given an increasing role in price-setting. Of the total sales in 1991, state-set prices accounted for only 33%. Prices that fluctuated within a range recommended by the state accounted for 21%, whereas prices set by supply and demand in the free market accounted for 46% of total sales. In the production field, rural or agricultural production has since 1991 been completely de-regularized and no more official production quotas or orders had been issued by the authority. In industrial goods, of the 858 items that were under central plans in 1978, only 127 remained under the command system in 1991. In 1980, there were 240 items of goods under official purchase plans; by 1991, this had dropped drastically to 8. Materials for production that used to be allocated under central plans amounted to 256 items in 1979 before the reform period. In 1991, they were reduced to 24 items only. The latitude of enterprise autonomy and the operation of economic forces in the market-place have thus been expanding very rapidly since the reform year of 1978 (*Beijing Statistical Yearbook*, 1992).

Is there a Chinese socialist city model? We say that there is, and it existed in and before the 1980s. The recent change of policy makes us uncertain of the future path of the development and nature of Beijing, except in very crude terms which we shall broadly describe in the following paragraphs. Beijing, being the national capital, may not be seen as typical of the Chinese socialist city of 1949–90, as it has incorporated a unique role as the political and cultural centre of the nation. Yet, taken in an overall sense, in both the Confucian and Soviet model centralism in authority and power makes the capital the 'model city', and what it is and what happened within it are often duplicated in lesser cities. Thus the difference between one Chinese city and another, put very generally, is in respect to their administrative rank rather than to qualitative or functional differences, as in Western contemporary cities where a resort town is distinctly different from an industrial city or a mining town. In traditional China, all cities were administrative in nature, responsible for passing on to their respective spheres of influence or hinterlands the blessing of Heaven for the potency of the land and orderliness of society. In socialist China, cities are markedly transformed by the socialist principles we have referred to earlier. Despite the existence of local uniqueness and differentiation according to administrative rank, they share a number of common factors:

1. *Centres of production.* The period of socialist rule has seen a drastic and consistent transformation of cities from consumptive to productive roles. In practice, cities have become foundation points for the implementation of central plans which emphasized the development of industries. In addition, they serve as central places for providing administrative, educational, cultural, medical and health support for their respective hinterlands. In this latter, and usually lesser role, the administrative rank does have a bearing on the scale and comprehensiveness of the services provided and the extent of their catchment areas.

2. *Maoist elements.* Secondly, Chinese socialist cities exhibit elements of Maoism in the form of the development of a large rural adjunct which with the central city forms a 'city-region', providing the space and other natural resources for enabling the city population to be 'self-sufficient' in food supply, as well as for convenient development along the leftist extremist idea of town–country convergence, i.e. the rural adjunct often became the ground for rustication of urban cadres and the intelligentsia.

3. *Socialist monotony.* At a lower level, one can point to the application of the equity rule and its consequences on the urban social space of generally low standard and uniform provision of housing, public transport and other facilities and services in a centrally coordinated and planned fashion. Social segregation exists, but to a much lesser extent than in even the East European countries formerly.

4. *Ideological symbolism.* Symbolism of the ruling ideology makes its imprint on the Chinese socialist city as well. This takes diverse forms. Most distinctive is the central square, often named the People's Square, fashioned after the reconstructed Tian An Men Square in nature and style of architecture, though its size varies according to the administration status of the respective city. The main street is invariably named 'People's Road' as well. In addition, from major municipal offices, factory buildings to residential blocks, similar layouts and architecture can be easily noted. An interesting

ideological symbolism is expressed in the form of planning standards, per capita urban land, road widths, per capita green and open space, etc., which are set variously against different administrative statuses of cities in a hierarchical manner.

As the national capital, Beijing has inherited the feudal role of being a 'model for the nation', which happens to be something subconsciously adopted by the socialist regime of China. Thus it not only bears the above characteristics of a Chinese socialist city, but has to be its model. It is in this 'model' role of Beijing that we find the city is different from the Soviet city model and is itself an element that is congruent with and being sourced from the traditional Chinese national capital under Confucianism. Thus we may say that the uniqueness of Beijing as a city model lies in its symbolism of the ruling ideology which also forms its primary role. Two other characteristics of traditional Chinese cities, i.e. they were administrative and politically determined, and they were not seats of production, are, however, greatly disrupted by the new socialist regime which emphasizes the productive role of cities. Thus there is both convergence and divergence between the traditional Chinese city concept and the Chinese socialist city concept.

The post-1978 Open Door and Economic Reform have ushered in a new stage of urban development in the PRC. Decentralization of authority and decision making, revival of economic and profit incentives, and the rule of the market have led to a rush of commercialism and drastic changes in the urban economy and urban landscape of China. Beijing has again been given the 'model' role in many of these aspects, once new policies have been tried out with success in the 'special' laboratories of the Special Economic Zones. Yet the new system has just started to evolve. There are still many imperfections and uncovered ground under the old system. Critical to this is the way to balance 'private' and 'public' interests, similar to the balance between 'flesh' and 'bones' or 'consumptive' and 'productive' roles of the 'former' (pre-1978) Chinese socialist city. If this is not handled well, the efficiency of the city and the welfare of its residents will suffer. As the situation is still in flux, the way ahead is not very certain.

We are already in the information age. Cities in many parts of the world have moved out of the industrial into the post-industrial stage of development. The USA in the 1970s witnessed the fast decline of the secondary sector within its major cities. New dynamics for city growth and prosperity lie with their command and possession of locational factors that attract international banking and finance, information and communication industries, and the headquarters of multi-national corporations (MNCs). New York, Chicago and San Francisco have been booming on this new platform ever since the 1970s, while most old industrial cities declined. With such changes, the population size, urban infrastructure and the building stock configuration of a city have experienced drastic changes (Hymer, 1975; Cohen, 1981; Friedmann, 1986). Indeed, a new notion of 'world city' has emerged. This category of cities are the foundation points for global capitalism. Friedmann (1986) claimed that world cities differ from each other not only by their mode of integration with the global economy, but also by their own historic past, national policy and cultural background, yet the economic variable is the decisive factor which gives them their common identity. He portrayed the world cities according to the 'seven hypotheses', that is:

1. The form and extent of a city's integration with the world economy and the functions assigned to the city in the New International Division of Labour (NIDL) will be decisive for any structural change occurring within it.
2. Key cities in the world are used by global capital as foundation points for the spatial organization and articulation of production and markets. The resulting linkages make it possible to arrange world cities into a complex spatial hierarchy of core cities and semi-peripheral cities.
3. The global control functions in world cities are directly reflected in the structure and dynamics of their production sectors and employment.
4. World cities are major sites for concentration and accumulation of international capital.
5. World cities are points of destination for a large number of both domestic and international migrants.
6. World city formation brings into force major contradictions of industrial capital, among them spatial and class polarization.
7. World city growth generates social costs at rates that tend to exceed the influx of poor workers into the world city itself.

Figure 13.1 illustrates the subcategories of world cities identified by Friedmann. Beijing has been developing in a closed Chinese environment for centuries under Confucianism, and then has further developed for about four decades, still in a closed-door manner, yet under the sway of a new ideology – socialism. It seems at present to be on the verge of yet another significant change. The PRC's opening to the world and its increasing participation in the community of nations and in the international market have already cleared the way for new dynamics in the formation of Friedmann's world cities. Indeed, Beijing, at a relatively

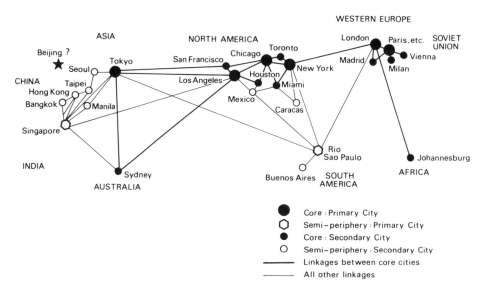

Figure 13.1 The hierarchy of world cities. Source: modified from Friedmann, 1986

central location in the prosperous and better developed third of China, serviced with the most dense air routes, railways and express-roads of the nation, as the headquarters of decision making of the CCP and the central government, in possession of the largest concentration of high-level manpower and R & D capacity, is an ideal regional headquarters for foreign MNCs and domestic (Chinese) MNCs, as well as for serving as the financial and business nerve or control centre for the vast Chinese territory. Chinese MNCs are already existing in small number and growing in size rapidly. The New Strategy of the Beijing Municipality of 1987 was formulated largely on dynamics within China. As the significant forces for the growth of the world's major cities in this age of rapid information transmission and international relatedness lie outside of China, the New Strategy will possibly have little relevance to guide Beijing's growth beyond 2000 if no new policies related to international capital and the international market have been sufficiently included in its deliberation.

We feel that the old industries of Beijing have to be quickly decentralized down or relocated to other places. Economic measures, in respect of the city charging market rates for land rent and services, have to be implemented to give the city financial strength for improving its infrastructure that is crucial to the development of high-level tertiary activities, particularly the airport, transport and communication services.

Post-industrial Beijing should emphasize its role as the nation's political centre. In the economic sphere, development of finance, business services, information and communication industries should be the leading activities. It should also be the regional headquarters of international and domestic MNCs. When Beijing will qualify as a world city, and what subcategory it should belong to, are still hard to guess (see Figure 13.1). Nevertheless, it is reasonably certain that Beijing could not be physically fashioned after the Ming T'ang, a product of the technology in use 4000 years ago, and its later development specified in *Kao Gong Ji* and basically followed in the layout of the old city of Beijing. Yet the spirit of Ming T'ang, i.e. that the national capital should be the nation's centre of information, communication and control, remains valid and crucial to Beijing's future growth. However, in future (even at present) the critical information is not 'blessing from Heaven', rather the critical information and decisions regarding the international market and flow of capital that organize economic and non-economic activities extending over the vast space beyond the limits of the city itself. This function of the national capital, or the prime city, is indeed in essence similar to 'blessing from Heaven', as it affects the welfare of the land through the 'demonstration effect' and 'filtering down' processes that work through the hierarchy of lesser cities.

The communication and control role is equally in agreement whether it is the new city concept of the world city or the Ming T'ang. World cities in Friedmann's mind are not production centres, they are primarily centres of finance and corporate decisions. Indeed, the world city reconfirms the origin of the city as represented by the Ming T'ang: information, communication and control are the primary roles of the city, whereas the productive role was either secondary, subsequent to the primary role, or outside it. Economics, when narrowly interpreted as physical production, never seems true of the making of the traditional Chinese national capital, nor is it generally true of the national capitals in the Western world in history as well as at present. The economics of the 'world city' lie not in such narrowly interpreted productive activities, but in the city's information, communication and control over material production all over the world. Do we see the shadow of the Ming T'ang in such a city?

The future of Beijing looks to us to lie in its being an international city, perhaps more inclined towards the 'world city' concept. As a cultural city, we hope that Beijing will preserve the old city as a life-sized museum of the traditional Chinese concept of a city, to the marvel and wide acclaim of all those who understand and are able to witness it, not simply as a page of important history, but also as a testimony to a living concept of what the city is.

References

Chapter 1

Agnew, J., Mercer J. and Sopher, D. (eds.) (1984) *The City in Cultural Context*, Allen & Unwin, Boston.

Bater, J.H. (1980) *The Soviet City*, Edward Arnold, London.

Berry, B.J. (1973) *The Human Consequences of Urbanization*, Macmillan, London.

Chang, Sen-dou (1977) 'The Morphology of Walled Capitals', in Skinner, G.W. (ed.), *The City in Late Imperial China*, Stanford University Press, California.

French, R.A. and Hamilton, F.E.I. (eds.) (1979) *The Socialist City*, Wiley, Chichester.

Ginsburg, N. (1972) 'Planning for South East Asian Cities', *Focus*, 22, 1–8.

Hauser, P.M. (1965) 'Urbanization: An Overview', in Hauser, P.M. and Schnore, L.F. (eds.) *The Study of Urbanization*, Wiley, N.Y., 1–48.

Ho, Kin-man (1937) 'Research on Ancient Chinese Cities', *Current Affairs*, 5, 9, 110–18 (Chinese text).

Johnson, J.H. (1967) *Urban Geography: An Introductory Analysis*, Pergamon, Oxford.

Ku, S.W. (1984) *The National Capital of Various Dynasties*, Zhonghua Books, Beijing (Chinese text, first published in the Qing Dynasty).

Lao, Zhen Yi (1942) 'On the Establishment of the National Capital and Its Planning Before the Six Dynasties', *Humanity Journal*, 1, 1, 19–31 (Chinese text).

Lim, W. (1982) *Zhou Li*, Commercial Press, Taipei (Chinese text, first published in Han Dynasty and written in Zhou Dynasty).

Liu, Pun Zhen (1980) *Archaeological History of Ancient China*, Chinese Construction Industry Press, Beijing (Chinese text).

Lo, K. (1992) *Chinese Society and Literature*, Literary Star, Taipei (Chinese text).

Mayer, H.M. (1971) 'Definitions of "City"', in Bourne, L.S. (ed.) *Internal Structure of the City*, Oxford University Press, N.Y., 28–31.

Meadows, P. (1957) 'The City, Technology, and History', *Social Forces*, 36, 141–47.

Mote, F.W. (1977) 'The Transformation of Nanking, 1350–1400', in Skinner, G.W. (ed.) *The City in Late Imperial China*, Stanford University Press, California, 101–54.

Mumford, L. (1961) *The City in History*, Pelican, London.

Murphy, R. (1984) 'City as a Mirror of Society: China, Tradition and Transformation', in Agnew, J., Mercer, J. and Sopher, D. (eds.) *The City in Cultural Context*, Allen & Unwin, Boston, 186–204.

Reissman, L. (1964) *The Urban Process*, Free Press, New York.

Sjoberg, G. (1960) *The Preindustrial City*, Free Press, New York.

Sjoberg, G. (1965) 'Cities in Developing and Industrial Societies: A Cross-cultural Analysis', in Hauser, P.M. and Schnore, L.F. (eds.) *The Study of Urbanization*, Wiley, N.Y., 213–63.

Skinner, G.W. (ed.) (1977) *The City in Late Imperial China*, Stanford University Press, California.

Smailes, A.E. (1967) *The Geography of Towns*, Hutchinson University Library, London.

Soothill, W.E. (1951) *The Hall of Light: A Study of Early Chinese Kingship*, Lutterworth, London.

Trewartha, G.T. (1952) 'Chinese Cities: Origins and Functions', *Annals of the Association of American Geographers*, 42, 1, 69–93.

Turner, R. (1949) *The Ancient Cities*, Vol. I, McGraw-Hill, N.Y.

Wang, M.G. (ed.) (1986) *Li Ji*, Commercial Press, Taipei (Chinese text, believed to have been first published in the Han Dynasty and written in the Zhou Dynasty).

Wheatley, P. (1971) *The Pivot of the Four Quarters*, Chicago, Aldine.

Wright, A.F. (1977) 'The Cosmology of the Chinese City', in Skinner, G.W. (ed.) *The City in Late Imperial China*, Stanford University Press, California, 33–75.

Ye, Yao Jun (1986) *History of the Development of the National Capital of China*, Vol. 1, Shenxi People's Press (Chinese text).

Yung Lo Da Din (1425) *Chronicles of the Reign of Yung Lo*, Vol. 9561, Ming Dynasty (Chinese text).

Chapter 2

Arlington, L.C. and Lewisohn, W. (1987) *In Search of Old Peking*, Oxford University Press, Hong Kong.

Chen, Gao Hua (1982) *Da Du of Yuan Dynasty*, Beijing Press (Chinese text).

Christaller, W. (1933) *Die Zentralen Orte in Süddeutschland*, Fischer, Jena. English edition translated by Baskin, C.W. (1966) *Central Places in Southern Germany*, Prentice-Hall, Englewood Cliffs.

Ciu, Ju Xian and Yang, Dong Shan (1989) *A Survey on National Capitals of China*, Henan University Press (Chinese text).

Cornish, V. (1922) *The Great Capitals*, Methuen London.

Farmer, E.L. (1976) *Early Ming Government: The Evolution of Dual Capitals*, Harvard University Press, Massachusetts.

Hou, Ren Zhi (1979) 'Tiananmen Square: Transition from Palace Square to People's Square', in Hou, Ren Zhi (ed.), *Theory and Practice in Historical Geography*, Shanghai People's Press, 227–250 (Chinese text).

Hou, Ren Zhi (1982) 'Beijing: Characteristics of History of Development and Its Restructuring', in *Historical Geography*, 2, 1–20 (Chinese journal).

Hou, Yong Jian (1989) 'Basic Siting Principles for National Capitals in Chinese History', in Shi, Nian Hai (ed.) *Research On Historical National Capitals of China*, Vol. 4, Gejiang People's Press, 37–53 (Chinese text).

Li, Bing Kuan and Liu, Gin Kuan (1986) 'Preliminary Study on Our Country's Characteristics in Siting of National Capitals in History and Its Relationship with Cultural Development', in Shi, Nian Hai (ed.) *Research on Historical National Capitals of China, Vol. 2,* Gejiang People's Press, 31–41 (Chinese text).

Liu, Wu Jun (1983) 'The Shifting National Capital of Various Dynasties in China in Relation to China's Changing Economic Foci', *Urban Issues,* 4, 20–3 (Chinese journal).

Sha, Xue Jun (1952) 'Types of National Capitals', *Continental Magazine,* Taipei, 5, 12, 422–7 (Chinese journal).

Shi, Nian Hai (1986a) 'Preface', in Shi, Nian Hai (ed.) *Research on Historical National Capitals of China,* Gejiang People's Press, 1–2 (Chinese text).

Shi, Nian Hai (1986b) 'Geographical Factor for Setting Up of National Capitals in the History of China', in Shi, Nian Hai (ed.) *Research on Historical National Capitals of China, Vol. 2,* Gejiang People's Press, 1–30 (Chinese text).

Shi, Nian Hai (1987) 'On the Setting Up of Ancient Capital Study', in Shi, Nian Hai (ed.) *Research on Historical National Capitals of China, Vol. 3,* Gejiang People's Press, 1–34.

Tam, Qi Xiang (1982) 'Seven Major National Capitals in Chinese History', *Issues In History Teaching,* 3, 5–9 (Chinese journal).

Wang, Pu Zi (1960) 'The Plan of Da Du of Yuan Dynasty', *Journal of the Museum of the Old Imperial Palace,* 2, 61–82 (Chinese text).

Xia, Xue Jin (1952) 'Typology of National Capitals', *Continental Magazine,* Taipei, 5, 1 (Chinese journal).

Ye, Yao Jun (1988) *History of the Development of National Capitals of China,* Shenxi People's Press (Chinese text).

Yu, De Yuan (1989) 'Cultural Characteristics of Beijing As An Ancient City', in Research Society on History of Beijing et al. (eds.) *Research On the History and Current Facts of Beijing,* Beijing Yan Shan Press, 131–141 (Chinese text).

Chapter 3

Cao, Ju Ren (1970) *Today's Beijing,* Hong Kong (Chinese text).

Chen, Zhen Xiang (1977) *Beijing,* International Research House on China, Hong Kong (Chinese text).

Ciu, Ju Xian and Yang, Dong Shan (1989) *A Survey on National Capitals of China,* Henan University Press (Chinese text).

Farmer, E.L. (1976) *Early Ming Government: The Evolution of Dual Capitals,* Harvard University Press, Massachusetts.

Ho, Ye Ju (1985) *Research on City Planning of the Kao Gong Ji,* China Construction Industry Press, Beijing (Chinese text).

Hon, Guang Hui (1984) 'Preliminary Study on the Population Geography Within the Present Day City Boundary of Beijing During the Three Hundred Years of Qing Dynasty and the Republic of China', Ph.D. Dissertation, Department of Geography, University of Beijing (Chinese text, mimeographed).

Hou, Ren Zhi (1979) 'Tiananmen Square: from Palace Square to People's Square', *Theory and Practice in Historical Geography,* Shanghai People's Press (Chinese journal).

Hse, Min Cong (1980) *Research on the Wall and Palace Design of Beijing of the Ming and Qing Dynasties,* Students Bookstore, Taipei (Chinese text).

Li, Jie Ping (1981) *Ancient National Capitals of China*, Heilongjiang People's Press (Chinese text).

Liang, Si Cheng (1989) *History of Chinese Architecture*, Ming Wen Press, Taipei (Chinese text).

Lim, Wan (1982) *Zhou Li*, Commercial Press, Taipei (Chinese text, believed to have been first published on the Han Dynasty and written in the Zhou Dynasty).

March, A.L. (1968) 'An Appreciation of Chinese Geomancy', *Journal of Asian Studies*, 27, 2, 253–67.

Ye, Yao Jun (1987) *Pictorial History on the Development of National Capitals In China, Vol. III: National Capitals of the Mature Period (Song to Qing)*, Lanzhou University Press (Chinese text).

Yoon, Hong-key (1980) 'The Image of Nature in Geomancy', *Geo Journal*, 4, 4, 341–7.

Yoon, Hong-key (1985) 'An Early Chinese Idea of a Dynamic Environmental Cycle', *Geo Journal*, 10, 2, 211–12.

Yu, Xi Xian (1990) 'Chinese Feng Shui Ideas and the Location and Layout of Chinese Cities', *Geography of the Earth*, 5, 92–107 (Chinese journal).

Chapter 4

Bater, J.H. (1980) *The Soviet City*, Edward Arnold, London.

Beijing Construction History Editorial Committee (1987) *City Construction Materials of Beijing Since Liberation, Vol. 1, City Planning*, Beijing (Chinese text).

Beijing of Contemporary China (1989) Chinese Social Sciences Press, Beijing (Chinese text).

Beijing Municipality (1991) 'Preliminary Summary Report on the Revision of the Scale and Layout of Beijing in Its General Plan', Beijing (Official Chinese document, mimeographed).

French, R.A. and Hamilton, F.E.I. (eds.) (1979) *The Socialist City*, Wiley, Chichester.

Hamilton, F.E.I. (1979) 'Spatial Structure in East European Cities', in French, R.A. and Hamilton, F.E.I. (eds.) *The Socialist City*, Wiley, Chichester, 195–262.

History of Chinese City Construction (1987), China Construction Industry Press, Beijing (Chinese text).

Milyutin, N.A. (1974) *Sotsgorod: the Problem of Building Socialist Cities*, MIT Press, Cambridge, MA.

Strumilin, S.G. (1961) 'Family and Community in the Society of the Future', *Soviet Review*, 11, 2, 3–29.

Chapter 5

Beijing Municipality (1982) 'General Plan of Beijing (draft) (September 1980)', (unpublished Chinese official document, Chinese text) (referred to in text as 1982 General Plan).

Beijing National Land Agency, Beijing Planning Commission (eds.) (1990) *Atlas of National Land Resources of Beijing Municipality*, Survey Press, Beijing (Chinese text).

Beijing Social and Economic Yearbook (various dates), China Census Press, Beijing (Chinese text).

Beijing Statistical Yearbook (various dates) China Census Press, Beijing (Chinese text).

Chen, Hai-yang (1989) 'On the Flexibility of Planning Targets: Reflection on the General Plan of Beijing', *Beijing City Planning & Construction Review*, 2, 11–13 (Chinese journal).

China Statistical Yearbook (various dates) China National Census Bureau, Beijing (Chinese text).

Ditu Chuban She (Atlas Press) (1984) *Atlas of China*, Beijing (Chinese text).

Hu, Zhaoliang (1990) 'Reasons and Solutions to the Inflation of City Size of Beijing Municipality', *Beijing City Planning & Construction Review*, 3, 2–4 (Chinese journal).

Hu, Zhaoliang (1992) 'Beijing' (unpublished paper, mimeographed).

Li, Gong and Liang, Qi Ping (1988) 'Strategic Considerations for the Layout of Beijing', *Beijing City Planning & Construction Review*, 4, 8–10 (Chinese journal).

Li, Gong and Liang, Qi Ping (1989) 'Strategic Considerations for the Layout of Beijing (continued)', in *Beijing City Planning & Construction Review*, 1, 9–11 (Chinese journal).

Li, Gong and Liang, Qi Ping (1992) 'Summary Report on the Revision of Beijing's General Plan', Beijing, (unpublished Chinese official document, Chinese text). (Referred to in text as 1992 General Plan).

Sit, V.F.S. (1985) 'Introduction: Urbanization and City Development in the People's Republic of China', in Sit, V.F.S. (ed.) *Chinese Cities*, Oxford University Press, Oxford, 1–66.

Wan, Lin Qing (1987) 'On the Expansion of the Municipal Territory of Beijing', Office of Changping County Government (unpublished Chinese document).

Wang, Tung (1991) 'Beijing's Future Urban Growth Pattern from the Perspective of its Rural Economic Development', in *Beijing City Planning & Construction Review*, 2, 6–9 (Chinese journal).

Wu, Yi Guang et al. (eds.) (1988) *Economic Geography of Beijing*, Xinhua Press, Beijing (Chinese text).

Yu, Xue Wen (1986) 'Application of Remote-sensing Technique to Study the Pattern of Development of Beijing's Built-up Areas', *City Planning*, 2, 9–14.

Zhou, Yu Zhen (1987) 'Beijing's Urban Land Use', in Beijing Municipality (ed.) *Beijing, Part II*, 80–84 (unpublished, Chinese text).

Chapter 6

Beijing Municipality (1992) 'Summary Report on the Revision of Beijing's General Plan', Beijing (unpublished Chinese official document).

Beijing Social & Economic Statistical Yearbook (various dates) China Census Press, Beijing (Chinese text).

Beijing Statistical Yearbook (various dates) China Census Press, Beijing (Chinese text).

Beijing Technology Management Research Centre (1991) 'On the Restructuring of Traditional Industries of Beijing By Means of High-level Technology', Research Report for the Municipal Government (Chinese text).

Chen, Hai Yang (1990) 'Problems Confronting the Development of Industries in Beijing', *Beijing City Planning & Construction Review*, 2, 17–19 (Chinese journal).

Forty Years of Beijing (1990) China Census Press, Beijing (Chinese text, internal circulation).

Li, Yau Hai (1990) 'Industry Development and Spatial Arrangement in Beijing', *Beijing City Planning & Construction Review*, 3, 23–6 (Chinese journal).

Lin, Pao, Ying, Run Lou and Mui, Li (1991) 'Ways To Develop Beijing's Industry By Year 2000', *Beijing City Planning & Construction Review*, 2, 27–30 (Chinese journal).

Ma, Ju (1991) 'Look Afar and Be Practical', *Beijing Daily*, 29 October (Chinese newspaper).

Regional Economic Development Strategy Research Institute, People's University (1991) 'Industrial Cooperation and Rational Location In the Capital City Region', (unpublished research report for the Seventh Five-Year Plan) (Chinese text).

Seventh Five-Year Plan Study (1991) 'Coordinated Spatial Development Between Regional Development and Beijing's Socio-economic Growth', Research Report of Beijing Municipality (unpublished, Chinese text).

Wu, Jiang (1990) 'Impact of Industrial Decentralization on Beijing's Rural and Urban Development', *Beijing City Planning & Construction Review*, 1, 18–20; 2, 20–22 (Chinese journal).

Wu, Yi Guang et al. (eds.) (1988) *Economic Geography of Beijing*, Xinhua Press, Beijing (Chinese text).

Yang, Sha Zhen (1984) 'Construct the National Capital To Make Prosperous the Economy', in Beijing Geographical Association (ed.), *Collected Essays on Symposium on Environmental Issues of Beijing*, 27–32 (Chinese text).

Zhang, Xing (1991) 'Analysis and Reflection on the Ten-Year Economic Efficiency of Beijing's Large and Medium Scale Industrial Enterprises', unpublished Research Report for the Municipal Government (Chinese text).

Chapter 7

Beijing Construction History Editorial Committee (1987) *City Construction Materials of Beijing Since Liberation, Vol. 1, City Planning*, Beijing (Chinese text).

Beijing Municipality (1981) 'Collected Essays on Issues of City Planning in Beijing' (unpublished Chinese text).

Beijing Municipality (1991) 'Summary Report on the Preliminary Revision on the Scale and Layout of Development in Beijing's General Plan' (unpublished official document dated 5 December).

Beijing Municipality Population and City Development Research Team (BMPCDRT) (ed.) (1984) *Collected Essays on Control of Size of Big Cities*, Beijing (mimeographed, Chinese text).

Beijing Social & Economic Statistical Yearbook (various dates) China Census Press, Beijing (Chinese text).

Cao, Lian Cun (1991) 'The City's Population Capacity Viewed From Per Capita Construction Area of the Planned Urban Area', *Beijing City Planning & Construction Review*, 3, 6–8 (Chinese journal).

Forty Years of Beijing (1990) China Census Press, Beijing (Chinese text, internal circulation).

Ji, Ping (1984) 'The Origin, Type and Age Structure of Beijing's In-migrants', in BMPCDRT (ed.), *Collected Essays on Control of Size of Big Cities*, Beijing (mimeographed, Chinese text).

Ji, Ping, Zhang, Kai Di and Liu, Da Wei (1984) 'Marriage Migration and Change of the Rural Population', in *Selected Essays on Beijing's Population Issues and Solutions* (unpublished official document, Chinese text).

Kelley, A.C. and Williamson, G. (1987) 'What Drives City Growth in the Developing World', in Tolley, G.S. and Thomas, V. (eds.), *The Economics of Urbanization and Urban Policies in Developing Countries*, World Bank, 32–46.

Li, Mu Zhen (1987) *The Population of Beijing*, China Financial Press, Beijing (Chinese text).

Li, Yu (1984) 'Survey and Analysis On Beijing's Out-migrants in the Three Recent Years', in *Selected Essays on Beijing's Population Issues and Solutions* (unpublished official document, Chinese text).

Liu, Da Wei (1986) 'Report on the Mobility of Beijing's Permanent Population', Research Unit, Beijing Municipality (unpublished, Chinese text).

McGee, T.G. (1971) 'The Urbanization Process in Asia', in Woodruff, A.M. and Brown, J.R. (eds) *Land for the Cities in Asia*, Harvard University Press, 28–67.

Rondinelli, D.A. (1988) 'Giant and Secondary City Growth in Africa', in Dogan, M. and Kasada, J.D. (eds.), *The Metropolis Era, Vol. 1*, Sage, California, 291–321.

Seventh Five-Year Plan Study (1991) 'Topical Research For the Social and Economic Development Projects for Revising Beijing's General Plan', Research Report to the Municipality (unpublished, Chinese text).

Sit, V.F.S. (1985) 'Introduction', in Sit, V.F.S. (ed.) *Chinese Cities*, Oxford University Press, Oxford, 1–66.

Sun, Hong Ming (1984) 'Reasonable Control Over the Size of the City Is Beijing's Key In Implementing Its General Plan', in *Selected Essays on Beijing's Population Issues and Solutions* (unpublished official document, Chinese text).

Sun, Hong Ming and Zhang Wei (1991) 'Beijing's Problem of Floating Population', *Beijing City Planning & Construction Review*, 3, 9–11 (Chinese journal).

Tolley, G.S. and Thomas, V. (1987) 'An Overview of Urban Growth: Problems, Policies and Evaluation', in Tolley, G.S. and Thomas, V. (eds.) *The Economics of Urbanization and Urban Policies in Developing Countries*, World Bank, 1–12.

Yang, Nai Chao and Liu, Da Wei (1984) 'Probing Into the Pattern of Beijing's Population Movements', in *Selected Essays on Beijing's Population Issues and Solutions* (unpublished official document, Chinese text).

Yeung, Yue-man (1988) 'Great Cities of Eastern Asia', in Dogan, M. and Kasada, J.D. (eds.) *The Metropolis Era, Vol. 1*, Sage, California, 155–186.

Zhang, Ji Si and Liu, Jie (1991) 'On the Mobility of Beijing's Permanent Residents', *Beijing City Planning & Construction Review*, 3, 12–15 (Chinese journal).

Zhang, Kai Di (1984) 'Population Migration and Control in Moscow', in BMPCDRT (ed.), *Collected Essays on Control of Size of Big Cities*, Beijing (mimeographed, Chinese text).

Zhang, Zhao Di, and An, Su Hua (1984) 'Control Measures and Decentralization of Beijing's Population', in BMPCDRT (ed.) *Collected Essays on Beijing's Population Problems and Their Solutions* (mimeographed, Chinese text).

Chapter 8

Bater, J.H. (1980) The Soviet City, Edward Arnold, London.

Beijing Construction History Editorial Committee (1985) *Beijing City Construction Since Liberation*, Beijing (Chinese text).

Beijing Construction History Editorial Committee (1987) *City Construction Materials of Beijing since Liberation*, Vol. 1, City Planning, Beijing (Chinese text).

Beijing Urban Housing Research Committee (1984) 'Survey Report of Urban Housing Problems of Beijing' (unpublished, Chinese text).

Dwyer, D.J. (1986) 'Urban Housing and Planning in China', *Transactions Institute of British Geographers*, 11, 479–89.

Fan, Yao Bang (1986) 'Fixed Planning Standards for Beijing's Residential Districts', *City Planning*, 5, 36–40 (Chinese journal).

Fan, Yao Bang (1987) 'The Situation of High-rise Housing As Revealed by a Recent Residents' Survey', *Beijing City Planning & Construction Review*, 2, 40–43 (Chinese journal).

Fan, Yao Bang (1988a) 'Development of Beijing's Residential High-rise Buildings', *Beijing City Planning & Construction Review*, 1, 36–8.

Fan, Yao Bang (1988b) 'Divergent Views on High-rise Residential Development', *Beijing City Planning & Construction Review*, 3, 33–5 (Chinese journal).

Fan, Yao Bang (1989a) 'Background For Beijing's Residential High-rise Development', *Beijing City Planning & Construction Review*, 3, 39–40 (Chinese journal).

Fan, Yao Bang (1989b) 'Beijing's Current Housing Situation and Housing Tasks', *Beijing City Planning & Construction Review*, 1, 30–33 (Chinese journal).

Fang, Xiao (1989) 'Establishment of Juer Hutong Housing Cooperative in Beijing', *Urban & Rural Construction*, 7, 18 (Chinese journal).

Feng, Wen Jiong and Zhou, Chang Xing (1990) 'Issues and Policies on Housing in the USSR', *Beijing City Planning & Construction Review*, 3, 52–4.

Gu, Yun Chang and Zhu, Hong (1989) 'Preferential Policy On Sale of Housing Units: Perspective from the Sixth Construction Company', *Urban & Rural Construction*, 4, 13–15 (Chinese journal).

Hamilton, F.E.I. and Burnett, A.D. (1979) 'Social Processes and Residential Structure', in French, R.A. and Hamilton, F.E.I. (eds.), *The Socialist City*, Wiley, Chichester, 263–304.

Lu, Kao Xiang (1989) 'Preliminary Enquiry Into Beijing's Problems and Development in High-rise Residential Housing', *City Planning*, 5, 18–21 (Chinese journal).

Lu, Kao Xiang, (1991) 'Planning Issues in the Redevelopment of Old and Dilapidated Housing', *Beijing City Planning & Construction Review*, 3, 16–18 (Chinese journal).

Ministry of Construction (1990) *Selected Legislation on Management Policy Regarding Housing in Towns and Cities*, Law Publication, Beijing (Chinese text).

Research Office, Urban Construction Bureau. Beijing Municipality (1984) 'Proposals on Speeding Up Urban Redevelopment of Beijing Municipality' (unpublished, Chinese text).

Research Office, Urban Construction Bureau, Beijing Municipality (1986) 'Development Targets and Strategy of Urban Housing Construction for the Capital in Year 2000' (unpublished, Chinese text).

Research Office, Urban Construction Bureau, Beijing Municipality (1991) 'Urban Redevelopment of Beijing: Situation, Problem and Solution' (unpublished, Chinese text).

World Bank Country Study (1992) *China: Implementation Options for Urban Housing Reform*, Washington, D.C.

Wu, Liang Yong and Liu, Yan (1989) 'Search For Ways to Redevelop Old Residential Areas in Beijing', *Beijing City Planning & Construction Review*, 3, 17–20 (Chinese journal).

Wu, Yu (1989) 'Success, Problem & Insights: A Review on 40–Years Housing Construction in Beijing', *City Planning*, 5, 13–17 (Chinese journal).

Chapter 9

Beijing Construction History Editorial Committee (1987) *City Construction Materials of Beijing since Liberation*, Vol. 1, City Planning, Beijing (Chinese text).

Beijing Metropolis (1985) (Chinese text, unpublished).

Beijing National Land Agency, Beijing Planning Commission (ed.) (1990) *Atlas of National Land Resources of Beijing Municipality*, Survey Press, Beijing (Chinese text).

Beijing Urban Ecological System Research Group (1991) *Beijing's Urban Ecological System Research*, PLA, Beijing (Chinese text).

Beijing Urban Systems Engineering Research Centre (BUSERC) (ed.) (1990) *A Collection of Scientific Research for Urban Development & Systems Engineering*, Vol. 2, Beijing Science Technology Press (Chinese text).

Fan, Yao Bang (1989) 'Distribution of Tall Buildings in Beijing and Building Height Zoning', *Beijing City Planning & Construction Review*, 2, 24–7.

Huo, Ya Zhen (1989) *Physical Geography of Beijing*, Beijing Normal University (Chinese text).

Jia, Li Jie (1990) 'Shortage of Water Resources – Reconstruction of the City of Beijing', in BUSERC (ed.), *A Collection of Scientific Research for Urban Development & Systems Engineering*, Vol. 2, Beijing Science Technology Press, 83–8 (Chinese text).

Li, Ren Yuan (1990) 'The Urban Cultural Value of Beijing', in BUSERC (ed.), *A Collection of Scientific Research for Urban Development & Systems Engineering*, Vol. 2, Beijing Science Technology Press, 55–61 (Chinese text).

Li, Ren Yuan and Li, Ying (1990) 'Analysis on Urban Nature and Function of Beijing', in BUSERC (ed.), *A Collection of Scientific Research for Urban Development & Systems Engineering*, Vol. 2, Beijing Science Technology Press, 47–54 (Chinese text).

Li, Zhun (1987) 'Strive for "Historical Cultural City, Modern Metropolis"', *Beijing City Planning & Construction Review*, 2, 2–4.

Li, Zhun (1990) 'Designing New Image for the Modern City Through Protecting the Characteristics of the Ancient Capital', *Beijing City Planning & Construction Review*, 3, 22–5.

Pang, Bin and Lin, Wen Pan (1987) 'Environmental Meaning of Urban Water Bodies', in Ying, Jia Min and Lin, Wen Pan (eds.) *Collected Essays on Environmental Research of Beijing–Tianjin Area*, Meteorological Press (Chinese text).

Pu, Chao Ming (1989) 'Protecting the Unique Characters of Beijing', *Beijing City Planning & Construction Review*, 3, 8–11.

Rui, Jing Wei (1989) 'Comprehensive Protection of Beijing's Old City', *Beijing City Planning & Construction Review*, 4, 5–6.

Tong, Guang Xi (1987) 'On Protection and Redevelopment of the Old City of Beijing', *Beijing City Planning & Construction Review*, 1, 12–15.

Wang, Yi (1989) 'On Beijing's Building Height Control Categories', *Beijing City Planning & Construction Review*, 4, 42–4.

Ying, Jia Ming (1988) *Ecological Environmental Study of the Beijing–Tianjin Region*, Meteorological Press, Beijing (Chinese text).

Zhao, Dong Ki (1989) 'On Protecting Beijing as a Cultural City and Its Modern Development', *Beijing City Planning & Construction Review*, 3, 5–7.

Zheng, Li Jie (1990) 'Beijing's Urban Reconstruction from the Perspective of Water Resources', in BUSERC (ed.) *A Collection of Scientific Research for Urban Development & Systems Engineering*, Vol. 2, Beijing Science Technology Press, 83–7 (Chinese text).

Zhou, Yon Cheng (1990) 'Elementary Discussion on Energy Development Strategy of Beijing', in BUSERC (ed.), *A Collection of Scientific Research for Urban Development & Systems Engineering*, Vol. 2, Beijing Science Technology Press, 156–63 (Chinese text).

Chapter 10

Banister, D. and Button, K. (eds.) (1993) *Transport, the Environment and Sustainable Development*, E & FN SPON, London.

Barat, J. (1990) 'Institutional Framework for Planning Transport in Third World Cities', in Dimitriou, H.K. (ed.), *Transport Planning for Third World Cities*, Routledge, London, 216–56.

Bater, J.H. (1980) *The Soviet City*, Edward Arnold, London.

Beijing Construction History Editorial Committee (1987) *City Construction Materials of Beijing since Liberation*, Vol. 1, City Planning, Beijing (Chinese text).

Beijing Construction History Editorial Committee (1985) *Beijing City Construction Since Liberation*, Beijing (Chinese text).

Beijing Public Transport Corporation (ed.) (1987) *Transport Surveys and Reports*, Vol. 1, (Chinese text, unpublished).

Button, K. and Ruthengatter, W. (1993) 'Global Environmental Degradation: the Role of Transport', in Banister, D. and Button, K. (eds.), *Transport, the Environment and Sustainable Development*, E&FN SPON, London, 19–52.

CCP of Beijing Municipality (1987) 'Beijing's Transport Problems: Surveys and Research Report', in Beijing Public Transport Corporation (ed.), *Transport Surveys and Reports*, Vol. 1, 2–16 (Chinese text, unpublished).

Chen, Jing Ren and Huang, Xiu Qing (1990) 'On Beijing's Expressways System', *Beijing City Planning & Construction Review*, 3, 36–8 (Chinese journal).

Civil Engineering Bureau, Beijing Municipality (1987) 'Report on Beijing's Road Network', in Beijing Public Transport Corporation (ed.), 26–48.

Compton, P.A. (1979) 'Planning and Spatial Change in Budapest', in French, R.A. and Hamilton, F.E.I. (eds.) *The Socialist City*, Wiley, Chichester, 461–92.

Dimitriou, H.K. (ed.) (1990a) *Transport Planning for Third World Cities*, Routledge, London.

Dimitriou, H.K. (1990b) 'Transport and Third World City Development', in Dimitriou, H.K. (ed.) *Transport Planning for Third World Cities*, Routledge, London, 1–49.

Dimitriou, H.K. (1990c) 'Transport Problems of Third World Cities', in Dimitriou, H.K. (ed.) *Transport Planning for Third World Cities*, Routledge, London, 50–84.

Dimitriou, H.K. (1990d) 'The Urban Transport Planning Process: Its Evolution and Application to Third World Cities', in Dimitriou, H.K. (ed.) *Transport Planning for Third World Cities*, Routledge, London, 144–83.

Forty Years of Beijing (1990) China Census Press, Beijing (Chinese text, internal circulation).

French, R.A. (1979) 'The Individuality of the Soviet City', in French, R.A. and Hamilton, F.E.I. (eds.), *The Socialist City*, Wiley, Chichester, 73–104.

Huang, Xiu Qing (1990) 'Analysis on Flyovers in Beijing', *Beijing City Planning & Construction Review*, Vol. 1, 38–40 (Chinese journal).

Li, Jing Tao (1987) 'Urban Bicycle Management in China', in *International Symposium on Engineering and Planning for Urban Transport*, Beijing, B16–4 (mimeographed, Chinese text).

Li, Wei (1990) 'Solution to Cross City Traffic Holds Key to Beijing's Transport Problem', *Beijing City Planning & Construction Review*, 2, 48–50 (Chinese text).

Lu, Jing Tao and Wang, Cun Lei (1987) 'Analysis on Beijing's Urban Transport System', in *International Symposium on Engineering and Planning for Urban Transport*, Beijing, A4–6 (mimeographed, Chinese text).

Ma, Gang (1988) 'Analysis On Beijing's Urban Traffic Volume', *Beijing City Planning & Construction Review*, 1, 10–12 (Chinese journal).

Municipal Public Transport Corporation (1987) 'Beijing Road Cargo Transport', in Beijing Public Transport Corporation (ed.), 129–59 (Chinese text).

Public Transport Corporation, Beijing Municipality (1987) 'Research and Surveys on Beijing's Public Transport', in Beijing Public Transport Corporation (ed.), 49–61 (Chinese text).

Qian, Lian He (1988) 'Improve Urban Planning to Enhance Transport Construction', *Beijing City Planning & Construction Review*, 2, 2–3 (Chinese text).

Quan, Yong Sun (1988a) 'Situation and Solution to Beijing's Urban Transport', *Beijing City Planning & Construction Review*, 1, 6–9 (Chinese text).

Quan, Yong Sun (1988b) 'Relieving Transport Pressure in the Central Area is An Urgent Task', *Beijing City Planning & Construction Review*, 4, 28–9 (Chinese journal).

Quan, Yong Sun (1990a) 'Demand Control Is Key to Beijing's Solution to Urban Transport', *Beijing City Planning & Construction Review*, 2, 43–5 (Chinese journal).

Quan, Yong Sun (1990b) 'Policy Suggestions on Beijing's Urban Transport', *Beijing City Planning & Construction Review*, 1, 34–7 (Chinese journal).

Quan, Yong Sun (1991) 'Analysis on Management and Operation of Beijing's Urban Transport Infrastructure', *Beijing City Planning & Construction Review*, 3, 42–4 (Chinese journal).

Ren, Bao Xing (1989) 'Beijing's Bicycle Problem', *Beijing City Planning & Construction Review*, 3, 30–1 (Chinese journal).

Ren, Bao Xing (1990) 'Solution to Transport Problems of Beijing', *Beijing City Planning & Construction Review*, 2, 46–7 (Chinese journal).

Rietveld, P. (1993) 'Policy Responses in the Netherlands', in Banister, D. and Button, K. (eds.), *Transport, the Environment and Sustainable Development*, E&FN SPON, London, 102–16.

Thomson, J.M. (1977) *Great Cities and Their Traffic*, Penguin, Harmondsworth.

Wang, Xiao Ming (1987) 'Cargo Vehicle Survey', *Beijing City Planning & Construction Review*, 2, 47–8 (Chinese journal).

Wang, Xu An (1991) 'Situation of Urban Transport in Moscow', *Beijing City Planning & Construction Review*, 1, 57–9 (Chinese journal).

Wang, Yu Ming (1988) 'Urban Public Transport Development in Beijing', *Beijing City Planning & Construction Review*, 1, 13–15 (Chinese journal).

White, P.R. (1990) 'Inadequacies of Urban Public Transport Systems', in Dimitriou (ed.), *Transport Planning for Third World Cities*, Routledge, London, 85–116.

World Bank (1975) *Urban Transport*, Washington.

Yu, Cun Cuan and Li, Shao Ming (1988) Raise the Level of Traffic Management to Increase Safety and Economies', *Beijing City Planning & Construction Review*, 2, 4–6 (Chinese journal).

Zhang, Jing Gan and Zhang, Yi De (1987) 'Probing Into the Problem of Difficulty In Getting Onto Public Transport in Beijing', *Beijing City Planning & Construction Review*, 1, 26–9 (Chinese text).

Zhang, Shu Jing (1987) 'Prospects on Urban Transport Engineering Development', in *International Symposium on Engineering and Planning for Urban Transport*, Beijing, R3–32 (mimeographed, Chinese text).

Zhang, Yi De (1988) 'On City Planning and Transport Planning of Beijing', *Beijing City Planning & Construction Review*, 4, 11–12 (Chinese text).

Zheng, Yong De (1988) 'Road Network Capacity Use of Beijing', *Beijing City Planning & Construction Review*, 2, 10–12 (Chinese text).

Zheng, Zu (1988) 'Review and Projections on Beijing's Urban Transport Planning', *Beijing City Planning & Construction Review*, 1, 2–5 (Chinese text).

Zhu, Jian Hang and Zhang, Zhi Jian (1987) 'Urban Transport with Chinese Character', in *International Symposium on Engineering and Planning for Urban Transport*, Beijing, A2–4 (mimeographed, Chinese text).

Chapter 11

Abu-Lughod, J.L. (1969) 'Testing the Theory of Social Area Analysis: the Ecology of Cairo, Egypt', *American Sociological Review*, 134, 198–212.

Beijing National Land Agency, Beijing Planning Commission (ed.) (1990) *Atlas of National Land Resources of Beijing Municipality*, Survey Press, Beijing (Chinese text).

Berry, B.J.L. and Rees, P.H. (1969) 'The Factorial Ecology of Calcutta', *American Journal of Sociology*, 74, 447, 491.

Dangschat, J. and Blasius, J. (1989) 'Social and Spatial Disparities in Warsaw in 1978: An Application of Correspondence Analysis to a "Socialist City"', *Urban Studies*, 24, 173–91.

Dwyer, D.J. (1986) 'Urban Housing and Planning in China', *Transactions Institute of British Geographers*, 11, 479–89.

French, R.A. (1987) 'Changing Spatial Patterns in Soviet Cities', *Urban Geography*, 8, 4, 309–20.

French, R.A. and Hamilton, F.E.I. (1979) 'Is there a Socialist City', in French, R.A. and Hamilton, F.E.I. (eds.), *The Socialist City*, Wiley, Chichester, 1–22.

Hamilton, F.E.I. and Burnett, A.D. (1979) 'Social Processes and Residential Structure', in French, R.A. and Hamilton, F.E.I. (eds.), *The Socialist City*, Wiley, Chichester, 263–304.

Harvey, D. (1974) 'Class-monopoly Rent, Finance Capital and the Urban Revolution', *Regional Studies*, 8, 239–55.

Hawley, A.H. and Duncun, O.D. (1957) 'Social Area Analysis: a Critical Appraisal', *Land Economics*, 33, 227–45.

Herbert, D.T. (1968) 'Principal Components Analysis and British Studies of Urban-Social Structure', *Professional Geographer*, 20, 280–83.

Jalowiechi, B. (1968) *Osiedle i Miasta, Studium Socjologiczno-Urbanystyczne Jednostek Mieszkaniowych*, Wroclawia P.W.N., Warsaw.

Johnston, R.J. (1973) 'The Factorial Ecology of Major New Zealand Urban Areas', *Transactions Institute of British Geographers*, special publication, 5, 143–68.

Jones, F.L. (1969) *Dimensions of Urban Social Structure*, ANU Press, Canberra.

Konrad, G. and Szelenyi, I. (1969) *Sociological Aspects of the Allocation of Housing, Budapest*, Sociological Research Group, Hungarian Academy of Sciences.

Kwiatkowska, E. (1973) *Preobrazenia Struktury Spoleczno-Przestrennej Miasta pod Wplynew Uprzemyslowienia*, Inst. Soejologii i Filozofii P.A.N., Warsaw.

Lo, C.P. (1972) 'A Typology of Hong Kong Census Districts: a Study in Urban Structure', in Sit, V.F.S. (ed.), *Urban Hong Kong*, Summerson, Hong Kong, 26–43.

Lo, C.P. (1980) 'Shaping Socialist Chinese Cities', in Leung, C.K. and Ginsburg, G. (eds.) *China: Urbanization and National Development*, Research Paper 196, Department of Geography, University of Chicago, 130–55.

Lo, C.P. (1986) 'The Evolution of the Ecological Structure of Hong Kong: Implications for Planning and Future Development', *Urban Geography*, 7, 2, 311–35.

Murdie, R.A. (1969) *Factorial Ecology of Metropolitan Toronto 1951–61*, Research Paper 116, Department of Geography, University of Chicago.

Pannell, C.W. (1973) 'Urbanization and City Growth in Taiwan', *Journal of Geography*, 72, 1, 5.

Pannell, C.W. (1977) 'Past and Present City Structure in China', *Town Planning Review*, Vol. 48, 157–72.

Pannell, C.W. (1980) 'The Internal Structure of Chinese Cities: Nanking', in Leung, C.K. and Ginsburg, G. (eds.), *China: Urbanization and National Development*, Research Paper 196, Department of Geography, University of Chicago, 187–214.

Pioro, Z. (1962) *Ekologia Spaleczna W Urbanistyce na Przykladzie Badan Lubelskich i Torunskich*, P.W.N., Warsaw.

Piotrowski, W. (1960) *Spoleczno-przestrzenne struktura m. Lodzi: stadium ekologiczne*, Wroclaw, Zaklad Narodowy im. Ossolinskich, Polish Academy of Sciences.

Shen, Daoqi and Yao, Shimou (1985) 'Nanjing: Evolution and Development', in Sit, V.F.S. (ed.) *Chinese Cities*, Oxford University Press, Oxford, 128–47.

Shevky, E. and Bell, W. (1955) *Social Area Analysis*, Stanford University Press.

Shevky, E. and Williams, M. (1949) *The Social Areas of Los Angeles*, University of California Press, Los Angeles.

Weclawowicz, G. (1979) 'The Structure of Socio-economic Space in Warsaw in 1931 and 1970: A Study of Factorial Ecology', in French, R.A. and Hamilton, F.E.I. (eds.), *The Socialist City*, Wiley, Chichester, 387–424.

Xu, Wei (1985) 'Spatial Structure of Inner City of Shanghai', M.A. Dissertation, East China Normal University, Shanghai (Chinese text, mimeographed).

Xu, X. et al. (1989) 'Spatial Structure of Guangzhou', *Geographical Journal*, 44, 4, 385–99 (Chinese journal).

Yu, Wei (1986) 'Urban Social Area Research and Planning', *City Planning*, 6, 25–8 (Chinese journal).

Zhu, Jun Ming (1992) 'Systematic Analysis on Shanghai's Urban Population', Ph.D. Dissertation, East China Normal University, Shanghai (Chinese text, mimeographed).

Chapter 12

Capital Social & Economic Development Research Institute (ed.) (1989) *Study on Development Strategy of the Capital*, Economic Management Press, Beijing (Chinese text).

Chen, Y.F. et al. (1989a) 'Main Report on Development Strategy of the Capital', in Capital Social & Economic Development Research Institute (ed.), *Study on Development Strategy of the Capital*, Economic Management Press, Beijing, 1–39 (Chinese text).

Chen, Y.F. et al. (1989b) 'Study on Social Development Strategy for Beijing', in Capital Social & Economic Development Research Institute (ed.), *Study on Development Strategy of the Capital*, Economic Management Press, Beijing, 163–77 (Chinese text).

Economic Committee of Beijing Municipality (1989) 'Strategy for Industrial Development in Beijing', in Capital Social & Economic Development Institute (ed.), 267–79.

Huang, D. (1987) 'Increasing Comprehensive Planning to Promote Coordinated Rural-urban Development in the Capital', *Beijing Planning & Construction Review*, 1, 20–3 (Chinese journal).

Huang, J.K. and Yang, X.C. (1984) 'Proposal on Economic Regional Planning for the Beijing–Tianjin–Tangshan Area', *City and Economic Regions*, 390–96 (Chinese journal).

Huang, N. (1991) 'Beijing's Historical Relationship with Surrounding Cities', in Research Reports on Planning for the Seventh Five Year Plan, 44–52 (Chinese text).

Huang, Yu and Bong, Yung Ji (eds.) (1992) *Rapid Construction of the Socialist Market Economy*, CCP Central Cadre School Press, Beijing (Chinese text).

Institute of Geography, Academia Sinica (1985) *Economic Geography of the Beijing–Tianjin–Tangshan Region*, Tianjin People's Press (Chinese text).

Li, Fu Yan (1985) 'Outline of National Land Planning of the Beijing–Tianjin–Tangshan Region', *Urban Planning*, 2, 24–8 (Chinese journal).

Liang, C.B. and Li, X. (1989) 'Structural Transformation and Sectorial Policy Study for Beijing', in Capital Social & Economic Development Research Institute (ed.), *Study on Development Strategy of the Capital*, Economic Management Press, Beijing, 125–62 (Chinese text).

Ma, J.Y. and Fan, I. (1989) 'Choice in Strategic Goals in the Economic and Social Development of Beijing', in Capital Social & Economic Development Research Institute (ed.), *Study on Development Strategy of the Capital*, Economic Management Press, Beijing, 40–73 (Chinese text).

Ma, J.Y. and Liu, Xue Wen (1989) 'Issues on Financing Beijing's Future Development', in Capital Social & Economic Development Research Institute (ed.), *Study on Development Strategy of the Capital*, Economic Management Press, Beijing, 125–62 (Chinese text).

Regional Development Strategy Research Institute, People's University (ed.) (1991) *Industrial Cooperation and Rational Location in the Capital City Region* (Chinese text, mimeographed).

Research Reports on Planning for the Seventh Five Year Plan, Beijing (1991) *Regional Development and Beijing's Coordinated Economic, Social and Spatial Growth* (Chinese text, mimeographed).

Sit, V.F.S. (1985) 'Introduction: Urbanization and City Development in the People's Republic of China', in Sit, V.F.S. (ed.), *Chinese Cities*, Oxford University Press, Oxford, 1–66.

Wan, Lin Qing (1987) 'On the Expansion of the Municipal Territory of Beijing', Office of Changping County Government (unpublished document).

Zhang, H.M. and Zhang, J. (1991) 'Study on Beijing's Growth from the Wider Perspective of the Beijing–Tianjian–Hebei Area', in Research Reports on Planning for the Seventh Five Year Plan', 1–7 (Chinese text).

Chapter 13

Asiaweek (1993) 'China's Supercity', June 30, 44–9 (Weekly magazine).

Beijing Statistical Yearbook (1992) China Census Press, Beijing.

Cohen, R.B. (1981) 'The New International Division of Labour, Multinational Corporations and Urban Hierarchy', in Dear, M. and Scott, A.J. (eds.) *Urbanization and Urban Planning in Capitalist Societies*, Methuen, London, 287–315.

Friedmann, J. (1986) 'The World City Hypotheses', *Development and Change*, 17, 69–83.

Hymer, S. (1975) 'The Multinational Corporation and the Law of Uneven Development', in Radice, H. (ed.) *International Firms and Modern Imperialism: Selected Readings*, Penguin, Harmondsworth, 37–62.

Mote, F.W. (1977) 'The Transformation of Nanking, 1350–1400', in Skinner, E.W. (ed.) *The City in Late Imperial China*, Stanford University Press, California, 101–54.

Index